Understanding Homelessness: New Policy and Research Perspectives

Edited by
Dennis P. Culhane and Steven P. Hornburg

Foreword
John K. McIlwain

Editors' Introduction
Dennis P. Culhane and Steven P. Hornburg 1

Section 1: Defining, Counting, and Tracking the Homeless

Introduction 5
Dennis P. Culhane

Homelessness Old and New: The Matter of
Definition 9
Kim Hopper

What's Behind the Numbers? Definitional
Issues in Counting the Homeless 69
David S. Cordray and Georgine M. Pion

Public Shelter Admission Rates in
Philadelphia and New York City:
The Implications of Turnover for Sheltered
Population Counts 101
*Dennis P. Culhane, Edmund F. Dejowski,
Julie Ibañez, Elizabeth Needham, and Irene Macchia*

Patterns of Homelessness: A Review of
Longitudinal Studies 135
Yin-Ling Irene Wong

Section 2: The Causes and Prevention of Homelessness

Introduction 165
Martha R. Burt

Causes of the Growth of Homelessness
During the 1980s 169
Martha R. Burt

Is Homelessness a Housing Problem? 205
James D. Wright and Beth A. Rubin

Where the Homeless Come From: A
Study of the Prior Address Distribution of
Families Admitted to Public Shelters in
New York City and Philadelphia 225
Dennis P. Culhane, Chang-Moo Lee,
and Susan M. Wachter

Toward a Comprehensive Homelessness-
Prevention Strategy 265
Eric N. Lindblom

**Section 3: Next Steps in Homelessness Research and
Public Policy**

Introduction 335
Nan P. Roman

Where to from Here? A Policy Research
Agenda Based on the Analysis of
Administrative Data 341
Dennis P. Culhane and Stephen Metraux

Future Directions for Programs Serving
the Homeless 361
Martha R. Burt

ISBN 0-9662039-0-9

© Fannie Mae Foundation 1997
All Rights Reserved

The opinions expressed in this publication are those of the authors
and do not necessarily represent the views of the Editors, Fannie Mae
Foundation, or its officers.

Foreword

John K. McIlwain
Fannie Mae Foundation

Homelessness is one of the more persistent, troubling social issues of our time. Virtually all Americans have been confronted with images of men and women sleeping and panhandling on the streets of our central cities, and of families with young children sleeping amidst their belongings in a shelter. Other, less visible facets of homelessness also demand attention: homelessness in rural areas, among victims of domestic violence, and among juveniles to name a few. Americans over the past two decades have been deeply troubled by this suffering and have responded with compassion, supporting countless shelters, soup kitchens, and other efforts to alleviate this destitution.

While such measures have been the foundation of the national response to homelessness, more is needed. Homelessness is not only indicative of extreme hardship, but also signals problems of a more structural nature affecting such areas as public welfare, health care, and, in particular, housing. Just as homelessness demands a response from Americans at an individual level, so must those entities involved with policy consider ways to address this social problem in a broader context.

Publication of *Understanding Homelessness: New Policy and Research Perspectives* represents the Fannie Mae Foundation's continuing commitment to pursuing informed policies that contribute to the amelioration of homelessness. Many of the chapters in this book first appeared in *Housing Policy Debate*, published originally by the Fannie Mae Office of Housing Research and now by the Fannie Mae Foundation. The journal has served as a forum for research that seeks to improve our understanding of the nature of homelessness, its causes, and how to best address it.

With the addition of several new, previously unpublished chapters, this volume extends that tradition. It reviews the state of knowledge regarding counting and tracking the homeless population in order to determine who the homeless are. We find, of course, that they come from many different backgrounds. The book then reviews what is known about the many different causes of homelessness. Importantly, the book then focuses on new research that suggests appropriate early intervention may prevent homelessness in many instances. The volume concludes with suggestions for next steps in research, programs, and legislation.

This book provides a valuable overview of homelessness research from both policy and methodological perspectives. It should appeal to a broad audience, including homelessness service providers, researchers, students, and policy makers. But from whatever perspective *Understanding Homelessness* is read, it will hopefully make clear that there remains much work to be done in designing and implementing effective responses to reduce and eventually eliminate homelessness. With this publication, the Fannie Mae Foundation continues its commitment to be part of such a response.

Author

John K. McIlwain is the President and Chief Executive Officer of the Fannie Mae Foundation. He began his career in housing in 1973 as Assistant Director for Finance and Administration, and then Deputy Director, of the Maine State Housing Authority. Prior to joining the Fannie Mae Foundation, he was the first Managing Director of the American Communities Fund, a venture capital fund founded by Fannie Mae and dedicated to investing in hard-to-finance affordable housing development and other community investment opportunities. He was formerly a partner at Powell, Goldstein, Frazer and Murphy where he represented a broad range of clients in the single-family and multi-family housing arenas. McIlwain is the immediate past President of the National Housing Conference, one of the nation's most respected organizations for low-income and affordable housing issues. He is also a past President of the National Housing and Rehabilitation Association and serves on the boards of the Center for Housing Policy and D.C. Agenda. He holds a law degree from New York University and an A.B. from Princeton.

Note

Several articles in this volume originally appeared in *Housing Policy Debate* between 1991 and 1996. They are reprinted here with no new editing for style or format, so each article appears in the style used when it was first published. For example, because endnotes were used in *Housing Policy Debate* in 1991, the articles first published that year have endnotes rather than footnotes, which are used in the current style. Authors' biographies have been updated if applicable and if new information was available. New articles commissioned for this volume were edited to the current style of *Housing Policy Debate*.

© Fannie Mae Foundation 1997. All Rights Reserved.

Editors' Introduction

Dennis P. Culhane
University of Pennsylvania

Steven P. Hornburg
Fannie Mae Foundation

As U.S. antipoverty programs undergo their most significant transformation since the New Deal, low-income communities and the organizations that serve them will need to prepare for the consequences. There is little doubt that a restructured public assistance system with greater work incentives will increase the rate at which families exit welfare for the labor market. But there is also little doubt that time limits and eligibility restrictions will lead to caseload terminations and income losses. How families and individuals will adjust to these cuts is unknown.

Reformers hope that the loss of benefits will compel people to return to the labor market. But local human service providers are wary that they will become the new safety net for the former welfare population, a role that they feel ill prepared to fill. Homeless shelter providers, in particular, are concerned about a potential increase in demand for their services. Indeed, there is already evidence that the rate of shelter admission increases significantly for individuals terminated from welfare—increasing 35 percent for one cohort in Philadelphia (Culhane et al. 1997). Shelter providers are further concerned because recent federal legislation has reduced resources for placing shelter residents in permanent housing, through both a reduction in new federal housing subsidies and the elimination of homeless "preferences" for public housing. As these placement opportunities shrink, people may remain in shelters longer, driving up daily demand for shelter, as indicated by data from New York City (Culhane, Metraux, and Wachter 1998).

The articles in this volume address homelessness issues in the context of the profound social policy transitions now under way and their likely impact on local service delivery systems. A range of new strategies will have to be developed to target the families and individuals for whom income entitlements and standard welfare-to-work programs have not led to self-sufficiency. These families and individuals will have special service needs, unique employment training and placement challenges, and housing instability issues. Given the recent evolution of local shelter systems into "continuums of care," one possibility is that these systems will try to assume (or will be saddled with) responsibility for these populations. More likely, given the costs of residential systems, is that shelters will become part of a broader mix of community-based programs ("homelessness prevention programs") that link people with specialized employment and housing resources, including nonshelter emergency assistance resources.

Whatever the strategies, an essential component of the design of effective approaches will be reliable information. In assembling this volume, we have considered the need of communities for reliable, policy-relevant information and have selected articles that discuss the methodological issues, as well as the policy questions they address, in three key homelessness research areas: (1) descriptive research (population size and characteristics, patterns of service use); (2) analyses of causal factors and efforts to address them; and (3) evaluative research on public policy and program effectiveness. Because more than a decade has been spent in studying homelessness and the programs that serve homeless people, the field is positioned to develop more effective programs and an improved knowledge base to address the problem—however daunting the social policy challenges ahead.

This volume begins its sampling of that rich literature by examining the central issues of problem definition and enumeration. For this, we have selected two sets of paired articles. The first pair includes Kim Hopper's historical review of the definitional quandaries created by the term "homelessness," both for academic researchers and public policy makers, and a parallel study by David Cordray and Georgine Pion of how varying operational definitions affect the results of empirical research. The second pair of articles accepts a limited definition of homelessness and focuses on the impact of viewing the problem from a longitudinal perspective. We have selected an article by Culhane and colleagues, who analyze administrative databases to document the period prevalence of shelter use, as opposed to the point prevalence, and a new review article by Irene Wong that is the first to summarize the emerging literature on the "patterns of homelessness." Together, these four articles provide readers with an understanding of the broad range of definitional and methodological issues in the area of population enumeration and composition, and the policy implications of varying definitional and methodological choices.

In the second section of the volume are four articles on the causes and prevention of homelessness. Although most homelessness programs and policies have focused on compensating for or remediating the individual risk factors of homeless people (e.g., substance abuse, mental illness, weak family supports), we have taken a step back to look at what the basic research on the structural causes of homelessness reveals. Moreover, given those results, what does the research literature suggest for strategies to *prevent* homelessness. We have invited Martha Burt to introduce the section and have republished her work on the factors associated with varying rates of homelessness by city. Burt's inter-city analysis is complemented by Culhane, Lee, and Wachter's study of the *intra*-city factors associated with the distribution of homeless families' previous addresses. James Wright and Beth Rubin examine how homelessness is linked to housing policy issues, particularly for people with special needs. These three articles provide a rich and textured picture of the causes of homelessness, and how they can be analyzed from a variety of methodological perspectives. The section concludes with the seminal article by Eric Lindblom that outlines a comprehensive policy approach for the prevention of homelessness.

The third section of the volume looks toward the future. Given the past 15 years of research and policy making devoted to this problem, what can we learn and where should it take us? Culhane and Metraux, in a newly published piece, lay out a policy research agenda for the future, based on their experience with the analysis of administrative data in New York City and Philadelphia. The authors see a major shift toward increased use of automated information systems to track the use of homeless services, and they describe the policy research that such comprehensive, longitudinal data can enable, particularly in light of recent transitions in social welfare policy. Martha Burt, in another newly developed piece, reviews the major signposts from the basic research and program evaluation literatures, and maps a direction for public policy and homeless programs. Nan Roman, the vice president for policy and programs at the National Alliance to End Homelessness, introduces the section and reviews the articles from the perspective of the current information needs of policy makers and advocates.

The strategic use of research and data will be critical to the success of communities attempting to respond to the restructuring of the social welfare system. Fortunately, more than a decade of research in the area of homelessness has helped to prepare the field to obtain and analyze the appropriate information. It is our hope that this volume will give policy analysts, advocates, researchers, and students an overview of the methodological and policy issues that should be considered in research designed to support more effective policies for the future.

Authors

Dennis Culhane is an associate professor of social welfare policy at the University of Pennsylvania and a senior fellow at the Leonard Davis Institute of Health Economics. His primary area of research is homelessness, about which he studies the prevalence and dynamics of public shelter use, the geographic and housing market factors associated with housing instability, and the health services utilization patterns of public shelter users. He is leading the development of several decision support software applications for public agencies, including the ANCHoR System for homeless services and various GIS (geographic information services) applications for housing agencies and community development organizations. He received his doctorate in social psychology from Boston College in 1990.

Steven P. Hornburg is Director of Policy for the Fannie Mae Foundation. He directs the Foundation's policy research and grants programs, including the Annual Housing Conference, the Policy Partners, and the Policy Events programs. Mr. Hornburg has been responsible for the Annual Housing Conference since 1990, working closely with national policy makers, academicians, trade and advocacy groups, and business leaders. He also serves as the Managing Editor for *Housing Policy Debate* and is Associate Editor of the *Journal of Housing Research*. He serves on the Advisory Boards of *Cityscape: A Journal of Policy Development and Research* and the Brookings Center on Urban and Metropolitan Policy. Mr. Hornburg also serves as Vice Chair of the International Committee of the National Association of Housing and Redevelopment Officials.

References

Culhane, Dennis P., Meg Koppel, Stephen Metraux, and Irene Wong. 1997. *Mitigating the Impact of State Welfare Cuts for Single Adults: The Implementation and Utilization of the Homelessness Prevention Pilot Project in the City of Philadelphia.* Philadelphia: University of Pennsylvania, School of Social Work.

Culhane, Metraux, and Wachter. 1998. Homelessness and Public Shelter Provision in New York City. In *Housing and Community Policy in New York City: Facing the Future*, ed. Michael Schill. Albany, NY: SUNY Press, forthcoming.

Section 1:

Defining, Counting, and Tracking the Homeless

Introduction
Dennis P. Culhane

Homelessness Old and New: The Matter of Definition
Kim Hopper

What's Behind the Numbers? Definitional Issues in
Counting the Homeless
David S. Cordray and Georgine M. Pion

Public Shelter Admission Rates in Philadelphia
and New York City: The Implications of Turnover
for Sheltered Population Counts
*Dennis P. Culhane, Edmund F. Dejowski, Julie Ibañez,
Elizabeth Needham, and Irene Macchia*

Patterns of Homelessness: A Review of
Longitudinal Studies
Yin-Ling Irene Wong

© Fannie Mae Foundation 1997. All Rights Reserved.

Section 1

Defining, Counting, and Tracking the Homeless: Introduction

Dennis P. Culhane
University of Pennsylvania

When advocates and journalists began to focus attention on the problem of "homelessness" in the 1980s, they opened a debate that was as much over research methodology as over political responsibility. Since then, little associated with the term has been free of controversy. Adoption of the term "homelessness," by policy analysts as well as academics, was the first tactical decision in bringing attention to an otherwise amorphous set of persons and circumstances. Unfortunately, as a term with few concrete referents, it could be construed to mean everything from inadequate or unstable housing to the lack of social and spatial attachments commonly associated with being "at home." As a result, the boundaries of who is included as "homeless" are under constant pressure, both to become more inclusive of groups who at best can be considered marginally housed and to be further restricted to only those who live in public spaces (shelters are homes!).

Defining homelessness is not the only problem; different methods for measuring the size and characteristics of the population produce very different portraits. Depending on the method chosen, one could conclude that most of the homeless are homeless for long periods or that most are homeless for short periods. Both conclusions would be true, even applying the same definition of homelessness. Similarly, one could find that most of the homeless have mental health or substance abuse problems or that such conditions affect a minority of the population, and again both would be equally valid results.

The articles in this section look at problems related to determining the nature and the extent of homelessness from different perspectives. In the first article, Kim Hopper reviews homelessness as a socially constructed concept from which a myriad of definitions and meanings have emerged, both in the present and through history. This inquiry is no mere academic exercise; his insistent questioning of why we, as a society, persist in setting the homeless as "a poor apart" cannot be ignored. The many definitions that are used to describe, group, and label this heterogeneous population collectively obscure a host of structural issues that create one basic "contemporary delineator of homelessness: income insufficient to afford available housing." In pointing this out, Hopper strips homelessness of the legal, sociological, and pathological connotations that have historically accompanied the problem and instead holds the term to its literal meaning as the need for a place to spend the night.

Hopper challenges the reader to examine how, from a general pool of poor persons forced to cope with the lack of a stable residence, the state designates a subset as "homeless." What results is a theoretical framework for homelessness that focuses on the process from which the parameters, and the resulting policies for this social problem, emanate. The inquiry becomes relocated to a point far from those who languish, disempowered, under this classification, for how the term *homeless* is applied is "a telling sign of the political dimensions of categorical need." Furthermore, as various interests struggle to bestow legitimacy on particular aspects of homelessness, "one must ask what it is about 'the rest of us' that has learned to ignore, then managed to tolerate, and now seeks to banish from sight the evidence of a present gone badly awry."

David Cordray and Georgine Pion take on the daunting task of determining how to use the conflicting interpretations and definitions that Hopper describes, and the array of data that results, to understand homelessness and craft policies to respond to it. They propose a process of "intelligent segmentation," in which data from relevant studies are grouped by the characteristics of homeless subpopulations and by the specific methods used to study them. The need here is not to achieve consensus but to facilitate three processes: comparison with other studies, debate about the merits of the definitions and procedures used, and an informed appraisal of the results and their implications. Cordray and Pion offer a practical approach to integrating various perspectives and interests related to homelessness and disseminating findings among research and policy camps.

The article by Dennis Culhane, Edmund Dejowski, Julie Ibañez, Elizabeth Needham, and Irene Macchia illustrates Cordray and Pion's point regarding how various perspectives can be integrated to achieve a broader understanding of homelessness. In contrast to the first two chapters, Culhane and his colleagues do not dwell on definition, but instead examine the impact of enlarging the time frame for measuring the size of the population, assuming a constant definition across time frames. This longitudinal approach to measuring homelessness depicts the dynamic nature of the problem more clearly than was possible in previous empirical studies.

Previously, the reliance on point-in-time studies for estimates of population size had consistently produced estimates sharply lower than those offered by homeless advocates. Cross-sectional studies of the characteristics of the population had also overestimated the number of chronically homeless persons relative to the larger population of people who experience temporary housing emergencies. On the basis of this research, some public officials could conclude that homelessness affected a "relatively small number of disturbed individuals" and not a broader segment of the poor population. A public response correspondingly small in scale and targeted to a narrow segment of the poor could therefore be justified. The Culhane et al. study offers alternative data documenting the broader population of persons affected by homelessness, which in turn could serve as the basis for examining the broader public policy issues that may mediate the risk of displacement.

Building on this longitudinal perspective, Yin-Ling Irene Wong's article (commissioned especially for this volume) is the first to assemble and analyze the results from the emerging literature on "patterns of homelessness." Using longitudinal data from nine studies, she argues that homelessness is but one outcome that occurs in a larger process of "residential instability." The people who are homeless at any one time are but a subset of those for whom housing constitutes a collection of makeshift adaptations to limited financial and housing resources. For many, shelters do not constitute "rock bottom," nor does a shelter stay represent the first step to a better life. Instead, shelters are one of a limited repertoire of options for keeping a roof over the heads of oneself and one's family.

Although Wong and Hopper take very different approaches, Wong's conclusions are consistent with Hopper's. Wong emphasizes the importance of a "prevention-oriented" approach to addressing homelessness that takes homeless policies into neighborhoods with high concentrations of residential instability and targets subgroups at particular risk for either experiencing or relapsing into homelessness. Homelessness is considered a consequence, as opposed to a label, and policy should focus on the larger number of persons with housing difficulties, as opposed to the somewhat arbitrary subset of persons who are in shelters or on the streets at any given time.

In summary, the four articles in this section offer different perspectives from which to understand homelessness. The first two articles focus on defining homelessness, both conceptually and practically, while the other two focus on what can be learned by examining a temporal dimension of homelessness that had been underemphasized in previous research. Each of the articles integrates previous homeless research in a way that enables the authors to present alternative approaches without reducing the range of dialogue on the subject. What emerges is a foundation for better-informed interventions and research.

Author

Dennis P. Culhane is an associate professor of social welfare policy at the University of Pennsylvania and a senior fellow at the Leonard Davis Institute of Health Economics. His primary area of research is homelessness, about which he studies the prevalence and dynamics of public shelter use, the geographic and housing market factors associated with housing instability, and the health services utilization patterns of public shelter users. He is leading the development of several decision support software applications for public agencies, including the ANCHoR System for homeless services and various GIS (geographic information services) applications for housing agencies and community development organizations. He received his doctorate in social psychology from Boston College in 1990.

© Fannie Mae Foundation 1991, 1997. All Rights Reserved.

Homelessness Old and New:
The Matter of Definition*

Kim Hopper
Nathan Kline Institute

Abstract

The contemporary emphasis on the pathologies of shelter denizens and street-dwellers tends to conceal the great variety of makeshift ways of life that have characterized "homelessness" over the centuries. Diversity notwithstanding, those considered "vagrants" were historically marked as suspect members of a poor apart, even when their numbers increased sharply. Because kin ties have consistently proven to be the first line of defense against "literal homelessness," skid row researchers thought their absence (along with the lack of associated ties to work and community) to be diagnostic of the condition. Indeed, earlier research tended to see as "homeless" any "disaffiliated" persons, housed or not, who lived alone in unconventional dwellings. Not only have the new homeless poor, by contrast, proven to be more diverse—their geographic locus, age, gender, ethnicity, and signal disabilities having all changed—but their common element is less often ascribed to faulty social connectedness than to sheer absence of shelter. This paper discusses such changes and reviews definitions of homelessness and several approaches to its social construction. The paper argues that, although definitions owe as much to political as to logical considerations, it makes both practical and historical sense to view the streets and shelters as but one variant of a class of informal or makeshift residential settings that increasingly characterizes the marginally situated.

Introduction

[A] distinction is drawn by arranging a boundary with separate sides so that a point on one side cannot reach the other side without crossing the boundary.
(G. Spencer-Brown, *Laws of Form*, 1972, 1)

Credible testimony has shown that the "homeless" bear certain common characteristics or "badges" which identify them. Examples [are] their clothing and use of shopping carts.... [They] also display certain common living habits such as returning to their living area at the end of the day, sleeping under bushes and in doorways, and carrying bags containing their worldly possessions.

---

*Originally published in *Housing Policy Debate* Volume 2, Issue 3.

(Judge B. Tam Nomoto, Opinion in *People v. Bell et al.,*
February 1991)

Medieval maps used to carry the warning "Here Be Dragons" to
mark the boundaries of the known world. It is a practice mim-
icked, if only inadvertently, in some recent commentaries on
homelessness.

In 1981, the *New York Times* commissioned novelist and travel
writer Paul Theroux to do a story on a group of people who, for
all intents and purposes, lived underground in the vast reticu-
late subterranean spaces of the city's subway system. Theroux
delivered. His account of what he called subway "skells"[1] is
riveting, an eerie evocation of a strange and unseen world.[2] It
wasn't the first such account; nor would it be the last.[3] But
Theroux sounded a theme that has menaced public perceptions
and discussion of homelessness in this country for a century now:
that such people constitute a distinct, even foreign species.[4] As if
to drive home the message, four years later in a futuristic novel
(O-Zone), Theroux reinvented the same term *(skell)* as the slang
epithet for an outcast group of misshapen, half-savage survivors
living in the ruined, contaminated remains of what used to be
Missouri in the days before a massive nuclear accident occurred.[5]

In the contemporary Western press,[6] the theme of estrangement
is sounded regularly in the evocation of Calcutta to describe
what otherwise might be mistaken for an American commonplace: the street-dwelling poor. But if the fact of their estrangement does not distinguish the contemporary homeless from those
in years past, other things do. In their sheer visibility, their
manifest diversity, the prevalence of evident (especially psychiatric) disabilities, the forces contending on their behalf (home-
grown champions and advocates from without) and the places in
which that struggle is staged (the streets, the press, and the
courts), and the terms of both popular and scholarly debate on
the problem and proposed solutions—in all these varied respects,
today's homeless poor are set apart from their forebears.

This paper proceeds in two stages. It puts off dealing with a
number of conceptual issues that are raised if one treats both
homelessness and its social import as problematic, although that
treatment should logically come first. Instead, the paper first
limns the historical range of phenomena to which the label has
been applied, takes note of anomalies in this mixed bag of groups
and practices, and then applies a finer lens to the American
scene of the past 50 years or so. The discussion touches on a
theme that is often ignored in today's analyses: the varieties of

unobtrusive aid, everyday practices of sharing and support, to which poor households have long resorted as a matter of course to avoid the indignities of public shelter. It is this theme that provides the skeletal frame for a larger, more ambitious argument that can only be sketched here. The argument that develops implicitly in the course of explicating several models of disenfranchisement is that it no longer makes sense (if it ever did) to treat the homeless as a poor apart. Poverty, especially as it occurs under the dramatically reconfigured conditions of housing and work that exist today, remains the most basic fact about homelessness. And it is within poverty's brace that the definition of homelessness should be located.

The paper begins, however, with a nod in the direction of this subject's contrary—home—if only to suggest some of the symbolic and affective resonances that typically have been ignored in the intense scrutiny of homelessness itself and to lay the groundwork for some concluding observations.

Varieties of homelessness

> *Home is where we start from.* (T. S. Eliot, *East Coker*)

> *[H]ome ... is ... the human point of ultimate return.*
> (John Hollander 1991, 33)

Definitions matter because they alert us to how things have changed. Even in the strict sense of the literally homeless,[7] caution should be exercised in applying the notion of homelessness across time, place, or culture. Although homelessness probably occurs in most societies, not only do the forces of displacement vary greatly but so do the configuration and meaning of the ensuing transient state. Moreover—and conceptually this is the most serious missing link in the contemporary discourse[8]—the reference point against which homelessness is measured (conventional dwelling) is not always clear. To take but one example, the rudimentary Western notion of home as a redoubt of domesticity and privacy (English *hearth,* German *heim) is* of comparatively recent origin. Rural housing for most of the population of the *ancien régime* was ruled by work and public sociability. Often such places amounted to little more than hovels shared with animals, and they "fulfilled no social function," not even the minimal one of "serv[ing] as homes for families."[9] Well into the 19th century, as the home took on the trappings of "a glorified domestic retreat in the urban middle class," it continued to serve decidedly more mundane purposes (e.g., as a site for household production) for rural and working-class families.[10]

Drawing the boundary between home and homelessness is further complicated when mobility, work, and tradition enter the picture. Resort to irregular forms of accommodations—what some may refer to as homeless ways of life—can describe the usual situation of whole communities (such as the Rom "gypsies," Irish "travelers," or nomadic hunters and gatherers), who would never think of telling a visiting anthropologist that they do not feel "at home." Uncertain domicile may designate the chosen practice of certain groups (e.g., religious mendicants, or warring or hunting parties) or the lot of specific occupations (migrant workers, prospectors, itinerant preachers). Occasionally, the distinctive niche recognized as homelessness is occupied by a miscellany of players, with little other than their mobility in common. In 14th-century England, for example, wayfaring was an established way of life. The minstrels, laborers, musicians, pardoners, "pedlars," and pilgrims who made up its ranks provided valuable communication links between distant regions, but even they could not escape the traditional suspicion of strangers, a suspicion aggravated by the predations of highwaymen and the lawless example of runaway serfs.[11] Affliction, artifice, and misfortune join forces in Braudel's catalog of the road population of 18th-century France:

> widows, orphans, cripples, … journeymen who had broken their contracts, out-of-work laborers, homeless priests with no living, old men, fire victims, … war victims, deserters, discharged soldiers and even officers, … would-be vendors of useless articles, vagrant preachers with or without licenses, "pregnant servant-girls and unmarried mothers driven from home," children sent out "to find bread or to maraud," … strolling players whose music was an alibi, "instrumentalists whose teeth were as long as their viols and whose bellies were as hollow as their double basses."[12]

Many others at the time, Braudel observes elsewhere, "were virtually homeless, living in makeshift shelters (what would be called shantytowns today)."[13] But note how much of a stretch it would be to consider "virtually homeless" those who inhabit contemporary "squatments" in Latin America: the *favelas* outside Rio de Janeiro, the *barricades* outside Lima, the *barrios* of Caracas. Their dwellings may not be conventional,[14] but they are surely customary and, informally at least, are accorded civil recognition. How else to account for the (conservatively

reckoned) 50,000 "pavement-dwellers" in Calcutta[15] or the
5 million (of a total city population of 12 million) who are "technically squatters"[16] in Bombay? Indeed, the official tolerance of
such settlements amounts to a tacit housing subsidy that plays
an undeniably essential role in the subsistence economy of the
workers who live there.[17]

Diversity in form and content is reflected in linguistic usage as
well. Victorian England would have recognized as homeless
those whom its Elizabethan forebears would have hunted down
as "masterless men." Each era would have readily identified the
other's "vagrants."[18] Late 19th-century America would castigate
as "tramps" those whom New England colonists somewhat more
delicately referred to as the "strolling poor."[19] In the early decades of the 20th century, America's "hobo" performed the same
economic functions as Canada's "bunkhouse man."[20] And, curi-
ously, when in 1959 the *Saturday Evening Post* asked, "Will ours
be the century of homeless people?" it had in mind not the dispossessed poor but the vast cohorts of political refugees of the
time.[21]

There is, then, a fundamental act of social production at work
here—namely, classification. Like "the poor," those whom we
understand to be "the homeless" historically "emerge when
society elects to recognize [homelessness] as a special status and
assigns specific persons to that category."[22] It is not need per se,
but a distinct set of practices and a formal social response—often
devised under circumstances of confrontation—that distinguish
these people in the most elementary fashion. Whether as recipients of emergency relief, as workers of a particularly rough and
disreputable sort, as dodgers of work, as wanderers or squatters,
as the merely (if cruelly) displaced, or as veterans of life on the
street, those who make up a period's official roster of "houseless
poverty"[23] are the product not of a natural distinction drawn but
of a cultural decision made. Conventions of recognition and
legitimation apply to the homeless no less than they do to those
who never leave the safe confines of hearth and home.

Homelessness past

The literature on homelessness in times past is voluminous and
varied.[24] Studies of the indigent on the European continent in
the late feudal period or *ancien régime*[25] make frequent mention
of an itinerant poor who at times were all but indistinguishable
from the poor at large. Owing to the dislocations after the disso-
lution of the monasteries, the tangled skein of Poor Laws, and

the upheavals caused by land enclosures and the rise of industrial towns, the English story is even more detailed and disputed.[26] Huge tomes have been assembled on the history of the vagrant, and fine studies have appeared more recently of the American tramp.[27] Some autobiographical and largely anecdotal material aside, however, very little is available on the history of the homeless woman.[28]

Themes in the social history of vagrancy. If only to highlight a number of enduring (though often disavowed) attitudes toward the homeless poor, a brief overview of core themes in the social history of vagrancy is instructive. The durability of these themes attests more to an underlying cultural ambivalence toward dependency—and, to take it a step deeper, toward work and the bonds of kinship—than to the periodic occurrence of some canonical set of circumstances that recreates the attitude anew each time. Historically in the West, these themes begin to take shape in the wake of the massive dislocations caused by the Black Death in the 14th century. Until that time, a residual, church-based attitude of mercy tempered secular discipline. But the sheer press of numbers and the concentrations of importuning beggars, along with fears of unrest and predation, soon led to measures concerned more with policing than with providing for the rootless poor.

A visible affront, insistent appeals, and the threat of contact and contamination[29]—such are the animating forces behind the call of the good citizens of Bruges in 1524 for a formal system of poor relief to succeed the messy imprecision of casual charity.[30] Although beggars tended to congregate in cities, it is hardly surprising to learn that mobility and unemployment figure strongly in their histories and come to dominate narratives of homelessness. The sources, however, of both their mobility and their lack of work are frequently considered suspect. So, too, is their cry of having nowhere else to turn. More darkly, from time to time allegations appear of outcast societies taking form in the nether ranks of the homeless poor, promulgating their own catechism of sedition and disorder; this occurred even as late as the mid-19th century in New York.[31] The broader danger, of course, was that a working class but newly broken to the wheel of the factory would be "demoralized" (indeed, tempted) by this example of a livelihood wrested without submitting to the regime of work.[32] Finally, given the suspect nature of the class itself, efforts to alleviate its plight— "indiscriminate charity" in particular—were also subject to suspicion, especially if those efforts were viewed as attracting still more of the rootless poor and enabling them to pursue their scurrilous trade.

Historically, then, to be penniless and on the road was to be marked as a member of a poor apart. "The tragedy of the tramp is his isolation," R. H. Tawney observed in 1912. "Every man's hand is against him; and his history is inevitably written by his enemies."[33] It took six depressions in the 19th century before American reformers began to question the wisdom of the idea that vagrancy was at the root of unemployment, rather than the reverse.[34] Another major depression would pass and a second would be well under way before this nation's cultural habit of holding men accountable (as they held themselves) for their lack of work would begin to abate. But by then, of course, the victims of unemployment were heads of households and of their families; single homeless men (and women) would once again have faded into the background of relief, there to be conveniently forgotten.

The legacy of the depression. Skid row in its classic form, the form that would fascinate a generation of American sociologists, was essentially a product of the war effort that had ended the Great Depression. After a decade that saw the numbers of the desperately poor rise to unprecedented levels, the gearing up of the war machine in the early 1940s effectively winnowed the ranks of those in the streets and shelters of all but the elderly and disabled. The 1930s had marked something of a watershed in the history of homelessness in this country: the newly dispossessed of that decade had included migrant families trekking westward, transients permanently on the move, squatter colonies sprouting along the rivers and in the parks of major cities, huge numbers of unemployed men, and a veritable army of young tramps riding the rails in hopeful transit to any place but home. Unprecedented numbers of local homeless made do, for the most part, by relying on family support and private charity. As their numbers grew, these "new poor"[35] surpassed, then displaced, the older, once-thriving communities whose ranks—by trade or by circumstance—had made up the legendary "knights of the road." The lore and lifeways of "hobohemia" proved no match for the realities of mass hardship. Demand for their rootless, specialized labor, already diminishing in the economy of the 1920s, plummeted thereafter. And although traces of that way of life may be found even today, its demise was a matter of record as early as 1940.[36]

Despite wholesale transformation in the ranks of the needy, the public response to homelessness during the depression, with a few notable exceptions,[37] remained hostage to some of the worst elements in the nation's relief tradition. Temporary and plainly inadequate makeshift measures evolved into virtual institutions and once set up, continued to channel program and policy directions through sheer inertial force. In cities everywhere, the common solution was massive congregate shelters as the cornerstone of homeless relief. Inventions[38] of emergency circumstance, such warehouses "crystallized into accepted forms of relief"[39] while the more intriguing (and politically threatening) work experiments were allowed to lapse. Even in the face of steadily mounting evidence of distress, the old American habit of self-blame on the part of the poor showed little sign of abating, except perhaps toward the end of the 1930s.[40] People may have recognized that "outside forces ... were in some vague way responsible, but not really. It was a personal guilt."[41] For some, adherence to the notion that, come what may, they were to be held individually responsible for whatever economic lot befell them may even have been the last "paradoxical ... minimum demanded by self-respect."[42]

The old distinction between neighbor (the local homeless) and stranger (the transient) resurfaced; relief efforts for the two categories were separate and ill-coordinated. Local officials, moreover, came to resent (for the brief period in which it was in existence) the qualitatively better accommodations that the Federal Transient Program offered.[43] Similarly, the distinction between the worthy and unworthy poor persisted, and the single homeless man once again virtually embodied the latter class. *Deterrence* remained the watchword of most of the shelters set up to serve him. He was barred not only from the original work relief program (the Civil Works Administration) but, for the most part, from the Works Progress Administration as well. Social casework bypassed him altogether.[44] Concern with the "demoralizing" effects of relief, moreover, at times seemed more pressing than a determined effort to see that all who were in need got help. Relief, no less than unemployment itself, was thought to breed "a subculture of fear and anxiety, a sallow acceptance of life, a bitter apathy."[45]

Nowhere, observers argued, was this more apparent than in the "shelterizing" effects of facilities for the homeless.[46] The unrelenting experience of failure, especially if constantly confirmed by the company one was forced to keep, rendered men "as open to the mental infection of dependency as they were to various physical infections."[47] Despite such warnings, the warehouse shelter, "social anachronism"[48] though it was recognized to be, proved the dominant form of homeless relief. Sheer economies of scale and an age-old reliance on deterrence[49] were, in all probability, both at stake.

The upshot was that the old debate—over whether character or the economy was the chief culprit in the persistence of unemployment—was revived. But the debate was never resolved. A reformist focus on the structural underpinnings gave way early on to one that looked instead to the needs of special populations of the dispossessed. Only rarely was it recognized, as research findings available at the time suggested, that "the real danger of a permanent relief roll is not that men will have no desire to work, but that such a desire will make no difference."[50] In the end, even in the face of mass hardship, it came down to that enduring staple of the American attitude toward the dependent, the uneasy amalgam of contempt and compassion for the unfortunate other that had marked poor relief since colonial days. Official efforts to suppress transiency while at the same time avoiding the spectacle of public starvation meant that policies and programs hummed with "ambivalence between repression and relief."[51]

For many in need, the stigma of relief and the conditions in shelters amounted to no choice at all. What choice there was came from kinship, real and fictive:

> Many of us know among our acquaintances, as well as among our clients, single men or women who have parents, married brother, or other close relative— sometimes dependent [i.e., receiving public relief]— living near at hand who have provided family association, perhaps a home and a common economic household. Many single individuals have lived for years with intimate friends, perhaps a landlord, or have other intimate associations which constitute a substitute family group.[52]

The postwar period: skid row as prosperity's discontents. In the long period of postwar prosperity, homelessness—even in its relatively degraded form of life on skid row—appeared to be on the verge of extinction. Unprecedented improvements took place in real income and housing conditions for the population at large. Between 1950 and 1970, for example, median family income (adjusted for inflation) nearly doubled. A housing problem did exist, but it was one typified by the remaining cold-water tenements or sharecropper shacks. Notably, the homeless skid row "derelicts" were not considered part of that problem; nor, but for a few pages in Michael Harrington's *The Other America* (1962), did they make much of an appearance in contemporary studies of poverty, except to be reckoned among the "disreputable poor."[53] These social "retreatists"[54]—along with, according to some, their distinctive "subculture"[55]—were relegated to the charge of the missions, detox units, flophouses, jails, and an occasional social work program. "Deviants" in trade and identity, occupants of the lowest social station extant—they stayed within a well-marked sanctuary. Skid row provided both refuge to men who drifted there and respite to communities unwilling to welcome them elsewhere. In this, as more than one observer noted, it was not unlike the asylums to which other classes of misfits and failures were committed.

Among the more telling indicators of this stereotypical "old homelessness" is the ease with which it lent itself to sociological scrutiny. In large part, it did so because the subsistence of such men was rarely in question. For the most part, studies of skid row denizens revealed that, though poor, such men were not penniless. A good number of skid row men (between a third and a half, depending on the local labor market) worked, typically at menial jobs. During the late 1950s in Chicago, for example, Bogue found that the average dweller on Madison Street was employed, at least intermittently, in any week; the median annual income was $1,058.[56] In *Subways Are for Sleeping* (1956), Edmund Love chronicled in fetching detail how a vagrant life could be managed on intermittent jobs (dishwashing, unloading trucks), two suits of clothes (one worn, the other at the laundry), and a berth in a public place (subways preferred) without ever resorting to public or private charity.[57]

More telling still: No matter which skid row one observed— whether in New York, Chicago, or Philadelphia (to take only those closely studied at the time)— "homeless" men were regularly housed. In any of those cities, a street census would have turned up only a few score men (perhaps a hundred at most) sleeping rough.[58] Except in isolated, well-bounded "zones of discard,"[59] their effective invisibility was their salient feature.[60] Indeed, if contemporary trends of urban renewal were any indication, the ecology of skid row itself seemed threatened and the fate of its inhabitants uncertain. The population of the skid row sections of 41 U.S. cities declined by half between 1950 and 1970.[61] Numerous commentators read in such signs the prospect of the imminent demise of skid row itself (or its dispersal in less concentrated areas). A few held out the possibility that such places might survive, on a much reduced scale, as

> a refuge for drop-outs from the working class who have psychic disabilities, a significant proportion of which involve alcoholism. If present trends continue, the population of skid row will continue to decline, and ...

[it] may come to function primarily as an open
asylum.[62]

It does not give away much of the ensuing story to note that,
15 years later, a journalist would reach for that same image of
an open asylum to characterize contemporary shelters for the
homeless.[63]

The resurgence of homelessness

Something was up when *Newsweek*'s inaugural issue for 1984
featured a grainy photograph of a homeless family whose mien
and posture, and even the weather-beaten clapboard wall in the
background, recalled those of the documentary record compiled
by the Farm Security Administration in the 1930s. The implication was unmistakable: were we as a nation about to traverse
that same hardscrabble corridor that the Joad family had trav-
eled during the Great Depression? Nowhere were such portents
clearer than in New York City.

New York City. As early as 1971, it was clear that the new vagrancy[64] would no longer be confined to its traditional precinct,
the Bowery. Indeed, the first and most salient feature of homelessness today is its disregard for the traditional boundaries of
skid row. Much of this no doubt reflects the spontaneous disper-
sion of the homeless poor themselves as they search for individual refuge, shunning the common sanctuaries that the old
zones of discard provided. But this centrifugal tendency is also
apparent in the geography of emergency relief, and it attests to
the press of sheer numbers. In May 1991 New York City operated 15 shelters for men (including one, Camp LaGuardia,
60 miles north of the city) and a dozen for women. Only two of
these facilities were located in the traditional Bowery area, and,
with the exception of those two and Camp LaGuardia, all of them
have been opened since December 1979. Following the pattern of
several years' standing, occupancy in the shelters tends to be
highest in late winter. On an average night in February 1991,
more than 8,700 men and women were lodged; on peak nights,
that figure rose by an additional 300 persons.[65] Thousands more
remain encamped on the streets and in other public spaces.

By comparison, in the mid-1960s the city's entire "shelter" population (including Camp LaGuardia) was estimated at roughly
8,000, and only 41 percent were being lodged at public expense
through emergency shelter funds. Another 7 percent stayed in
the missions or slept rough; perhaps 300 otherwise homeless

men were in city hospitals; an additional 50 were in jail. Homeless women were rare in public, and provisions for their lodging
were confined to a single 46-bed facility on the Bowery.[66]

More striking still is the picture for homeless families. Twice in
the postwar period, New York City has had to turn to commercial hotels, at great public expense, to quarter homeless families
displaced by fires or inhospitable living conditions. Both crises,
in 1947 and again in 1970–71, were relatively short-lived. In the
latter instance, the city managed to relocate 95 percent of a
thousand homeless families within a year, almost all of them in
public housing units.[67] No such option exists today. Affordable
housing is scarce, and informal resources have been taxed beyond capacity. In the early 1980s, the demand for emergency
shelter on the part of homeless families accelerated, rising
24 percent from 1981 to 1982 and then doubling in the next year.
The city now operates 20 shelters for homeless families and
contracts with a number of commercial hotels to lodge additional
families. By the beginning of summer 1986, the number of families lodged in such emergency accommodations had surpassed
4,200. In September 1986, the city was forced to turn to hotels in
New Jersey (for the second time in three years) to meet the
demand. But late in 1988, the city vowed to step up its relocation
efforts and move 17,000 parents and children out of welfare
hotels and into permanent housing in the next two years. By late
summer of 1990, although the homeless family population was
still more than 4,000, only 142 families were left in three hotels.
Eight months later, that figure was back up to 682 families in
14 hotels, and another 516 in congregate shelters. City studies
suggest that two-thirds of the total homeless family population—
or more than 10,000 individuals—are children.[68] This means
that in New York, children constitute a larger proportion of the
sheltered population than do unattached men, a fact replicated
in poverty statistics.

These figures pertain only to those homeless people who have
found their way to public shelters. Large numbers persist in
fending for themselves outside that system, for reasons that
historically have had more to do with the terms and conditions of
the offer of public shelter than with the impaired capacity of
potential clients. Estimates of the numbers of people who regularly sleep on the street; in transportation depots, public parks,
or shanty structures; on the subways; or in any of the innumer-
able fastnesses of the city hidden from sight are notoriously
unreliable. The latest attempt—the Census Bureau's S-Night
effort in 1990 to enumerate those who were visible on the street
in preidentified locations—was fraught with difficulties in

definition, design, and implementation.[69] Even so, a total of
10,447 individuals were counted.[70] Seasoned observers—whether
outreach workers seeking to engage these street dwellers, mobile
soup-and-sandwich teams, or the long-term homeless themselves—are uniformly of the opinion that the numbers continue
to grow.

The national picture. Changes of the order described above
are not specific to New York City, although they appear to be
unusually pronounced there.[71] Nationwide, in the 1980s, the
specter of homelessness proved one of the few embarrassing
realities that proponents of a new morning in America could not
conjure away.[72] Whatever the precise magnitude,[73] scenes of men
and women foraging in garbage cans, conversing earnestly with
unseen companions, catching catnaps along the well-lit lanes of
public commerce and transport, or simply lumbering along with
tattered parcels of belongings in tow have become almost clichéd
fixtures in the urban landscape. Their insistent, obtrusive presence in the rhythms and avenues of everyday life, together with
the marked heterogeneity of the population, signals what is
distinctive about urban homelessness today.[74]

Already by the mid-1980s, reports from city officials in 20 municipalities across the nation confirmed what earlier studies had
predicted. Requests for emergency food and shelter assistance
had continued to climb despite the improved economic climate
after 1983; four years later, at the end of the decade, substantially the same story was told.[75] As the numbers rose, it became
increasingly clear that the contemporary reality of homelessness
accorded poorly with received images of skid row society. Local
studies have documented the differences in great detail.[76]

Today's homeless poor are a far more heterogeneous group than
their immediate skid row predecessors. Indeed, if the reports of
local researchers are any indication, in the past 15 years
homelessness has undergone a transformation of a scale and
complexity not seen since the Great Depression. What had been
treated as a version of the rogues' gallery is now widely recognized as the staging ground for a new kind of poverty. And
although it would be hazardous to take the map as too faithful a
rendition of the territory, local studies have documented a good
deal of regional variation. Today, the homeless population counts
men, women, and children—alone, in small groups, and as families—among its ranks. Geographical mobility is the rule in some
areas while, in other areas, most of the homeless hail from the
immediate surrounds. Encampments of transients have sprung
up in some places, reminiscent of the Hoovervilles of the thirties;

in other places, nomadism prevails on the street. Reflecting the changing composition of poverty at large, today's homeless poor are younger and more ethnically diverse than their counterparts of the 1950s and 1960s. If certain of their number have been found to have problems of substance abuse or a pronounced degree of psychiatric disability, it is also the case that others are distinguishable from the settled poor chiefly by the fact of their displacement.[77]

Within the class as a whole, certain subpopulations may be identified, whose relative proportions vary from region to region:

1. Single-parent households, many of which were receiving public assistance when they became homeless, who have been evicted for failure to pay rent, removed on vacate orders, burned out, or turned out by friends or family with whom they had been doubling up[78]

2. Single men, either indigenous or on the road, who are out of work, are increasingly of ethnic minority status, and often have rudimentary or obsolete job skills, the younger men tending to have job histories concentrated in the peripheral labor market[79]

3. Single women of all ages, who have lost husbands or mates, have been turned out by friends or family, or simply cannot keep up with rising rents[80]

4. Individuals with serious disabilities, severe and persisting mental illness, or long-standing substance abuse problems in particular[81]—some of them having been hospitalized, others not, and all having lost whatever precarious accommodations they once had and being now at a severe disadvantage in competing for the affordable housing that remains

5. Ex-offenders released from jail or prison to fall back on their own meager resources, who face discrimination in securing jobs[82]

6. Homeless youths, who are especially vulnerable to the depredations of the street—some having been ejected from households unwilling or unable to support them any longer, and some having been victims of abuse or graduates of foster care[83]

7.   A host of smaller groups, including the displaced elderly, victims of domestic violence, and legal and undocumented immigrants

Frayed ties to kin, poor prospects of employment, problems of eligibility for assistance, inadequate public assistance levels, and compromised health[84] are circumstances that are distributed throughout these subgroups. Their categorical relationship rests on the single distinction of their seeking public or private shelter or having to trust to their wits on the streets. Though recognized as serious and widespread for nearly a decade now, the problem of homelessness remains consigned largely to the roster of emergency relief, on what is still a largely nonexistent domestic agenda.[85] Uncertainties over the precise scale notwithstanding, it does seem safe to hazard that not since the Great Depression have so many Americans been homeless.[86]

Roots of the new homelessness. Whatever personal quirks, ailments, or deficiencies may put individuals or households at increased risk of becoming homeless, the structural roots of the problem lie in the changes that have taken place over the past two decades in the labor and housing markets in the United States. The net effects of these trends are exacerbated by declining welfare, unemployment, and disability benefit levels for those who qualify and by persisting inequities in federal housing subsidy programs. The upshot, terrible in its simplicity, is the contemporary delineator of homelessness: income insufficient to afford available housing.

The shift of the American economy from goods production to finance, information processing, and services over the past quarter century has dramatically altered labor markets and the demand for work, especially in cities of the Midwest and the Northeast.[87] Wage-based incomes have become increasingly polarized, a fact reflected in growing income disparities. Intensified competition from abroad, coupled with the influx of immigrants (both legal and undocumented) and part-time workers willing to accept the low-wage jobs that remain at home, has placed those Americans with low skills and poor schooling at a significant disadvantage. Minority men of age to enter the labor market have been especially hard hit by the loss of manufacturing jobs: Their earnings and labor market participation rates have plummeted for the past two decades.[88] The quality of life in inner cities has deteriorated—a consequence of both fiscal cutbacks and outmigration of more affluent households—and poverty has become more geographically concentrated. For many young minority men, the shadow economy offers virtually the only source of income; a declining pool of marriageable males has meant, in turn, that many women see female-headed households (at least as they are officially reported) as the sole option for a family life. And what has been described as a sort of "tramping" rite of passage for young African-American males, temporarily between family affiliations,[89] may today frequently include a stint in the public shelters.

As with work, so with housing: Disabilities and social deficits may handicap a given tenant's or family's chances in the market, but it is the game of housing itself that is rigged.[90] Growing numbers of poor households are competing for a shrinking supply of affordable stock. In the past 20 years, the rental housing gap—the number of available and affordable rental units relative to the need—has widened ominously. In 1970, a total of 6.6 million units were reasonably affordable (at 30 percent of income) by about 5.9 million very poor households (those in the bottom income quartile). In 1990, the comparable figures were 8.5 million households chasing 4.3 million units—a gap of 4.2 million units. Huge numbers of inexpensive, unsubsidized units have disappeared from the market, casualties of rising operating costs and decisions to warehouse, convert, or abandon low-rent units. Not surprisingly, then, in 1987, more than a fifth of this nation's rental households devoted more than half their income to meeting housing costs; 4 million households spent more than 70 percent.[91] By an alternative reckoning, 27 million households, or a third of the nation's total, are so tightly strapped that once they settle housing costs each month, they are unable to meet other necessities.[92]

Housing subsidies fall far short of offsetting such difficulties for poor families. In 1989, only 2.2 million (or fewer than a fifth) of those households below the federal poverty line lived in subsidized units. Today, nearly two-thirds of households receiving Aid to Families with Dependent Children (AFDC) live in unsubsidized dwellings, a third of which are substandard, and these residents pay more than half their income for the privilege.[93] Usually unrecognized as "housing assistance," the bulk of such federal help is indirect, buried in the tax structure in the form of income tax deductions for mortgage interest payments, property taxes, or deferred capital gains. Such write-offs greatly favor the better-off Americans: the top fifth income group accounts for 60 percent of all housing subsidies.[94] Another form of subsidy— direct additions to the stock of affordable housing—has declined precipitously in the 1980s in favor of rental vouchers. In the past decade, the federal government has significantly reduced support for new rental construction; even adding "commitments" to existing units, the federal outlay fell by more than 70 percent between 1979 and 1989.[95]

Alternatives to decent work and affordable housing rely on a variety of makeshifts and buffers. Census data indicate that loss of a job was less often a ticket to poverty in the 1960s, when families could afford to take on additional members,[96] but families today are finding themselves increasingly hard-pressed to make ends meet. Since 1970, welfare benefits have badly failed to keep pace with inflation, their real value declining by 39 percent; today, the maximum value of combined cash and food stamp benefits amounts on average to less than three-quarters of the poverty threshold.[97] Similarly, unemployment benefits are reaching a smaller proportion of the jobless than they have at any time in the past 20 years.[98] Thus, it is clear that the first line of defense against the streets remains the support of kin and friends. In Chicago, for example, the average duration between loss of a steady job and literal homelessness was almost four years; like General Assistance clients at large, "these people managed to stay in homes mainly through the generosity of family and perhaps friends, supplemented by casual employment."[99] Perhaps the best index of the precarious situation of those living at the margins are figures that come from nonhomeless comparison groups; such figures have had the inadvertent effect of showing how unexceptional is the literal homelessness of the study group.[100]

The social construction of homelessness

When Harrington undertook to chronicle that "other America" more than a quarter of a century ago, he confronted a poverty that was "invisible ... hidden ... off the beaten track." Tellingly, his account omits sustained attention to homelessness; the subject is confined to a nine-page treatment of "the alcoholic poor," drawing on his experience with *The Catholic Worker* on the Bowery in the early 1950s. Yet even here, in this "place of incredible physical and moral desolation," Harrington departs from convention. Skid row denizens, he notes, "have long been defined as a major problem in our society, but they have not been understood as a problem of poverty, and that is an important fact about them." Whatever the specific contributions of alcoholism, little progress would be made until "the fact that these people are poor" was recognized and dealt with.[101]

Here is an early lesson that society would do well to recover: the link between homelessness and poverty. It is one all too easily missed in the spate of epidemiological studies that dominate contemporary research on homelessness. The problem is not the specificity of such studies. Rather, it is their neglect of larger structural "givens" within which the decisive encounters between individual need and available resources occur. Only by attending to such circumstances can we begin to get at the factors determining how and to what degree personal disabilities become social handicaps.

The definition quandary

> Every definition available to us in the literature on the homeless man becomes in the end an attempt to classify.... All such terms, like "hobo," "tramp," or "bum," are really designations for conditions in which a man may find himself at any time. (Nels Anderson, *The Homeless in New York City* 1934, 151–52)

Although it is a welcome advance over earlier epithets, the studied imprecision of the term *homelessness* has resulted in much confusion—not so much because the distinctions are difficult to state clearly, but because their implications are seen to commit their users to radically different political agendas. In a word, what is understood as legitimate need may be prosecuted as a warrant of entitlement. Put differently, disputes over the definition of homelessness have their roots not in conceptual difficulties but in practical utilities. This section reviews some of the alternative definitions now in circulation and tries to clarify what is at stake in the manifest and tacit disputes.

Classification and reification

Definitions matter because they tell us not only where to look for what we seek but also how to recognize it when we find it. A perennial problem, and one that continues to dog labels even after their users have been apprised of it, is that of reification: the tendency to transform into *things* certain phenomena that are better understood as *relationships or processes.* Most relevant here are phenomena that not only get named and attached to an individual, but also come to dominate the person's social identity and to locate his or her effective world at the margins of the world that so-called normals share.[102] The problem is that in the process, contingent and mutable social forces—by virtue of their being unrecognized—become invisible players on the cultural stage. As Rainwater has observed with specific relevance to the poor, "variables" get attached to "populations" with scarcely a thought given to the social circumstances under which these variables are invoked or to the response that they, in turn, provoke in others.[103] The upshot is that circumstances can be transformed into traits; makeshift, often transient ways of coping with difficulties become lasting attributes of the person coping.[104]

All definitions are matters of convention, but that does not mean that they are simply conjured up out of thin air.[105] Political agendas, for example, may shape the discussion in both subtle and heavy-handed ways. In 1983, the United Nations Commission on Human Settlements announced that it had designated 1987 as the International Year of Shelter for the Homeless. It called on governments worldwide to submit demonstration programs—"ranging from self-help building activities to means of strengthening training, financial and management systems"—that would help others "to improve the grim shelter conditions of the majority of the poor." The U.S. entry—"Freeing the Spirit of Enterprise"—reflected the almost *laissez faire* attitude that characterized federal policies toward the relief of homelessness at that time.[106]

The range of contemporary attentions

Even a casual acquaintance with the contemporary literature or legislation dealing with homelessness is enough to reveal the range of definitions in use. Most definitions pertain to the population, not to the problem, and are at pains to distinguish these "new homeless poor" from their less honorable predecessors.[107] Some definitions, still bearing the dust of field notes, take the form of homespun declarations about the homeless:

> those whose primary nighttime residence is either in the publicly or privately operated shelters or in the streets, in doorways, train stations and bus terminals, public plazas and parks, subways, abandoned buildings, loading docks and other well-hidden sites known only to their users.[108]

Others boast the operationalized precision of survey research, either distilled—

> "without shelter on the night of measurement." Some-
> one using a shelter for the homeless on the night of
> measurement is assumed to be "without shelter."[109]

> not having customary and regular access to a conven-
> tional dwelling.... A person who does not own or rent a
> dwelling and is not a regular member of a household
> that does so is homeless.[110]

or elaborated—

> those currently residing for at least one day but for less
> than fourteen with a friend or relative, not paying rent,
> and not sure that the length of stay will surpass four-
> teen days; those current[ly] residing in a shelter,
> whether overnight or transitional; those currently
> without normal, acceptable shelter arrangements and
> thus sleeping on the street, in doorways, in abandoned
> buildings, in cars, in subway or bus stations, in alleys,
> and so forth; those residing in a treatment center for
> the indigent who have lived at the facility for less than
> 90 days and who claim that they have no place to go,
> when released.[111]

Legislative efforts at definition can also be fairly exhaustive (as
in the McKinney Act), although more narrowly drawn statutory
language is the rule.[112]

Finally, there are those who argue that what is distinctive about
today's homeless poor is the same thing that has been true from
time immemorial: not "an absence of proper housing" but a
pronounced social deficit, "a condition of disaffiliation, a lack of
bonds, a pathology of connectedness."[113]

Definitions matter because, depending on how the boundaries are
drawn, the number in the class can vary substantially. Take the
case of people using soup kitchens in Baltimore.[114] If one adopts
a strict criterion of the homeless—those whose usual residence is
in the street or shelters—only 32 percent of the soup kitchen
patrons are counted. If the definition is broadened to take in
persons who spent at least one night of the past two weeks on
the street or in a shelter, the figure rises by an additional
5 percent. If one includes those whose current residential status
is uncertain and of limited duration, the figure climbs by another
10 to 18 percent (owing to gaps in the data). Finally, if one adds
in those who have been doubled up for six months or more, the
figure rises by an additional 18 percent. (Another 11 percent said

they had been interviewed elsewhere; they are not tabulated here.) Netted out, by the narrow but commonsense gauge of "a place of one's own," fewer than a fifth of the soup kitchen patrons were *not* homeless.

Some views of disenfranchisement

If one turns to the broader models of disenfranchisement within which the subject of homelessness is embedded and interpreted, three approaches may be discerned.

Sociological: a question of ties. Dominating the field of skid row scholarship for at least a decade was the disaffiliation school, bolstered by the heroic research efforts of the Columbia Bowery Project of the late 1960s.[115] In the hands of those analysts, the term *homeless* referred to anyone without the usual social ties to family, work, or community life; it could be applied to the settled as well as to the unsettled (or "literally homeless") poor.[116] There is, moreover, an abiding trait/state ambiguity in the use of the term *disaffiliation.* By contrast, *homelessness* today usually refers only to a condition of subsistence fleeting, recurring, or stable, as the case may be—rather than to a property of persons.

The skid row depicted (or stereotyped, often unfairly)[117] by these scholars was an anticommunity of exiles—the listless, aimless haunt of old men void of ambition or bonds, for whom the empty ritual of a shared bottle provided the only semblance of sociability. Its inhabitants were textbook cases of career retreatists. The place was less interesting for its social forms (typically perceived as perfunctory and evanescent) or its institutional elements than for the personal profiles of its gallery of misfits and failures. Later work[118] laid greater stress on the processes of resocialization into skid row as a way of life. But because so little of this subculture was shared in other than fugitive fashion, a true sociology of skid row proved an awkward undertaking,[119] a cul-de-sac that eventually led to the curious depiction of its social organization in terms of the dynamics, not of group behavior, but of aggregative behavior.[120]

How much of the fault lay with men's souls and how much with their circumstances remained unclear, an ambiguity that goes to the heart of the disaffiliation thesis. In their study of Bowery residents, Bahr and Caplow hypothesized that men who severed ties with the institutions of work, church, and family were more likely to drift into homelessness and remain there. But their survey data showed only that homeless men were likely to have cut such ties, not that their disaffiliation preceded (let alone caused) their homelessness. Even if it begins as a condition, somewhere along the line homelessness acquires the status of a trait if it persists long enough; hence, the meaning of disaffiliation shifted over the course of Bahr and Caplow's analysis— sometimes denoting a social state, other times a personal attribute.[121] However obscure its origins and uncertain its locus, "disaffiliation" is something that is "wrong" with such men; their homelessness, in turn, is only one manifestation of that something.

But the legacy of the disaffiliation school cannot be dismissed so easily. In its selective attention to the dimension of connectedness and its concentration on family and kin ties, the disaffiliation school both informs and misleads. It is, to this author's thinking, a serious error to reduce the dimensions of contemporary homelessness to "a pathology of connectedness" (as Bahr continues to insist), given the mounting evidence that both homeless single persons and homeless families have drawn upon, continue to draw upon, and in some cases have exhausted family and friends in their struggle to survive. Simply put, "family and kinship ties, friendship constellations, and organizational participation" are indeed "critical foci" in the dynamics of homelessness, even if they are not the essential elements in defining it.[122] As was true in the 1930s, such makeshifts still account for the bulk of emergency shelter provided today and frequently spell the difference between a shared home among friends and the anonymous kindness of strangers.

Social-ecological: needs and practices. To say what "living in poverty" means practically, one must not only specify a (somewhat arbitrary) threshold of hardship,[123] but also describe coping behaviors: those practices that enable a household to survive below the official floor of subsistence. The same is true of homelessness. To the extent that public shelter lends itself to a variety of utilities—some of which are distinct from, if not at odds with, its declared purpose—recurring use of this resource may be included within the class of makeshifts that emerge under conditions of housing scarcity.[124]

For purposes of policy, the broader definition of homelessness is preferable because it more accurately reckons the universe of need. Such an approach takes in the precarious lodgings of those who double up with friends or family, or the situation of those facing release from hospital or jail or a rehabilitation program without a residence.[125] It also accords with the findings of longitudinal studies only now beginning to yield results. Sosin and his colleagues in Minneapolis, for example, tracked a cohort of nearly 500 homeless individuals. They conclude that

> the state of homelessness appears to be more a drift
> between atypical living situations and the street
> than between normality and street life. In other words,
> the typical pattern of homelessness seems to be one of
> *residential instability* rather than constant homeless-
> ness over a long period.[126]

Statutory definitions, with the notable exception of that con-tained in the McKinney Act, have generally been drawn in more restrictive terms. And although it can be argued that a more flexible definition of homelessness—say, along the lines of "resi-dential instability," as suggested by Sosin and colleagues—is more faithful to the phenomenon, neither consistency nor conceptual clarity is primarily at issue here. The definition of the class is also, potentially at least, the staking of an entitlement. And historically, in matters that concern redistribution, politics—not logic—plays the dominant role.[127]

A social-ecological approach may also serve to redirect attention to necessary ingredients that are otherwise consigned to the status of background variables. Take, for example, Rossi and Wright's catalog of factors affecting the numbers of those on the street or in shelters:

> the size of the literally homeless population is driven by
> those macroprocesses that affect the availability of low-
> skilled employment, the ability of poor families to help
> their less fortunate members, the market conditions
> affecting the supply of very low cost housing for single
> persons, and the coverage of income-maintenance pro-
> grams for disabled and single persons.[128]

Strictly speaking, homelessness in this view takes on the socio-logical character of an ascribed status: a public recognition that follows an explicit or (as may be the case with some of those on the street) implicit declaration of need. This usage derives from Simmel's sociology of *Der Arme*, in which he argues that the poor come into existence, as it were, by social fiat. Not absolute priva-tion but relative deprivation, recognized as such, is the *sine qua non* for the emergence of the class:

> It is only from the moment they are assisted—perhaps
> already when their total situation would normally
> require assistance, even though it has not yet been

given—that they become part of a group characterized
by poverty. This group does not remain united by interaction among its members, but by the collective attitude
which a society as a whole adopts toward it.[129]

Simmel's approach has the advantage of preserving the historic
association of homelessness with vagrancy. It does not fix the
definition of homelessness to either work (as was historically
done with men) or sexuality/marital history (as was the case
with women). It is flexible enough to accommodate the broad
class of shelterless individuals in evidence today. It suggests
that the terms and conditions under which need is recognized as
valid may be contested, subject to a host of competing interests
that may be foreign (if not hostile) to the determination of actual
need. It suggests further that the contingencies of service delivery are a better guide to actual policy than are officially es-
poused principles. And at the same time that it draws attention
to the conceivably vast reservoir of unmet need, to a kind of
shadow homelessness, it also raises questions about the utility of
such a distinction.

Makeshift economies: homelessness and marginality. The boundary between the frankly homeless and those in imminent risk of
becoming so has become increasingly porous in recent years, as
the situation of the settled poor has become more tenuous. So
striking is this development that the notion of a staged, one-way
process, according to which individuals living at the edge of
subsistence are pushed by some crisis over the threshold of
homelessness, has been called into question.[130] An alternative
hypothesis holds that within the subsistence world of the marginally situated, bouts of homelessness—like repeated moves
into and out of the welfare system[131]—are increasingly common.
Episodic in nature and affecting the lives of large numbers of the
poor beyond those overtly without shelter on a given night,
homelessness may be a recurrent fact of life, of varying degrees
of frequency and severity, for members of these households.
Indeed, researchers in Los Angeles have suggested that cyclical
homelessness may now be the modal type of homelessness in
that city.[132]

Viewed in this way, homelessness is a contingent state defined
against a shifting background of an array of conditional shelter
arrangements (time-limited caretaking, doubling up with friends
or family, seasonal employment with on-premises housing, and
so on). Such a "makeshift economy" perspective[133] treats informal social support less as a capital asset than as a strategic good
to be deployed in what may be complex and carefully calibrated

ways. How such reserves are traded on is a function of both the press of circumstance and the operant rules of relationship and reciprocity. Turning to such resources is not without costs, nor can their availability be taken for granted. Decisions about their use over time must weigh considerations well beyond the surmise of casual inquiry. Thus, what strikes an observer as a depleted informal support network or an immediate lack of housing may instead reflect a decision to reserve a privileged resource for later use.

Implications. This last approach not only accommodates those everyday means of coping with adversity and shortages that have long characterized life among the poor and very poor, but also suggests that homelessness of the scale and complexity evident today is best viewed as one manifestation of contemporary poverty.[134] Once this linkage is recognized, another one follows. The attachment of meanings to persons always involves the exercise of power, but that does not ensure that the act will be uncontested. Implicit here is the allowance for unexpected, even counterintuitive, action on the part of the subject class itself.

For example, the poor may (1) reject the terms or conditions of official definitions; (2) thwart official detection or verification rules (e.g., man in the house); or (3) organize, protest, riot, or appear to be threatening to do so, thereby shaking a little more out of the redistribution tree. The recognition of this possibility serves as a corrective to a too-dogmatic reading of the "social construction" position and honors a latent capacity that, when exercised by the poor, can "undermine the very status that they occupy."[135] Poor people have done precisely that several times in the recent past, and even within the most disenfranchised of their ranks today, similar movement may be stirring again—as occurred in an organization of New York City's homeless families, Parents on the Move.[136]

The point is not simply that there is a moral (or cultural) dimension to relative deprivation that exists above and beyond whatever structural forces are posited. Rather, it is that the deprived themselves, people who are potential recipients of aid, may well play a determining role in setting the terms and conditions of legitimate need. Any account of the social construction of poverty must reckon with the "moral economy of the poor." Discussing the food riots in 18th-century England, E. P. Thompson writes that

> these grievances operated within a popular consensus
> as to what were legitimate and what were illegitimate
> practices in marketing, milling, baking, etc. This in its
> turn was grounded upon a consistent traditional view of
> social norms and obligations, of the proper economic
> functions of several parties within the community,
> which, taken together, can be said to constitute the
> moral economy of the poor. An outrage to these moral
> assumptions, quite as much as actual deprivation, was
> the usual occasion for direct action.[137]

No doubt, matters are not always so clear, and the dictates of a consistent traditional view—especially with respect to what constitutes a conventional dwelling—may be disputed. Nor has historical analysis succeeded in clarifying the circumstances under which moral outrage is fired. But in the troubled course of public shelter in the United States in the 1980s, the role of such indignation has been critical, and the tools at its disposal have ranged from public demonstrations to judicial petition to legislation.

Finally, such a position allows for the historically well-documented redefinition of public utilities—be they open spaces, jails, treatment facilities, or specialized shelters—by their users, as well as by frontline staff and the officials in charge of protecting order or recycling surplus property.[138] It thus credits the poor with more of a role in the day-to-day shaping of institutional routines and functions than is typically the case in social welfare histories.

Reprise: the functional space of shelter. Suppose one were to revise the social-ecological approach to homelessness to include a pattern of intermittent resort to informal housing resources, supplied on an ad hoc basis by one's network of family and friends. From this standpoint, homelessness is not a trait, an impairment, or even a social deficit (as various positions have claimed). Rather, it is a circumstance, arising from a variety of causes, that presents a problem to be solved: where to stay that night. It may be solved for better or worse, by design or default, in temporary or more lasting fashion, in seen and unseen ways, by a variety of makeshifts. Public shelter is one such makeshift—the most prominent but probably not the most substantial (in terms of actual carrying capacity).

This point may become clearer if the institutional space spanned by the category of functional emergency shelter is mapped in a two-by-two matrix, along the axes of visibility and formality (fig. 1). Four cells result, within which may be located the arrangements that pass for emergency shelter today:

Figure 1. **The Functional Space of Shelter**

Visible   Invisible

	Visible	Invisible
Formal	1	3
Informal	2	4

1. Formal/visible: public shelter facilities and private refuges, the declared purpose of which is to offer emergency accommodations to those who have none

2. Informal/visible: jury-rigged emergency lodging provided by institutions whose avowed function is something else (although it may be related), such as churches and synagogues offering shelter in their basements, schools, or function rooms

3. Formal/invisible: public institutions whose primary function is not to provide shelter but to treat illness or trauma (hospitals, emergency rooms), to detain people accused of crimes (jails), or to confine the mentally disabled (psychiatric facilities), but that may, inadvertently, solve an individual's problem of homelessness for the duration of his or her stay

4. Informal/invisible: the makeshift arrangements provided by friends and family in their own dwellings, often illicitly

Regardless of the outcome of the scholastic debates, the thrust of current research is that homelessness in the most encompassing sense of the term has to do with various kinds and degrees of residential uncertainty and instability. In the absence of secure and stable dwelling, people have devised makeshifts that span everything from shared (and overcrowded) living arrangements to a nomadic life on the streets. Officially, only those makeshifts that are on display in public spaces, and the need that declares itself to public or charitable authorities, are classified as homelessness. Up to that point, hardship may exist, but it exists as coping, as at-risk populations, or as unmet need. It is not defined as homelessness.

This approach accords the official definition of homelessness a certain face validity that, as ethnographic fact, is bound to be respected. It also draws our attention to subtler shaping currents. Culturally, the condition that the state defines as homelessness[139]—like the acts it defines as crime—is not only interesting in its own right (whatever misgivings the members of the culture at large may have about the bias of that definition); it is also a telling sign of the political dimensions of categorical need. But the official definition is not the only one. The precise dimensions of the problem and the kinds of makeshifts that are to be sanctioned as legitimate homelessness are contested matters. Tradition too has its political aspects, and power—not logic—takes center stage in reasoning the need.

What kind of social problem?

Given the welter of studies, testimony, and reports the new vagrancy has occasioned—and, at times, the highly politicized nature of the discussion—it is not surprising that explanatory accounts have multiplied. Among the few constants is a consensus that homelessness today poses a serious problem in urgent need of redress. To any but the professionally contrary, the presence of large numbers of citizens living on the streets or in emergency shelters readily satisfies Merton's criterion of a social problem: "a sizeable discrepancy between what is and what people think ought to be."[140] Beyond that, little about the nature or locus of the problem is uncontested. If indeed some "cherished value" is being challenged, there is, as one of Merton's colleagues insists, no agreement about "what that value really is and ... what it is that really threatens it."[141]

The idiom of pathology. In some quarters, the tendency to resort to the discourse of disease has been pronounced, and it serves to link what is thought to be the one novel feature of the contemporary problem—the presence of large numbers of the mentally ill among the homeless—to the problem of the indigent alcoholic. In other quarters, the new deviance has entirely eclipsed the old. Indeed, it is not uncommon to see virtually the entire problem of homelessness reduced to the dimension of deranged street dwellers.[142] Although some analysts insist that the failures of deinstitutionalization must be placed within the context of a larger fiscal crisis and of a severely depleted low-income housing market,[143] common folk wisdom remains hostage to the notion that were it not for the mass release of psychiatric patients, there would be no crisis of homelessness.

Nor have imputations of pathology been limited to the florid psychoses of the street. The rapid increase in homeless families in some areas has revived debates about the nature of such "disordered" families and about the reasons for the preponderance of single-parent households among them. In some of these analyses are echoes of the culture-of-poverty thesis, which posits a relatively autonomous system of values and behavior passed on from parent to child. It had been suggested, for example, that families in emergency shelters might be transmitting "a heritage of homelessness" from one generation to the next;[144] more recent studies dispute that interpretation.[145]

A still-suspect class. There are, in other quarters of commentary, discernible traces of 16th-century tracts that aimed at penetrating the ruses and disguises of "counterfeit beggars." One analyst warns cities against following New York's lead in instituting a more adequate system of public shelter because, in his view, such a policy only encourages people who could otherwise manage on their own to take up permanent lodgings in emergency facilities. Despite much evidence to the contrary, this position sees the problem as a simple example of Say's Law: A supply of emergency shelters is creating a demand that otherwise would not exist. The same argument has recently been extended to the situation of homeless families in New York, where the evidence of this happening has been met with an equal measure of disbelief.[146]

For their part, advocates for the homeless have resisted any analysis that recalls the blame-the-victim approaches that have been applied to disenfranchised groups in the past. Instead, the advocates insist that homelessness must be seen as evidence that fundamental needs-meeting mechanisms—those in the market and those in government—have failed. The advocates' fear is not without historical grounding. Reducing structural problems in the economy to the fault or burden of special populations is a familiar gambit in official policy and one that has long been applied to the wandering poor of this country.[147] Usually, but not invariably, such a reduction occurs in the service of a disciplinary agenda. Homelessness has been variously construed as the hapless plight of impaired minds, as the deviant subculture of the chronically marginal poor, and as the latest trick of the idle and unscrupulous. There is a common theme to such claims: Its origins may be varied, but homelessness, once it takes hold, persists—like the "pauperization" or "demoralization" of earlier eras—because it transforms character. Therefore, corrective measures must have a moral as well as a therapeutic cast: "The majority of the homeless need intensive services, mental health care, discipline and order in their lives."[148]

Seeking to redress the balance, advocates (this author among them) have emphasized the victimization of the homeless. If this emphasis sometimes occurs at the expense of recognizing their specific humanity, here, too, the advocates have followed historical suit. Heirs to the documentary tradition of American cultural criticism,[149] they have also fallen prey at times to the strains of paternalism and sentiment that have marred that tradition in the past. With few exceptions, the homeless poor have played little role in these analyses, appearing rather as mute casualties of forces beyond their ken or control.[150]

From the new homelessness to enduring pouerty. The necessary corrective will be found only by returning the discussion of homelessness to that of poverty as a whole. There are, to be sure, significant risks in such a move. But it does seem fair to say that the harrowing simplicity of the term *homeless* may have outlived its utility. Whatever specific immediate gains are to be won by arguing for targeted programs for specific exceptional populations, it may be prudent in the long run to shift the definition of the problem, the focus of advocacy efforts, and the scope of analysis to more universal themes.[151] Such a deliberate redirection would have the added advantages of moving from remedial programs to preventive measures[152] and of engaging a potentially much larger constituency. But it will first have to contend with the legacy of a decade that saw misery return to the streets on a scale that had not been seen for 50 years. It must contend, that is, with the forces of distancing and dismissal with which this paper opened and to a discussion of which, in closing, it must return.

Conclusion

> *Thou art the thing itself; unaccommodated man is no more but such a poor, bare, forked animal as thou art (King Lear, act 3, sc. 4, line 106)*

Largely because of seismic changes in the labor and housing markets, the cultural landscape shifted in the 1980s, allowing researchers and average citizens—as the Great Depression had allowed James Agee, Walker Evans, and their readers—a glimpse into "a portion of unimagined existence"[153] ordinarily unavailable. In neither case was the poverty new; in neither case was its normal unavailability accidental. Whether the poor were tenant farmers in Alabama in the 1930s, African-American families in contemporary Chicago or Boston,[154] or, for that matter, working-class families in 19th-century Massachusetts,[155] such travails were part and parcel of what it meant to scrape by on the rough edge of subsistence. Out of such contrivances, unseen and unheralded, did the poor manage to survive. That this was largely unknown, at times even actively concealed, was as it should be: This was the way cultural (and class) boundaries were supposed to work.

When such boundaries are eroded, the shock of meeting poverty on the street— "houseless," its hand outstretched, and the plea for assistance made personal and immediate—is both real and disingenuous. It is real because people who have lived with the convenience of not seeing poverty can prove to be quick studies when they finally confront it in the flesh. There is, after all, a linkage to be prized in the sudden realization of a Presbyterian elder at a Salt Lake City soup kitchen that she was "one job and one divorce away" from the people she was serving.[156] It is disingenuous because the poverty plainly had always been there for the seeing. It was not the case (much press to the contrary) that some previously unknown, long-festering underclass had emerged.[157] What was new, in a word, was that, as a fact of everyday life, poverty had become unavoidable. Shielding it from sight was no longer something that the culture took care of; to turn a blind eye to suffering these days, one had to cultivate the habit of not seeing. That takes time, and it is neither simple nor painless.

If, as Lilian Brandt[158] once argued, there is little that is new in the corrective measures each era adopts to cope with the burden of the displaced poor, it is also the case that recycled policy often goes unrecognized as such. Forced to cultivate the habit of not seeing, Americans have rediscovered how difficult that is and how easily resentment displaces sympathy. Like the citizens of Bruges in the 16th century, society has rushed to institutionalize measures that, whatever their long-term costs, at least promise the short-term gain of removing the spectacle of poverty from the street. Like their counterparts in the 19th century, New York City agencies, reading portents of general disorder in the example of unrestricted panhandling, have gone to court to secure a ban against begging in the subways.[159] Like irate townsmen combating the tramp menace, local governments have returned to the practice of "warning out" the undomiciled on the premise that it is so much cheaper to move them on than to assist them or to suffer their presence. And like relief officials in the 1930s, states and municipalities have turned first to private charity and then to the long-discredited practice of storing surplus persons in warehouses and armories.

Driven by a mounting sense of things tumbling out of control, such measures have as their object, whether as underlying logic or explicit design, the reestablishment of proper boundaries between a well-hidden poor and a no-longer-uneasy settled citizenry.[160] Whatever their immediate value as instruments of relief, these measures stop far short of seeking to rectify—or even to address—the structural roots of the poverty attested to by mass homelessness. More damaging still, they may have the effect of easing the abrasion needed to motivate the search for a more lasting and inclusive resolution. To borrow Lear's phrase, "the thing itself" is not mere lack of shelter. It is not the absence of a prescribed set of rules, services, and medications in a carefully structured environment that will enable the chronically ill or afflicted to live decently, if apart from the rest of us. It is not the lack of specialized assistance for troubled families. It is something far more fundamental than that: the barely noticed loss of a sustained and determined commitment to make available to all at least the material resources and social tools needed to participate fully in this society.[161]

In closing, what are the core elements to this line of argument? The opposite of homelessness is not shelter but home, and, socially understood, home must entail some claim to solidarity.[162] The question underlying homelessness policy, then, is not, what does charity demand? but rather, what does solidarity require? It is not sufficient to ask what it is about the homeless poor that accounts for their dispossession. One must also ask what it is about "the rest of us" that has learned to ignore, then managed to tolerate, and now seeks to banish from sight the evidence of a present gone badly awry.[163]

Phrased this way, the question is deeply disturbing. For some time now, aside from those infrequent and horrifying preparations for Third World invasions, this country has been markedly short on solidarity. It is not that common decency has become such an uncommon commodity. Rather, it is that mobilizing common decency, animating it, and putting it to constructive use in collective action require both a will and a stalwart sense of urgency that seem patently absent, embarrassing even to mention, in the ranks of the nation's political leadership. With rare exceptions, there has never been (in William James's fine phrase) "the moral equivalent of war"[164]—at *home,* on the *domestic front.* How easily and misleadingly those terms have come to signify shared heritage in so consistently divided a nation.

That Lear was banished to the heath was a transgression of kinship. He took refuge there in the cave of Poor Tom, himself masquerading as a homeless lunatic to escape the treachery of his half-brother. Is this as far as the legacy of tradition can take us—that answers are to be found in disciplining kinship to meet its obligations? Or in trusting to the comfort found only in the hovels of similarly kinless strangers? Grant that the welfare state has made some progress since Elizabethan times and assume that the word is something more than a slogan to be cheered safely on foreign shores: What would solidarity require here, at home?

Author

Kim Hopper is a medical anthropologist working as a Research Scientist at the Nathan S. Kline Institute for Psychiatric Research, and the Center for the Study of Issues in Public Mental Health, in Orangeburg, New York. He is also a lecturer at the Columbia University School of Public Health and past president of the National Coalition for the Homeless. [1997]

Endnotes

1. Possibly a corruption of the 17th-century English *skellum,* meaning "rascal, devil, pestilence, carcase, etc." (*Oxford English Dictionary*).

2. P. Theroux, "Subway Odyssey," *New York Times Magazine,* January 31, 1982, 20.

3. Anthony Muto wrote an article for the *New York Telegram* in 1929 describing "a new tribe of mendicants ... young and old, male and female, white and black" living in the subways (*Literary Digest,* June 8, 1929, pp. 54–55); compare Theroux's account with Jennifer Toth's article on New York's "mole people" in the *Los Angeles Times,* September 2, 1990, 1.

4. For a tracing of this theme in New York's history, see Kim Hopper, "A Poor Apart: The Distancing of Homeless Men in New York's History," *Social Research* 58(1991):107–32.

5. P. Theroux, *O-Zone* (New York: Putnam, 1986). Strikingly, it is the discovery of their residual humanity, even in the most primitive surrounds, that sounds the novel's core and quite traditional theme.

6. See, for example, a running series of *New York Times* editorials (begun on July 15, 1987, A26) entitled "The New Calcutta." Compare with a fine piece in the *Washington Post* by Michael Specter (March 3, 1991, p. C1)

that, while succumbing to the Orientalist trope, manages to make exactly the opposite point. The image of Calcutta (especially with reference to "the black hole of Calcutta") occurs in the press as early as the 1870s with respect to the denizens of the police stations (that period's effective shelters).

7.   That is, those who do "not [have] customary and regular access to a conventional dwelling" (P. Rossi, *Down and Out in America: The Origins of Homelessness* [Chicago: University of Chicago Press, 1989], 10)—essentially, those who live in shelters or on the street.

8.   It is an issue recently and usefully explored by a range of scholars at a New School for Social Research conference, "Home: A Place in the World," the proceedings of which have been published in *Social Research* 58(Spring 1991).

9.   See P. Aries, *Centuries of Childhood* (New York: Knopf, 1962), 392.

10. See T. K. Hareven, "The Home and the Family in Historical Perspective," *Social Research* 58(1991):273.

11. See J. Jusserand, *English Wayfaring in the Middle Ages,* rev. ed. (London: Ernest Benn, 1920), and A. L. Beier, *Masterless Men: The Vagrancy Problem in England, 1560–1640* (New York: Methuen, 1985).

12. F. Braudel, *Civilization and Capitalism, 15th–18th Century,* vol. 2, *The Wheels of Commerce* (New York: Harper and Row, 1982), 510–11.

13. F. Braudel, *Civilization and Capitalism, 15th–18th Century,* vol. 1, *The Structures of Everyday Life* (London: Collins, 1981), 285.

14. Such "houses are not docketed in the city registries either as individual houses or as aggregates of houses, or places" (A. Leeds, "The Concept of the 'Culture of Poverty,' " in *The Culture of Poverty: A Critique,* ed. E. Leacock [New York: Simon and Schuster, 1971], 237).

15. S. Mukherjee, *Under the Shadow of the Metropolis: They Are Citizens Too* (Calcutta: Calcutta Metropolitan Development Authority, 1975), 68. This is the official census figure and, even then, a hopeless underestimation.

16. *New York Times,* April 25, 1991, p. 15.

17. See, for example, J. Perlman, *The Myth of Marginality* (Berkeley: University of California Press, 1976). Closer to home, a *New York Times* editor has recently endorsed "legalized limited squatting" as an expedient for returning to use thousands of city-owned housing units for which there are no immediate development plans (October 30, 1990, p. A24).

18. C. J. Ribton-Turner, *A History of Vagrants and Vagrancy and Beggars and Begging* (London: Chapman and Hall, 1887).

19. D. L. Jones, "The Strolling Poor: Transiency in Eighteenth-Century Massachusetts," *Journal of Social History* 8(1975):28–54.

20. N. Anderson, *The Hobo* (Chicago: University of Chicago Press, 1923); E. W. Bradwin, *The Bunkhouse Man* (New York: Columbia University Press, 1928).

21. *Saturday Evening Post,* September 12, 1959. When the magazine did run a story on the predecessors of today's homeless, it observed vernacular practice: "Skid Row: Junk Heap for Human Beings" (*Saturday Evening Post,* December 20, 1952). This distinction is one the disaffiliation school tends to elide: "Migrants and refugees" and "chronic wanderers and alcoholics" are seen as two subgroups of the larger class (H. M. Bahr, *Skid Row: An Introduction to Disaffiliation* [New York: Oxford University Press, 1973], 18, 285).

22. L. Coser, "The Sociology of Poverty," *Social Problems* 13(1965):141.

23. The phrase appears in *King Lear* (act 3, sc. 4, line 26), a play freighted with images of homelessness, and introduces Lear's famous "poor naked wretches" speech (cf. M. Ignatieff, *The Needs of Strangers* [New York: Viking, 1984]).

24. See H. M. Bahr, ed., *Disaffiliated Man: Essays and Bibliography on Skid Row, Vagrancy, and Outsiders* (Toronto: University of Toronto Press, 1970) for an instructive selection.

25. See N. Z. Davis, "Poor Relief, Humanism and Heresy: The Case of Lyon," *Studies in Medieval and Renaissance History* 5(1968):217–75; O. Hufton, *The Poor in Eighteenth Century France, 1750–1789* (Oxford, England: Clarendon Press, 1974); M. Mollat, *The Poor in the Middle Ages* (New Haven: Yale University Press, 1986).

26. R. H. Tawney, *The Agrarian Problem in the Sixteenth Century* (London: Longmans, Green, 1912); S. Webb and B. Webb, *English Poor Law History, Part I: The Old Poor Law,* rev. ed. (Hamden, CT: 1927; Archon, 1963); Beier.

27. P. T. Ringenbach, *Tramps and Reformers, 1873–1916* (Westport, CT: Greenwood Press, 1973); K. L. Kusmer, "The Underclass in Historical Perspective: Tramps and Vagrants in Urban America, 1870–1930," in *On Being Homeless: Historical Perspectives,* ed. R. Beard (New York: Museum of the City of New York, 1987), 20–31; E. H. Monkkonen, ed., *Walking to Work* (New York: Cambridge University Press, 1984).

28. In part, this lack appears to be because both local chroniclers and later historians have tended to be more interested in her common trade— prostitution—than in the destitution and homelessness she would otherwise suffer, as Stephanie Golden's work in progress (*Woman on the Outside*) should show.

29. That is, contamination from—not to put too fine a point on it—"pollution": fears of physical and moral infection were often symbolically confounded, if not fused (see M. Douglas, *Purity and Danger* [London: Routledge and Kegan Paul, 1966]).

30. See F. R. Salter, *Some Early Tracts on Poor Relief* (London: Methuen, 1926) for the relevant documents.

31. P. Boyer, *Urban Masses and Moral Order in America, 1820–1920* (Cambridge: Harvard University Press, 1978), 89–90. At that time, unattached paupers were considered the moral equivalent of the plague (see J. L. Hagen, "Whatever Happened to 43 Elizabeth I, C2?" *Social Service Review* 56[1982]:111).

32. Kusmer.

33. Tawney, 275.

34. Ringenbach.

35. To my knowledge, the term was first used by Pauline Young ("The New Poor," *Sociology and Social Research* 17[1933]:56–64) to characterize the Great Depression's casualties of unemployment, was later revived (and disputed) during the Johnson administration's War on Poverty (S. Thernstrom, "Is There Really a New Poor?" *Dissent* 15 [January-February 1968]:59–64), and then found new life on the heels of the 1981–82 recession.

36. For representative accounts, see N. Anderson, *Men on the Move* (Chicago: University of Chicago Press, 1940); T. Caplow, "Transiency as a Cultural Pattern," *American Sociological Review* 5(1940):731–39; K. A. Lovald, "From Hobohemia to Skid Row: The Changing Community of the Homeless Man" (Ph.D. diss., University of Minnesota, 1960); R. A. Bruns, *Knights of the Road* (New York: Methuen, 1980).

37. I have in mind chiefly the short-lived work camp experiments and the Federal Transient Program.

38. Or, more accurately, reinventions: the model was the age-old one of the almshouse, effectively retrofitted for emergency use (see D. Rothman, *The Discovery of the Asylum* [Boston: Little, Brown, 1973], and T. Finnegan, "The Once and Future Poorhouse," *Empire State Report* [May 1991]:48–54).

39. M. Lewis, "You Can't Stay Here. Washington Ditches the Transient." *Social Work Today* 3:8–10, 1935; R. S. Wilson, "Problems in Coordinating Service for Transient and Resident Unattached from the Point of View of Individual Service," Proceedings of the National Conference of Social Work (Chicago: University of Chicago Press, 1935), 219.

40. See R. S. McElvaine, *Down and Out in the Great Depression: Letters from the Forgotten Man* (Chapel Hill: University of North Carolina Press, 1983), 11–12, and J. T. Patterson, *America's Struggle Against Poverty, 1900–1980* (Cambridge: Harvard University Press, 1981), 52–53, for discussions.

41. S. Terkel, *Hard Times* (New York: Avon, 1970), 20.

42. E. W. Bakke, *The Unemployed Worker* (New Haven: Yale University Press, 1940), 25–26.

43. See J. M. Crouse, *The Homeless Transient in the Great Depression: New York 1929–1941* (Albany: State University of New York Press, 1986), for an authoritative discussion of the program as it took shape in New York State.

44. W. McMillan, "Single Blessedness," *Survey* 70(March 1934):74–75; E. F. Reed, *Federal Transient Program: An Evaluative Survey* (New York: Committee on Care of Transients and Homeless, 1934), 35; I. Seligson, "The Case of the Homeless Man in New York City" (Thesis, New York

School of Social Work, 1940); W. W. Bremer, *Depression Winters* (Philadelphia: Temple University Press, 1984), 6.

45. T. Minehan, *Boy and Girl Tramps of America* (New York: Farrar and Rinehart, 1934), xii.

46. The locus classicus is E. H. Sutherland and H. J. Locke, *Twenty Thousand Homeless Men* (Chicago: J. B. Lippincott, 1936). For the contemporary version, see J. Grunberg and P. F. Eagle, "Shelterization: How the Homeless Adapt to Shelter Living," *Hospital and Community Psychiatry* 41(1990):521–25, and the exchange of letters in *Hospital and Community Psychiatry* 41 (December 1990).

47. L. Brandt, *An Impressionistic View of the Winter of 1930–1931 in New York City* (New York: Welfare Council, 1932), 24.

48. R. S. Wilson, 219.

49. At times, deterrence was formalized: In 1938, New York City rejected over half the applicants for emergency shelter simply by intensifying the intake inquiry to discover, for example, how many had relatives in the area (W. B. Herlands, *Administration of Relief in New York City* [New York: City of New York, Department of Investigation, 1940], 125).

50. E. W. Bakke, "Fifth Winter of Unemployment," *Yale Review* 24(1934–35):268.

51. Caplow, 732.

52. R. S. Wilson, 214.

53. D. Matza, "The Disreputable Poor," in *Class, Status and Power: A Reader in Social Stratification,* ed. Reinhard Bendix and Seymour M. Lipset, 2d ed. (New York: Free Press, 1966), 289–302.

54. R. K. Merton, "The Sociology of Social Problems," in *Contemporary Social Problems,* ed. R. K. Merton and R. Nisbeth, 4th ed. (New York: Harcourt Brace Jovanovich, 1976), 7; Bahr, *Disaffiliated Man,* 42–44.

55. S. E. Wallace, *Skid Row as a Way of Life* (Totowa, NJ: Bedminister Press, 1965).

56. D. Bogue, *Skid Row in American Cities* (Chicago: University of Chicago Press, 1963). By contrast, Rossi's research team found that only 39 percent of those interviewed had worked in the past month, and the adjusted annual median income amounted to less than a third of that of their 1950s counterparts (P. H. Rossi, G. A. Fisher, and G. Willis, *The Condition of the Homeless of Chicago* [Amherst, MA: Social and Demographic Research Institute, and Chicago, National Opinion Research Council, 1986]).

57. E. G. Love, *Subways Are for Sleeping* (New York: Harcourt Brace, 1956).

58. A single rough contrasting index is irresistible at this point: in New York City in March 1990, the U.S. Bureau of the Census enumerated 10,447 individuals in its street count.

59. R. E. Murphy, J. E. Vance, and B. J. Epstein, "Internal Structure of the CBD," *Economic Geography* 31(1955):21–46, as cited in J. C. Schneider, "Skid Row as an Urban Neighborhood, 1890–1920," in *Housing the Homeless,* ed. J. Erickson and C. Wilhelm (New Brunswick, NJ: Rutgers University Press, Center for Urban Policy, 1986), 181.

60. Arguably, it was only because homelessness—and poverty generally—differed in this way that so astute an observer of the urban scene as E. B. White could sensibly remark: "New York is peculiarly constructed to absorb anything that comes along without inflicting the event on its inhabitants, so that every event is, in a sense, optional, and the inhabitant is in the happy position of being able to choose his spectacle and so conserve his soul" (as cited by K. T. Jackson, "The Capital of Capitalism: The New York Metropolitan Region, 1890–1940," in *Metropolis: 1890–1940,* ed. A. Sutcliffe [London: Alexandrine Press, 1984], 348). For the fierce and indignant contrast, consult M. Magnet, "Homeless: Craziness, Dope and Danger," *New York Times,* January 26, 1990, A31, among many others.

61. B. Lee, "The Disappearance of Skid Row: Some Ecological Evidence," *Urban Affairs Quarterly* 16(1980):81–107.

62. J. F. Rooney, "Societal Forces and the Unattached Male," in *Disaffiliated Man,* ed. Bahr (1970), 34.

63. *In These Times,* January 23–29, 1985.

64. See J. Darnton, "Alone and Homeless, 'Shutouts' of Society Sleep in Doorways," *New York Times,* October 26, 1971, p. 82. Ten years later, the city was said to be facing a "crisis" on vagrants. D. Carmody, "New York Is Facing 'Crisis' on Vagrants" *(New York Times,* June 28, 1981, p. 1). Until 1983, the index to the *Times* listed all articles pertaining to homeless people and shelters under the heading "Vagrants and Vagrancy."

65. New York City Human Resources Administration, nightly shelter statistics.

66. Figures were culled from M. A. Baker, *An Estimate of the Population of Homeless Men in the Bowery Area, New York City, February 28, 1965* (New York: Columbia University, Bureau of Applied Social Research, 1965), 6–7, 19; N. Markel, "A Preliminary Study of New York City's Hospitals and Their Contacts with Homeless Men ... [and] of New York's Legal Agencies and Their Effect on Homeless Men" (New York: Columbia University, Bureau of Applied Social Research, 1964); Bahr, *Skid Row,* chap. 6.

67. For the full account, see D. Gordon, *City Limits* (New York: Charterhouse, 1973).

68. Figures reported by the Crisis Intervention Service (New York: Human Resources Administration, July 1986); *New York Times,* September 27, 1986, A1; *New York Newsday,* November 7, 1988, p. 21; and *New York Observer,* April 29, 1991, 11.

69. For a detailed treatment, see the evaluation reports submitted to the Census Bureau. The count of those visible in public spaces of projected

occupancy of at least six occupants is estimated to have fallen short by a factor of more than 40 percent. The national picture was examined in a hearing before the Senate Committee on Governmental Affairs on May 9, 1991.

70. Recall that, by comparison, on a warm summer night in the mid-1960s, at most a hundred or so men could be seen sleeping on the street (G. Nash, *The Habitats of Homeless Men in Manhattan* [New York: Columbia University, Bureau of Applied Social Research, 1964]).

71. Nor are they confined to the United States. In 1985, the subject came up at a meeting of Common Market delegates: "The Homeless of Europe: A Scourge of Our Time" (*New York Times,* October 7, 1985, p. 2). It has more recently surfaced—and been christened one of the "backfires of capitalism"—in Eastern Europe, Hungary in particular *(New York Times,* October 23, 1990, A8).

72. Though God knows they tried: the Reagan administration coupled crass dissembling with outlandish dodges in its handling of homelessness. In June 1982, Philip Abrams, a senior offcial of the Department of Housing and Urban Development (HUD), proclaimed publicly that "no one is living in the streets" *(Boston Globe,* June 17, 1982). White House adviser (and later attorney general) Edwin Meese chose the Christmas season of the following year to observe that reports of persisting hunger were merely anecdotal and that people patronized soup kitchens "because the food is free ... and that's easier than paying for it" (R. McFadden, "Comments by Meese on Hunger Produce a Storm of Controversy," *New York Times,* December 10, 1983, A12). Early the following year, the president himself opined that some of those on the street were there, "you might say, by their own choice" (F. X. Clines, "Reagan, in Chicago Speech, Assails Critics of His Tax-Cutting Plan," *New York Times,* February 1, 1984, A16). And later that June, the same hapless Mr. Abrams newly turned out as anthropologist, characterized overcrowding in Hispanic households as a cultural preference (R. Pem, "Housing Official Defends Remarks," *New York Times,* May 15, 1984, A25). The administration's apologists were joined by Thomas Main, who took to the pages of the *Wall Street Journal* to argue that many of the people in New York City shelters were not "truly homeless," but—in their resort to these dirty, dangerous and degrading places—were simply "exploiting a good housing deal" ("New York City's Lure to the Homeless," September 12, 1983). Compare with R. C. Ellickson, "The Homelessness Muddle," *The Public Interest 99*(1990):45–60.

73. For a discussion of both the difficulties of measurement and a number of attempts to overcome them, see W.R. Breakey and P. J. Fischer, "Homelessness: The Extent of the Problem," *Social Forces* 46(1990):31–47.

74. The rural picture still lacks a good deal of detail, but preliminary indications from an Ohio study are that it differs in some respects from the urban one. Specifically, women (nearly half of them with children) are more common; the homeless population itself is better educated than its urban counterpart and is more often white; and economic factors figure highly as causes of their homelessness. See B. Toomey and R. First, *Preliminary Findings on Rural Homelessness in Ohio* (Columbus: Ohio State University, November 1990).

75. U.S. Conference of Mayors, *The Continued Growth of Hunger, Homeless-ness and Poverty in America's Cities: 1986* (Washington, DC: U.S. Confer-ence of Mayors, 1986); U.S. Conference of Mayors, *A Status Report on Hunger and Homelessness in America's Cities: 1990* (Washington, DC: U.S. Conference of Mayors, 1990). Compare with National Coalition for the Homeless, *American Nightmare: A Decade of Homelessness in the United States* (New York: National Coalition for the Homeless, December 1989).

76. By now the studies are myriad. A representative sample would include Brown et al., *The Homeless of Phoenix: Who Are They? And What Should Be Done?* (Phoenix, AZ: Consortium for the Homeless, 1983); M. J. Robertson, R. H. Ropers, and R. Burger, *The Homeless of Los Angeles County: An Empirical Assessment* (Los Angeles: UCLA School of Public Health, 1985); New York State Department of Social Services, *Homelessness in New York State*, 2 vols. (Albany: New York State De-partment of Social Services, 1984); D. J. Baumann et al., *The Austin Homeless* (Austin: University of Texas, Department of Psychology, 1985); G. Morse et al., *Homelessness in St. Louis: A Mental Health Program Evaluation, Field Study, and Follow-up Investigation* (Jefferson City: Missouri Department of Mental Health, 1985); V. Mulkern et al., *Homelessness Needs Assessment Study* (Boston: Massachusetts Depart-ment of Mental Health, 1985); D. Roth et al., *Homelessness in Ohio: A Study of People in Need* (Columbus: Ohio Department of Health, 1985); R. K. Farr, P. Koegel, and M. A. Burnam, *A Study of Homelessness and Mental Illness in the Skid Row Area of Los Angeles* (Los Angeles: Los Angeles County Department of Mental Health, 1986); Rossi, Fisher, and Willis; D. Snow et al., "The Myth of Mental Illness Among the Homeless," *Social Problems* 33(1986):407–13; E. Struening, *A Study of Residents of the New York City Shelter System* (New York: New York State Psychiat-ric Institute, 1986); C. Hoch and R. A. Slayton, *New Homeless and Old: Community and the Skid Row Hotel* (Philadelphia: Temple University Press, 1989); W. R. Breakey et al., "Health and Mental Problems of Homeless Men and Women in Baltimore," *Journal of the American Medical Association* 262(1989):1352–57. J. A. Momeni has compiled a set of state reports (J. A. Momeni, ed., *Homelessness in the United States* [New York: Greenwood Press, 1989]).

77. And, as a result of the "leveling" effects of homelessness itself, the differences between the subsistence strategies of those with chronic disorders and those without are not great (P. Koegel, "Subsistence Adaptation among Homeless Adults in the Inner City of Los Angeles," *Journal of Social Issues* 46[1990]:104).

78. In New York City, a significant proportion of them (44 percent) have never managed their own household (B. C. Weitzman, J. R. Knickman, and M. Shinn, "Pathways to Homelessness among New York City Fami-lies," *Social Forces* 46[1990]:125–40).

79. For the situation in New York City, see K. Hopper, E. Susser, and S. Conover, "Economies of Makeshift: Homelessness and Deindus-trialization in New York City," *Urban Anthropology* 14, nos. 1–3 (1985):183–236.

80. Some of these women are more accurately classified as from "broken" families, having been forced to place their children under public care or

to arrange for alternative homes with friends or family for the duration of their homelessness.

81. For reviews, see R. Tessler and D. L. Dennis, *A Synthesis of NIMH-Funded Research Concerning Persons Who Are Homeless and Mentally Ill* (Rockville, MD: National Institute of Mental Health, 1989); S. Ridgely, H. H. Goldman, and J. Talbott, *Chronic Mentally Ill Young Adults with Substance Abuse Problems* (Baltimore: University of Maryland, Department of Psychiatry, 1986); P. Koogel, M. A. Burnam, and R. K. Farr, "The Prevalence of Specific Psychiatric Disorders among Homeless Individuals in the Inner City of Los Angeles," *Archives of General Psychiatry* 45(1988):1085–92; E. Struening and D. K. Padgett, "Physical Health Status, Substance Use and Abuse, and Mental Disorders among Homeless Adults," *Journal of Social Issues* 46(1990):65–82; P. J. Fischer and W. R. Breakey, "The Epidemiology of Psychiatric and Substance Use Disorders among the Homeless," *American Psychologist,* in press; Baumohl and Huebner.

82. "Serious" criminal activity among the homeless turns out to involve crimes of survival for the most part, such as petty theft (often shoplifting) and entry into vacant buildings and warehouses for shelter (P. J. Fischer, "Criminal Activity among the Homeless: A Study of Arrests in Baltimore," *Hospital and Community Psychiatry* 39[1988]:46–51; D. A. Snow, S. G. Baker, and L. Anderson, "Criminality and Homeless Men: An Empirical Assessment," *Social Problems* 36[1989]:532–49).

83. See Breakey and Fischer, 38.

84. See J. D. Wright, "Poor People, Poor Health: The Health Status of the Homeless," *Social Forces* 46(1990):49–64.

85. The Bush administration's contempt for taking the issue of poverty seriously bids fair to become legendary. It is perhaps best exemplified in the remark of a White House official asked to characterize the administration's poverty policy: "Keep playing with the same toys ... but paint them a little shinier" (*New York Times,* July 6, 1990, A1).

86. Nor is the allusion simply an amateur historian's flourish: for some of those who donate to charities today, the same comparison beckons from living memory (*New York Times,* February 18, 1987, B4).

87. See F. Levy, *Dollars and Dreams* (New York: Russell Sage, 1987); W. J. Wilson, *The Truly Disadvantaged* (Chicago: University of Chicago Press, 1987); and J. D. Kasarda, "Urban Industrial Transition and the Underclass," *Annals of the American Academy of Political and Social Science* 501(1989):26–47, for discussion and analysis. Trends discussed in this paragraph are documented in contributions to *The Urban Underclass,* ed. C. Jencks and P. Peterson (Washington, DC: The Brookings Institution, 1991).

88. Interestingly, where local economies have flourished, giving rise to tight labor markets, employers have shown few scruples about recruiting from within an alleged underclass—and the men have responded (R. B. Freeman, "Employment and Earnings of Disadvantaged Young Men in a Labor Shortage Economy," 103–21, and P. Osterman, "Gain from

Growth? The Impact of Full Employment on Poverty in Boston," 122–34, in *The Urban Underclass,* ed. Jencks and Peterson [1991]). Nor does an unwillingness to work seem to be the problem (M. Tienda and H. Stier, "Joblessness and Shiftlessness: Labor Force Activity in Chicago's Inner City," in *The Urban Underclass,* ed. Jencks and Peterson [1991], 135–54).

89. Such men, owing to what is seen as their naturally disruptive tendencies and unwillingness to assume domestic responsibilities, are often encouraged to leave even the flexibly configured support of their families in the inner city. For a while, they "live a kind of vagabonding existence with age mates ... [who] support and help each other, as they live 'on the street,' often as 'homeless' people in abandoned buildings, in low rent apartments with their 'brothers,' or moving around in and out of various family apartments" (P. Hainer, "Sharing Kith and Kin: A Study of Kinship Behavior, An Approach to Explanation" [Ph.D. diss., Brandeis University, 1991], 223–24).

90. The game has been recently likened by two analysts to that of "musical chairs" (K. Y. McChesney, "Family Homelessness: A Systemic Problem," *Journal of Social Issues* 46[1990]:191–206; E. Sclar, "Homeless and Housing Policy," *American Journal of Public Health* 80[1990]:1039–40).

91. Figures in this paragraph are taken from the analysis of J. Alker and C. Dolbeare, *The Closing Door: Economic Causes of Homelessness* (Washington, DC: National Coalition for the Homeless, 1990). As these authors point out, the gap in any locale may well be larger, owing to many units being substandard, of the wrong size, or in the wrong location. Furthermore, many inexpensive units are occupied by households with incomes above the limit charted here.

92. M. E. Stone, *One-third of a Nation* (Washington, DC: Economic Policy Institute, 1990). The number of such shelter-poor households grew 42 percent between 1970 and 1987.

93. In 33 states, the fair-market rent level set by HUD is higher than the entire AFDC grant (C. Dolbeare, *Out of Reach: Why Everyday People Can't Find Affordable Housing* [Washington, DC: Low Income Housing Information Service, 1989]).

94. Alker and Dolbeare, 22.

95. U.S. House of Representatives, Committee on Ways and Means, *Overview of Entitlement Programs: 1990 Green Book* (Washington, DC: U.S. Government Printing Office, 1990), 1309; compare with S. Levitan and S. Schillmoeller, *The Paradox of Homelessness in America* (Washington, DC: George Washington University, Center for Social Policy Studies, 1991), 15–16.

96. C. Jencks, "Is the American Underclass Growing?" in *The Urban Underclass,* ed. Jencks and Peterson (1991), 50. However, census data have well-documented limitations when used to characterize the resource sharing and residential patterns of the inner-city poor (see P. Hainer, "Census Definitions and the Politics of Census Information," *Practicing Anthropology* 7, no. 3[1985]:7–8).

97. K. Hopper and J. Hamburg, "The Making of America's Homeless: From Skid Row to New Poor, 1945–1984," in *Critical Perspectives on Housing*, ed. R. Bratt, C. Hartman, and A. Meyerson (Philadelphia: Temple University, 1986); Alker and Dolbeare, 15; House Committee on Ways and Means, 555.

98. Benefits today reach about a third of out-of-work men and women. During the recessions of 1975 and 1982, the comparable figures were three-quarters and one-half, respectively. The reduction in covered workers is due largely to two factors: tightened eligibility requirements imposed by states, and a higher percentage of the work force employed in the service sector, where part-time work, frequent shifts in jobs, and lack of unionization (leading to more employer challenges to benefit claims) have meant that fewer laid-off workers qualify for benefits *(New York Times*, December 2, 1990, p. A1).

99. Rossi, 114–16. In New York, three-quarters of a high-risk group of welfare recipients had been involuntarily displaced in the past and never showed up in the emergency shelter system; they simply made do with friends or family until they secured replacement housing (G. L. Berlin and D. Baillargeon, *The Housing Alert Program: A One Year Evaluation* [New York: Human Resources Administration, 1989]).

100. Sosin and his colleagues, for example, found that half of an extremely poor comparison group in Chicago had been homeless in the past, some of them repeatedly (M. Sosin, P. Colson, and S. Grossman, *Homelessness in Chicago: Poverty and Pathology, Social Institutions and Social Change* [Chicago: University of Chicago, School of Social Service Administration, 1988]). A more recent study in Los Angeles found that 39 percent of a comparison group of housed welfare families had been forced to double up (with "strangers") at some point in the past five years and a fifth had been literally homeless (Wood et al., "Homeless and Housed Families in Los Angeles: A Study Comparing Demographic, Economic, and Family Function Characteristics," *American Journal of Public Health* 80[September 1990]:1049–52).

101. M. Harrington, *The Other America* (1962; rev. ed., Baltimore: Penguin, 1971), 2–3, 94, 86, 100.

102. Obvious physical (R. Murphy, *The Body Silent* [New York: H. Holt, 1987]) or mental (S. Estroff, *Making It Crazy* [Berkeley: University of California, 1981]) disability and its ensuing stigma is one such master status, effectively displacing all other attributes and constituting, in effect, that person's public "identity."

103. "All of the research which relates personal characteristics of the poor to some outcome tends to assume that when a significant coefficient for that characteristic is discovered it is something about the person's behavior or culture or personality or whatever that is productive of the given outcome. But in fact it may be that it is the definition of that characteristic by others with whom the individual deals which is productive of the outcome" (L. Rainwater, "Class, Culture, Poverty and Welfare" [Unpublished manuscript, 1987, 71]).

104. It was the Great Depression that forced Nels Anderson, in *The Homeless in New York City* (New York: Welfare Council, 1934), to reconsider the

wisdom of such divisions; he himself had earlier devised one of the most widely used taxonomies of homeless men.

105. As T. Bethell suggests, "It was the invention of the concept itself ... the word 'homelessness' ... *which hitherto had not really existed*" that provides "the key to the detection of a problem" (T. Bethell, "Remarks in the Heritage Foundation," in *Rethinking Policy on Homelessness* [Washington, DC: Heritage Foundation, 1989], 2, emphasis added). But how this social problem "emerged," as recently charted by M. Stern ("The Emergence of the Homeless as a Public Problem," *Social Service Review* 58[1984]:291–301), is both more complex and less arbitrary than that.

106. *UN Chronicle*, July 1983, 107. Notably, a UN film produced as part of the year's activities was forced to omit footage of two American projects (the only ones to appear). The U.S. mission had objected that the film neglected to mention the "individual rights element" of homelessness in the United States (*New York Times,* December 29, 1987, A7). A State Department memo on the subject concludes that public homelessness is "not a function of poverty but rather of disorientation and of the toleration of American society for such aberrant behavior" (U.S. Department of State 1988, 5).

107. And, in the process of defending the "moral integrity" of the new homeless, such analyses often obscure the "social continuity" between the two groups (see Hoch and Slayton, chap. 10).

108. E. Baxter and K. Hopper, *Private Lives, Public Spaces* (New York: Community Service Society, 1981), 6–7; compare with G. Morse, "Homeless People: A Typological Analysis and Gender Analysis" (Ph.D. diss., University of Missouri, 1984); Baumann et al.; Farr, Koegel, and Burnam.

109. M. R. Burt and B. E. Cohen, *America's Homeless: Numbers, Characteristics, and Programs That Serve Them* (Washington, DC: The Urban Institute, 1989), 17.

110. Rossi, 10, 12.

111. Sosin, Colson, and Grossman, 22; compare with Roth, 1989:148–9.

112. See, for example, M. M. Cuomo, *1933–1983: Never Again* (Albany: Executive Chamber, 1983).

113. H. M. Bahr, "Introduction," in *Homelessness in the United States*, ed. J. Momeni (New York: Greenwood Press, 1989), xx–xxi. Strictly speaking, this is an analysis of homelessness as an expression of some deeper deficiency, not a definition per se. See next section for discussion.

114. I draw here on the unpublished work of P. Campanelli et al., "Research on Enumerating Homeless Persons: Results of a Census Bureau Test of Alternative Methods" (Washington, DC: U.S. Bureau of the Census, 1990).

115. See Bahr, *Skid Row;* H. Bahr and T. Caplow, *Old Men Drunk and Sober* (New York: New York University Press, 1973). Of course, the disaffiliation thesis was anticipated by some earlier sociological and historical work on homelessness. H. Warren Dunham's brief study (*Homeless Men*

and Their Habitats [Detroit, MI: Wayne State University, 1953]), for example, made use of the notion of "undersocialization" to explain the original deficits from which such men suffered (cf. Wallace, 132ff.).

116. See, for example, Nash. Tellingly, an earlier version of disaffiliation appears here as "responsibilitilessness." In the Columbia Bowery Project, homelessness was operationalized as anyone who lived "without kin of any sort in his housing unit, is 21 years old or older, spends a limited amount or nothing on his living quarters ... [and] is not currently employed in the higher ranks of occupations" (Nash, A-1).

117. Again, see Hoch and Slayton 1989.

118. For example, Wallace.

119. A "culture" of the "disaffiliated" would appear to be a contradiction in terms.

120. Bahr, *Skid Row,* 162f.

121. Bahr and Caplow, 5–6, 55–56, 305.

122. Bahr, *Skid Row,* 313.

123. See, for example, Harrington's discussion of the federal poverty level ("The New Gradgrinds," *Dissent* [Spring 1984]:171–81).

124. Note, too, that this shifts the question away from personal attribute and toward strategic practice.

125. Rossi's pragmatic use of "literal homeless" should not mask the more inclusive scope of his notion of homelessness as a "condition that describes persons who do not have customary and regular access to a conventional dwelling unit" (p. 10).

126. M. Sosin, I. Piliavin, and H. Westerfelt, "Toward a Longitudinal Analysis of Homelessness," *Journal of Social Issues* 46(1990):171, emphasis in original. Along similar lines, other researchers have referred to homelessness as "a recurring waystation" for the marginally situated poor (Hopper, Susser, and Conover).

127. See D. Stone, *The Disabled State* (Philadelphia: Temple University, 1984).

128. P. H. Rossi and J. D. Wright, "The Urban Homeless: A Portrait of Urban Dislocation," *Annals of the American Academy of Political and Social Science* 501(1989):141.

129. G. Simmel "The Poor," *Social Problems* 13(1908, orig.; 1965):138–39. The roots of this "collective attitude" may be disputed. Some argue, for example, the necessity of maintaining social harmony by placating the poor in a society characterized by structured inequality. But until the decision to aid an officially needy group is taken—at least in principle and allowing for its defiance in practice—"poverty is individual suffering, without social consequence" (ibid.).

130. See, for example, Farr, Koegel, and Burnam, 256–59; Sosin, Colson, and Grossman; Sosin, Piliavin, and Westerfelt.

131. See M. Sullivan, *Teen Fathers in the Inner City* (New York: Vera Institute, 1985), 70; D. Ellwood, *Poor Support* (New York: Basic, 1988).

132. Farr, Koegel, and Burnam; P. Koegel and M. A. Burnam, "Traditional and Nontraditional Homeless Alcoholics," *Alcohol Health and Research World* 11, no. 3(1987):28–34.

133. To my knowledge, the term was originally used in a study commissioned by the National Federation of Settlements to look into the effects of "broken work" on families of the unemployed (H. Hall, "Introducing Our Neighbors," in *Case Studies of Unemployment,* National Federation of Settlements [Philadelphia: University of Pennsylvania Press, 1931], xxiii–1). It was later revived by Olwen Hufton in her study of the 18th-century French poor and was applied to homelessness by Hopper, Susser, and Conover in a study of New York's sheltered men.

134. See also Rossi, Hopper and Hamberg; and M. Hope and J. Young, *The Faces of Homelessness* (Lexington, MA: D.C. Heath, 1986).

135. Coser, 148.

136. See the chronicle of this organization in A. Mathieu, "Parents on the Move: Families Resist" (Ph.D. diss., New School for Social Research, 1991).

137. E. P. Thompson, "The Moral Economy of the English Crowd in the Eighteenth Century," *Past and Present* 50(1971):79.

138. For discussion of this phenomenon in the settings indicated in the text, see P. Marin, "Helping and Hating the Homeless," *Harper's Magazine,* January 1987, 39–49; J. Spradley, *You Owe Yourself a Drunk* (Boston: Little, Brown, 1970); J. Wiseman, *Stations of the Lost* (Englewood Cliffs, NJ: Prentice-Hall, 1970); D. L. Dennis, K. Gounis, and J. P. Morrissey, "Housing the Homeless Mentally Ill," *Research Notes* (New York State, Office of Mental Health) 2, no. 5(1987):1–4; M. Lipsky, *Street-Level Bureaucracy* (New York: Russell Sage, 1980); and R. Warner, *Recovery from Schizophrenia* (Boston: Routledge and Kegan Paul, 1985), 91.

139. Again, a repeatedly contested matter: HUD offcials are currently challenging the expansive definition of homelessness contained in the McKinney Act. They would prefer to see the dimensions of the problem restricted to the bounds of the literal homeless—those in shelters or on the street. From a programmatic standpoint, the latter is a problem more susceptible to being solved (S. A. Kondratas, "Presentation to the National Coalition for the Homeless," March 16, 1991).

140. Merton, 7.

141. C. W. Mills, *The Sociological Imagination* (New York: Grove Press, 1959), 7.

142. See C. Krauthammer, "When Liberty Really Means Neglect," *Time,* December 2, 1985; J. Perkins, "New Institutions for the Homeless," *Wall Street Journal,* February 26, 1985; S. A. Kondratas, "Myth, Reality and the Homeless," *Insight* 14(April 1986):78; E. F. Torrey, "Finally, A Cure for the Homeless," *Washington Monthly,* September 23–27, 1986.

143. H. H. Goldman and J. P. Morrissey, "The Alchemy of Mental Health Policy," *American Journal of Public Health* 75(1985):727–31; National Institute of Mental Health, *Deinstitutionalization Policy and Homelessness* (Rockville, MD: National Institute of Mental Health, 1990).

144. E. L. Bassuk, L. Rubin, and A. S. Lauriat, "Characteristics of Sheltered Homeless Families," *American Journal of Public Health* 76(1986): 1097–1101.

145. Bassuk's current work should shed additional light; that of Weitzman et al. already has.

146. T. Main, "The Homeless of New York," *The Public Interest* 72(1983):3–23; R. K. Filer, "What Really Causes Family Homelessness?" *The City Journal* (Fall 1990):31–41.

147. See P. Marcuse, "A Shame of Cities," *The Nation* 244(1987):426–29, for discussion.

148. Kondratas, "Myth, Reality and the Homeless," 78.

149. W. Stott, *Documentary Expression in Thirties America* (New York: Oxford University Press, 1973).

150. Ironically, too, in this respect, the advocates are heirs to the scholarly bequest of skid row researchers.

151. As T. Skocpol has recently argued in "Targeting within Universalism: Politically Viable Policies to Combat Poverty in the United States," in *The Urban Underclass,* ed. Jencks and Peterson (1991), 411–36; compare with R. Greenstein's response, "Universal and Targeted Approaches to Relieving Poverty" (437–59), in the same volume.

152. McChesney.

153. J. Agee and W. Evans, *Let Us Now Praise Famous Men* (1941; New York: Ballantine, 1970).

154. N. Lehmann, *The Promised Land* (New York: Basic, 1991); Hainer, "Sharing with Kith and Kin."

155. A. Keyssar, *Out of Work: The First Century of Unemployment in Massachusetts* (New York: Cambridge University Press, 1986).

156. *Iowa Press-Citizen,* May 7, 1983.

157. Jencks and Peterson.

158. Brandt, *An Impressionistic View,* 2.

159. *Walley* v. *New York City Transit Authority,* Index No. 177/91, 1991.

160. For close documentation of the case in New York, see C. Vergara, "Ghettoes: No Way Out," *New York Daily News,* February 11, 1990; C. Vergara, "Showdown in Drug City," *Village Voice,* March 27, 1990; C. Vergara "Lessons Learned, Lessons Forgotten," *The Livable City* (New York: Municipal Art Society) 15(1991):2–9; and Finnegan.

161. Not all will want to belong, as Marin reminds us, and room must be made "on the margins" to accommodate that decision. My argument is that the option should be there.

162. As I read J. Berger, *And Our Faces, Dear Heart, Brief as Photos* (New York: Pantheon, 1984), and Ignatieff.

163. See also G. Blasi, "Social Policy and Social Research on Homelessness," *Journal of Social Issues* 46(1990):207–19.

164. W. James, "The Moral Equivalent of War," *Popular Science Monthly,* October 1910, reprinted in *Pragmatism and Other Essays* (New York: Washington Square Press, 1968), 289–301. But recall that the attempt to revive the phrase itself was a miserable failure on the part of the Carter administration.

References

Agee, J., and W. Evans. *Let Us Now Praise Famous Men.* 1941. Rev. ed. New York: Ballantine, 1970.

Alker, J., and C. Dolbeare. *The Closing Door: Economic Causes of Homelessness.* Washington, DC: National Coalition for the Homeless, 1990.

Anderson, N. *The Hobo.* Chicago: University of Chicago Press, 1923.

———. *The Homeless in New York City.* New York: Welfare Council, 1934.

———. *Men on the Move.* Chicago: University of Chicago Press, 1940.

———. *Report on the Municipal Lodging House of New York City.* New York: Welfare Council, 1932.

Aries, P. *Centuries of Childhood.* New York: Knopf, 1962.

Bahr, H. M., ed. *Disaffiliated Man: Essays and Bibliography on Skid Row, Vagrancy, and Outsiders.* Toronto: University of Toronto Press, 1970.

———. "Introduction." In *Homelessness in the United States,* edited by J. Momeni, xvii–xxv. New York: Greenwood Press, 1989.

———. *Skid Row: An Introduction to Disaffilation.* New York: Oxford University Press, 1973.

Bahr, H., and T. Caplow. *Old Men Drunk and Sober.* New York: New York University Press, 1973.

Baker, M. A. *An Estimate of the Population of Homeless Men in the Bowery Area, New York City, February 28, 1965.* New York: Columbia University, Bureau of Applied Social Research, 1965.

Bakke, E. W. "Fifth Winter of Unemployment." *Yale Review* 24(1934–35): 253–73.

————. *The Unemployed Worker.* New Haven: Yale University Press, 1940.

Bassuk, E. L., L. Rubin, and A. S. Lauriat. "Characteristics of Sheltered Homeless Families." *American Journal of Public Health* 76(1987):1097–1101.

Baumann, D. J., C. Beauvais, C. Grigsby, and D. F. Schultz. *The Austin Homeless.* Austin: University of Texas, Department of Psychology, 1985.

Baumohl, James, and Robert B. Huebner. "Alcohol and Other Drug Problems Among the Homeless: Research, Practice, and Future Directions." *Housing Policy Debate* 2, no. 3(1990):837–66.

Baxter, E., and K. Hopper. *Private Lives, Public Spaces.* New York: Community Service Society, 1981.

Beier, A. L. *Masterless Men: The Vagrancy Problem in England, 1560–1640.* New York: Methuen, 1985.

Berger, J. *And Our Faces, Dear Heart, Brief as Photos.* New York: Pantheon, 1984.

Berlin, G. L., and D. Baillargeon. *The Housing Alert Program: A One Year Evaluation.* New York: Human Resources Administration, 1989.

Bethell, T. "Remarks in the Heritage Foundation." *Rethinking Policy on Homelessness.* Washington, DC: Heritage Foundation, 1989.

Blasi, G. "Social Policy and Social Research on Homelessness." *Journal of Social Issues* 46(1990):207–19.

Bogue, D. *Skid Row in American Cities.* Chicago: University of Chicago Press, 1963.

Boyer, P. *Urban Masses and Moral Order in America, 1820–1920.* Cambridge: Harvard University Press, 1978.

Bradwin, E. W. *The Bunkhouse Man.* New York: Columbia University Press, 1928.

Brandt, L. *Glimpses of New York in Previous Depressions.* New York: Welfare Council, 1933.

————. *An Impressionistic View of the Winter of 1930–1931 in New York City.* New York: Welfare Council, 1932.

————. "Relief of the Unemployed in New York City, 1929–1937." New York: Welfare Council, 1939. Draft.

Braudel, F. *Civilization and Capitalism, 15th–18th Century.* Vol. 1, *The Structures of Everyday Life.* London: Collins, 1981.

————. *Civilization and Capitalism, 15th–18th Century.* Vol. 2, *The Wheels of Commerce.* New York: Harper and Row, 1982.

Breakey, W. R., and P. J. Fischer. "Homelessness: The Extent of the Problem." *Social Forces* 46(1990):31–47.

Breakey, W. R., P. J. Fischer, M. Kramer, G. Nestadt, A. J. Romanoski, A. Ross, R. M. Royall, and O. C. Stine. "Health and Mental Problems of Homeless Men and Women in Baltimore." *Journal of the American Medical Association* 262(1989):1352–57.

Bremer, W. W. *Depression Winters.* Philadelphia: Temple University Press, 1984.

Brown, C., S. M. MacFarlane, L. Stark, and R. Paredes. *The Homeless of Phoenix: Who Are They? And What Should Be Done?* Phoenix, AZ: Consortium for the Homeless, 1983.

Bruns, R. A. *Knights of the Road.* New York: Methuen, 1980.

Burt, M. R., and B. E. Cohen. *America's Homeless: Numbers, Characteristics, and Programs That Serve Them.* Washington, DC: The Urban Institute, 1989.

Campanelli, P., M. Salo, L. Schwede, and E. Martin. "Research on Enumerating Homeless Persons: Results of a Census Bureau Test of Alternative Methods." Washington, DC: U.S. Bureau of the Census, 1990.

Caplow, T. "Transiency as a Cultural Pattern." *American Sociological Review* 5(1940):731–39.

Carmody, D. "New York Is Facing 'Crisis' on Vagrants." *New York Times,* June 28, 1981, p. 1.

Clines, F. X. "Reagan, in Chicago Speech, Assails Critics of His Tax-Cutting Plan." *New York Times,* February 1, 1984, p. A16.

Cohen, C., and J. Sokolovsky. *Old Men of the Bowery.* New York: Guilford Press, 1989.

Coser, L. "The Sociology of Poverty." *Social Problems* 13(1965):140–48.

Crisis Intervention Service. Monthly reports. New York City Temporary Housing Program for Families with Children. New York: Human Resources Administration, 1986.

Crouse, J. M. *The Homeless Transient in the Great Depression: New York 1929–1941.* Albany: State University of New York Press, 1986.

Cuomo, M. M. *1933–1983: Never Again.* Albany: Executive Chamber, 1983.

Darnton, J. "Alone and Homeless, 'Shutouts' of Society Sleep in Doorways." *New York Times,* October 26, 1971, p. 82.

Davis, N. Z. "Poor Relief, Humanism and Heresy: The Case of Lyon." *Studies in Medieval and Renaissance History* 5(1968):217–75.

Dennis, D. L., K. Gounis, and J. P. Morrissey. "Housing the Homeless Mentally Ill." *Research Notes* (New York State, Office of Mental Health) 2, no. 5 (1987):1–4.

Dolbeare, C. *Out of Reach: Why Everyday People Can't Find Affordable Housing.* Washington, DC: Low Income Housing Information Service, 1989.

Douglas, M. *Purity and Danger.* London: Routledge and Kegan Paul, 1966.

Dunham, H. W. *Homeless Men and Their Habitats.* Detroit, MI: Wayne State University, 1953.

Ellickson, R. C. "The Homelessness Muddle." *The Public Interest* 99(1990):45–60.

Ellwood, D. *Poor Support.* New York: Basic, 1988.

Estroff, S. *Making It Crazy.* Berkeley: University of California, 1981.

Farr, R. K., P. Koegel, and M. A. Burnam. *A Study of Homelessness and Mental Illness in the Skid Row Area of Los Angeles.* Los Angeles: Los Angeles County Department of Mental Health, 1986.

Filer, R. K. "What Really Causes Family Homelessness?" *The City Journal* (Fall 1990):31–41.

Finnegan, T. "The Once and Future Poorhouse." *Empire State Report* (May 1991):48–54.

——— . Fischer, P. J. "Criminal Activity among the Homeless: A Study of Arrests in Baltimore." *Hospital and Community Psychiatry* 39(1988):46–51.

———. and W. R. Breakey. "The Epidemiology of Psychiatric and Substance Use Disorders among the Homeless." *American Psychologist,* in press.

Freeman, R. B. "Employment and Earnings of Disadvantaged Young Men in a Labor Shortage Economy." In *The Urban Underclass,* edited by C. Jencks and P. E. Peterson, 103–21. Washington, DC: The Brookings Institution, 1991.

Golden, Stephanie. *Woman on the Outside.* In progress.

Goldman, H. H., and J. P. Morrissey. "The Alchemy of Mental Health Policy." *American Journal of Public Health* 75(1985):727–31.

Gordon, D. *City Limits.* New York: Charterhouse, 1973.

Greenstein, R. "Universal and Targeted Approaches to Relieving Poverty." In *The Urban Underclass,* edited by C. Jencks and P. E. Peterson, 437–59. Washington, DC: The Brookings Institution, 1991.

Grunberg, J., and P. F. Eagle. "Shelterization: How the Homeless Adapt to Shelter Living." *Hospital and Community Psychiatry* 41(1990):521–25.

Hagen, J. L. "Whatever Happened to 43 Elizabeth I, C 2?" *Social Service Review* 56(1982):108–19.

Hainer, P. "Census Definitions and the Politics of Census Information." *Practicing Anthropology* 7, no. 3(1985):7–8.

———. "Sharing Kith and Kin: A Study of Kinship Behavior, An Approach to Explanation." Ph.D. diss., Brandeis University, 1991.

Hall, H. "Introducing Our Neighbors." In *Case Studies of Unemployment,* National Federation of Settlements. Philadelphia: University of Pennsylvania Press, 1931.

Hareven, T. K. "The Home and the Family in Historical Perspective." *Social Research* 58(1991):253–86.

Harrington, M. "The New Gradgrinds." *Dissent* (Spring 1984):171–81.

———. *The Other America.* 1962. Rev. ed. Baltimore: Penguin, 1971.

Herlands, W. B. *Administration of Relief in New York City.* New York: City of New York, Department of Investigation, 1940.

Hoch, C., and R. A. Slayton. *New Homeless and Old: Community and the Skid Row Hotel.* Philadelphia: Temple University Press, 1989.

Hope, M., and J. Young. *The Faces of Homelessness.* Lexington, MA: D.C. Heath, 1986.

Hopper, K. "A Poor Apart: The Distancing of Homeless Men in New York's History." *Social Research* 58(1991):107–32.

Hopper, K., and J. Hamberg. "The Making of America's Homeless: From Skid Row to New Poor, 1945–1984." In *Critical Perspectives on Housing,* edited by R. Bratt, C. Hartman, and A. Meyerson, 12–40. Philadelphia: Temple University, 1986.

Hopper, K., E. Susser, and S. Conover. "Economies of Makeshift: Homelessness and Deindustrialization in New York City." *Urban Anthropology* 14, nos. 1–3(1985):183–236.

Hutton, O. *The Poor in Eighteenth Century France, 1750–1789.* Oxford, England: Clarendon Press, 1974.

Ignatieff, M. *The Needs of Strangers.* New York: Viking, 1984.

Jackson, K. T. "The Capital of Capitalism: The New York Metropolitan Region, 1890–1940." In *Metropolis: 1890–1940,* edited by A. Sutcliffe, 319–53. London: Alexandrine Press, 1984.

James, W. "The Moral Equivalent of War," *Popular Science Monthly,* October 1910. Reprinted in *Pragmatism and Other Essays.* New York: Washington Square Press, 1968.

Jencks, C. "Is the American Underclass Growing?" In *The Urban Underclass,* edited by C. Jencks and P. Peterson, 28–100. Washington, DC: The Brookings Institution, 1991.

Jencks, C. and P. Peterson, eds. *The Urban Underclass.* Washington, DC: The Brookings Institution, 1991.

Jones, D. L. "The Strolling Poor: Transiency in Eighteenth-Century Massachusetts." *Journal of Social History* 8(1975):28–54.

Jusserand, J. *English Wayfaring the Middle Ages.* Rev. ed. London: Ernest Benn, 1920.

Kasarda, J. D. "Urban Industrial Transition and the Underclass." *Annals of the American Academy of Political and Social Science* 501(1989):26–47.

Keyssar, A. *Out of Work: The First Century of Unemployment in Massachusetts.* New York: Cambridge University Press, 1986.

Koegel, P. "Subsistence Adaptation among Homeless Adults in the Inner City of Los Angeles." *Journal of Social Issues* 46(1990):83–108.

Koegel, P., and M. A. Burnam. "Traditional and Nontraditional Homeless Alcoholics." *Alcohol Health and Research World* 11, no. 3(1987):28–34.

Koegel, P., M. A. Burnam, and R. K. Farr. "The Prevalence of Specific Psychiatric Disorders among Homeless Individuals in the Inner City of Los Angeles." *Archives of General Psychiatry* 45(1988):1085–92.

Kondratas, S. A. "Myth, Reality and the Homeless." *Insight* 14(April 1986):78.

———. "Presentation to the National Coalition for the Homeless," March 16, 1991.

Krauthammer, C. "When Liberty Really Means Neglect." *Time,* December 2, 1985.

Kusmer, K. L. "The Underclass in Historical Perspective: Tramps and Vagrants in Urban America, 1870–1930." In *On Being Homeless: Historical Perspectives,* edited by R. Beard, 20–31. New York: Museum of the City of New York, 1987.

Lee, B. "The Disappearance of Skid Row: Some Ecological Evidence." *Urban Affairs Quarterly* 16(1980):81–107.

Leeds, A. "The Concept of the 'Culture of Poverty.'" In *The Culture of Poverty: A Critique,* edited by E. Leacock, 226–84. New York: Simon and Schuster, 1971.

Lehmann, N. *The Promised Land.* New York: Basic, 1991.

Levitan, S., and S. Schillmoeller. *The Paradox of Homelessness in America.* Washington, DC: George Washington University, Center for Social Policy Studies, 1991.

Levy, F. *Dollars and Dreams.* New York: Russell Sage, 1987.

Lewis, M. "You Can't Stay Here. Washington Ditches the Transient." *Social Work Today* 3(1935):8–10.

Lipsky, M. *Street-Level Bureaucracy.* New York: Russell Sage, 1980.

Lovald, K. A. "From Hobohemia to Skid Row: The Changing Community of the Homeless Man." Ph.D. diss., University of Minnesota, 1960.

Love, E. G. *Subways Are for Sleeping.* New York: Harcourt Brace, 1956.

McFadden, R. "Comments by Meese on Hunger Produce a Storm of Controversy." *New York Times,* December 10, 1983, p. A12.

Magnet, M. "Homeless: Craziness, Dope and Danger." *New York Times,* January 26, 1990, p. A31.

Main, T. "The Homeless of New York." *The Public Interest* 72(1983):3–23.

———. "New York City's Lure to the Homeless." *Wall Street Journal,* September 12, 1983.

Marcuse, P. "A Shame of the Cities." *The Nation* 244(1987):426–29.

Marin, P. "Helping and Hating the Homeless." *Harper's Magazine,* January 1987:39–49.

Markel, N. "A Preliminary Study of New York City's Hospitals and Their Contacts with Homeless Men ... [and] of New York's Legal Agencies and Their Effect on Homeless Men." New York: Columbia University, Bureau of Applied Social Research, 1964.

Mathieu, A. "Parents on the Move: Families Resist." Ph.D. diss., New School for Social Research, 1991.

Matza, D. "The Disreputable Poor." In *Class, Status and Power: A Reader in Social Stratification,* 2d ed. Edited by R. Bendix and S. M. Lipset, 289–302. New York: Free Press, 1966.

McChesney, K. Y. "Family Homelessness: A Systemic Problem." *Journal of Social Issues* 46(1990):191–206.

McElvaine, R. S. *Down and Out in the Great Depression: Letters from the Forgotten Man.* Chapel Hill: University of North Carolina Press, 1983.

McMillan, W. "Single Blessedness." *Survey* 70(March 1934):74–75.

Merton, R. K. "The Sociology of Social Problems." In *Contemporary Social Problems,* 4th ed. Edited by R. K. Merton and R. Nisbeth, 5–43. New York: Harcourt Brace Jovanovich, 1976.

Mills, C. W. *The Sociological Imagination.* New York: Grove Press, 1959.

Minehan, T. *Boy and Girl Tramps of America.* New York: Farrar and Rinehart, 1934.

Mollat, M. *The Poor in the Middle Ages.* New Haven: Yale University Press, 1986.

Momeni, J. A., ed. *Homelessness in the United States.* New York: Greenwood Press, 1989.

Monkkonen, E. H., ed. *Walking to Work.* New York: Cambridge University Press, 1984.

Morse, G. "Homeless People: A Typological Analysis and Gender Analysis." Ph.D. diss., University of Missouri, 1984.

Morse, G., N. M. Shield, C. R. Hanneke, R. J. Calsyn, G. K. Burger, and B. Nelson. *Homelessness in St. Louis: A Mental Health Program Evaluation, Field Study, and Follow-up Investigation.* Jefferson City: Missouri Department of Mental Health, 1985.

Mukherjee, S. *Under the Shadow of the Metropolis: They Are Citizens Too.* Calcutta: Calcutta Metropolitan Development Authority, 1975.

Mulkern, V., V. J. Bradley, R. Spence, S. Allein, and J. E. Oldham. *Homelessness Needs Assessment Study.* Boston: Massachusetts Department of Mental Health, 1985.

Murphy, R. *The Body Silent.* New York: H. Holt, 1987.

Murphy, R. E., J. E. Vance, and B. J. Epstein. "Internal Structure of the CBD." *Economic Geography* 31(1955):21–46.

Nash, G. *The Habitats of Homeless Men in Manhattan.* New York: Columbia University, Bureau of Applied Social Research, 1964.

National Coalition for the Homeless. *American Nightmare: A Decade of Homelessness in the United States.* New York: National Coalition for the Homeless, December 1989.

National Institute of Mental Health. *Deinstitutionalization Policy and Homelessness.* Rockville, MD: National Institute of Mental Health, 1990.

New York State Department of Social Services. *Homelessness in New York State.* 2 vols. Albany: New York State Department of Social Services, 1984.

Osterman, P. "Gain from Growth? The Impact of Full Employment on Poverty in Boston." In *The Urban Underclass,* edited by C. Jencks and P. E. Peterson, 122–34. Washington, DC: The Brookings Institution, 1991.

Patterson, J. T. *America's Struggle Against Poverty, 1900–1980.* Cambridge: Harvard University Press, 1981.

Pear, R. "Housing Official Defends Remarks." *New York Times,* May 15, 1984, p. A25.

Perkins, J. "New Institutions for the Homeless." *Wall Street Journal,* February 26, 1985.

Perlman, J. *The Myth of Marginality.* Berkeley: University of California Press, 1976.

Rainwater, L. "Class, Culture, Poverty and Welfare." Unpublished manuscript, 1987.

Reed, E. F. *Federal Transient Program: An Evaluative Survey.* New York: Committee on Care of Transients and Homeless, 1934.

Ribton-Turner, C. J. *A History of Vagrants and Vagrancy and Beggars and Begging.* London: Chapman and Hall, 1887.

Rice, S. A. "The Failure of the Municipal Lodging House." *National Municipal Review* 11(1922):358–62.

———. "The Homeless." *American Academy of Political and Social Science* 77(1918):140–53.

Ridgely, S., H. H. Goldman, and J. Talbott. *Chronic Mentally Ill Young Adults with Substance Abuse Problems.* Baltimore: University of Maryland, Department of Psychiatry, 1986.

Ringenbach, P. T. *Tramps and Reformers, 1873–1916.* Westport, CT: Greenwood Press, 1973.

Robertson, M. J., R. H. Ropers, and R. Burger. *The Homeless of Los Angeles County: An Empirical Assessment.* Los Angeles: UCLA School of Public Health, 1985.

Rooney, J. F. "Societal Forces and the Unattached Male." In *Disaffiliated Man: Essays and Bibliography on Skid Row, Vagrancy, and Outsiders,* edited by H. M. Bahr, 13–38. Toronto: University of Toronto Press, 1970.

Rossi, P. *Down and Out in America: The Origins of Homelessness.* Chicago: University of Chicago Press, 1989.

Rossi, P. H., G. A. Fisher, and G. Willis. *The Condition of the Homeless of Chicago.* Amherst, MA: Social and Demographic Research Institute, and Chicago: National Opinion Research Council, 1986.

Rossi, P. H., and J. D. Wright. "The Urban Homeless: A Portrait of Urban Dislocation." *Annals of the American Academy of Political and Social Science* 501(1989):132–42.

Roth D., J. Bean, N. Lust, and T. Saveanu. *Homelessness in Ohio: A Study of People in Need.* Columbus: Ohio Department of Mental Health, 1985.

Rothman, D. *The Discovery of the Asylum.* Boston: Little, Brown, 1973.

Salter, F. R. *Some Early Tracts on Poor Relief.* London: Methuen, 1926.

Schneider, J. C. "Skid Row as an Urban Neighborhood, 1890–1920." In *Housing the Homeless,* edited by J. Erickson and C. Wilhelm, 167–89. New Brunswick, NJ: Rutgers University Press, Center for Urban Policy, 1986.

Sclar, E. "Homeless and Housing Policy." *American Journal of Public Health* 80(1990):1039–40.

Seligson, I. "The Case of the Homeless Man in New York City." Thesis, New York School of Social Work, 1940.

Simmel, G. "The Poor." *Social Problems* 13(1908, orig.; 1965):118–40.

Skocpol, T. "Targeting within Universalism: Politically Viable Policies to Combat Poverty in the United States." In *The Urban Underclass,* edited by

C. Jencks and P. E. Peterson, 411–36. Washington, DC: The Brookings Institution, 1991.

Snow, D. A., S. G. Baker, and L. Anderson. "Criminality and Homeless Men: An Empirical Assessment." *Social Problems* 36(1989):532–49.

Snow, D., S. Baker, L. Anderson, and M. Martin. "The Myth of Mental Illness am⟨ ng the Homeless." *Social Problems* 33(1986):407–13.

Sosin, M., P. Colson, and S. Grossman. *Homelessness in Chicago: Poverty and Pathology, Social Institutions and Social Change.* Chicago: University of Chicago, School of Social Service Administration, 1988.

Sosin, M., I. Piliavin, and H. Westerfelt. "Toward a Longitudinal Analysis of Homelessness." *Journal of Social Issues* 46(1990):157–74.

Spradley, J. *You Owe Yourself a Drunk.* Boston: Little, Brown, 1970.

Stern, M. "The Emergence of the Homeless as a Public Problem." *Social Service Review* 58(1984):291–301.

Stone, D. *The Disabled State.* Philadelphia: Temple University, 1984.

Stone, M. E. *One-third of a Nation.* Washington, DC: Economic Policy Institute, 1990.

Stott, W. *Documentary Expression in Thirties America.* New York: Oxford University Press, 1973.

Struening, E. *A Study of Residents of the New York City Shelter System.* New York: New York State Psychiatric Institute, 1986.

Struening, E., and D. K. Padgett. "Physical Health Status, Substance Use and Abuse, and Mental Disorders among Homeless Adults." *Journal of Social Issues* 46(1990):65–82.

Sullivan, M. *Teen Fathers in the Inner City.* New York: Vera Institute, 1985.

Sutherland, E. H., and H. J. Locke. *Twenty Thousand Homeless Men.* Chicago: J. B. Lippincott, 1936.

Tawney, R. H. *The Agrarian Problem in the Sixteenth Century.* London: Longmans, Green, 1912.

Terkel, S. *Hard Times.* New York: Avon, 1970.

Tessler, R., and D. L. Dennis. *A Synthesis of NIMH-Funded Research Concerning Persons Who Are Homeless and Mentally Ill.* Rockville, MD: National Institute of Mental Health, 1989.

Thernstrom, S. "Is There Really a New Poor?" *Dissent* 15 (January–February 1968):59–64.

Theroux, P. *O-Zone.* New York: Putnam, 1986.

———. "Subway Odyssey." *New York Times Magazine,* January 31, 1982.

Thompson, E. P. "The Moral Economy of the English Crowd in the Eighteenth Century." *Past and Present* 50(1971):76–136.

Tienda, M., and H. Stier. "Joblessness and Shiftlessness: Labor Force Activity in Chicago's Inner City." In *The Urban Underclass,* edited by C. Jencks and P. E. Peterson, 135–54. Washington, DC: The Brookings Institution, 1991.

Toomey, B., and R. First. *Preliminary Findings on Rural Homelessness in Ohio.* Columbus: Ohio State University, November 1990.

Torrey, E. F. "Finally, A Cure for the Homeless." *Washington Monthly,* September 23–27, 1986.

Toth, Jennifer. "NY's 'Mole People' Shun Society in Transit Tunnels." *Los Angeles Times,* September 2, 1990, A1.

U.S. Conference of Mayors. *The Continued Growth of Hunger, Homelessness and Poverty in America's Cities: 1986.* Washington, DC: U.S. Conference of Mayors, 1986.

———. *A Status Report on Hunger and Homelessness in America's Cities: 1990.* Washington, DC: U.S. Conference of Mayors, 1990.

U.S. House of Representatives. Committee on Ways and Means. *Overview of Entitlement Programs: 1990 Green Book.* Washington, DC: U.S. Government Printing Office, 1990.

Vergara, C. "Ghettoes: No Way Out." *New York Daily News,* February 11, 1990.

———. "Lessons Earned, Lessons Forgotten." *The Livable City* (New York: Municipal Art Society) 15(1991):2–9.

———. "Showdown in Drug City." *Village Voice,* March 27, 1990.

Wallace, S. E. *Skid Row as a Way of Life.* Totowa, NJ: Bedminister Press, 1965.

Warner, R. *Recovering from Schizophrenia.* Boston: Routledge and Kegan Paul, 1985.

Webb, S., and B. Webb. *English Poor Law History, Part I: The Old Poor Law.* 1927. Rev. ed. Hamden, CT: Archon, 1963.

Weitzman, B. C., J. R. Knickman, and M. Shinn. "Pathways to Homelessness among New York City Families." *Social Forces* 46(1990):125–40.

Wilson, R. S. "Problems in Coordinating Service for Transient and Resident Unattached from the Point of View of Individual Service." Proceedings of the National Conference of Social Work. Chicago: University of Chicago Press, 1935, 210–23.

Wilson, W. J. *The Truly Disadvantaged.* Chicago: University of Chicago Press, 1987.

Wiseman, J. *Stations of the Lost.* Englewood Cliffs, NJ: Prentice-Hall, 1970.

Wood, D., B. Valdez, T. Hayashi, and A. Shen. "Homeless and Housed Families in Los Angeles: A Study Comparing Demographic, Economic, and Family Function Characteristics." *American Journal of Public Health* 80(September 1990):1049–52.

Wright, J. D. "Poor People, Poor Health: The Health Status of the Homeless." *Social Forces* 46(1990):49–64.

Young, P. "The New Poor." *Sociology and Social Research* 17(1933):59–64.

© Fannie Mae Foundation 1991, 1997. All Rights Reserved.

What's Behind the Numbers?
Definitional Issues in Counting the Homeless*

David S. Cordray and Georgine M. Pion
Vanderbilt University

Abstract

Any estimate of the number of homeless persons involves several definitional
issues, including the underlying conceptual definition of "homelessness," the
intended use of and rationale for the count, how the conceptual definition is
translated into operational procedures, and methodological choices. These
issues are at least partially responsible for the variation in existing estimates
of homeless individuals. To best serve multiple constituencies and demands for
information, the adoption of a broad definition is recommended. Furthermore,
it is necessary to develop and report estimates for specific policy-relevant
subgroups of homeless persons, as well as to develop a family of research
studies that can yield an understanding of the conditions facing the homeless
and identify "markers" for those who are at risk of becoming homeless.

Introduction

Definitional issues pertinent to counting homeless individuals,
including who *has been* counted and who *could be* counted, play
an integral and controversial role in shaping estimates of the
homeless population. At the same time, an exclusive focus on
these issues can prove unproductive, often serving as just one
more interesting intellectual exercise. Such a concern with
definitions rapidly becomes devoid of meaning unless it is linked
explicitly to practices of counting homeless persons. Thus, in
delineating issues embodied in the task of defining homelessness
(e.g., "Who could or should be counted?"), a broader approach
that examines the interplay among definitions, methods, and
reasons for counting the homeless is essential. As with any
attempt to count or estimate the magnitude of a phenomenon, an
understanding of estimates of the size of the homeless population requires information about how the estimates were produced, who is and is not represented, and why the estimates
were undertaken in the first place. By using this broader lens
(one that focuses on what's behind the numbers), it is possible to
better understand the points of convergence and divergence in

---

*Originally published in *Housing Policy Debate* Volume 2, Issue 3.

estimates produced by different investigators, and to identify methodological implications for improving our knowledge about homelessness, along with the quality of information that is generated.

What's behind the numbers?

As evidence in both scholarly journals and the popular press proves, considerable variation exists among national estimates of homeless individuals in the United States.[1] A cursory examination of the bases for these varying estimates highlights the fact that definitional issues are partly responsible for their diversity. However, definitional issues are only one element; therefore, it is useful to briefly review the set of factors that may contribute to the differing estimates.

Some examples

Nearly ten years ago, Hombs and Snyder, members of the Community for Creative Non-Violence, estimated that there were 2.2 to 3 million homeless persons in the United States.[2] What's behind these numbers? According to Rossi, they essentially represent "extrapolations from local estimates by knowledgeable persons."[3] It appears that the definition of homelessness was left to the discretion of the 100 key informants residing in the 25 cities that CCNV contacted.[4] Rossi further concludes that "not enough information is given about the Hombs and Snyder estimates to let us evaluate their worth."[5] Kondratas levels a much stronger judgment, calling the numbers a "clear leap of fantasy."[6] She also points to the "staying power" of these numbers and their political significance in setting the stage for further debate about the size of the homeless population.

Using similar methods (key informant plus other "count-like" strategies), the U.S. Department of Housing and Urban Development (HUD) placed the number of homeless during any given night during December 1983 and January 1984 at between 250,000 and 350,000.[7] Although this study was conducted shortly after Hombs and Snyder's effort, HUD's estimate was about one-tenth that of Hombs and Snyder. What factors account for this difference? Although identifying all the disparities is arduous, HUD researchers, unlike Hombs and Snyder, did provide experts with a definition of what they meant by homelessness (i.e., individuals in shelters or public/private places not designed for human habitation), a specific time frame (one average night), and a specific period for which the basic estimates were derived.

The data collected by HUD serve as the basis for three additional estimates. Tucker, extrapolating from data gathered in the HUD study, estimated the 1987 homeless population at 700,000.[8] What's behind this number? Tucker's procedure essentially involved using the estimates in "the most reliable range" obtained by HUD from service organizations for 35 individual cities, and duplicating HUD's procedures to develop estimates for 15 additional cities; in contrast to HUD, however, he based his projected "homeless rate per thousand" for each of the 50 cities on the population of the city itself rather than the population for the Standard Metropolitan Statistical Area (SMSA). A different estimate was put forth by Freeman and Hall, who developed their own street-to-shelter ratios, applied these estimates to the HUD estimates of the shelter population, and then adjusted this total based on an assumed growth rate.[9] Using these procedures, Freeman and Hall estimated 343,000 to 363,000 homeless persons in 1985.

Drawing on the 1984 HUD estimates, the National Alliance to End Homelessness estimated that as many as 736,000 persons were homeless on any particular night, with between 1.3 million and 2 million different individuals experiencing homelessness at some point during 1988.[10] The Alliance's nightly prevalence estimate was based on a presumed 20 percent annual increase in the number of homeless, stemming from the reported annual growth in the demand for shelters.[11] The latter, in turn, was based on an estimate taken from a report by the U.S. Conference of Mayors.[12] Thus, these three numbers are essentially estimates based on estimates.

In a separate data collection effort, the Urban Institute recently estimated that 567,000 to 600,000 individuals in the United States were homeless on any given night in 1987.[13] The figure is derived from a probability-based national estimate of the number of homeless persons using shelters or soup kitchens in cities with populations over 100,000. Rather than assuming that all users of soup kitchens were homeless, the Urban Institute researchers screened respondents using these guidelines:

- Not having a home or a permanent place to live;

- Residing in a shelter or hotel/motel paid for by a voucher or other instrument;

- Staying in an indoor or outdoor space that was not intended for habitation; and

- Staying with a relative or friend "with whom they did not have a regular arrangement to stay for five or more days a week."[14]

Based on these definitions, the study found 229,000 persons homeless over a seven-day period. To develop the national estimate of 567,000 to 600,000, projections were made, using findings from within the target cities and shelter/soup kitchen locations that were sampled. Based on new information and assumptions about the distribution of homeless in other places and the nonutilization of services by homeless individuals, additional analyses have resulted in a new estimate of about 350,000 to 500,000 homeless in the United States.[15]

In his recent book *Down and Out in America: The Origins of Homelessness,* Peter Rossi concluded that the best estimate of the *literally homeless* (i.e., those in shelters and on the streets) was 250,000 to 350,000, and that another four to seven million individuals were extremely poor and thus at risk of becoming homeless.[16] This estimate of the literally homeless is based on what Rossi regards as the most reliable evidence collected. Because the majority of previously reported estimates are not actual counts, he is not sanguine about the analytic basis for his choice of the best estimate of the literally homeless. On the other hand, his appraisal of the size of the group that others have found difficult to estimate (i.e., those at risk of homelessness) is grounded in analyses of rather firm national data bases.

Some definitional issues accounting for variation in estimates

The examples cited above suggest several definitional issues that have been previously confronted by researchers. With regard to the estimate offered by Hombs and Snyder,[17] we can see where definitional issues appear to have been skirted altogether. In other instances, different definitions have been adopted by different investigators. The numbers reported by the Urban Institute reflect a broader view of who is homeless (i.e., they include those who are doubled up) than those produced by either HUD or Rossi. We will refer to this as an issue associated with the *conceptual definition* of homelessness. Even when the definitions are the same, however, researchers possess considerable latitude in how they operationalize their conceptual definitions— a point we will revisit later. For example, selecting a specific time of year to conduct the count is an operational detail that can influence the resulting numbers. Would HUD's figures have been smaller if the time frame chosen for sampling had been spring or summer? This issue was explicitly addressed by Rossi and his colleagues, who incorporated into their study of the Chicago homeless provisions for estimating the use of shelters and streets in winter and fall.[18]

Looking across the examples, several other definitional issues emerge. The time span associated with the estimate is important. For the most part, previous estimates have referred to the prevalence of homelessness at *any given point in time* (i.e., on an average night), although the National Alliance to End Homelessness did attempt to project the number of individuals who would experience homelessness during a given year. Given the frequent movement of this population into and out of homelessness,[19] it is not surprising that vast differences exist between the prevalence estimates and this annual incidence figure. Upon which criteria should definitions be based? Is one set of definitions preferable over another? Do some definitions bias results in a predictable fashion? In general, the answer to these questions is "It depends."

Other reasons for variation

As previously noted, multiple factors have contributed to varying estimates. In the case of technical culprits, some definitions impose biases that tend to understate or overstate the size of the population. Yet with regard to other contributing factors, bias is not the correct attribution. Rather, the estimates are based on different conceptions of the problem or estimation task. So as not to leave the impression that estimates depend only on definitional issues, a brief review of other contributors to varying estimates appears in order.

Since estimates address different time periods, actual growth in the size of the population could certainly account for the disparities between estimates derived in the early 1980s compared to those produced for the latter part of the decade. The methodological difficulties confronting efforts to identify and count this transient and ever-changing population, along with the technical transgressions actually committed, have been admirably catalogued in the literature.[20] In addition, it is clear that some methods produce more bias than others.[21] Also well-articulated have been the obvious and more subtle roles played by such factors as prevailing views about the causes of homelessness.[22] Time and resource constraints are culpable in terms of limiting the methodological choices that are available.[23]

Interplay among definitions, intended uses, and methods

Scratching even slightly below the surface to see what lies behind a given estimate of the number of homeless persons reveals a rather complex interplay among definitions, methods, and the reasons for counting or estimating in the first place (see figure 1).

Figure 1. **What's Behind the Numbers?**

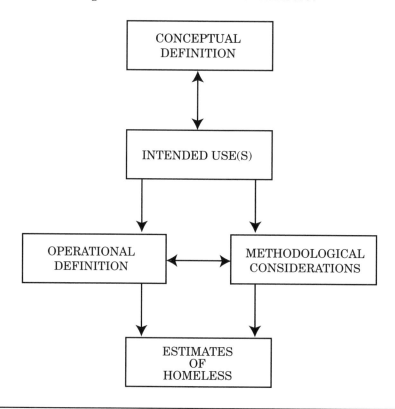

In a nutshell, our scheme asserts that conceptual definitions of homelessness establish the foundations upon which subsequent assessments are built. Important research issues, that is, the specification of operational definitions and methods of enumeration, flow more or less directly from this initial conceptual definition. Simply stated, it is impossible to make meaningful decisions about whom to count as homeless and how to derive that estimate without a firm grasp of the concept that one intends to measure. Of course, this assumes that an agreed-upon definition of homelessness is possible—a dubious assumption in many minds.

The authors adopt a different perspective by arguing that waiting for consensus to develop around a *singular* conceptual definition is not productive. There are simply too many political pushes and pulls associated with desires to expand or contract any definition. What is more important for researchers is that counts be reported in a fashion that allows users to understand who, on the continuum of homelessness, has and has not been included. The authors refer to this method of reporting counts as *intelligent segmentation*. That is, total estimates, regardless of the conceptual definition embraced, would be reported for meaningful subgroups (e.g., shelter residents, persons on the streets, and residents of institutions). Thus, the conceptual definition of homelessness is comprised of an ordered series of subconstructs, each with its own conceptual meaning. Throughout the articles in this journal, homelessness seems to be presented as the anchor point of a continuum that is probably best labeled as a standard of living. Although the line between those who have adequate living arrangements and those who do not is often fuzzy, the real difference among researchers appears to be the extent to which they are willing to count as homeless the persons who are further up this continuum.

There are several reasons for abandoning the idea of an agreed-upon definition for homelessness. Hopper notes that conceptions of homelessness have changed dramatically over time, and the conditions that serve as "markers" are culturally determined.[24] This does not mean, however, that we should forsake our concerns about definitions. Rather, what is needed is a perspective that will permit us to avoid "chasing our tails" over such definitional issues as which definition is correct. As shown in figure 1, the authors depart from the customary idea that operationalizations and methods of enumeration flow directly from a singular conceptual definition (as typically embodied in classical measurement notions) by recognizing that these relationships are moderated by the notion of the intended use or the rationale for the estimate.

The reasoning behind this position is simple. A primary obstacle to defining homelessness by consensus is that multiple purposes exist for embarking on an estimation task, along with many constituencies clamoring for different kinds of information. For example, Congress may be interested in obtaining a count of all homeless individuals, and this broad ambition dictates the use of a broad conceptual definition. On the other hand, some requestors may have more modest demands involving a specific subgroup of the homeless population. Their purposes would be adequately served by a more circumscribed definition (e.g., the literally homeless). Thus, the intended use of and impetus for asking the question "How many?" plays a role in framing the parameters for a particular study.

Similarly, the anticipated uses of a count enlarge or shrink the conceptual definition that is entertained, which in turn influences the development of operational procedures. As an illustration, if the main impetus for counting homeless persons is to discern current and future service needs, a broad conceptual definition is necessary—one that includes multiple subgroups, such as those who are literally homeless and those who are precariously housed. For planning purposes, the logic of adopting a broad definition is that it supplies the means for assessing the needs of both today's homeless and those who are at risk (tomorrow's potential homeless population). Long-term resource planning would be of little value if those who were vulnerable now and likely to need supportive assistance in the future were disregarded. If, on the other hand, the requestor's needs are more discrete (e.g., knowing how many shelter beds are needed or how many meals must be prepared), only the relevant portion of the homeless continuum would be considered. The operational definition would be highly filtered in this circumstance.

Of course, it is not only the operational definition of homelessness that is altered by the breadth of the conceptual definition adopted and the uses to which the results are to be applied; the methodologies for counting are also affected (see figure 1). A broad definition in all likelihood will require the development of multiple sampling frames (e.g., for shelters, for nonconventional dwelling spaces, and for soup lines). Thus, the methodological complexity expands dramatically when national estimates, based on a broad definition, are stipulated. Time and resources often are insufficient for carrying out such ambitious enumeration efforts, so methodological trade-offs must then be made, involving the use of projection procedures and other less precise or rigorous methods.[25] Therefore, it should be clear that methodological decisions are not independent of the impetus for the study or its scope, but rather are conditional upon these previous decisions.

How might conceptual definitions be generated?

The generally accepted practice in social science research is first to articulate what is intended to be measured, that is, to state the conceptual definition of the phenomenon to be investigated. For example, studies aimed at examining the causes and consequences of chronic mental illness must clearly state what "chronic mental illness" means;[26] similarly, efforts to investigate the relationship between stress and diathesis for the onset of depression must delineate what the term "stress" encompasses.[27] For knowledge to most effectively be accumulated and advanced through the work of multiple and independent researchers, a consensus regarding the proper definition is ideal. At the very least, however, it is imperative that researchers be conscientious and forthright about specifying the definition(s) that guide their individual studies.

The conceptual definitions underlying previous efforts to characterize the size and composition of the homeless population often have been ambiguously or incompletely articulated. In some cases, no such definition is provided, and thus the definition may or may not be understood by the bulk of researchers and/or users of the results. In other cases, studies suffer from "semantic imprecision,"[28] allowing interpretational degrees of freedom on the part of investigators. Thus, it comes as no surprise that no generally agreed-upon definition of homelessness exists.[29] In fact, some would suggest that there is little merit in arriving at a definition of homelessness. For the purposes of the decennial census, the Census Bureau studiously avoided providing any definition of homelessness. As Taeuber and Siegel asserted, "the 1990 Census did not impose one";[30] rather, it skirted the issue by simply designating locations where and time when persons would be counted (e.g., at shelters in the evening and in the street and open public locations in the early hours of the morning). The establishment of a conceptual definition was bypassed, and the Census Bureau proceeded directly to developing an operational definition. Although it is difficult to envisage that the Census Bureau's selection of where to look was devoid of any conceptual underpinning, however tacit, such definitional "leap-frogging" is in all likelihood common in homelessness research.

Common-sense approaches

One way to define homelessness is to rely on common sense or natural language. The mere mention of the term *homeless* generates a variety of images. The most obvious one is of a person who has no home. In fact, the *Oxford English Dictionary*'s definition of *homeless* is a common-sense one: "having no home or permanent shelter."

Other sources also are instructive for obtaining insight into the meaning and circumstances customarily associated with homelessness. As shown by a casual perusal of the subject index for newspaper articles on homelessness, journalists have contributed to the process of defining homelessness. Some headlines underscore the more standard view of the literally homeless: "Alone and Homeless, 'Shutouts' of Society Sleep in Doorways," "New York City Resists State on Shelters for Homeless," "Police Close Down Makeshift Home for Skid Row Residents."[31] Other circumstances associated with homelessness also are revealed by newspaper accounts ("A devastating typhoon ... left 180 people dead, 370,000 homeless").[32] More recently, those who are temporarily displaced and have doubled up with family or friends have sometimes been considered homeless by the press. Other conditions highlighted by the press include families living in motels on an apparently permanent basis due to their inability to find affordable housing or to accumulate the cash deposits required for rentals, and those in which there is a significant gap between income and rents.[33] While journalistic accounts can be helpful, each represents a limited segment of the homeless population. It remains unclear how these segments could be stitched together to provide a broader and more workable conceptual definition. Another strategy for exploring how homelessness has been defined, and thus who should or could be counted, is to consult definitions that have been developed previously.

Formal definitions

The *Oxford English Dictionary* is often viewed as the ultimate source for definitions, but its definition of *homeless* ("having no home or permanent shelter") is in fact somewhat blurry. In trying to apply this definition to enumeration efforts, we would immediately have questions concerning what exactly is meant by the terms *home* and *permanent*.[34]

Defining *home* could be relatively straightforward, if one wished to rely on the Internal Revenue Service (IRS). In its 1990 income tax filing instructions, *home* is defined as "a house, condominium, cooperative, mobile home, boat, or similar property. It must provide basic living accommodations, including sleeping space and toilet and cooking facilities."[35]

Obviously, any dwelling that is missing one or more of these features provides a definitional rationale for classifying a resident of that dwelling as homeless. This source is less instructive in terms of elucidating what is meant by permanence, but operational parameters could be identified. And, while the spirit of the IRS definition is consistent with common-sense notions of what constitutes a home, one could easily imagine a shelter for the homeless, which may contain shared sleeping, toilet, and cooking facilities, as qualifying as a home within the letter of the definition. Clearly, reliance on this definition is inadequate for the purposes of providing a conceptual framework for enumerating the homeless.

One researcher who has articulated a conceptual definition of homelessness is Rossi: "Homelessness, at its core, means not having customary and regular access to a conventional dwelling; it mainly applies to those who do not rent or own a residence."[36]

This definition focuses on the "literally homeless" population. Rossi recognizes that other conditions put individuals at risk of homelessness (e.g., precarious housing situations such as being doubled up or being weakly attached to the housing market), but prefers to label these persons as "the extremely poor." The literally homeless are considered to occupy the lowest level of this standard-of-living continuum.

The definition incorporated by the McKinney Act (P.L. 100–77, sec 103(2)(1), 101 stat. 485 (1987)) adopts a somewhat broader view of homelessness:

> The term "homeless" or "homeless individual" includes an individual who (1) lacks a fixed, regular, and adequate nighttime residence and (2) has a primary nighttime residence that is (a) a supervised, publicly or privately operated shelter designed to provide temporary living accommodations (including welfare hotels, congregate shelters, and transitional housing for the mentally ill), (b) an institution that provides a temporary residence for individuals intended to be institutionalized, or (c) a public or private place not designed for, or ordinarily used as, a regular sleeping accommodation for human beings.

In addition to the literally homeless, this definition also allows inclusion of individuals who are in such institutions as psychiatric hospitals (prisons are explicitly excluded in the act's definition), if they have no specific dwelling to return to upon their release; this expanded coverage is similar to that incorporated by other federal statutes.[37] The National Institute of Alcohol Abuse and Alcoholism (NIAAA), in its recent Cooperative Research Demonstration Project for Homeless Individuals with Alcohol and Other Drug Problems, further broadens the McKinney definition by stating that those "doubled up" should be eligible for services funded by its project.[38] Although it is not clear whether Burt and Cohen or Sosin, Colson, and Grossman specified a conceptual definition prior to conducting their research, their operational practices are consistent with this broadest conceptual framework.[39]

Operational definitions

What should be clear from the preceding section is that conceptual definitions can guide decisions to include or exclude an individual by limiting or expanding the target population to be counted.[40] In making the translation between explicit or implicit conceptual definitions and the specific operational procedures to be employed, several additional definitional issues must be addressed. These include the relevant *individual characteristics* (e.g., age) and the *settings* in which appropriate individuals are likely to be located (e.g., in shelters, in institutions, or on the streets). Persons in those settings often may not be homeless; for example, Burt and Cohen and Sosin, Colson, and Grossman found that not all clients of soup kitchens and meal programs are homeless.[41] Such findings support the need to implement specific rules for identifying who should be counted, including the development and use of *screening questions* that may ask whether the individual is homeless and the *duration of homelessness*. Counts also can vary depending upon the time frame covered by the enumeration process (*incidence* versus *prevalence*). Specifically, estimates can be derived for a particular point in time (e.g., a given night) or over an extended period of time (e.g., in a given year); for the latter, the unduplicated count provides an estimate of the total number of individuals experiencing transitory or extended periods of homelessness.

Individual characteristics. Given that the homeless population is diverse and becoming more so, the central question, beyond the total number of homeless individuals, addresses the composition of the population. For planning services, such concerns are important because not all populations are likely to require the same set of services. Individual characterization of the population can assume an endless number of configurations; for example, key subgroups include homeless substance abusers, homeless chronically mentally ill, homeless families, and unaccompanied youths. In its most recent report, the Interagency Council on the Homeless catalogues the important subgroups and summarizes the federal initiatives that have been undertaken.[42]

For the purposes of this paper, what is important is the recognition that segmenting the total homeless population into policy-relevant components is central and has methodological implications. In particular, an interest in describing the population requires individual-level data; therefore, a reliance on settings as a means of determining who is homeless is insufficie t. Nevertheless, settings provide a rough (i.e., probabilistic), *a priori* categorization scheme for framing the enumeration task.

Settings where homeless persons are likely to be found. In an effort to summarize prior studies aimed at providing estimates of the homeless population, Burt and Taeuber surveyed the authors of seven studies.[43] To identify who had been counted by the researchers, Burt and Taeuber compiled an extensive listing of possible settings and conditions where homeless individuals might be found. These were classified into seven generic categories with numerous specific subcategories:

1. *Shelter-type institutions.* These include homeless shelters, domestic violence shelters, subsidized temporary hotels/motels/apartments, and runaway and homeless youth centers.

2. *Non-shelter institutions.* In this category are jails, mental health facilities, detoxification centers, and quarter-way, half-way, and three-quarters-way houses.

3. *"Gray area" institutions.* These include single-room-occupancy dwellings, hotels that are paid with the individual's own resources (e.g., YMCAs and residential hotels with long-term occupants), and transitional/permanent housing projects (e.g., group homes and arrangements targeted at the "once homeless").

4. *Long-standing institutions.* This group includes hospitals housing boarder babies, facilities designed to shelter victims of natural disasters, and housing facilities for other emergency situations (e.g., facilities for abused and neglected children).

5. *Nonresidential institutions.* This category is different from the previous settings in that it does not include sleeping arrangements, but rather service settings specifically targeted at homeless individuals: soup kitchens, mobile food vans, drop-in centers, and health clinics.

6. *Noninstitutional locations.* These are nonconventional dwellings, including streets, parks, transportation depots,

abandoned buildings, parked cars, sections of highways (e.g., underpasses), public transportation (e.g., subways), parking garages, and railroad boxcars.

7. *Conventional dwelling units.* The focus here is on identifying those individuals who are doubled up or otherwise precariously housed.

While the list is daunting, it is instructive in terms of the potential scope of the search process. It should be noted that Burt and Taeuber did not identify the conceptual definitions used in these seven studies or in developing this list; rather, these settings appear to be based on logical and plausible locations.

The number of sites that served as the basis for enumeration varied dramatically across the seven studies reviewed, and not surprisingly, no study included all of the settings listed earlier. The choice of settings that were investigated appears to have been influenced by different conceptual definitions (either tacit or explicit). For example, Rossi, Fisher, and Willis focused on homeless shelters (both short-term and transitional) and nonconventional dwelling locations (e.g., streets, parks, and abandoned buildings).[44] Rossi has articulated the clearest linkage between the conceptual and operational definitions.[45] Stemming from his notion of literal homelessness, "conventional dwellings" include homes, apartments, mobile homes, rented rooms in hotels, rooming houses, or private homes, but exclude such public places as subway stations, scrap-material shacks, abandoned buildings, and dormitory arrangements (as in shelters). In addition, the identification of appropriate settings is also defined by his notion of "customary and regular access"; this access is granted to those who rent or own a home or who are members of a household that occupies a dwelling (e.g., children). Individuals who fall outside these boundaries are considered literally homeless. However, Rossi's definition excludes those residing in institutions (e.g., hospitals and jails), and those doubled up or precariously housed fall into the extremely poor, rather than literally homeless, category.

Adhering to the McKinney definition provides additional latitude, given that such terms as "fixed, regular, and adequate nighttime residence" are subject to interpretation in terms of who should be counted. In fact, this definition explicitly states that those in institutions can be classified as homeless. Our reading of the definition suggests that the McKinney Act incorporates a compound definition. That is, not only must an individual lack a fixed, regular, and adequate nighttime residence, but also the individual's nighttime residence must fall into one of the three categories identified in the act. Therefore, the institutionalized should be counted only if they lack a fixed, regular, and adequate residence upon discharge.

Some efforts have understood the McKinney definition to encompass persons who double up. For example, NIAAA explicitly views those doubled up as at risk for homelessness and eligible for services provided by NIAAA research demonstration projects. Similarly, space in which persons are doubled up may be viewed as *not* "fixed, regular, and adequate" because of the potential of extremely overcrowded and unsafe conditions. In contrast, other efforts to enumerate homeless persons (e.g., those of some state departments of education) have more rigidly construed the definition to exclude those who are doubled up from their reporting to the U.S. Department of Education on homeless children and youths.[46]

Screening questions. The list of settings is introduced by a key phrase— "likely to be found." This phrase implies that not all individuals observed in those settings are in fact homeless. Therefore, simply counting the number of occupants in a particular setting at a given time may overestimate the size of the homeless population. For example, some residents of prisons are unlikely ever to be released, and thus their housing status is immaterial. Others may have families and spouses (and homes) to return to, and others may have sufficient resources to procure housing upon their release. The methodological implications are straightforward: it is necessary to interview residents of certain locations. For other settings (e.g., homeless shelters), the use of screeners is less important; in fact, most researchers have merely assumed that an individual's presence in a shelter is sufficient to classify him/her as homeless.

Duration and prior history of homelessness. It is well recognized that homelessness is dynamic, with some individuals cycling in and out of various settings that represent more or less extreme forms of deprivation. For example, of those using meal programs or in treatment programs, nearly two-thirds of Sosin, Colson, and Grossman's Chicago sample were not currently homeless, although a large majority of these had previously been homeless.[47] Santiago et al. published similar findings, and their expanded definition (from "currently homeless" to "homeless within the last three months") increased the number of individuals classified as homeless by 50 percent.[48] The determination of duration and prior history of homelessness hinges on the investigator's initial definition of homelessness.

Incidence versus prevalence. As noted earlier, counts of homeless individuals vary depending upon whether they are counts for a particular night or point in time (point prevalence), counts of the number becoming homeless within a given year (annual incidence), or counts of the cumulative total (annual prevalence). In deriving these estimates, it is necessary to take into account the duration and prior history of homelessness, which are generally self-reported and subject to all the limitations of this approach.

The intended uses of the estimates and their methodological implications

The complexities associated with defining, locating, and counting the number of homeless individuals are unlikely to be the result of serendipitous or whimsical decisions, regardless of whether the estimate is for local or national use. Furthermore, for each estimate, there are one or more specific requestor(s) of the information who have a plan for how this information will be used (e.g., Congress might want to determine financial allocations required for services to the target population). For example, Section 722 of the McKinney Act requires each state to gather data on the number and location of homeless children and youths for reporting to Congress via the Secretary of Education. This information is then to serve as a basis for ensuring that this group has access to free and appropriate education.

If the main reason for attempting to understand the size and composition of the population is to improve service delivery, the definitions (who gets counted and where) and methods (how the estimate is derived) are likely to differ from those used if the goal is simply to derive a figure for ascertaining the magnitude of the problem. If the primary reason for conducting a count of the homeless is to develop a short-term plan for delivering services (e.g., to ensure adequate numbers of beds in local shelters), the focus will be on counting those individuals who are potential shelter occupants. Thus, the effort is directed toward counting the literally homeless, rather than those marginally housed or on the streets and not likely to use shelters. In contrast, the design of a long-term delivery plan requires that the definition of "homeless" include not only shelter users but also those likely to become homeless in the near future (those at imminent risk). To accommodate these various interests and uses, it is desirable to have a conceptual definition that is inclusive.

But as the definition of homelessness is expanded, methods for gathering data become more complex. Rossi makes this point quite clearly and argues that a definition must "cover the essence of that term and [be] also *practical to use in actual research*"[49] (italics added). There are good technical reasons for constraining the definition in such a way that it can be studied, but political arguments exist for not restricting definitions in accordance with methodological convenience.

One important practical consideration is the cost of obtaining statistically sound estimates. Although it is possible to construct an elegant study for each component embodied in the broadest definition imaginable, the breadth of settings outlined above would make such an undertaking formidable and tremendously expensive. Even with adequate time and money, the rapid transition in the composition of this population would almost certainly call precise estimates into question. Although longitudinal studies (panel and cross-sectional) could be undertaken, political changes in the acceptability of definitions suggest additional sources of slippage. So, although money and time are important, and good studies take both, they are not sufficient to solve all problems.

If we lower our sights somewhat, we can reduce the time and resources needed to conduct a study in a variety of ways. For example, a precise national estimate could be obtained if we imposed a limited definition of homelessness (e.g., only those individuals located in shelters or on the streets). As the Census Bureau knows so well, concentrating on specific segments of the population invites accusations of bias.

To counter these claims requires a broadening of the definition of homelessness. However, this does not resolve the problem. Embracing a broad definition of homelessness—one similar to that specified in the McKinney Act or NIAAA's expansion—is desirable, but not practical for all purposes. It appears unlikely that every estimate would or could include members of all possible groups that meet a broad definition's criteria for inclusion. Therefore, unless research practices are altered, estimates will continue to be based on selected subgroups of the homeless population. Confusion will prevail.

Intelligent segmentation

The definition of homelessness—regardless of its breadth—is not really as intractable a problem as it may appear. The real problem is in how the resulting numbers are reported. Two issues are important—the completeness of reporting and the level at which

components or segments of the homeless population are reported. First, "counters" can be clearer about who is being
counted and who is not. It is often quite difficult to ascertain
with confidence exactly who was included in the enumeration (or
estimation) process. In some cases, it is impossible to tell.[50]
Second, even when operational definitions (e.g., settings and
conditions) are described, the numbers found in each segment
are not disclosed separately. The authors use the term *intelligent
segmentation* to denote how reporting of estimates could be
carried out. In particular, a total estimate of the homeless would
be broken into individual estimates for each of the subgroups
examined. Rossi provides a nearly perfect example of this strategy in reporting his results on the shelter and street components
of his Chicago study.[51] In a later section of this paper, an illustration incorporates a broader definition than Rossi's literal
homelessness concept.

The need for a family of studies

Counting the number of homeless in the various settings encompassed by a broad definition will require the use of multiple
methodological tactics. We refer to this as a *family of studies,*
with each member targeted at a specific component of the conceptual definition. Because of the uncertainty associated with
each method and the difficulty of implementing these strategies
with transient populations, the necessary family of studies must
also include "side studies" that check on the quality of each
"member" study. This tactic is readily seen in the work of
Taeuber and Siegel, Dennis, and James, to name a few.[52] The
constellation of member studies will, in all likelihood, pattern
the complexity of the definition that is used. The specific locations where the homeless are likely to be found entail sampling
designs that are tailored to each segment. In other words, multiple studies are needed. Unlike conventional household surveys,
probability-based estimates of individuals in settings involving
nonconventional dwellings require an alteration in the traditional way we think about sampling frames. Dennis provides an
accounting of these modifications.[53] For example, blocks need to
be sampled. Because not all blocks in a given geographical area
will have the same probability of containing homeless individuals, it is necessary, for the purposes of sampling efficiency, to
rely on informants to classify blocks; in this manner, differential
probabilities of finding homeless individuals can be obtained so
that stratifications can be built into the sampling design. The
sampling frame developed for shelters is likely to be more similar, in practice, to conventional survey tactics. At the same time,

constructing the list is likely to depend on multiple sources (e.g., key informants, listing of community service agencies, and telephone contacts).

Establishing the technical credibility of each member study is the primary intent of the second type of study within our so-called family. This focus is not novel, of course, inasmuch as almost every competent survey researcher is aware that transgressions can occur in the execution of the various study phases. Sampling frames are not always complete,[54] interviewers do not always follow instructions, respondents may not cooperate, and some respondents are incapable of providing accurate information on their prior sleeping arrangements or shelter status. The list of sampling and nonsampling errors and biases that might be encountered is substantial. Estimating the magnitude of these concerns is the primary objective underlying this type of methodological study.

Intelligent segmentation and multiple methods: an illustration

To make the idea behind intelligent segmentation clear and to show how the family of studies might be configured, the next section provides an illustration. This two-pronged approach was used in a recently completed study issued by the U.S. General Accounting Office (GAO).[55] Although some of the issues were idiosyncratic to the particular question of interest, others were generic and have immediate application to other issues in the field (e.g., estimating prevalence of subgroups). Similarly, the analytic tactics (e.g., sensitivity analysis) are sufficiently general to be useful in other areas. It should be noted that we do not believe that this illustration necessarily represents the best way to estimate the number of homeless children and youths. However, we are convinced that it provides a useful illustration of how future results should be reported.

Origins of the GAO study

In reauthorizing the McKinney Act (P.L. 100-77), Congress requested that GAO provide an estimate of the number of homeless children and youths in all 50 states. That same law also required the Secretary of Education to compile and submit to Congress, through state education agencies, data on the number and location of homeless children and youth. The Department of Education issued its report on February 15, 1989, and in essence, the mandated count assigned to GAO was intended to function as a check on the accuracy of the department's efforts. On June 15, 1989, GAO issued its report. It should be noted that the congressional language basically requested complete, national enumeration within 12 months. Through a series of negotiations, an estimate based on a representative sample was deemed sufficient to meet congressional needs. Other trade-offs will be made clearer as the example unfolds.

In a nutshell, different methods were used to derive an overall estimate. Because not all methods were equally trustworthy (actual enumerations, expert opinion, and population extrapolations contain different strengths and weaknesses), the accuracy of the results produced by each method needed to be documented and disclosed. This differential trustworthiness resulting from statistical and nonstatistical sources of error and bias can be incorporated into confidence intervals or ranges based on sensitivity analyses.

The bottom line

Using a variety of methods, GAO estimated that on a given night (October 24, 1988), about 68,000 children and youths aged 16 years or younger were members of families that are literally homeless (see table 1). As argued earlier, a broad interpretation of the McKinney Act would suggest that the estimated 68,000 homeless children and youths represent only part of the potential homeless population, namely, that part that is literally homeless. Many advocates and stakeholders view this as a fairly narrow conceptualization of the problem. As a means of broadening the definition, GAO attempted to estimate those believed to be precariously housed (e.g., those doubled up with relatives or friends). This group is quite large, representing an additional 186,000 children and youths who could be considered homeless on any given day. GAO stated that these estimates did not include homeless runaway children and youth, nor did they account for those families who may be on the brink of homelessness by virtue of their economic situation. Despite these omissions, adding the number of precariously housed to the number of individuals who are literally homeless reveals that, on any given night, more than 250,000 children and youth might be considered homeless.

Table 1. **Estimated Number of U.S. Homeless Children and Youths at Any Given Time**

Category	Best Estimate	Range[a]		Source[b]	Confidence[c]
		Low	High		
Literally homeless					
Urban					
Shelters, hotels	25,522	18,265	32,779	Surveys	High
Churches	4,094	2,340	6,570	Opinion	Low
Public places	9,016	4,512	24,072	Opinion	Low
Other	7,651	5,168	10,446	Opinion	Low
Suburban	14,427	7,213	21,641	Population Rates	Moderate
Rural	7,357	3,678	11,035	Population Rates	Moderate
Total	68,067	41,176	106,543	All	Moderate
Precariously housed (doubled up)	185,512	39,362	296,452	Opinion	Low

Source: U.S. General Accounting Office, *Children and Youths: About 68,000 Homeless and 186,000 in Shared Housing at Any Given Time* (Washington, DC: U.S. Government Printing Office, 1989), page 2.

[a] The low and high estimates represent a plausible range of values based on various assumptions.

[b] The three primary sources of information upon which estimates were based were surveys of shelter providers and agencies providing vouchers (conducted on October 24, 1988), the application of homeless rates to a population base, and expert opinion.

[c] The confidence rating reflects an assessment of the level of certainty that can be expected of the estimates, given the reliability of the data sources and the range of estimates provided.

An illustration of intelligent segmentation

Simply reporting an aggregate figure (say 250,000) would have made it impossible to know how much each component of the definition contributed to the overall total. Segmentation of this estimate into its component parts makes it clear that the numbers differ across settings. As might be expected, homeless children and youths were not evenly distributed across the different locations where homeless families are thought to congregate or "reside." Nationwide, urban shelters and hotels housed families with roughly 25,500 children and youths; about 21,800 were likely to be in suburban and rural areas; churches accounted for about 4,000; abandoned buildings, cars, or public places were likely to be called home by about 9,000; and about 7,000 may have been in various other settings (e.g., institutions). Not only is the utility of survey results greatly enhanced if data are presented setting by setting, as shown in table 1, but such practices sidestep the issue of which definition is correct. Furthermore, such reporting implies (and indeed, encourages) that the broadest possible definition (within resource constraints) should be used in future surveys. When idiosyncratic definitions and operationalizations of homelessness are used across different sites, presenting separable estimates (by subgroup) is essential if the results of such estimation exercises are to be used intelligently.

An illustration of the family of studies

Opting for a broad definition of homelessness and one that fairly represented the settings where the literally homeless were likely to be found had substantial consequences for the estimation procedures that could be employed. The purist in all of us would probably like to use a common set of procedures (across settings) that could be defended on statistical grounds. In attempting to meet the request of Congress, GAO had to rely on a unique mixture of methodological strategies in piecing together its overall estimates. Basically, the strategy involved three steps and multiple methods (a count, expert opinions, and population-based extrapolations).

The first phase was very traditional. It entailed the use of survey methods whereby an unduplicated estimate of the number of children and youths in shelters and hotels (or motels) in 40 large urban areas (populations in excess of 250,000) was obtained, representing 27 cities. A multistage probability sample was drawn to select shelters; a telephone survey was used to obtain counts of the number of children housed in shelters on a particular night (October 24, 1988); and the number of vouchers for hotel or motel accommodations issued by the county were obtained for that same night. This method was intended to provide a nationally representative estimate of the number of children and youths in shelters and hotels or motels in urban counties. It also served as the foundation for the other estimate procedures.

To use a sample-based methodology for obtaining estimates in other settings (e.g., streets) would have been prohibitively expensive and time-consuming. GAO opted for an approximation. In particular, the second phase of the study involved developing separate estimates of the number of children and youths in some of the other settings used to define literal homelessness. These were derived by using the survey-based county estimates in conjunction with expert opinion. The experts' ratings reflect their estimates of the proportions of homeless children and youths in each of these other settings. The same procedures were used to obtain estimates of the number of children and youths who might be precariously housed (e.g., doubled up).

Using sampling methods to simply identify children and youths in urban and suburban areas would have been too time-consuming and expensive. Again, GAO used an approximation based on a different methodology. For estimates of children and youths in rural and suburban areas, actual survey-based counts were used in conjunction with other estimates (derived from the empirical literature) and population counts in nonurban areas. Here, estimates based on the median homelessness rate across the 27 cities were used to project the homelessness rate relative to the population base in rural and suburban areas. Rather than relying on expert opinion, these estimates used extant data on population size in nonurban areas and estimates from the study's first phase. The third phase assessed the accuracy of the estimates produced by these procedures by comparing the results with those reported in other national studies.

Side studies on methodological adequacy

Although estimates were produced for each setting within the definition of homelessness, they were obviously not of equal integrity. To account for the precision of each estimate, the GAO study also calculated ranges similar to confidence intervals (see table 1). With the exception of the survey results, these were not ordinary confidence intervals in the sense of classical statistics. Rather, sensitivity analyses were used as a basis for determining the robustness of each estimate. This produced an upper and lower boundary for each setting × method combination. Whereas an ordinary confidence interval uses the error of estimate as the basis for specifying the interval within which the true population value will be found, the interval estimation procedures altered key parameters or assumptions underlying each calculation. In this way, GAO was able to provide the user with a sense of the stability and sensitivity (to alternative assumptions) of each value. GAO also supplied a verbal description of the overall confidence placed in each estimate; ratings ranged from "low" to "high."

Little is known about the prevalence of homelessness in suburban and rural areas. Because the initial sampling frame was restricted to large urban areas, it would have underestimated the number of homeless children and youths by omitting suburban and rural areas. Prior studies of the homeless population in suburban areas assumed that prevalence is about one-third the rate of that for central cities. In creating the lower boundary for the confidence interval or range, one-third of the median rate of homelessness found in the sample of cities was used. In constructing the upper boundary, the assumption was made that the median rate was appropriate. Here, the best-guess point estimate ended up being the average of the high and low boundary values. Although these values are derived from extrapolations of estimates (GAO's own estimates from the survey results) and compounded estimates (an estimate from another study was applied to its survey-based estimate), the confidence that might be placed in these values was judged as moderate. That is, it was judged to be below the confidence level placed in the survey results and above the confidence level ascribed to the opinion-based estimates for the number of individuals housed in churches, in public places, in other settings (such as institutions), and those in doubled-up situations (see table 1).

Specifically, the opinion-based estimates were derived from interviews with shelter providers, advocates, and knowledgeable government officials in the sample of 40 counties (covering 27 cities). More than 300 individuals provided their countywide estimates of the relative number of homeless families residing in settings other than public or privately sponsored shelters and hotels. These responses were converted to ratios that, when applied to the estimated number of families in shelters, provided estimates of the number of families in other settings. The median ratios for each county were computed along with lower and upper bound values (first and third quartile, respectively). The results showed that opinion-based estimates were very sensitive to the choice of values (median, first, or third quartile), depicting a substantial range in values. As seen in table 1, using the median ratios derived within counties produced an estimate of approximately 186,000 doubled-up children and youths nationwide. The range, however, suggests that there may be from 39,000 to 296,000, depending upon how the data are analyzed at the individual county level. The ranges for other estimates using this method are also quite broad. This is especially true for expert-based assessments of the number of children and youths that are likely to be in public places. Because of this hypersensitivity, the GAO report judged the confidence that should be placed in opinion-based estimates as low.

Sensitivity analyses are helpful to a certain extent, but they cannot establish with certainty the overall sensibleness of a set of calculations. The decisions that were made on high versus low estimates—although based on logic and, where possible, prior data—are but a subset of all the possible values that could have been chosen. And, although it is better to provide the client or user with a sense of the confidence that should be placed in the numbers that have been produced, bracketing in this way does have inherent limitations.

As a means of judging the adequacy of these methods, a second form of multimethod research can be used—namely, comparing competing estimates from parallel studies. Two recent reports served as the basis for other national estimates of the number of homeless children and youths. The Institute of Medicine (IOM), using data from the National Alliance to End Homelessness, estimated that 100,000 children and youth were literally homeless, in contrast to the GAO estimate of roughly 68,000.[56] A careful review of the IOM methodology suggests several noncomparabilities across procedures. Adjusting the IOM estimate to reflect new information on service utilization[57]—a key assumption in the IOM estimate—reveals an adjusted estimate of 87,000; although this figure is closer to GAO's best-guess value of 68,000, it is about 23 percent higher than GAO's. However, it is well within the confidence range established for the estimate of the number of literally homeless.

In another report, the Urban Institute, under contract to the U.S. Department of Agriculture, conducted a study of homeless in shelters and soup kitchens in 20 cities with populations greater than 100,000, and extrapolated its findings to the nation.[58] The Urban Institute reported approximately 61,500 homeless children in cities and suburban areas. GAO's comparable estimate was 60,710, excluding rural settings. Although none of these three studies is, by itself, able to stand up to close technical scrutiny, the fact that they differ in approach and converge within a reasonably close confidence range suggests that GAO probably derived a sensible understanding of the magnitude of the problem.

Conclusions

In this paper, the authors have shown that several definitional issues must be addressed to achieve an understanding of what's behind the numbers. The thorniest of these issues concerns conceptual definitions—that is, what is meant by "homeless."

Some definitions are quite literal, whereas others are more expansive, including individuals who technically have shelter but are tenuously housed. Which definition is correct is not an easy question to answer. Should we worry about such definitions? Of course. Are definitional issues worth agonizing over? Probably not. Rather, we see several sensible rationales for incorporating a broad definition at the onset; there are a variety of legitimate reasons for being concerned about the size of various subgroups that compose the segment of the population labeled the "extremely poor."[59] In particular, policy formulation and services planning require a broad look at who is homeless and who may be homeless in the future.

However, broad conceptual definitions expand the number and types of locations within which homeless persons are likely to be found, and this diversity constitutes a sizable methodological challenge. This situation should not restrict inquiry as to the size and composition of the population. We would prefer to see more concerted efforts to clearly delineate which segment(s) of the population compose any aggregate numbers. The concept of *intelligent segmentation* as a vehicle for reporting estimates of the components of a broad definition is a means of dealing with the obstacles inherent in developing a consensus as to who should be counted in the aggregate. Having a broad definition that can be decomposed into its separate segments allows for a better understanding of who has and who has not been included in any particular study. This facilitates the understanding of differences across studies and the use of the numbers by other interested policy makers, researchers, and the public.

We also suggest that the complexity inherent in broad definitions will require the development of a family of studies to capture the full range of conditions facing the homeless and those who are at risk. The methods underlying each study within the family are likely to be uncertain due to a host of sampling and nonsampling biases that we may know little about for particular subpopulations. The values that are reported should reflect these conceptual and methodological uncertainties. In this way, consumers will be better informed about the likely "true" range of homeless individuals in the United States.

Authors

David S. Cordray is professor of public policy and psychology and chair of the Department of Human Resources at Vanderbilt University. He also is director of the Center for the Study of At-Risk Populations and Public Assistance Policy at the Vanderbilt Institute for Public Policy. Georgine M. Pion is research associate professor of psychology and human development at Vanderbilt University and fellow in the Center for the Study of At-Risk Populations and Public Assistance Policy. Both are involved in a national, NIAAA-funded evaluation of 14 research demonstration projects to examine the effectiveness of interventions for homeless individuals with alcohol and other drug abuse problems.

The authors would like to thank Peter Rossi, Howard Sandler, and Mark Appelbaum for their helpful comments on this paper and Kelly Johnson, Ann Dismukes, and Nell Thelin for their assistance in its preparation and production. The U.S. General Accounting Office study discussed here as an illustration of the use of intelligent segmentation and multiple methods was conducted while David Cordray served as assistant director within the Program Evaluation and Methodology Division of the U.S. General Accounting Office. The work summarized here was a collaborative effort involving Lois-Ellin Datta, James Onken, and Peggy Murray, among others.

Endnotes

1.   Martha R. Burt and Barbara E. Cohen, *Feeding the Homeless: Does the Prepared Meals Provision Help?* (Washington, DC: The Urban Institute, 1988); Carl F. Horowitz, "Mitch Snyder's Phony Numbers: The Fiction of Three Million Homeless," *Policy Review* 49(1989):66–69; Peter H. Rossi, *Down and Out in America: The Origins of Homelessness* (Chicago: University of Chicago Press, 1989).

2.   Mary E. Hombs and Mitch Snyder, *Homelessness in America: A Forced March to Nowhere* (Washington, DC: Community for Creative Non-Violence, 1983).

3.   Rossi, *Down and Out in America,* 53.

4.   U.S. General Accounting Office, *Homeless Mentally Ill: Problems and Options in Estimating the Numbers and Trends,* GAO/PEMD-88-24 (Washington, DC: 1988).

5.   Rossi, *Down and Out in America,* 54.

6.   Anna Kondratas, "Estimates and Public Policy: The Politics of Numbers," this journal.

7.   U.S. Department of Housing and Urban Development, *A Report to the Secretary on the Homeless and Emergency Shelters* (Washington, DC: Office of Policy Development and Research, 1984).

8.   William Tucker, "Where Do the Homeless Come From?" *National Review,* September 25, 1987, 32–43.

9.   Richard B. Freeman and Brian Hall, *Permanent Homelessness in America?* Working Paper No. 2013 (Cambridge, MA: National Bureau of Economic Research, 1986).

10.   National Alliance to End Homelessness, *Housing and Homelessness: A Report of the National Alliance to End Homelessness* (Washington, DC: National Alliance to End Homelessness, 1988).

11. U.S. General Accounting Office, *Children and Youths: About 68,000 Homeless and 186,000 in Shared Housing at Any Given Time,* GAO/PEMD-89-14 (Washington, DC: 1989).

12. U.S. Conference of Mayors, *The Continued Growth of Hunger, Homelessness, and Poverty in America's Cities: A 25-City Survey* (Washington, DC: U.S. Conference of Mayors, 1986).

13. Martha R. Burt and Barbara S. Cohen, *America's Homeless: Numbers Characteristics, and Programs That Serve Them* (Washington, DC: The Urban Institute, 1989).

14. Martha R. Burt, "Developing the Estimate of 500,000–600,000 Homeless People in the United States in 1987," in *Conference Proceedings for Enumerating Homeless Persons: Methods and Data Needs,* ed. Cynthia M. Taeuber (Washington, DC: Bureau of the Census, 1991).

15. Ibid.

16. Rossi, *Down and Out in America,* 81. Although no specific dates were provided by Rossi, we assume that he refers to the year just prior to the publication of his book.

17. Hombs and Snyder, *Homelessness in America.*

18. Peter H. Rossi, Gene A. Fisher, and Georgiana Willis, *The Condition of the Homeless in Chicago* (Amherst, MA, and Chicago: Social and Demographic Research Institute and National Opinion Research Center, 1986).

19. Michael Sosin, Paul Colson, and Susan Grossman, *Homelessness in Chicago: Poverty and Pathology, Social Institutions, and Social Change* (Chicago: Chicago Community Trust, 1988).

20. M. Audrey Burnam and Paul Koegel, "Methodology for Obtaining a Representative Sample of Homeless Persons," *Evaluation Review* 12(1988):117–52; Charles D. Cowan, William R. Breakey, and Pamela J. Fischer, "The Methodology of Counting the Homeless," in *Homelessness, Health, and Human Needs,* Institute of Medicine (Washington, DC: National Academy Press, 1988); Alice K. Johnson, "Measurement and Methodology: Problems and Issues in Research on Homelessness," *Social Work Research and Abstracts* (December 1989):12–20; Ezra Susser, Sarah Conover, and Elmer L. Struening, "Problems of Epidemiologic Method in Assessing the Type and Extent of Mental Illness Among Homeless Adults," *Hospital and Community Psychiatry* 40(1989):261–65; U.S. General Accounting Office, *Homeless Mentally Ill.*

21. Rossi, *Down and Out in America;* U.S. General Accounting Office, *Homeless Mentally Ill.*

22. Brent B. Benda and Patrick Dattalo, "Homelessness: Consequence of a Crisis or a Long-Term Process?" *Hospital and Community Psychiatry* 39(1988):884–86; Charles Hoch, "A Brief History of the Homeless Problem in the United States," in *The Homeless in Contemporary Society,* ed. Richard D. Bingham, Roy E. Green, and Sammie B. White (Newbury Park, CA: Sage, 1987); Sosin, Colson, and Grossman, *Homeless in Chicago.*

23. David S. Cordray, "Counting the Homeless: What Counts?" in *Conference Proceedings for Enumerating Homeless Persons: Methods and Data Needs,* ed. Cynthia M. Taeuber (Washington, DC: Bureau of the Census, 1991); Rossi, *Down and Out in America.*

24. Kim Hopper, "Homelessness Old and New: The Matter of Definitions," this journal. Hopper provides a nice account of the historical changes in definitions of homelessness. He takes a social constructionist perspective on problem definition, also pointing out cultural differences in defining terms such as *conventional dwelling.*

25. Cordray, "Counting the Homeless."

26. Howard H. Goldman, Antoinette A. Gattozzi, and Carl A. Taube, "Defining and Counting the Chronically Mentally Ill," *Hospital and Community Psychiatry* 32(1981): 21–27.

27. Scott M. Monroe and Anne D. Simons, "Diathesis-Stress Theories in the Context of Life Stress Research: Implications for the Depressive Disorders," *Psychological Bulletin* (in press).

28. Cynthia M. Taeuber and Paul M. Siegel, "Counting the Nation's Homeless Population in the 1990 Census," in *Conference Proceedings for Enumerating Homeless Persons: Methods and Data Needs,* ed. Cynthia M. Taeuber (Washington, DC: Bureau of the Census, 1991).

29. Johnson, "Measurement and Methodology"; James D. Wright, *Address Unknown: The Homeless in America* (Hawthorne, NY: Aldine de Gruyter, 1989).

30. Taeuber and Siegel, "Counting the Nation's Homeless Population," 93.

31. John Darnton, "Alone and Homeless, 'Shutouts' of Society Sleep in Doorways," *New York Times,* October 25, 1975; Robin Herman, "New York City Resists State on Shelters for Homeless," *New York Times,* October 11, 1980; Janet Clayton, "Police Close Down Makeshift Home for Skid Row Residents," *Los Angeles Times,* May 11, 1985.

32. Bob Drogin, "Typhoon Dims a Philippine Bright Spot," *Los Angeles Times,* May 11, 1985.

33. Mark I. Pinsky, "A New Class of Homeless on the Horizon," *New York Times,* March 27, 1985; Kirsten Downey, "Renters Called Vulnerable in Downtown," *Washington Post,* December 29, 1990.

34. As noted by Rossi in his comments on this paper, the *Oxford English Dictionary*'s definition of home also is saturated with references to family, intimacy, acceptance, and other feelings of social support. In contrast, current definitions of homelessness contain no such allusions. This is a shift from definitions held by social scientists prior to 1980, in which homelessness often was equated with familylessness and spouselessness.

35. Internal Revenue Service (IRS), "Instructions for Form 1040A" (Washington, DC: IRS, 1990).

36. Rossi, *Down and Out in America,* 10.

37. David Dreier, "What Does 'Homelessness' Really Mean?" (Letter to the editor), *Washington Post,* May 10, 1990.

38. National Institute on Alcohol Abuse and Alcoholism (NIAAA) and National Institute on Drug Abuse (NIDA), *Cooperative Agreements for Research Demonstration Projects on Alcohol and Other Drug Abuse Treatment for Homeless Persons* (Washington, DC: NIAAA and NIDA, 1989).

39. Burt and Cohen, *Feeding the Homeless;* Sosin, Colson, and Grossman, *Homelessness in Chicago.*

40. A small-scale study that also supports the ways in which definitional criteria affect the number of individuals viewed as homeless was conducted by James Morrison, "Correlations Between Definitions of the Homeless Mentally Ill Population," *Hospital and Community Psychiatry* 40(1989):952–54.

41. Burt and Cohen, *Feeding the Homeless;* Sosin, Colson, and Grossman, *Homelessness in Chicago.*

42. *The 1990 Annual Report of the Interagency Council on the Homeless* (Washington, DC: Interagency Council on the Homeless, 1991).

43. Martha R. Burt and Cynthia M. Taeuber, "Overview of Seven Studies," in *Conference Proceedings for Enumerating Homeless Persons: Methods and Data Needs,* ed. Cynthia M. Taeuber (Washington, DC: Bureau of the Census, 1990).

44. Rossi, Fisher, and Willis, "The Condition of the Homeless."

45. Rossi, *Down and Out in America,* 11.

46. U.S. General Accounting Office, *Children and Youths,* 31.

47. Sosin, Colson, and Grossman, *Homelessness in Chicago.*

48. Jose M. Santiago, et al., "Defining the homeless mentally ill: A methodological note," *Hospital and Community Psychiatry* 39(1988):712–19.

49. Rossi, *Down and Out in America,* 11.

50. Hombs and Snyder, *Homelessness in America.*

51. Rossi, *Down and Out in America.*

52. Taeuber and Siegel, "Counting the Nation's Homeless"; Michael L. Dennis, "Changing the Conventional Rules: Surveying Homeless People in Nonconventional Locations," this journal; Franklin J. James, "Counting Homeless Persons With Surveys of Users of Services for the Homeless," this journal.

53. Dennis, "Changing the Conventional Rules."

54. Taeuber and Siegel, "Counting the Nation's Homeless."

55. U.S. General Accounting Office, *Children and Youths.*

56. Institute of Medicine, *Homelessness, Health, and Human Needs* (Washington, DC: National Academy Press, 1988).

57. U.S. General Accounting Office, *Children and Youths,* 31.

58. This estimate is based on information in Burt and Cohen's *Feeding the Homeless.* Additional information is contained in a memorandum from the Urban Institute to the U.S. Department of Agriculture, and information obtained in a telephone conversation with an Urban Institute researcher.

59. Rossi, *Down and Out in America,* 53.

© Fannie Mae Foundation 1994, 1997. All Rights Reserved.

Public Shelter Admission Rates in Philadelphia and New York City: The Implications of Turnover for Sheltered Population Counts*

Dennis P. Culhane
University of Pennsylvania

Edmund F. Dejowski and Julie Ibañez
City of New York

Elizabeth Needham
University of Pennsylvania

Irene Macchia
City of Philadelphia

Abstract

Previous estimates of the size and composition of the U.S. homeless population have been based on cross-sectional survey methodologies. National enumeration efforts have yielded point-prevalence estimates ranging from 0.11 to 0.25 percent of the population. This study reports data from shelter databases in Philadelphia and New York City that record identifiers for all persons admitted and so make possible unduplicated counts of users.

Unduplicated counts of shelter users yield annual rates for 1992 of about 1 percent for both cities and rates near 3 percent over three years in Philadelphia (1990–92) and over five years (1988–92) in New York. The annual rates are three times greater than rates documented by point-prevalence studies. Shelter bed turnover rates are reported, as are average monthly first admission and readmission counts over a two-year period. Implications for future research and public policy are discussed.

Introduction

For the past decade, researchers, policy analysts, advocates for the homeless, and officials from the federal government have been engaged in the daunting challenge of estimating the size of the homeless population in the United States. Unfortunately, the imprecision in defining and locating a transient, often hidden population has frustrated enumeration efforts. Divergent

---

*Originally published in *Housing Policy Debate* Volume 5, Issue 2.

estimates have inspired debate as to whether homelessness affects thousands or millions of Americans and, consequently, whether the problem requires emergency remedies or more fundamental changes in the nation's social policies. This article demonstrates that the homelessness numbers debate has been inappropriately framed from the outset. Using estimates at a single point in time (point-prevalence estimates), derived from cross-sectional survey methodologies, as the primary approach to measuring the size and composition of the population does not capture the magnitude of the problem over time; is likely to overrepresent persons with long periods of homelessness (e.g., people with disabilities; see Dennis et al. 1993); and, by implication, portrays the population as more stable than dynamic. This article reviews existing estimates of the homeless population and reports shelter utilization data from New York City and Philadelphia that provide new evidence on the scope of the homelessness problem.

Literature review

Advocates for the homeless have consistently maintained that the number of homeless people in the United States is far greater than that reported by government researchers or other social scientists. The numbers debate began in 1983, when members of the Community for Creative Non-Violence (CCNV) in Washington, D.C., issued a report (Hombs and Snyder 1982) placing the number of homeless Americans at 2.2 million, or 1 percent of the population. The estimate was based on an extrapolation of data from a key-informant survey of 14 cities conducted by CCNV, but the survey lacked any explicit, let alone uniform, data standards. The CCNV report was advanced primarily for advocacy purposes and led Kondratas (1991, 633) to conclude that "this [methodology] was a clear leap of fantasy." It nevertheless established a benchmark that was widely reported in the media and against which subsequent estimates have been measured.

The U.S. Department of Housing and Urban Development (HUD 1984) provided a counterpoint to the CCNV estimate in 1984 with the first study of homelessness by the federal government. HUD estimated that 250,000 to 350,000 people (0.11 to 0.15 percent of the U.S. population) were living either in shelters or on the streets on an average night between December 1983 and January 1984. However, HUD researchers, while using four different estimation techniques, also relied on a key-informant survey methodology. Results were derived from a larger sample of cities (N = 60) and applied to the nation's metropolitan and nonmetropolitan populations, but were still based on the estimates of experts and shelter providers, not on a systematic count. Consequently, the methodology was criticized by advocates and by members of the subcommittee in testimony before the U.S. House of Representatives Subcommittee on Housing and Community Development (1984) and later by researchers (Appelbaum 1987; Parsons 1986) and the U.S. General Accounting Office (GAO 1988). HUD's and CCNV's divergent estimates (0.11 versus 1 percent) served as the frame of reference for the numbers debate that ensued.

Results from succeeding enumeration studies by social scientists have been far more convergent, but have nonetheless conflicted with estimates by advocates for the homeless. Rossi, Fisher, and Willis's (1986) study in Chicago was among the more widely cited local surveys, particularly because it included a systematic count of street homeless as well as a shelter census. The researchers were able to document 2,344 homeless people, or 0.09 percent of the population, although advocates from the Chicago area had maintained that the number was closer to 15,000 (Rossi 1987). Similarly, a one-night survey of the street and shelter population in Boston in 1986 (City of Boston 1986) enumerated 2,863 homeless people, or a rate of 0.50 percent, although the Massachusetts Coalition for the Homeless had estimated the number to be 15,000. In a summary of other local counts, Burt and Cohen (1989) report a range of estimates from 0.02 percent in rural Ohio to 0.41 percent in Washington, D.C., as well as the 0.50 percent found in Boston. A more recent enumeration by Dennis et al. (1993) in the Washington metropolitan area found that 1.05 percent of the population aged 12 and older were homeless—the highest rate among the enumerations to date. Nevertheless, despite the wide variation in local estimates, reported homelessness rates have consistently been closer to HUD's estimate than to CCNV's (Kondratas 1991).

Although there is agreement that the homeless or "sheltered" population on a given night more than doubled in the 1980s (Burt 1992; Freeman and Hall 1987; HUD 1989; Kondratas 1991), two recent national studies have again confirmed that while there is significant local variation in the rate of homelessness, the national numbers do not approach advocates' estimates of 2 million to 3 million persons. One study (Burt and Cohen 1989) was based on a probability sample of shelter providers and people using shelters and soup kitchens in U.S. cities of 100,000 or more population. The authors estimated that 229,000 people, or 0.37 percent of the population of these 178 cities, used homeless services in March 1987. Projecting to the United States as a whole, adjusting for urban and nonurban areas, and assuming that for every 100 who used homeless services there were 50 who did not, Burt and Cohen reported a national estimate of 567,000 to 600,000 homeless, or a national rate of 0.235 to 0.249 percent. This estimate has since been accepted by federal officials for planning purposes, although Kondratas (1991) regarded it as an overestimate.

As part of the 1990 census, the Census Bureau conducted a count of homelessness in the nation. The bureau reported that in the 200 largest cities, approximately 230,000 people were identified as living in shelters, on the streets, or in public places not intended for habitation (U.S. Department of Commerce 1991). In an analysis of results for the 50 largest cities, Barrett, Anolik, and Abramson (1992) found sheltered population rates below 0.20 percent for 35 cities and between 0.20 and 0.40 percent for 11 cities. Only four cities had sheltered population rates exceeding 0.40 percent: Seattle (0.44); San Francisco (0.57 percent); Atlanta (0.62 percent); and Washington, D.C. (0.78 percent). The Census Bureau estimates were denounced by advocates and social scientists, some of whom evaluated the enumeration by surveying homeless people to ascertain whether they had been interviewed by census takers and by placing confederates in street locations to see whether they would be counted (see National Coalition for the Homeless 1991 for a summary). The evaluations revealed that the Census Bureau's effort, albeit the largest and most ambitious of its kind, failed to count many of the street homeless and even missed entire shelters. However, as Kondratas (1991, 640–41) has remarked, "even if the count were increased by 100 percent, that would mean 460,000 homeless persons; a 200 percent increase would result in a figure of 690,000.... The bottom line is that the range of legitimate estimates of the homeless population is 230,000 to 600,000."

The convergence of enumerations near 230,000 by Burt and Cohen (1989; largest 178 cities) and the Census Bureau (U.S. Department of Commerce 1991; largest 200 cities) led Kondratas (1991) to conclude that advocates overstated the numbers to support a structuralist interpretation of homelessness and that, in reality, the problem afflicts a small number of troubled individuals, not the new homeless of ordinary working Americans described by advocates. According to Kondratas (1991, 634), advocates' inflated estimates are partly to blame for a misguided federal homelessness policy:

The concept "millions of homeless" was inconsistent with a relatively small proportion of extremely poor persons beset with multiple ongoing problems. If millions were homeless, it was plausible that unemployment and social program cuts were driving ordinary working Americans to the streets.... In other words, the exaggerated number had a strong bearing on this misperception of the causes of homelessness and characteristics of the homeless, which in turn led to ill-conceived policy.

Kondratas goes on to declare that "for those who understand numbers, the so-called numbers debate has long been over" (p. 643).

The evidence appears to suggest that a much smaller number of people is homeless at any point in time than advocates have claimed. However, cross-sectional methods for measuring homelessness have been applied primarily for research, not advocacy, and have been the preferred approach to date because they avoid the duplication problems inherent in longer time frames and because they are useful for meeting immediate planning needs (i.e., planning shelter capacity). Unfortunately, cross-sectional methods also have limitations. They do not capture the magnitude of the problem over time, and they are likely to overrepresent people with long periods of homelessness, such as those with disabilities (see Dennis et al. 1993), relative to longitudinal research designs. Consequently, some people may use the results of cross-sectional research to conclude erroneously that the population over time is composed of more disabled and chronically homeless persons than is actually the case. Indeed, Kondratas's declaration that the numbers debate is over and that unemployment and cuts in social programs are not causes of homelessness appears to derive from a belief that most homeless people are persistently homeless and beset with multiple ongoing problems. A number of empirical findings suggest that those assumptions deserve more careful examination.

Demographic surveys of the homeless have consistently shown that, in addition to being younger and including families with children, the recent homeless report having been homeless for a far shorter duration than their skid row counterparts of the 1950s and 1960s. For example, while Blumberg, Shipley, and Shandler (1973) report that 78 percent of their skid row sample from Philadelphia in 1960 had been skid row residents for more than 1 year and 33 percent for more than 10 years, a survey of Philadelphia's homeless in 1988 (Ryan, Bartelt, and Goldstein 1989) found that 75 percent had been homeless for less than

1 year and 50 percent for less than six months. A study in Phoenix (Brown et al. 1983) found that 60 percent had been homeless for less than six months. In Ohio, Roth et al. (1985) reported that 49 percent had been homeless for less than 60 days. Similar findings in New York (Hoffman et al. 1982) and Chicago (Rossi, Fisher, and Willis 1986), as well as a meta-analysis by Shlay and Rossi (1992) covering 14 studies, confirm that a majority of the recent homeless report having been homeless for relatively brief periods (less than six months).

Researchers have applied estimation techniques to data on length of homelessness to project the annual prevalence of homelessness (that is, the number or proportion of persons experiencing homelessness over the course of a year) by varying assumptions regarding turnover. Rossi's (1989) method yielded annual prevalence estimates 2.3 to 3.4 times greater than point-prevalence estimates, and Vernez et al. (1988) estimated annual turnover rates in California of 5.8, 3.4, and 2.3 in Orange, Alameda, and Yolo Counties, respectively. Unfortunately, because these data are derived from cross sections of the population, there is no way to accurately estimate actual rates of turnover, particularly since such rates would be influenced by the proportion of shelter users with short episodes of homelessness. Nevertheless, these data suggest that turnover among the homeless population is significant and that many more people are likely to be homeless over time than at a single point in time.

Longitudinal research would provide more conclusive evidence of the dynamic nature of homelessness, although little such research has been published. The one published study to date, by Sosin, Piliavin, and Westerfelt (1990)—two additional longitudinal studies are in progress (Burnam, Koegel, and Duan 1990; Robertson, Piliavin, and Westerfelt 1990)—was based on a two-wave, two-sample survey of homeless adults in Minneapolis. In a preliminary analysis of their data, Sosin, Piliavin, and Westerfelt found that homelessness is much more episodic than chronic and that neither previous episodes of homelessness nor an episode of long duration reduce a person's chance of making a stable exit from homelessness. These findings led the authors to conclude that "attempts to enumerate the homeless population through counts at any point in time clearly underestimate the intermittently homeless population" (Sosin, Piliavin, and Westerfelt 1990, 172). This conclusion was consistent with their critique of cross-sectional studies that "tend to misrepresent the length of time individuals are in one status [and] tend to overestimate the proportion of individuals who have long stays"

(p. 158). The results also led the authors to question the efficacy of the current emphasis on temporary and transitional approaches to reversing homelessness and to argue instead that "policy strategies...might focus attention on moving individuals from temporary dwellings to *permanent* ones, or...turn[ing] temporary exits [from homelessness] into permanent ones" (p. 172, emphasis in original).

The final and perhaps most interesting evidence of the turnover in the homeless population comes from a rather unexpected source: telephone surveys of the general population assessing their attitudes toward homelessness. Three such surveys have been conducted, in each of which respondents were asked whether they had ever been homeless. Quite surprisingly, researchers have found convergent and high estimates of prior homelessness among the general population. Toro and McDonell (1992) report that among their sample of persons from Buffalo, New York, selected by a random-digit dialing method, 4.2 percent indicated having been homeless in the past. Novacek et al. (1991) found that 5 percent of a random sample of people from the Tulsa, Oklahoma, telephone directory reported a prior experience of homelessness. A national study by Link et al. (1993) polled 1,507 people and found that 12 percent reported having been homeless. Because these data are significantly qualified by respondents' interpretation of the term "homeless," Link et al. specifically asked whether the respondents had been homeless while living doubled up with friends or relatives, whether they had stayed in a shelter, and whether they had slept in public spaces. The researchers found that if they excluded persons who have doubled up with friends or relatives and included only those who have stayed in a shelter or slept in public spaces (the "literal" homeless), then more than half, or 7 percent of the total, had a prior homelessness episode. The authors reported that 3.2 percent of the respondents had suffered literal homelessness in the past five years.

Compared with point-prevalence surveys, these prevalence estimates are remarkably high, particularly when one considers that only people with telephones are interviewed in such studies. Assuming that most of the prior homelessness episodes occurred after 1980, when the nation's shelter capacity experienced its largest growth (Burt 1992; HUD 1989), this evidence—combined with data on the reported length of time homeless from the longitudinal research of Sosin, Piliavin, and Westerfelt (1990)— suggests that point-prevalence studies may have captured only a fraction of the population that has experienced homelessness in the past decade.

The research question

Would data systems that register every person who stays in a shelter over a specified period and within a defined geographic area help to reconcile the 4 to 7 percent rates of prior homelessness from telephone surveys with the 0.1 to 0.4 percent point-prevalence estimates from enumeration studies? This article addresses that question by reporting shelter utilization data from Philadelphia and New York City, both of which register every person who enters the public shelter system.

Data and methods

Shelter systems and databases

Both Philadelphia and New York City have standardized admissions procedures for persons requesting public shelter. Public shelters are defined as emergency housing facilities for the homeless that are owned, administered, or contracted through city government; this definition does not include transitional housing facilities. Philadelphia's public shelter system had a census of 2,490 persons (including children) at the end of the 1992 fiscal year.[1] By contacting not-for-profit shelter providers listed with local charitable agencies, we identified an additional 451 private beds, or 15.3 percent of the total ($N = 2,941$), as outside Philadelphia's public shelter system and thus untracked by the city's shelter registry system (see table 1). In New York

Table 1. **Average Daily Census in Philadelphia and New York City Shelters, 1992**

Type of Shelter	Philadelphia[a]		New York City	
	Persons	Percent	Persons	Percent
Public (tracked)[b]	2,490	84.7	23,752	82.1
Private (untracked)[c]	451	15.3	5,179	17.9
Total	2,941	100	28,931	100

[a] The census of the Philadelphia shelter system at the end of the 1992 fiscal year (June 30, 1992) is used as a proxy for Philadelphia's average daily census.
[b] The public shelter census is equivalent to the number of people using the shelter system, because each city contracts for occupied beds only.
[c] The average daily census of private, untracked facilities is a measure of bed capacity at a single point in time.

---

[1] See footnotes to table 1 for explanation of censuses.

City the average daily census of the public shelter system in
fiscal 1992 was 23,752 persons (including children). A match of
the New York City public shelters with facilities listed as homeless shelters by the New York City Department of City Planning
(1992) yielded a count of 5,179 private beds, or 17.9 percent of
the total (N = 28,931), outside the public shelter system. Thus,
the reported data for both cities underestimate the actual
number of shelter users because client movement in private
facilities is not included, although it is noteworthy that the
proportion of untracked beds in the two cities is similar.

New York City Adult Shelter System. When single adults enter
the New York City Adult Shelter System, they go through an
intake process that establishes their file in the Shelter Care
Information Management System (SCIMS); at that time, a system identification number is assigned to each new client. Next,
the client's needs are assessed to determine whether the client is
better suited to a specialized or general shelter. Intake and
assessment take place at designated assessment shelters. A
client who makes initial contact with a nonassessment shelter is
given a subway token, directions, and a referral to an assessment shelter.

During the intake process, a client is asked for name, Social
Security number, date of birth, citizenship, and veteran status to
open the SCIMS record. (A client who declines or is unable to
provide any of the information is logged in as John or Jane Doe.)
In addition, data are collected on presenting medical and psychiatric conditions, previous residence, marital and family status,
status of children, and reasons for termination or suspension of
services.

Since its inception in 1986, SCIMS data entry has been done by
social service staff (or designated data entry staff) in the shelters. During client interviews, information is written on paper
forms for later data entry. The data entry system has continued
to operate as designed, with only minor changes. Since April
1989 new client entries are generally done only at assessment
shelters.[2] Record updates are done at the clients' shelter location. Lodging history is preserved and includes dates of admission and authorized discharge. For the period encompassed by
this study, if a client still required service at the end of one
authorization period, a new authorization period was added to

---

[2] A few exceptions exist, such as clients referred to the system by a hospital
and identified as requiring specialized services (e.g., wheelchair accessibility);
these clients are entered into the system by administrative staff.

the client's lodging history. If a client left before the end of the authorization period, the "end date" is the date the client left. Readmission and subsequent discharge dates were thus similarly maintained.

New York City Family Shelter System. The New York City Family Shelter System database, the Homeless Emergency Referral System (HOMES), was designed primarily as a reservation system. Its secondary function is to provide information for case management. Since HOMES' inception, its data entry has been done through a centralized data entry unit. All information is transmitted by telephone or fax to this unit, where entries are made. This centralization has provided a higher level of quality control than is available for SCIMS. Family clients and household members must report identifiers (name, date of birth, Social Security number, and citizenship) and other demographic information (e.g., race, marital status). Additional information tracked in HOMES includes pregnancy and newborn status, referral sources, reasons for homelessness, last known address, income support (welfare) status, and types of permanent housing placements. The database tracks entry and exit from the system by recording dates of admission, discharge, and subsequent readmission and discharge.

Homeless families enter the New York City shelter system through either Income Support (IS) Centers or Emergency Assistance Units (EAUs). Families must prove their legal or biological relationships. To be considered a family, cohabiting adults must be legally married or be on the same IS grant; a marriage certificate or proof of a shared IS grant must be provided to the EAU or IS staff. In the case of children, parents must provide documentation that the children are their own. Information can be compared with entries in the New York State public assistance database[3] if the family is recorded in that system. If adults are not legally married and no children or pregnancy is involved, they are referred to the Adult Shelter System. Every woman who states that she is pregnant is given a urine test to substantiate the pregnancy before placement. Only families or pregnant women are allowed into the Family Shelter System.

Philadelphia Office of Services to the Homeless and Adults. Philadelphia has a centrally administered shelter system that includes a single portal of entry for all adults and families

---

[3] A state-owned and state-maintained database, the Welfare Management System, is used by the IS program. The database maintains records on all persons applying for and receiving public assistance in New York State.

requesting shelter between 7:30 a.m. and 4:30 p.m. Both families and single adults seeking shelter during these hours must go to the Office of Services to the Homeless and Adults (OSHA) office in downtown Philadelphia, which coordinates shelter placements. To be seen by caseworkers at OSHA, a client must present two forms of identification, which together must include a Social Security number and a Philadelphia street address. A client who presents appropriate identification is assigned to a caseworker for an intake interview. A client who lacks verification of a Social Security number is directed to a nearby Social Security Administration office to obtain a temporary identification card. A client who lacks a Philadelphia address or has been in Philadelphia for less than six weeks is referred to the Travelers Aid Society.

Intake interviews are designed to assess client needs, record client information, and, whenever possible, help clients avoid shelter placement. At intake, caseworkers record client information directly in the Client Information System (CIS). This information includes identifiers (name, date of birth, Social Security number, and Medicaid number), initial intake date, demographics, marital and family status, reasons for homelessness, last two addresses, characteristics of prior housing arrangement, emergency contact persons, names and ages of accompanying children, medical problems, reasons for restricted access to shelter (if any), case close date, and subsequent and current intake dates. A maximum of two readmission dates can be recorded in CIS; the most recent readmission overwrites the last when a client has had more than two readmissions.

If a shelter assignment is deemed necessary at intake, caseworkers call shelter facilities to locate beds. In general, the Philadelphia shelter system has two types of beds: short term and long term. A short-term bed is assigned and renewed on a day-by-day basis; a long-term bed is assigned and renewed monthly. Depending on the client's needs and what is available, matches between client and facility are attempted (Culhane 1993). However, because long-term beds are usually scarce, most clients must first cycle through a series of short-term beds. Short-term and long-term beds are reimbursed on the same per diem basis. A client's status can be determined by the length of time indicated on the Purchase of Services (POS) form obtained at intake.

Two shelters, one for single men and one for single women and families, are designated as the after-hours intake sites and offer both initial intake and short-term shelter placements. Both sites collect identifying information from clients and require identification for admission. The data are later entered at the central intake site (OSHA). To obtain a long-term shelter placement, after-hours clients must go through the more thorough intake process with caseworkers at Adult Services. Families and single women are not admitted to a short-term bed on the next night if they have not gone through the intake process at OSHA during the day. Single men, however, may access short-term beds through the after-hours intake site indefinitely, thus avoiding an intake interview at OSHA.

Because this study was designed to calculate rates of admission and readmission to the shelter system—not to analyze patterns of stay—discharge or case closure dates were not part of this analysis. Although it is possible to derive discharge dates that accurately indicate the day a client left New York City shelters, in Philadelphia case closure dates are recorded either at the end of the client's authorization period (the client may have left before that date) or after 45 days without follow-up contact by a case manager. To correct for this problem and the limited readmission fields in the Philadelphia case registry, a separate shelter tracking database was created in Philadelphia on July 1, 1991. Those data were not analyzed for this study, although the authors are planning future longitudinal data analyses to compare stay patterns in New York City and Philadelphia.

Unduplication and aggregation procedures

Because the databases were designed to create one record per client, they theoretically should not include duplicate cases. Identification requirements for families and singles in the Philadelphia shelter system and for families in the New York City shelter system provide some assurance that duplication is minimized. However, given the potential for data entry errors and the use of nicknames, an unduplication procedure was undertaken at both sites. Unfortunately, the procedure may not detect the use of pseudonyms or false identification, so some duplication may remain.

In Philadelphia, automated sorting was employed to identify matches by last name and first initial. All matches were then searched manually by first name, birth date, and Social Security number. Any match of last name with Social Security number (seven of nine numbers) or with first name (variants included) *and* birth date (month and year) was noted as a duplicate case.

An overall duplication rate of 1.2 percent was found, most of which appeared to result from keystroke errors in the entry of Social Security numbers. For this study, only the record with the earliest initial intake date was retained among the duplicate records.

In New York City, both the Family Shelter System and the Adult Shelter System have identified duplicate entries through Social Security number, name, and birth date matches.[4] The Family Shelter System cross-checks all entries at the time of data entry against Social Security numbers, the first five letters of the last name plus the first four letters of the first name, and the year and month of birth. Possible duplicate entries appear on the monitor and are checked before the intake process continues. In addition, all records are verified for duplication each month, and a monthly overlay of Social Security numbers from the Welfare Management System database identifies any children or adults who are included in the database under a different name. Because the Adult Shelter System, unlike the Family Shelter System, requires no personal identification for admission, it had a greater problem with multiple records caused by aliases and misspellings. A built-in safeguard prevents two entries from being made with the same Social Security number. Periodic matches produce suspect lists of duplicates for a final manual determination of whether the records are duplicates. Records of people suspected of using aliases are matched by all existing personal identification fields, including mother's maiden name.

The Philadelphia case registry was initiated on December 21, 1989, for singles and families. The New York City databases were initiated in three stages: First on line were women (December 12, 1985), followed by men (September 8, 1986), and finally the Family Shelter System (April 1, 1987). However, the Family Shelter System, unlike the Adult Shelter System, not only included known origination dates for the system but back-entered lodging information for all families active in the system when the database went on line.

For this study, two years of admissions data were selected: June 1, 1990, through May 31, 1992. To make the data on first admissions roughly comparable between the two sites, the New York City databases were reset to a January 1, 1990, start date (by disregarding any admission or discharge activity before that

---

[4] Either an eight- or nine-digit Social Security number match or a match with the first five letters of the last name, the first four letters of the first name, and the birth month and year identify duplications.

date). First admission counts by month were created from both databases by aggregating client records by initial intake date over the selected period. Readmission counts by month were similarly created by aggregating client records by readmission dates. In New York City, discrete episodes of shelter use were obtained by consolidating individual uses of the facilities into stays. The end of a stay is defined by at least one day out of the shelter system before the start of a subsequent stay; one stay may include the use of multiple shelter facilities. In Philadelphia, an episode of shelter use ends (case closure) only when the client has been out of the shelter system for 45 days, and a maximum of two readmissions can be recorded per client. Both these factors are likely to result in the Philadelphia database showing fewer readmissions than New York City.

In addition to two years of admission and readmission counts by month, an unduplicated annual count for the second year of the study period (June 1, 1991, to May 31, 1992) was calculated for Philadelphia, and yearly unduplicated counts by calendar year (from 1988 to 1992) were calculated for New York City. The unduplicated annual count in Philadelphia was determined by adding all first admissions in the second year of the study period (year 2) to the number of people in the database having both a first admission before year 2 and any readmission in year 2. (For this purpose, the presence of a readmission in year 2 in the Philadelphia data was accurately determined because the Philadelphia data were current only to the end of the selected study period—that is, before they could be overwritten by later readmissions.) The unduplicated count for New York City was determined by adding all persons with any shelter service record for the 1992 calendar year. The family person count by month in New York City was derived by multiplying the number of families each month by the average family size each month.

The likelihood that a person with a first admission in year 1 would be readmitted in year 2 was also calculated for both cities. Annual rates of turnover were calculated by dividing the unduplicated client counts in year 2 (or 1992 for New York City) by the average daily census (New York City) or the end-of-year bed capacity (Philadelphia) of the systems. Finally, unduplicated counts over three and five years of the New York City data and three years of the Philadelphia data were calculated, and select race/ethnicity- and age-adjusted rates were determined by dividing unduplicated counts by population data from the 1990 census (U.S. Bureau of the Census 1991).

One final caveat should be noted regarding the data. The Philadelphia CIS does not reliably distinguish between persons receiving shelter and those requesting but not receiving shelter. In
part, this is because the more recently established tracking
system was intended to track shelter assignment and usage.
Therefore, while the Philadelphia data accurately reflect the
number of people requesting shelter, approximately 5 percent of
those requesting shelter every month do not receive it but are
still included in this study's results. The New York City data do
reliably distinguish between those receiving and those not receiving shelter, and only those receiving shelter are included in
the data reported here.

Results

Unduplicated counts and population-adjusted rates

As shown in figure 1, nearly 1 percent of Philadelphia's population and more than 1 percent of New York City's population used
the public shelter system in 1992. Nearly 3 percent of Philadelphia's population requested services from the city shelter
system from 1990 to 1992, and more than 2 percent of New
York's population received shelter over the same period. Over
five years, 3.27 percent of New York City's population spent time
in a public shelter. Even though data before 1988 are incomplete,
4.37 percent of New York City's population has been registered
in a public shelter since the inception of the databases. Given
that these data exclude private, untracked facilities
(15 percent of the bed total in Philadelphia and 18 percent in
New York City [table 1]), these data presumably reflect an
undercount of shelter users, although the data remain qualified
by clients' potential use of pseudonyms and false identification.

Although both cities have previously reported point-prevalence
rates for people in shelters (between 0.22 and 0.3 percent; see
figure 1) that are within the point-prevalence range reported
nationally, both cities have annual prevalence rates exceeding
any previously published estimate. Roughly three to four times
as many people were registered as shelter users in Philadelphia
and New York City over the course of a year as were enumerated
at a single point in time by two recent studies (Burt 1992; U.S.
Department of Commerce 1991).

Three-year and five-year data adjusted for selected race/
ethnicity and age groups are presented in table 2 (five years of

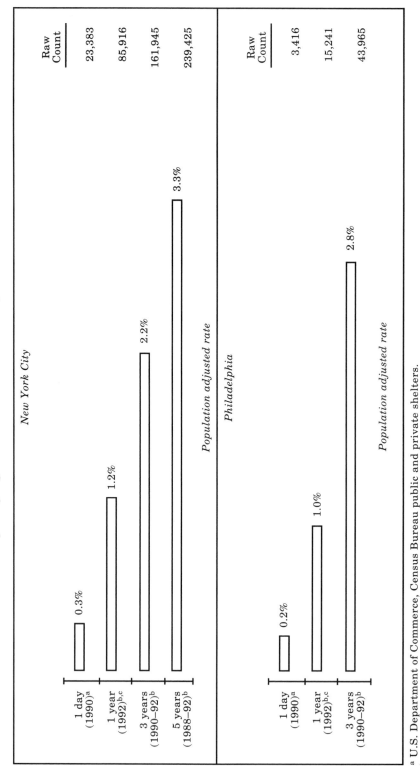

Figure 1. Unduplicated Shelter, Population Counts, and Admission Rates in Philadelphia and New York City, by Varying Sources and Time Frames, in Persons

[a] U.S. Department of Commerce, Census Bureau public and private shelters.
[b] Present authors, rates use 1990 population.
[c] Philadelphia data are for 6/1/91 – 5/31/92, and include all persons requesting shelter. New York City data are for calendar year 1992 and include only persons sheltered.

Table 2. **Unduplicated, Population-Adjusted Shelter Utilization Rates in Philadelphia and New York City**

	Philadelphia[a] 3 years (1990–92)		New York City[a,b] 3 years (1990–92)		New York City[a,b] 5 years (1988–92)	
	Pop.-Adjusted Number[a]	Raw Percent	Pop.-Adjusted Number[a,b]	Raw Percent	Pop.-Adjusted Number	Raw Percent
Total persons	43,965	2.77	161,945	2.21	239,425	3.27
Black (not of Hispanic origin)	38,557	6.18	103,995	5.63	147,469	7.98
White (not of Hispanic origin)	3,473	0.42	8,846	0.28	14,663	0.46
Hispanic	1,495	1.68	44,001	2.47	63,589	3.57
Other	440	0.94	5,102	0.96	13,702	2.59
Total children (< 18)	15,053	3.97	55,114	3.27	77,782	4.61
Black (not of Hispanic origin)	14,270	7.88	34,887	5.76	47,353	7.82
White (not of Hispanic origin)	467	0.30	1,274	0.26	2,086	0.43
Hispanic	256	0.77	17,454	3.20	24,399	4.48
Other	60	0.57	1,499	3.28	3,944	8.64
Poverty[c]						
Persons	43,965	14.00	161,945	11.69	239,425	17.29
Families	6,402	10.50	31,315	10.97	44,194	15.48
Children	15,053	13.60	55,114	11.24	77,782	15.86

Note: Subtotals may not total because of rounding.
[a] The number of children by race/ethnicity was interpolated by distributing the total number of children across racial/ethnic groups according to the distribution of family households by race/ethnicity (assumes family sizes are equal across groups). Philadelphia includes all persons requesting shelter and New York City includes only persons receiving shelter.
[b] The number of homeless children in New York City was calculated by multiplying the number of families by race by the average family size (1.760), derived from a random sample of daily census reports from 1990 to 1992.
[c] Poverty population figures are based on 1990 data (U.S. Department of Commerce 1991a). The poverty rate is based on a single-point-in-time measure and does not capture the number of people experiencing poverty longitudinally; therefore, the proportion reported as experiencing homelessness over time will be inflated.

data are not yet available for Philadelphia). The data demonstrate the disproportionate impact of homelessness on minorities
(particularly African Americans) and children, as well as the
similar risk for homelessness by subgroup in the two cities. In
both cities, African Americans are more than twice as likely to
become homeless as the general population. In a three-year
period, African Americans are 15 times more likely than whites
in Philadelphia and 20 times more likely than whites in New
York City to become homeless. In both cities, about 6 percent
of the African-American population has been registered in the
shelter system in the past three years, and the number reaches
almost 8 percent in New York City over five years. Children are
also more likely to become homeless than the general population.
Indeed, African-American children represent the most vulnerable of the subpopulations listed here; nearly 8 percent of both
cities' African-American children have used the public shelter
system (over three years in Philadelphia and five years in New
York). Poverty-adjusted rates were also calculated, although it
should be noted that the poverty rate is measured at a single
point in time and will therefore overestimate the proportion of
poor who become homeless. Thus, assuming stability in the
poverty population, between 11 and 14 percent of the poor in
both cities have used the shelters in the past three years, with
comparable proportions among poor families and poor children.
The similarity in rates reported for both cities, across demographic groups, is noteworthy.

In table 3 is presented the distribution of client demographic
characteristics at a single point in time and over three years,
showing how turnover affects the proportionate representation of
subpopulations. Of particular note is the reduction in the proportion of sheltered households among families when viewed over
time, suggesting that the higher turnover among single adults
leads to their lower proportionate representation at a given point
in time. Likewise, the proportion of clients who are children in
both cities decreases to approximately one-third of the total
when viewed over three years, because families turn over at a
lower rate than single adults.

Admission patterns

Although the above data are suggestive of the significant turnover in the shelter system, those patterns can be more clearly
shown by examining monthly admissions to shelters. In table 4
are shown the average number of persons admitted monthly to
the New York and Philadelphia public shelter systems over the

two-year study period and the average daily census in the second year of the study period. As can be seen by comparing the total admissions with total average daily census, in both cities approximately half the beds turn over, on average, every month. In Philadelphia nearly half the beds are emptied and filled again every month with people *new* to the shelter system.

Table 3. **Characteristics of Shelter Users, Single Point in Time versus Three-Year Counts, Philadelphia and New York City**

	Philadelphia[a]		New York City[b]	
	Point in Time	3 Years	Point in Time	3 Years
Household type (%)				
Single	66	77	54	67
Families	34	23	46	33
Race of household head (%)				
Black	91	88	65	65
White	6	8	5	8
Hispanic	3	3	29	24
Other	0	1	1	3
Children (% of total)	46	35	41	34
Single adults (%)				
Male	69	77	83	82
Female	31	23	17	18

[a] Philadelphia's single point in time was December 21, 1993. The count includes all active cases; thus, people who may have left shelter but have not been out for the 45-day cutoff period are included.
[b] New York City's point in time was January 9, 1993.

Table 4. **Average Monthly Shelter Admissions for Philadelphia and New York, in Persons, June 1990 through May 1992**

	First Admissions		Readmissions		Total Admissions		Average Daily Census
	Mean	SD	Mean	SD	Mean	SD	1992
Philadelphia							
Singles	592	90	279	55	871	110	1,249
Families	572	109	218	83	790	134	1,241
Total	1,164	172	497	128	1,661	214	2,490
New York City							
Singles	1,401	242	5,686	369	7,086	500	7,286
Families	1,796	493	3,719	612	5,515	496	16,466
Total	3,197	690	9,405	666	12,601	698	23,752

Note: Subtotals may not sum to totals because of rounding.

Because the two sites have different definitions of readmission, readmission counts are not comparable between the cities. New York's data reveal a much higher proportion of the total admissions considered readmissions because, for the purposes of this study, an episode ends with one day out of the shelter system and another episode may begin the next day. For this reason, the New York data illustrate how frequently people leave and reenter the shelter system, with three times as many readmissions as first admissions. Philadelphia, on the other hand, while potentially experiencing the same phenomenon, shows a much lower monthly average readmission count. The count is lower because Philadelphia counts readmissions only after the client spends 45 consecutive days out of the shelter system and because Philadelphia's data code for a maximum of two readmissions. Provisionally, the New York figures could be considered a better estimate of the administrative burden of turnover to providers and clients because they better capture the frequency of exit and reentry. However, the Philadelphia figures may be a more accurate measure of the number of episodes of homelessness served by providers, since one day out of the system is not considered a true exit from homelessness.

Until now, data have been reported in persons, not household units. However, because people entering the shelter system are typically treated as households, for policy planning and management purposes it is often more useful to examine shelter utilization counts by household. For example, caseloads for intake workers and social workers are likely to be determined by household rather than person units. The differences that result when the two-year total admission counts are calculated by persons and households in Philadelphia and New York are presented in table 5 (recall that "total admissions" combines first admissions and readmissions and therefore is not an unduplicated count). The resulting difference is primarily a consequence of children included as members of family households not being counted as separate persons, which reveals that, in both sites, approximately one-third of the total admissions in persons are accounted for by children and other family members (although, again, because of the different definitions of readmission, the total admission rates for Philadelphia and New York are noncompa-rable). For Philadelphia singles, the number of households is slightly lower than the number of persons because married couples without children were previously coded as two single adult households in the database, while in New York City they were treated as members of one family household.

Table 5. **Total Admissions to Shelters in Philadelphia and New York City, June 1990 to May 1992 (in Persons and Households)**

City	Persons	Households
Philadelphia		
Singles	20,910	20,130
Families	18,969	5,701
Total	39,879	25,831
New York City		
Singles	170,074	170,074
Families	132,358	42,572
Total	302,432	212,646

In figures 2 and 3, household units are used to show the trend of monthly admissions and readmissions for families and single adult households for the two-year study period. In general, and disregarding any potential effects of policy changes on admission rates, the trend for first admissions would be predicted to decline and the trend for readmissions to increase over time as the persons at risk for homelessness experience their first episode and are counted as readmissions on subsequent episodes. However, if the pool of potential homeless households replenishes or even increases over time, then this downward trend among first admissions would be attenuated and possibly reversed.

Time series regression analyses were conducted on first admission and readmission rates for singles and families in both cities over the two-year study period, adjusting for seasonal variation. Results reveal that first admission rates for families in both cities show a significant downward trend (Philadelphia, adjusted $R^2 = 0.23$, $F = 7.87$, $p < 0.02$, $\beta = -0.513$; New York, adjusted $R^2 = 0.46$, $F = 20.66$, $p < 0.001$, $\beta = -0.695$). Thus, the pool of families experiencing a first-time shelter stay in Philadelphia and New York City has been declining. For singles, however, only New York City had a significant downward trend of first admissions (adjusted $R^2 = 0.70$, $F = 54.01$, $p < 0.0001$, $\beta = -0.843$), suggesting either that Philadelphia's pool of single adults experiencing a first shelter admission has been replenishing over time or that there simply is no discernible trend among single admissions in Philadelphia. Results for the analyses of readmission rates similarly reveal the predicted increasing trend for families in both cities (Philadelphia, adjusted $R^2 = 0.57$, $F = 31.63$, $p < 0.0001$, $\beta = 0.768$; New York, adjusted $R^2 = 0.66$, $F = 45.58$, $p < 0.0001$, $\beta = 0.821$). Because of definitional differences, the trends for family readmissions are not comparable for

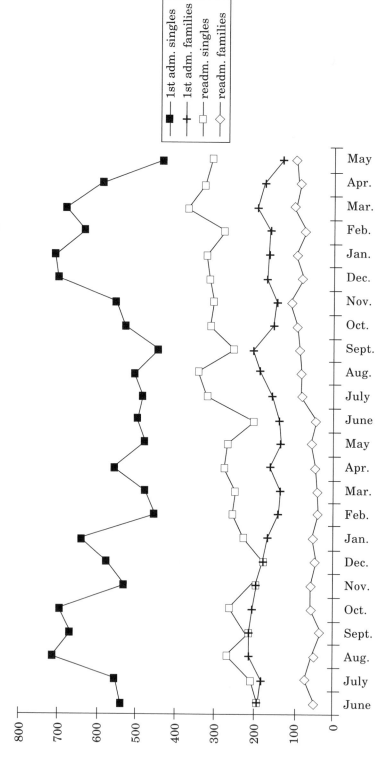

Figure 2. **First Admission and Readmission Counts for Singles and Families (in Households) for Philadelphia, June 1990 to May 1992**

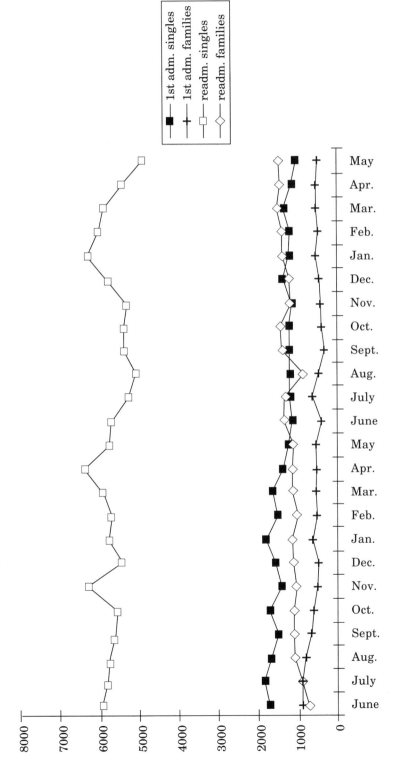

Figure 3. **First Admission and Readmission Counts for Singles and Families (in Households) for New York City, June 1990 to May 1992**

the two cities; however, both demonstrate the predicted increasing proportion of admissions accounted for by readmissions over time as families with first admissions reappear in the system. For single adults, however, only Philadelphia had the predicted increasing rate of readmissions (adjusted $R^2 = 0.60$, $F = 35.02$, $p < 0.0001$, $\beta = 0.784$); in New York, single adults with previous shelter experience had a nonsignificant decreasing rate of readmission over the study period (adjusted $R^2 = 0.03$, $F = 1.63$, $p = 0.2145$, $\beta = -0.263$).

Because New York City has five complete years of admission data, unduplicated first admission and system user counts by year for the past five years were also computed (table 6).

Table 6. **Unduplicated First Admissions and System Users in New York City, in Households (by Calendar Year)**

	1988	1989	1990	1991	1992
First admissions[a]					
Singles	42,658	20,989	14,326	12,862	11,337
Families	13,827	7,106	7,925	7,834	7,830
Total households	56,485	28,095	22,251	20,696	19,167
System users[b]					
Singles	42,658	42,822	35,334	32,508	29,259
Families	13,827	14,144	14,957	15,205	18,220
Total households	56,485	56,966	50,291	47,713	47,479

[a] Represents clients' first stay in the shelter system. Shelter stay history is traced as if no client entered the system before January 1, 1988. Only the first stay during the period is counted.
[b] Represents annual users of shelter system. Clients may be represented in multiple years.

The data on first admissions show much higher counts for 1988 than for the other years because the database was reset to a January 1, 1988, start date. Thus, people whose first admission was before 1988 and who had a readmission in 1988 are counted in 1988 as a first admission, inflating the number of first admissions. While the number of first admissions appears relatively stable for families across the remaining four years (aggregated by year rather than month), the first admissions for single adults again show a significant downward trend. The unduplicated count of system users by year similarly shows a substantial decline in the number of homeless singles who have used the New York City shelter system, dropping 31 percent from 1988 to 1992. In contrast, the unduplicated annual number of families has been steadily rising across the five-year period, increasing 32 percent from 1988 to 1992. Because families include more than one person, the total number of system users by year has been increasing.

Annual turnover and readmission rates

If annual turnover is defined as the unduplicated count of persons served in a year divided by the average daily census in that year, Philadelphia had an annual rate of turnover of 6.12 in 1992 (15,241/2,490), while New York City had an annual rate of turnover of 3.62 (85,916/23,752).[5] Thus, for every person in shelter on a given night of 1992, more than six people in Philadelphia and nearly four people in New York used the shelter system at some time during the year. Three-year turnover rates could be calculated similarly, dividing the unduplicated three-year count by the average daily census from 1992. In Philadelphia the three-year turnover rate is 17.66, and in New York City the three-year turnover rate is 6.82.

While shelter stay patterns were not the focus of study here, the likelihood of a household experiencing an admission in both years of the data was examined as a preliminary to more extensive longitudinal analyses of stay patterns by the authors. A readmission rate was therefore calculated for households with a first admission in year 1 (June 1, 1990, to May 31, 1991) in the two-year study period and a readmission in year 2 (June 1, 1991, to May 31, 1992). In Philadelphia 11.6 percent of the households first admitted in year 1 had another admission in year 2, which compares with the overall readmission rate (readmission could occur in the same year) of 27 percent. In the aggregate (without adjusting each client to his or her own baseline admission date), most households with a readmission in Philadelphia are likely to experience that readmission in the same year as the first admission, and a much smaller proportion of households (less than half) experience a readmission in the year following the first admission.

---

[5] The Adult Shelter System in New York City has one large facility that shelters persons who tend to have long stays. On an average night it accommodates approximately 1,000 persons on long-term stays. The stay patterns of these clients will skew turnover rates and systemwide average lengths of stay. The population at this facility comprises primarily older men. The actual turnover rate in Philadelphia is likely to be closer to New York's than this comparison indicates because the numerator is inflated (approximately 5 percent) by persons requesting but not receiving shelter and the denominator is a proxy for average daily census taken from a single-night count in the summer (and therefore is lower than it would be if it accounted for the higher numbers sheltered in winter months).

The corresponding measure in New York was calculated for family households, revealing that 27 percent of the families with a first admission in year 1 had a readmission in year 2, while the overall readmission rate (readmission could be in the same year as first admission) for families was 65 percent. Hence, in New York as in Philadelphia, fewer than half the families with a readmission will have a readmission in the year following their first admission, although families in New York City are more than twice as likely as those in Philadelphia to enter a shelter in the year following their first admission (again, note that definitional differences make readmission data noncomparable between the two cities). In general, however, shelter use in consecutive years appears to be the exception, not the rule, in both cities.

Discussion

Although social scientists have repeatedly "proved" them wrong, advocates for the homeless appear to have been correct in insisting that homelessness affects a much larger pool of persons than has been documented by cross-sectional research. Indeed, more people have stayed in New York and Philadelphia shelters in the past several years than have ever been enumerated on a single night in the United States. While public shelters in Philadelphia and New York have average daily utilization rates of 0.16 and 0.31 percent of the population, respectively, on an annual basis the rates approach 1 percent in Philadelphia and exceed 1 percent in New York City. These annual homelessness rates are three times greater than rates previously documented for either city by point-prevalence studies (Burt 1992; U.S. Department of Commerce 1991). Those rates increase for multiple years, to nearly 3 percent in three years in Philadelphia and to 3.3 percent in five years in New York—consistent with the five-year estimate from the national telephone survey by Link et al. (1993).[6]

---

[6] It is interesting to note that despite significant differences in the average daily census between New York City and Philadelphia, the cities have comparable one- and three-year rates of shelter utilization. Thus, the different rates of turnover probably reflect differences in local shelter policies (which in turn influence admission and stay patterns) as much as variations in local conditions that produce homelessness. Several policy differences between the two cities might help explain the differences in turnover. In 1988 Philadelphia had a public shelter system similar in size (32 beds per 10,000 population) to the New York City public shelter system in 1992. But in response to city budget cuts, the number of public shelter beds in Philadelphia declined by nearly half

The critical factor that cross-sectional enumerations cannot capture but that is clearly demonstrated in this study is the magnitude of turnover in the sheltered population. It is this high rate of turnover that accounts for much higher rates of homelessness over time than at a single point in time and that demonstrates a substantially higher risk for homelessness in the community.

Because this study does not include persons in privately funded shelters or on the street—the Census Bureau enumerated the point prevalence of street homelessness at 10,447 in New York City and 1,069 in Philadelphia in 1990 (U.S. Department of Commerce 1991)—the findings underestimate the true prevalence of homelessness in both cities. Moreover, because this study is limited to two cities, and given the wide intercity variability found in previous research (Burt 1992; U.S. Department of Commerce 1991), the shelter utilization rates identified here cannot be generalized to other cities. However, recent data from St. Paul, Minnesota (Chase 1993), and from the state of Rhode Island (Rhode Island Emergency Food and Shelter Board 1992), as well as unpublished data from other municipalities (see comment by Burt, this issue), confirm that similar and even higher rates of turnover have been found elsewhere. Thus, convergent with other sources of evidence, this study demonstrates that homelessness is a far more common experience among poor people, particularly African Americans and their children (at least in these two cities), than has been evidenced by

---

between 1988 and 1990, from 5,100 to 2,800. To continue serving even roughly the same number of clients annually, shelter stays would have had to have declined proportionately to the bed decline. Philadelphia achieved this shortened average length of stay by significantly qualifying its previous commitment to a right to shelter (renegotiated through a consent decree) and by establishing much more restrictive shelter policies, including the creation of a copayment and savings requirement and stricter enforcement of behavioral standards, such as mandated participation in mental health and substance abuse treatment programs (see Culhane 1992). In contrast, the New York City shelter system has generally continued to provide some level of shelter even to persons who refuse to participate in treatment programs. There are no limitations on how long clients may stay or how frequently they may use the system. Single adults are provided shelter in a general or specialized shelter (e.g., veterans' shelters, short-term substance abuse treatment, employment shelters). Specialized shelters have various restrictions—such as savings requirements, length-of-stay limitations, and program participation requirements—that general shelters do not. However, clients can move between specialized and general shelters as availability and readiness allow. The Family Shelter System has also established standards for shelter conditions that can include a private room with private bath and kitchen facilities. These standards and the lack of stay restrictions have likely led to a greater daily census and longer lengths of stay in the Family Shelter System.

point-prevalence enumerations. These findings suggest that future research and policy should consider the implications of turnover when estimating the risk for homelessness.

Regarding future research directions, the turnover identified here suggests that our conceptions of the relative proportion of subpopulations among the homeless, informed as they are by a large body of cross-sectional research, may now be open to reassessment. For example, there is evidence that people with mental disabilities or substance abuse problems are homeless for longer periods than others and so turn over at a lower rate (see Dennis et al. 1993), which would significantly inflate their proportionate representation among the population when examined at a single point in time. Correspondingly, employed and recently unemployed people—the "ordinary working Americans" hypothesized as nonrepresentative of the homeless by Kondratas (1991)—may turn over at a higher rate, meaning that their proportionate representation has been significantly underestimated in cross-sectional research.

Further longitudinal analyses of shelter stay patterns are needed to clarify the personal characteristics associated with varying lengths of stay, the probability of multiple admissions, and the time between admissions. Event history or survival analyses can be used to develop profiles of client characteristics associated with various stay histories, enabling planners to target services designed to reduce lengthy shelter stays and the likelihood of readmission. Longitudinal analyses of stay patterns can also be used to examine the costs of various stay patterns and how stays are influenced by various types of shelter facilities. In addition, interrupted time series analysis can be used to examine how policy changes affect stay patterns and admission rates. The tracking databases described in this study are ideal for these purposes, and given the information they would provide researchers and planners, their replication in other sites should be considered.

Registry and tracking databases are useful not only for shelter system-specific analyses; their potential for answering other important questions regarding subpopulations among the homeless expands substantially if they are integrated with other service system databases. For example, the client identifiers from these databases can be matched with identifiers in welfare, mental health, housing, AIDS, and other service system databases, allowing researchers to identify the eligibility and service utilization patterns that predict homelessness and to assess the impact of homelessness on those service systems. Likewise, the prior address information reported by those who enter the shelter system can be used to calculate admission rates by neighborhood or census tract and to identify the factors from other geographic databases (census, housing, health statistics, crime, etc.) that correspond to that distribution. Thus, geographic areas with high homelessness rates or with socioeconomic characteristics that predict high homelessness rates can be identified for the targeting of homelessness prevention and residential stabilization interventions, and the efficacy of these interventions can be measured by assessing changes in shelter admission rates.

From a policy perspective, the results of this study provide a basis for questioning the emphasis of recent reform proposals that argue for reducing homelessness primarily through the creation of transitional housing and other programs that provide a "continuum of residential care" (HUD and District of Columbia 1993; New York City Mayoral Commission on the Homeless 1992). In both Philadelphia and New York, most people who use shelters do so on a short-term or intermittent basis and are therefore not chronically homeless. Forcing such persons into a continuum-of-care system in order to access housing support and social services is likely to lead to many unintended consequences while doing little to reduce homelessness. Assuming that reduced utilization of the emergency housing system is a goal, one must presumably decrease lengths of stay in and admissions to that system. By linking more services to the shelter and transitional housing system, a municipality risks increasing both lengths of stay and admissions, either of which alone would significantly increase the daily demand for emergency housing. Anecdotal evidence suggests that some families already enter shelter to receive priority placement on Section 8 or public housing waiting lists (Dugger 1991). Similarly, requiring that people be homeless to be eligible for transitional housing or continuum-of-care services is likely to tap significant latent demand for such services and could even lead to the dumping of clients on the shelter system by other agencies. Indeed, converting the shelter system into a more service-intensive system risks institutionalizing a costly and potentially substandard secondary public health, welfare, and housing system while failing to address directly the deficiencies in the existing systems that presumably contribute to shelter utilization. Finally, given the volume of shelter users identified in this study, such a system would also require significant new resources to site new facilities and to develop the administrative capacity necessary to monitor provider performance and contain system costs.

An alternative policy, while recognizing the need for transitional housing for the long-term homeless, might seek to support people with short-term or intermittent housing emergencies in maintaining and stabilizing their residential options in the community, rather than provide incentives for entering a separate institution of residential care. As Hopper (1990, 444) has observed, the dominant adaptation of the poor and unemployed to displacement and housing instability historically has been through the maintenance of "makeshift" arrangements of "custom and kinship," with family members "bearing the brunt of makeshift shelter." Hopper therefore asks, "Can [we] mute the damage and enhance the supportive capacity of such networks, and thus avoid the ever more costly mushrooming of the shelter system?"

A community-based strategy could be envisioned that would have the goal of reducing shelter utilization by rebuilding (or creating) the community and social support infrastructure that would enable people to stay in their own homes when possible or that would attempt to resettle them as soon as possible. Such a strategy could be targeted geographically (based on the distribution of the prior addresses of people currently entering the shelter system) or demographically (based on household risk factors for homelessness). Intervention programs might include the provision of case management, community-based health, mental health, substance abuse, and other social services (including crisis intervention, respite services, home care, and residential treatment programs); time-limited and permanent housing subsidies; benefits counseling; employment training and placement; and other targeted economic and community development programs. By placing those programs outside the shelter system and under the authority of existing health, housing, and human service departments, such a policy would have the advantages of addressing the more proximal community conditions leading to homelessness and of addressing the gaps in the existing systems that need to be bridged, rather than duplicating those systems in shelters. It would also reduce some of the perceived incentives for shelter admissions and lengthy shelter stays that would likely come with a continuum-of-care initiative. The present "shelter diversion" initiative under way in New York City—in which most families are assessed before or soon after shelter admission to determine whether they can be diverted from shelter with a time-limited housing subsidy or other intervention—is one example of movement in this direction. Other homelessness prevention program models have been described (Jahiel 1992; Lindblom 1991; U.S. Department of Health and Human Services 1991).

In conclusion, future policy should reconsider the scope of the homelessness problem and the role of turnover when conceptualizing appropriate interventions. In particular, this study's findings suggest the potential benefits of a prevention-oriented approach to reducing homelessness. Programs that attempt to divert people from shelters or to reduce unnecessarily long shelter stays are integral to such an approach, as are transitional housing programs that help long-term homeless persons reconnect with community housing and services. However, such programs may have little effect without more broad-based social welfare policies that increase opportunities for and access to affordable housing, jobs, income supports, social services, and quality health care.

Authors

Dennis P. Culhane is Assistant Professor of Psychiatry and a Senior Fellow at the Leonard Davis Institute for Health Economics at the University of Pennsylvania. Edmund F. Dejowski is Director and Julie Ibañez is Deputy Director of the Office of Management Planning, City of New York Human Resources Administration. Elizabeth Needham is Research Assistant and a student in Urban Studies at the University of Pennsylvania. Irene Macchia is Manager of Information Systems for the Department of Records, City of Philadelphia. [1997]

The authors wish to acknowledge Heidi Lange-Joe and Delano Kimbrough for their technical assistance with this project.

References

Appelbaum, Richard P. 1987. *Counting the Homeless*. Chicago: Center for Urban Research and Policy Studies, University of Chicago.

Barrett, Diane F., Irwin Anolik, and Florence H. Abramson. 1992. The 1990 Census Shelter and Street Night Enumeration. Paper read at the annual meeting of the American Statistical Association, Boston.

Blumberg, Leonard, Thomas Shipley, and Irving Shandler. 1973. *Skid Row and Its Alternatives: Research and Recommendations from Philadelphia*. Philadelphia: Temple University Press.

Brown, Carl E., Steven W. McFarlane, Ronald Paredes, and Louisa Stark. 1983. *The Homeless of Phoenix: Who Are They? And What Should Be Done?* Phoenix: Phoenix South Community Mental Health Center.

Burnam, M. Audrey, Paul Koegel, and T. S. Duan. 1990. Los Angeles Study of Mental Illness among Homeless People. National Institute of Mental Health grant application. Santa Monica, CA: RAND Corp.

Burt, Martha R. 1992. *Over the Edge: The Growth of Homelessness in the 1980s.* New York and Washington, DC: Russell Sage Foundation and The Urban Institute Press.

Burt, Martha R., and Barbara E. Cohen. 1989. *America's Homeless: Numbers, Characteristics, and the Programs That Serve Them.* Washington, DC: The Urban Institute Press.

City of Boston. 1986. *Making Room: Comprehensive Policy for the Homeless.* Boston: Emergency Shelter Commission.

Chase, Richard A. 1993. *Emergency Shelters, Transitional Housing, and Battered Women's Shelters Data Collection Project, Second Annual Report.* St. Paul, MN: Wilder Research Center.

Culhane, Dennis P. 1992. The Quandaries of Shelter Reform: An Appraisal of Efforts to Manage Homelessness. *Social Service Review* 66(3):428–40.

Culhane, Dennis P. 1993. The Organization and Utilization of the Shelter System in Philadelphia: Estimating Average Length of Stay and Annual Rate of Turnover. *Journal of Health and Social Policy* 4(4):55–78.

Dennis, Michael L., Ronaldo Iachan, Jutta P. Thornberry, Robert M. Bray, Lisa E. Packer, and Gayle S. Bieler. 1993. *Prevalence and Treatment of Drug Use and Correlated Problems in the Homeless and Transient Population: 1991.* Final report under NIDA contract no. 271-89-8340. Rockville, MD: National Institute on Drug Abuse.

Dugger, Celia. 1991. Benefits of System Luring More Families to Shelters. *New York Times*, September 4, A1.

Freeman, Richard B., and Brian Hall. 1987. Permanent Homelessness in America? *Population Research and Policy Review* 6:3–27.

Hoffman, Stanley, David Wenger, J. Nigro, and R. Rosenfeld. 1982. *Who Are the Homeless? A Study of Randomly Selected Men Who Use the New York City Shelters.* New York: State Office of Mental Health.

Hombs, Mary E., and Mitch Snyder. 1982. *Homelessness in America: A Forced March to Nowhere.* Washington, DC: Community for Creative Non-Violence.

Hopper, Kim. 1990. The New Urban Niche of Homelessness: New York City in the Late 1980s. *Bulletin of the New York Academy of Medicine* 66(5):435–50.

Jahiel, René. 1992. *Homelessness: A Prevention-Oriented Approach.* Baltimore: Johns Hopkins University Press.

Kondratas, Anna. 1991. Estimates and Public Policy: The Politics of Numbers. *Housing Policy Debate* 2(3):631–47.

Lindblom, Eric N. 1991. Toward a Comprehensive Homelessness-Prevention Strategy. *Housing Policy Debate* 2(3):957–1025.

Link, Bruce G., Ezra Susser, Anne Stueve, J. Phelan, R. Moore, and Elmer L. Struening. 1993. Reconsidering the Debate about the Numbers of Homeless People in the United States. Paper read at the annual meeting of the American Public Health Association, October, San Francisco.

National Coalition for the Homeless. 1991. *Fatally Flawed: The Census Bureau's Count of Homeless People*. Washington, DC.

New York City Department of City Planning. 1992. *Residential Facilities in New York City, 1992: An Index of Beds by Type of Facility and Community District*. New York.

New York City Mayoral Commission on the Homeless. 1992. *The Way Home: A New Direction in Social Policy*. New York: Office of the Mayor.

Novacek, Jill, Robert Raskin, David Behlinger, Suzanne Rybicki, Christie Nail, and Linda Firth. 1991. *Citizens' Opinions about Tulsa's Homeless*. Tulsa, OK: Tulsa Institute of Behavioral Sciences.

Parsons, Lynn. 1986. *Literature Review of Studies Which Deal with Estimating the Size of the Homeless Population*. Amherst: University of Massachusetts Social and Demographic Research Institute.

Rhode Island Emergency Food and Shelter Board. 1992. *Serving Rhode Island's Homeless: Three-Year Report of the Rhode Island Emergency Shelter Information Project*. Providence.

Robertson, Marjorie, Irving Piliavin, and Herb Westerfelt. 1990. Alameda County Study of Mental Illness among Homeless Adults and Families. National Institute of Mental Health grant application. San Francisco: Alcohol Research Group.

Rossi, Peter H. 1987. No Good Applied Social Research Goes Unpunished. *Society* 25:73–80

Rossi, Peter H. 1989. *Down and Out in America: The Origins of Homelessness*. Chicago: University of Chicago Press.

Rossi, Peter, Gene A. Fisher, and Georgiana Willis. 1986. *The Condition of the Homeless in Chicago*. Amherst: University of Massachusetts Social and Demographic Research Institute.

Roth, Dee, Jerry Bean, Nancy Lust, and Saveanu Trian. 1985. *Homelessness in Ohio: A Study of People in Need*. Columbus: Ohio Department of Mental Health, Office of Program Evaluation and Research.

Ryan, Phyllis, David Bartelt, and Ira Goldstein. 1989. *Homelessness in Pennsylvania: How Can This Be?* Philadelphia: Temple University Institute for Public Policy Studies.

Shlay, Anne, and Peter H. Rossi. 1992. Social Science Research and Contemporary Studies of Homelessness. *Annual Review of Sociology* 18:129–60.

Sosin, Michael, Irving Piliavin, and Herb Westerfelt. 1990. Toward a Longitudinal Analysis of Homelessness. *Journal of Social Issues* 46(4):157–74.

Toro, Paul A., and Dennis M. McDonell. 1992. Beliefs, Attitudes, and Knowledge about Homelessness: A Survey of the General Public. *American Journal of Community Psychology* 20(1):53–80.

U.S. Bureau of the Census. 1991. *Statistical Abstracts of the United States, 1991*. 111th ed. Washington, DC: U.S. Government Printing Office.

U.S. Department of Commerce. 1991. Census Bureau Releases 1990 Decennial Census Counts for Persons Enumerated in Emergency Shelters and Observed on the Streets. *U.S. Department of Commerce News* CB91:117.

U.S. Department of Health and Human Services. 1991. *Homelessness Prevention Programs.* Washington, DC: Office of the Inspector General.

U.S. Department of Housing and Urban Development. 1984. *A Report to the Secretary on the Homeless and Emergency Shelters.* Washington, DC: Office of Policy Development and Research.

U.S. Department of Housing and Urban Development. 1989. *A Report on the 1988 National Survey of Shelters for the Homeless.* Washington, DC.

U.S. Department of Housing and Urban Development and District of Columbia. 1993. *The D.C. Initiative: Working Together to Solve Homelessness.* Washington, DC: HUD Office of Community Planning and Development.

U.S. General Accounting Office. 1988. *Homeless Mentally Ill: Problems and Options in Estimating Numbers and Trends.* GAO/PEMD-88-24. Washington, DC.

U.S. House of Representatives Subcommittee on Housing and Community Development. 1984. *Joint Hearing on the HUD Report on the Homeless, House Subcommittee on Housing and Community Development with the Subcommittee on Manpower and Housing of the Committee on Government Operations.* 98th Cong., 2nd sess., May 24.

Vernez, George, M. Audrey Burnam, Elizabeth A. McGlynn, Sally E. Trude, and Brian S. Mittman. 1988. *Review of California's Programs for the Homeless Mentally Disabled.* Santa Monica, CA: RAND Corp.

© Fannie Mae Foundation 1997. All Rights Reserved.

Patterns of Homelessness: A Review of Longitudinal Studies

Yin-Ling Irene Wong
University of Pennsylvania

Abstract

This article reviews nine research projects that tracked the residential status of homeless people. Two types of studies were analyzed: (1) studies based on shelter administrative records and (2) studies using panel study designs. The review identifies methodological issues raised, summarizes findings, and discusses the implications for social policy.

The review points to several important findings. First, homelessness is part of an experience of residential instability involving a patchwork of contingent housing strategies. Although the majority of the urban homeless were able to move from the streets to conventional housing, most would experience another homeless episode. Second, demographic characteristics are important predictors for exits from and returns to homelessness as well as for the type of domicile obtained. Third, access to material resources is critical for facilitating exit from homelessness and preventing the recurrence of homeless episodes. These findings underscore the importance of a prevention-oriented approach in combating homelessness.

Keywords: Residential instability; Homelessness prevention; Resource utilization; Homeless shelters

Introduction

The character of homelessness has undergone significant change during the past half-century. Whereas the homeless were once seen as an aging, immobile group contained in skid row neighborhoods of urban communities, the contemporary homeless are a more diverse population, demonstrating a higher degree of mobility and transiency. Indeed, research on the contemporary homeless has documented a great deal of movement in and out of the homeless state. This finding suggests that a larger-than-expected proportion of the U.S. population either has experienced or is at risk of experiencing bouts of homelessness (Burt 1994; Culhane et al. 1997; Link et al. 1995).

Data collection efforts seeking to document patterns of residential transitions among the homeless and identify conditions and circumstances leading to such transitions have not taken into account the dynamic nature of homelessness. The first generation of research on the urban homeless was mostly cross-sectional studies. Using self-reports of prior homelessness history, a number of studies found that many of the homeless had made multiple transitions between the streets and conventional housing. But single-point-in-time research is known for its methodological inadequacy in capturing dynamic phenomena such as poverty and homelessness (Bane and Ellwood 1986; Shinn 1992; Sosin, Piliavin, and Westerfelt 1990). Findings from standard cross-sectional surveys, if accepted uncritically, construct a "truncated, decontextualized, and overpathologized" picture of the homeless (Snow, Andersen, and Koegel 1994), which may inadvertently lead to misguided and ill-conceived social policy that fails to address the diverse needs of homeless people (Shinn 1992).

Recently, with the development of shelter-based management information systems and public sponsorship of longitudinal research on homelessness, a number of studies have sought to understand the process of homelessness. Although these studies are few in number, they offer a unique opportunity to examine the residential status and patterns of homelessness among people deprived of conventional shelter. In this article, I review nine research projects that tracked the residential status or residential transitions of initially homeless people. Specifically, I identify the methodological questions raised by these research projects, and I discuss the implications for social policy and design of programs to diminish the incidence and duration of homelessness.

Cross-sectional analysis of homelessness patterns and its limitations

Research on the contemporary homeless documents substantial diversity in the U.S. homeless population. One aspect of this newfound diversity relates to sociodemographic characteristics, as illustrated by the large numbers of families with children and single women who seek shelter at private and public social agencies (Rossi 1994). Another aspect—the focus of this article—centers on variations in the duration and incidence of homelessness.

The 1983 study by Arce et al. in Philadelphia represents the first published study to classify the contemporary homeless according to length of time spent on the streets and domicile experiences prior to homelessness. From a snapshot survey of one adult emergency shelter that operated for two months during the winter of 1981–82, Arce et al. identified three distinct groups of homeless people: "the habitual street people, the episodic homeless, and those who did not usually live on the street but were undergoing an acute crisis" (p. 812). Despite the study's limited scope and lack of definitional clarity, surprisingly similar classifications of homeless people appeared in other cross-sectional studies conducted later (see Wong 1995 for a review).[1]

Residential data derived from cross-sectional studies can provide some information for assessing the needs of homeless people at a given point in time, but these data are inherently misleading and imprecise. In cross-sectional studies, chronically and cyclically homeless people tend to be overrepresented, and those who have one-time short homeless episodes, underrepresented (Shinn 1992; Sosin, Piliavin, and Westerfelt 1990). As a result, social programs tend to heavily target the former groups, while overlooking the needs and problems experienced by the short-term transitionally homeless. For example, individual disabilities are more prevalent among the long-term and the episodic homeless than among the short-term homeless (Grigsby et al. 1990; Koegel, Burnam, and Farr 1988; Kuhn and Culhane 1998). Social programs designed on the basis of cross-sectional data would pay more attention to palliative and remedial measures, at the expense of prevention efforts that could benefit a wider constituency of individuals who have no apparent disabilities, but who are at risk of homelessness because of poverty and a shortage of low-income housing.

Moreover, since cross-sectional studies intercept respondents during an ongoing homeless episode, no information is available on episode length and permanency or on whether the observed episode would be followed by others. Some researchers extrapolate the "typical" spell of homelessness by doubling the observed episode duration, assuming that homeless people are interviewed at the middle of their homeless spells (Freeman and Hall 1987; Rossi 1989). Although such extrapolation may be a plausible method for estimation, it does not take into consideration another phenomenon of interest—transitions into and out of the

---

[1] In seeking to understand the patterns of homelessness, cross-sectional research uses three snapshot measures to construct prototypes of homeless people: (1) the elapsed time since the first homeless episode, (2) the number of homeless episodes ever experienced, and (3) the duration of the current homeless episode. Using these measures, I have compared cross-sectional data on homelessness patterns reported in six community-based and two national studies (Wong 1995). The comparison results suggest that although variation exists in the relative proportions, the recently short-term homeless, the episodic homeless, and the long-term homeless each constitute a significant portion in any communities under study.

homeless state. It is also questionable whether doubling the observed spell length is an appropriate method, given its insensitivity to the changing policy and program environment of the community under study.

Single-point-in-time research has little relevance to social policy making because of its inability to identify antecedents that may be associated with the duration, ending, and recurrence of homelessness. Therefore, while several cross-sectional studies have identified gender and family-status differences in the duration and incidence of homelessness (Burt and Cohen 1989; Calsyn and Morse 1990; Rossi, Fisher, and Willis 1986; Roth, Toomey, and First 1992; Wright 1989), no further inquiry has been conducted to explore factors that may account for such differences. The problem of interpreting cause-and-effect relationships can be overcome by the use of longitudinal designs, in which the same individuals are followed from their entry into one status until their move into another status.

Methodological characteristics of longitudinal research on homelessness

The methodological characteristics of the nine longitudinal research projects included in this review are summarized in table 1. The studies are grouped by the type of data collection method used for tracking residential status or homeless-domicile transitions. Within each of the two primary types of data sources—shelter administrative databases and multiwave panel surveys—the studies are listed in chronological order based on the year of data collection.

Of the nine research projects I was able to identify and locate, five used data from shelter administrative records and three collected their data from multiwave survey interviews. Stretch and Kreuger's 1992 study differs from the others in that researchers conducted a follow-up survey of formerly homeless families who had resided in a public shelter in St. Louis between 1983 and 1987. For convenience, I grouped Stretch and Kreuger's study with the other five shelter-based research projects. All the research projects were community-based studies located in urban areas. Interestingly, the first longitudinal data collected were from a local authority's homeless families unit in a major British city (Kelly, Mitchell, and Smith 1990). A total of 10 articles—most published or accepted for publication—on residential status or transitions were generated from eight research projects (Culhane and Kuhn 1998; Kelly, Mitchell, and Smith 1990; Kuhn

Table 1. **Methodological Characteristics of Nine Longitudinal Studies on the Urban Homeless**

Studies on the Urban Homeless	Kelly, Mitchell, and Smith 1990	Rocha et al. 1996	Culhane and Kuhn 1998; Kuhn and Culhane 1998	Wong, Culhane, and Kuhn 1997	Stretch and Kreuger 1992	Culhane and Kuhn 1998; Kuhn and Culhane 1998	Sosin, Piliavin, and Westerfelt 1990; Piliavin et al. 1996	Course of Homelessness Study (personal communication)	Wong and Piliavin 1997; Wong, Piliavin, and Wright forthcoming
Year(s)	1981–82	1983–92	1987–95	1988–95	1989	1991–95	1985–86	1990–93	1991–93
Location	A major British city	St. Louis	New York City	New York City	St. Louis	Philadelphia	Minneapolis	Los Angeles County	Alameda County, CA
Study design	Administrative data	Administrative data	Administrative data	Administrative data	Administrative data and follow-up survey	Administrative data	Two-wave panel study	Multiwave panel design	Three-wave panel study
Target population	Families in a local authority's homeless families unit	Shelter families that secure permanent or temporary housing	Adults unaccompanied by children entering homeless shelters the first time	Adults accompanied by dependent children and married couples entering homeless shelters the first time	Shelter families best served and placed in permanent housing	Adults unaccompanied by children entering homeless shelters the first time	Service-using homeless adults	Sheltered and unsheltered homeless adults	Homeless adults residing in shelters or served by meal programs
Sampling method	Population, one family shelter	Population, two family shelters	Population	Population	Population, one family shelter	Population	Convenience sampling	Stratified sampling procedure	Multistage design
Numbers	526 families	1,156 families	Culhane and Kuhn, 136,657 individuals; Kuhn and Culhane, 73,263 individuals	27,919 families	450 families	Culhane and Kuhn, 16,435 individuals; Kuhn and Culhane, 6,897 individuals	Recent arrivals sample, 113 individuals; cross-sectional sample, 338 individuals	Cross-sectional sample, 1,563 adults; longitudinal sample, 520 adults	564 homeless adults
Definition of homelessness	Homeless people temporarily housed in local hostels and privately rented flatlets	Stay in one of the two family shelters between 1983 and 1992	Residence in a public shelter for at least one night	Residence in a public shelter for at least one night	Stay in a family shelter between 1983 and 1987	Residence in a public shelter for at least one night	(1) Residence in shelter or unconventional accommodations; (2) temporary residence with a friend or relative, or in board-and-lodge facilities	During the 30 days preceding the baseline interview resided (1) on the streets, (2) in temporary shelter, (3) program for the homeless in which stays are temporary	During the 30 days preceding the baseline interview resided (1) on the streets, (2) in temporary shelters, (3) in hotel or motel room paid for by a voucher

Table 1. **Methodological Characteristics of Nine Longitudinal Studies on the Urban Homeless** *(continued)*

Studies on the Urban Homeless	Kelly, Mitchell, and Smith 1990	Rocha et al. 1996	Culhane and Kuhn 1998; Kuhn and Culhane 1998	Wong, Culhane, and Kuhn 1997	Stretch and Kreuger 1992	Culhane and Kuhn 1998; Kuhn and Culhane 1998	Sosin, Piliavin, and Westerfelt 1990; Piliavin et al. 1996	Course of Homelessness Study (personal communication)	Wong and Piliavin 1997; Wong, Piliavin, and Wright forthcoming
Sampling sites	A local authority's homeless families unit	Two family shelters	All public shelters in the Single Client Information Management System (accounted for 82% of all shelter beds)	All public shelters in the New York City Family Shelter System	One family shelter	All public shelters in the Single Shelter System (accounted for 84% of all shelter beds)	4 drop-in centers, 8 overnight shelters, 5 free-meal programs	(1) Shelter services; (2) meal services; (3) street locations or other unconventional dwellings	29 out of 75 facilities located in the community
Attrition	Not applicable	Not applicable	Not applicable	Not applicable	44.6%	Not applicable	42.4% for recent arrivals sample; 40.1% for cross-section sample	13%	15%
Participation rate	100%	100%	100%	100%	100%	100%	Not known	Cross-sectional sample, 87%; longitudinal sample, 96.5%	90%
Method of data collection	Schedules completed by social workers	Case records	Computerized client registry system	Computerized client registry system	Case records; field interviews	Computerized client registry system	Face-to-face structured interview	Face-to-face structured interview	Face-to-face structured interview
Methods of analysis	Log-linear analysis	Logistic regression	Survival analysis; cluster analysis	Survival analysis	Bivariate analysis using cross-tabulations and t tests	Survival analysis; cluster analysis	Bivariate analysis; logistic regression; survival analysis	Survival analysis	Survival analysis; event sequence analysis; bivariate analysis

Note: The studies are organized according to research sites.

and Culhane 1998; Piliavin et al. 1996; Rocha et al. 1996; Sosin, Piliavin, and Westerfelt 1990; Stretch and Kreuger 1992; Wong, Culhane, and Kuhn 1997; Wong and Piliavin 1997; Wong, Piliavin, and Wright forthcoming). In addition, preliminary information on residential transitions was obtained from personal communication with Paul Koegel of the Course of Homelessness Study.[2]

The research designs and sampling strategies varied widely across the nine research projects, as did the scope of study and number of respondents included in each. Of the six projects that used shelter-based data, the number of respondents varied as a function of city size, duration of study, and number of shelters included in the study. The numbers ranged from 450 families in Stretch and Kreuger's study to 136,657 adults in the Single Shelter System in New York City (Culhane and Kuhn 1998). By contrast, the sample sizes for the three projects that used panel design were quite similar. Although the Course of Homelessness Study in Los Angeles had a cross-sectional sample of 1,563 individuals, only one-third, or 520 individuals, were selected for the longitudinal sample. Thus, the sample size for the three multiwave panel studies ranged from 451 persons in the Minneapolis study to 564 persons in the Alameda County study.

There is virtually no sampling design in the studies that used shelter-based administrative data. All eligible persons who entered shelter facilities were tracked over time for the number and length of shelter stays. Two out of the three panel studies used a probability sampling method.

The Course of Homelessness Study used a method to draw a sample that combined aspects of Burnam and Koegel's service-setting sampling approach (Burnam and Koegel 1988) and aspects of Rossi's "blitz" sampling approach (Rossi, Fisher, and Willis 1986). This involved randomly sampling individuals in three nested strata: those who used shelter beds, those who used meal services but not shelter beds, and those who slept on the streets and other places not meant for sleeping and who did not use either meal or shelter services. From the cross-sectional sample, 520 adults were randomly selected for the longitudinal sample. The method of selection involved disproportionate stratification so that 50 percent of the longitudinal sample had severe mental disabilities and one-third were newly

---

[2] The Course of Homelessness Study is currently in the process of submitting its longitudinal results for publication. Until they appear, it is only possible for the investigators to discuss findings in very general terms.

homeless—that is, were in their first homeless episode, which had started within the past 12 months (Koegel, Burnam, and Morton 1996; Koegel, Melamid, and Burnam 1995).

Compared with the Course of Homelessness Study, the Alameda County study employed a less inclusive design by sampling from the service-using population only. A multistage sample design was used to select homeless adults who either resided in shelters or were served by agencies providing meals to people in poverty.[3] Similarly, the Minneapolis study drew its sample exclusively from the service-using population. The Minneapolis study, however, differs from the other two panel studies in that it selected a convenient sample of all homeless individuals present in social agencies serving the homeless at the time of the interviewers' visit.

As can be expected, the scope and type of information collected varies widely according to the data collection method used. Shelter registry systems are designed primarily for administrative purposes and service delivery. It is not surprising, therefore, that the particular variables available to researchers from administrative databases were not recorded with the express purpose of addressing their research questions (Kelly, Mitchell, and Smith 1990). Worse, administrative databases may be constructed in such a way that variables relevant to the understanding of residential transitions are omitted altogether (Wong, Culhane, and Kuhn 1997). In this respect, all three panel survey studies are outstanding in the richness and complexity of their collected information.[4]

Specification of variables of interest

As shown in table 2, the measures researchers used in each study were quite different and depended on the types of residential information available. Kelly, Mitchell, and Smith (1990) focused on the length of stay in publicly funded temporary shelters.

---

[3] Sample selection involved three stages: (1) sampling agencies from two strata representing shelters and meal programs based on size and clientele (i.e., families and single adults), (2) sampling meal times with food-providing agencies, and (3) random sampling of homeless users within shelters and at food providers (Piazza and Cheng 1993).

[4] The topic areas included in these surveys are prior and current homelessness, childhood and family history, physical and behavioral health status, current functioning, social and medical service utilization, enrollment status in income support programs, and subjective satisfaction with various life spheres.

Table 2. **Specification of Variables of Interest**

Studies on the Urban Homeless	Kelly, Mitchell, and Smith 1990	Rocha et al. 1996	Culhane and Kuhn 1998	Wong, Culhane, and Kuhn 1997	Stretch and Kreuger 1992	Kuhn and Culhane 1998	Sosin, Piliavin, and Westerfelt 1990; Piliavin et al. 1996	Course of Homelessness Study (personal communication)	Wong and Piliavin 1997; Wong, Piliavin, and Wright forthcoming
Variable of interest	Length of stay in shelter for homeless families	Type of housing placement obtained upon leaving shelter: (1) permanent placement; (2) temporary housing	Exit from public shelter: those shelter stays that ended without a subsequent shelter admission within the next 30 days	(1) Exit from shelter: a departure from shelter for at least 30 days; (2) types of exit: unknown arrangements, own housing, subsidized housing, and others; (3) return: stay in to shelter: stay in shelter for 1 day or more after exit	(1) Housing status at the time of follow-up interviews; (2) number of residences taken since leaving shelter; (3) additional shelter episodes after leaving shelter	Typology of homelessness by number of shelter days and number of shelter episodes	(1) Exit: stay in a dwelling (except a shelter or institution) for at least 14 or 30 consecutive days; (2) types of exit: independent and dependent; (3) return: stay 1 day in the homeless status after an exit	(1) Exit: stay in domicile (excluding temporary arrangement) for at least 30 or 90 days; (2) types of exit: independent and dependent; (3) return: stay 1 day in the homeless status after an exit	(1) Exit: stay in domicile (excluding institutions) for a continuous 30 days or more; (2) types of exit: independent and dependent; (3) return: stay 1 day in the homeless status after an exit
Duration of observation	Not specified	Not specified	2-year period	2-year period	An average of 3.5 years since leaving the shelter	3-year period for New York; 2-year period for Philadelphia	6-month period	14-month period	1-year period

Note: Culhane and Kuhn's (1998) and Kuhn and Culhane's (1998) studies reported research findings on both New York City and Philadelphia public shelter systems for single homeless adults.

Stretch and Kreuger (1992) examined three measures of residential experience: (1) housing status at the time of the follow-up
interview, (2) number of residences taken, and (3) any additional
shelter episodes experienced since leaving the public shelter.
Rocha et al. (1996) used a categorical dependent variable with
two outcomes of housing placement: permanent placement and
temporary housing. Kuhn and Culhane (1998) used multiyear
data on shelter utilization in New York City and Philadelphia to
develop a typology of homelessness based on the number of
shelter days and shelter episodes.

All three panel studies examined the phenomena of exit from
and return to homelessness. So did two studies conducted by
Culhane and colleagues in New York City and Philadelphia
(Culhane and Kuhn 1998; Wong, Culhane, and Kuhn 1997). The
five studies that examined exit and reentry used survival analysis (see table 1). Survival analysis requires event history data
that specify the timing of transition from one status to another.

The specification of an exit from and a return to homelessness is
contingent on the method used in data collection. Analyses that
were based on shelter registries focused exclusively on the incidence of shelter discharge and readmission. In contrast, the
definition of homelessness used by panel studies extended beyond shelter use to include residence in unconventional accommodations and other temporary arrangements (see table 1). For
these studies, an exit from homelessness is indicated by a report
of a stay in a conventional dwelling.

Irrespective of how an exit is defined—as a departure from
public shelter or an entry into a domicile state—a "duration
threshold" is needed in order to determine which transitions
constitute exits (Piliavin et al. 1996). Interestingly, most studies
converged on a threshold of 30 days' continuous stay away from
the shelter or stay in a domicile. An earlier study by Sosin,
Piliavin, and Westerfelt (1990), however, used a 14-day threshold. Researchers in the Course of Homelessness Study, on the
other hand, used both 30- and 90-day thresholds in their analysis of transition patterns. The Course of Homelessness Study is
particularly useful for determining the sensitivity of research
findings to varying duration thresholds of exits.

Methodological issues and limitations

The appraisal of the findings on residential status and
residential transitions should be considered in light of the

methodological compromises in each of these studies. The methodological issues arising from shelter-based tracking data are distinct from those that are common in panel surveys.

Obvious deficiencies in administrative databases correspond to two fundamental questions: who is being studied and what is being studied. Administrative databases track sheltered populations only, thereby neglecting the residential transitions of their nonsheltered counterparts who do or do not use services such as meal programs or day centers. While Koegel, Burnam, and Morton (1996) showed that less inclusive sampling frames, such as those derived from homeless shelters, do not consistently produce biased estimates of population characteristics, no data are available to address the question of whether sheltered and nonsheltered populations differ in their trajectories of residential transitions.

Moreover, information on residential status and transitions that is recorded in shelter databases is limited to movements into and out of homeless shelters and is not indicative of the state of homelessness. Without systematic records of discharge locations, it is not known whether shelter exiters were able to locate temporary or permanent housing or were simply discharged to the streets. On the other hand, even if shelter-based administrative systems keep reliable records of discharge destinations for each shelter user, the incidence of return to homelessness is likely to be underestimated. Former shelter users who cannot sustain their domicile status may choose to live on the streets rather than seek readmission to the shelter.

Multiwave panel studies rectify these shortcomings by adopting a broader definition of homelessness and using follow-up interviews to obtain histories of various housing transitions experienced by sample members. Despite this obvious advantage, panel surveys are not immune from other sources of bias and limitation. First, since residential histories are based on retrospective reports by respondents, their reliability depends on the lapse of time between interviews and the degree of residential stability experienced. Other things being equal, it is reasonable to believe that shorter intervals between interviews and less residential instability are associated with more reliable data. With regard to interview intervals, the Course of Homelessness Study—using bimonthly follow-up interviews—may provide more dependable residential information than either the Minneapolis study or the Alameda County study, which scheduled their follow-up interviews 4 to 12 months apart.

Second, sample attrition, a phenomenon common in panel studies, may significantly compromise research results. Probably because of improvements in sample tracking strategies, the attrition rates are much lower for the two recent studies (around 15 percent) than for the Minneapolis study (40 percent). However, lower attrition rates and a lack of apparent differences between the follow-up and the baseline samples do not necessarily guarantee that research findings based on follow-up samples are unbiased, because researchers may omit from their analyses phenomena relevant to residential transitions. The biases arising from attrition can be corrected with statistical procedures that control for the probability of attrition in the baseline sample (Piliavin et al. 1996).

Third, panel studies on homeless populations often encounter difficulty in identifying recently homeless persons. An ideal panel study should be based on a sample of homeless people who are just entering their current homeless episodes. Such a design would reduce the problem of "left-hand censoring," which inadvertently results in an underrepresentation of people who experience short-term homelessness.[5] However, in both the Minneapolis and the Alameda County studies, sampling plans that originally sought to include only the recently homeless were subsequently expanded to include a cross-section of homeless people because of the insufficient flow of recently homeless individuals into the sampling sites.[6]

Demographic profiles of sample members

Table 3 gives basic demographic information—age, race, gender, and household composition—of sample members from the nine research projects. Of the six shelter-based studies, two focused on homeless people unaccompanied by dependent children and four focused on sheltered homeless families. The Minneapolis and the Course of Homelessness studies were made up primarily

---

[5] "Left-hand censoring" refers to the failure to include in the sample individuals who began their homeless episodes at the same time as included individuals but exited their homeless episodes prior to the sampling period.

[6] The Alameda County study originally targeted a sample of "recent arrivals" who had become homeless within 30 days preceding the interview. After the first month of data collection, it became clear that the flow of recently homeless individuals into the sampling sites was very low. The target population was thus expanded to include the cross-section of homeless individuals. In the Course of Homelessness Study, the definition of the "newly homeless" was quite broad and included people who had had their first homeless episode within the past 12 months.

Table 3. **Demographic and Background Information**

Studies on the Urban Homeless	Kelly, Mitchell, and Smith 1990	Rocha et al. 1996	Culhane and Kuhn 1998; Kuhn and Culhane 1998 (New York City part)[a]	Wong, Culhane, and Kuhn 1997	Stretch and Kreuger 1992	Culhane and Kuhn 1998; Kuhn and Culhane 1998 (Philadelphia part)[a]	Sosin, Piliavin, and Westerfelt 1990; Piliavin et al. 1996[b]	Course of Homelessness Study (personal communication)[c]	Wong and Piliavin 1997; Wong, Piliavin, and Wright forthcoming[b]
Age	20 & under (23.5%); 21–30 (45.4%); over 30 (21.4%)[d]	26.6 (mean)	Under 30 (34.9%); 30–50 (56.4%); over 50 (8.7%)	28.6 (mean)	No information reported	Under 30 (29.2%); 30–50 (63.3%); over 50 (7.5%)	32 (mean)	38 (mean)	Overall mean: 36.6 (mothers, 31.2; single females, 36.0; single males, 38.0)
Race	No information reported	86% African American	62.4% black; 37.6% nonblack	59.2% African American; 34.6% Hispanic	80% African American	85.1% black; 14.9% nonblack	43% white; 26% black	59% African American	65.5% African American
Gender	No information reported	Predominantly women; no statistics on percentages	Male, 81.6%; female, 18.4%	No information reported	Predominantly women; no statistics on percentages	Male, 82.9%; female, 17.1%	Male, 85%; female, 15%	Male, 79%; female, 21%	Male, 66.4%; female, 33.6%
Household composition	All families; no information on family structure	All families; 91% women with children	All single homeless adults not accompanied by dependent children	90.9% single-mother families	All families; 73% women with children	All single homeless adults not accompanied by dependent children	Predominantly single homeless adults; only 5% were currently accompanied by dependent children	Predominantly single homeless adults; only 2% were currently accompanied by dependent children	Mothers with children, 14.9%; single female, 18.7%; single male, 66.4%

[a]Basic demographic data are based on the Kuhn and Culhane (1998) study.
[b]Basic demographic data are based on the cross-sectional sample. Statistics on individual characteristics differ slightly for the "recent arrivals" sample.
[c]Part of the information is provided by the descriptive data on the Course of Homelessness Study reported in Marshall et al.'s (1996) study of objective life circumstances and life satisfaction.
[d]Age is unknown for the remaining 9.7 percent of the sample.

of single homeless people. Only 5 and 2 percent of their respective samples were accompanied by children. The Alameda County study has the most diverse sample of all nine studies in terms of household structure. One-third of its sample was mothers with children and single females, and two-thirds were single males.

As shown in table 3, the average age of sample members ranged from 27 years in Rocha et al.'s St. Louis study to 38 years in the Course of Homelessness Study. On average, heads of homeless families are much younger than single homeless individuals, a finding consistent with the results of two meta-analyses of other homeless populations (Rossi 1994; Shlay and Rossi 1992). Even considering the racial and ethnic compositions of the different communities involved, there is an obvious overrepresentation of the minority populations. Finally, two contrasting gender patterns are noted for single homeless adults and homeless families: The majority of families are headed by females, and males make up the majority of the single homeless populations.

Residential status and patterns of homeless-domicile transitions

Salient findings describing the residential status and patterns of homeless-domicile transitions are reported in table 4. The findings are presented separately for shelter-based studies and panel surveys.

Findings from shelter-based studies

Exit from shelter: Rate and duration. Regardless of whether the clients served were single persons or families, all six studies using shelter administrative data reported a shelter exit rate of 100 percent. The exit rate can be construed as an artifact of the shelter systems, whose policies concerning admission and length of stay dictate the flow of single individuals or families into and out of the system (Rossi 1994; Wong, Culhane, and Kuhn 1997).

Given the lack of variation in the incidence of shelter exit, length of stay provides a more appropriate measure of residential transition. All but the two St. Louis studies reported shelter stay lengths of their sample members. Although the findings from shelter-based studies are not strictly comparable because of the idiosyncratic features of their settings, it is worthwhile to note the difference in the duration of shelter stays between homeless families and single homeless individuals.

Table 4. **Residential Status and Patterns of Homeless-Domicile Transitions**

Study on the Urban Homeless	Kelly, Mitchell, and Smith 1990	Rocha et al. 1996	Culhane and Kuhn 1998	Wong, Culhane, and Kuhn 1997	Stretch and Kreuger 1992	Kuhn and Culhane 1998	Sosin, Piliavin, and Westerfelt 1990; Piliavin et al. 1996*	Course of Homelessness Study (personal communication)	Wong and Piliavin 1997; Wong, Piliavin, and Wright forthcoming*
Exit from and return to homelessness (rate)	Exit rate: 100%	Exit rate: 100%	(1) Exit rate: 100% within two years of shelter admission; (2) return rate: men 50% and women 33% within two years of shelter admission	(1) Exit rate: 100% within two years of shelter admission; (2) return rate: 22% within two years of shelter discharge	(1) Exit rate: 100%; (2) return rate: 16%	No information reported	(1) Exit rate: 76%; (2) return rate: 51%	(1) Exit rate: more than 50% exited under any 30-day exit, independent 30-day exit, and any 90-day exit definitions; (2) return rate: the majority returned to homelessness at least once	(1) Exit rate: overall 82%, mothers with children 94%, single females 89%, single males 76%; (2) return rate: overall 65%, mothers with children 38%, single females 65%, single males 77%
Exit from and return to homelessness (duration data)	Average length of stay in shelter: 62 days	No information reported	(1) 50% of shelter users stayed less than 45 days; (2) 18% of New York shelter users consumed 53% of the system days; (3) median time taken for returning to shelter: 100–140 days	Mean length of shelter stay: 79 days	No information reported	No information reported	Consistent decrease in both exit and return hazard rate with time	Information in prepublication status and thus not available	(1) Median days homeless before experiencing an exit: mothers with children 54 days, single females 78 days, single men 93 days; (2) median days domiciled before returning to homelessness: single females 88 days, single men 87 days
Other measures of residential outcome	No other measures	Pattern of housing placements upon exit: permanent housing 60%, temporary housing 40%	No other measures	(1) Percent discharged from shelter to different locations: unknown arrangements 41%, own housing 8%, subsidized housing 48%, others 4%; (2) families that were discharged to subsidized housing stayed in shelter longer but had the lowest rate of shelter readmission	(1) Current residences: Section 8 housing 64%, private rental or purchased units 17%, other assisted housing 17%, homeless 2%; (2) average number of residences taken since leaving shelter: 2.28	Typologies of homelessness: (1) New York: transitional 81%, episodic 9%, chronic 10%; (2) Philadelphia: transitional 79%, episodic 12%, chronic 10%	(1) Most of the exits were to dependent dwellings; (2) it took longer to make a transition to semi-independent (rent-paying) exit; (3) average domiciled time before returning to homelessness: 65 days	Information in prepublication status and thus not available	(1) Homelessness pattern: continuous homeless 18%, exit with no return 37%, episodic homeless 46%; (2) women with children more likely to have own apartment exit; (3) average number of residences taken among exiters: 1.7

*Data on homeless-domicile transitions are based on survival analyses performed on the "recent arrivals" sample. Using data from the "recent arrivals" sample reduces the problem of left-hand censoring.

On average, homeless families in Kelly, Mitchell, and Smith's study stayed two months in shelter accommodations before they were placed in permanent housing. The mean length of stay among homeless families in New York City was higher, amounting to 79 days during their first episode in the shelter system. The shelter stays experienced by homeless families, albeit relatively brief, were generally longer than those experienced by single homeless people. In Culhane and Kuhn's study of the pattern of public shelter utilization among single adults in New York City and Philadelphia, the researchers documented that 50 percent of shelter users spent less than 45 days in the system within a period of two years. In another study using the same databases, Kuhn and Culhane (1998) found that about 80 percent of the single adult homeless population in both cities can be classified as short-term transitionally homeless people. The mean length of stay for the transitionally homeless in Philadelphia is as brief as 20 days within a two-year period.

Residential status and housing placement. Three out of the four databases on homeless families recorded some information on the residential status or housing placement of their sample members after leaving homeless shelters. Neither of the two administrative databases on single homeless adults provided such information. At the time of their follow-up interviews—two to six years after shelter admission—only 2 percent of previously homeless families in St. Louis were currently living in a family shelter (Stretch and Kreuger 1992). In contrast, 81 percent were living in Section 8 or other public assisted housing. The remaining 17 percent were in private rental or purchased units. Despite the seemingly favorable housing outcome, Stretch and Kreuger's sample reported an average of 2.3 different residences since leaving shelter, indicating some residential instability.

On the basis of 10-year shelter utilization records of two facilities in St. Louis, Rocha et al. (1996) reported that 60 percent of the homeless families found long-term housing by renting from the public or private sector (53 percent) or making permanent "live-in" arrangements (7 percent). The 40 percent of the families that were discharged to temporary housing included 21 percent who went to another shelter or a transitional housing program, 16 percent who sought shared housing arrangements with friends or family, and 3 percent who went to institutions or motels. Administrative data from the New York City Family Shelter System reported a similar proportion of their shelter users discharged to permanent housing placement (Wong, Culhane, and Kuhn 1997). Among families who had left the shelter system between 1988 and 1995, 48 percent obtained government-subsidized housing and 8 percent either found their own housing or returned to their former residences. Because of the coding system used for shelter discharge, the residential status of families not discharged to permanent housing is unclear.[7]

Aside from records of housing placements, the New York City family shelter database also reported the duration of shelter stay by type of shelter discharge or housing placement. Contrasting patterns of shelter discharge for the two primary routes out of homeless shelters—discharges to unknown arrangements and discharges to subsidized housing—were noted. The study found that families exiting homeless shelters to unknown arrangements had relatively short stays in the shelters, but families discharged to subsidized housing stayed in the shelters for substantially longer periods. Such a differential pattern is obviously an artifact of the city's rehousing policy, which established eligibility for subsidized housing only after 90 days of stay in family shelters.

Readmission to shelter: Rate and duration. Four studies reported data on shelter readmission among their sample members. The rates of shelter readmission were similar for single shelter users in New York City and Philadelphia. One-half of male and one-third of female shelter users experienced another shelter episode within two years of shelter admission. The median time for returning to homeless shelters reported in these two shelter systems ranged from 100 to 140 days.

Homeless families had a lower rate of shelter readmission than single homeless people. The 201 families in a St. Louis shelter reported a 16 percent readmission rate, and first-time users of family shelters in New York City reported a 22 percent readmission rate within a two-year period.

Findings from panel surveys

Exit from homelessness: Rate and duration. Under most definitions of exit, a majority of sample members in all three panel studies reported an exit from the homeless state to a

---

[7] As the administrative record shows, 41 percent of all first-time shelter users were discharged to unknown arrangements (there was no record in the database of the type of housing obtained). In addition, about 4 percent of first-time shelter stays ended in "other exits," which included involuntary exits (such as arrests), discharges to shared lodging (with friends or family), and discharges to shelters for victims of domestic violence.

conventional domicile.[8] Seventy-six percent of all recently home-less people in the Minneapolis study were able to make a transition from homelessness to domicile, compared with 82 percent in the Alameda County study.[9]

The inclusion of subsamples of female-headed families, single females, and single males in the Alameda County study provides an opportunity to compare the homeless-domicile transition rates by gender and family status. Within a period of one year, mothers with children had the highest rate of exiting home-lessness (94 percent), followed by single females (89 percent) and single males (76 percent). Families in Alameda County also spent less time homeless before making a transition to a conven-tional domicile. The average number of days that homeless families spent on the streets before making a transition to a domicile was 54 days, compared with 78 days for single females and 93 days for single males.

Residential status and housing placement. The Minneapolis and the Alameda County studies also reported data on the type of accommo-dations their sample members obtained after leaving homelessness. Exit locations can be classified according to the financial responsi-bility—including rent payment, mortgage payment, or contribution to household expenses—assumed by the respondents as well as the permanency of the domicile arrangement.

Most of the exits reported in the Minneapolis study were to housing arrangements in which the respondents did not assume any financial responsibility. Transitions from homelessness to these "dependent exits" also took less time than transitions to more independent exits, in which the respondent contributed to housing costs. In sharp contrast, the majority of exits reported in the Alameda County study were supported at least in part by respondents' rent payments. There was, moreover, a higher incidence of residence in permanent housing, particularly among female-headed families with dependent children.

Returns to homelessness: Rate and duration. All three panel studies found that most of their sample members experienced a return to the streets after making a transition to a domicile. For

---

[8] The only exception is one of the four definitions of exit in the Course of Home-lessness Study. Under the 90-day independent exit definition, less than 50 percent of the Los Angeles homeless sample reported an exit from homelessness.

[9] The exact proportion of sample members who exited homelessness is unavail-able for the Course of Homelessness Study.

the Minneapolis and Alameda County studies, in which data on returns were available, the proportions of domiciled sample members reporting another homeless episode were 51 and 65 percent, respectively.[10]

Consistent with findings from shelter administrative data, families reported a lower rate of returning to homelessness than single individuals. The proportions of domiciled families, single females, and single males in the Alameda County study who returned to another homeless episode were 38, 65, and 77 percent, respectively. Despite the difference in proportion, the median number of days domiciled before returning to homelessness was almost identical for single females and males.

Multivariate analysis of predictors of residential outcome

Six research papers employed multivariate analysis to identify individual characteristics and circumstances associated with various indicators of residential outcome, including length of shelter stay, type of housing placement, and exit from and return to homelessness.[11] For the Course of Homelessness Study, findings on the correlates of exit from a homeless spell were based on personal communication.[12] Table 5 lists the outcome variables and their predictors. The predictor variables were organized into four categories: basic demographics, homelessness-related variables, personal deficit variables, and resource utilization variables.[13] The predictor variables used in the research projects reflect largely the type of data available as well as the research objectives of each study.

---

[10] The higher return rate reported in the Alameda County study is probably an artifact of the longer study period. Most Alameda County respondents were in the study at least twice as long as their counterparts in the Minneapolis study.

[11] Stretch and Kreuger's St. Louis study employed bivariate analyses to identify correlates of returns to homelessness. Three variables were found to be associated with a higher rate of return to homelessness: longer interval between shelter exit and follow-up interview, not receiving Section 8 housing, and sharing lodging with extended families. Kuhn and Culhane's study cross-tabulated the various sociodemographic variables with the three types of homeless people identified by cluster analysis. These variables included age, gender, race, physical health, substance abuse, and mental health.

[12] The findings on the correlates of exit from a homeless spell are in prepublication status. They are discussed in very general terms in this section.

[13] Time-related variables that are relevant to multiyear shelter-based tracking data sets are not included in this review. Although these variables may

Table 5. **Multivariate Analyses of Predictors of Residential Status and Homeless-Domicile Transitions**

Studies on the Urban Homeless	Kelly, Mitchell, and Smith 1990	Rocha et al. 1996	Culhane and Kuhn 1998	Wong, Culhane, and Kuhn 1997	Piliavin et al. 1996	Course of Homelessness Study (personal communication)[a]	Wong and Piliavin 1997
Dependent variables	Length of stay in shelter	Permanent placement versus temporary housing	Probability of exit from homeless shelter	(1) Hazard rates of various types of discharge from family shelter; (2) hazard rate of return to shelter	(1) Hazard rates of independent and dependent exits; (2) hazard rate of return to homelessness	Hazard rate of exit from homeless spell	(1) Hazard rate of exit from homeless spell; (2) hazard rate of return to homelessness
Basic demographics	Number of children; age of woman; pregnancy status	Number of children[b]; age of head of household; race[b]	Race[c]; U.S. citizenship; veteran status; age[c]	Family type; number of adults[c,d]; number of children[c,d], age of family head[c,d]; race[c,d]; pregnancy status[c,d]	Age; race[c]; gender[d]	Age[c]; gender[c]; race[c]	Age[c,d]; race[c,d]
Homelessness-related variables	Prior homelessness; reason for homelessness; whether intentionally homeless	Not included in study	Number of prior shelter stays	Reasons for homelessness[c,d]; length of shelter stay	Prior homelessness[c]; current homeless spell length	Lifetime and current measures of homeless	Prior homelessness[d]; current homeless spell length
Personal deficit variables	Not included in study	Education	Marital status; physical health; substance abuse[c]; mental health status[c]	Not included in study	Foster care placement; criminal history; marital status; living alone; social support; education and training[c]; work history[d]; current work status[c]; physical health; mental disabilities; substance abuse; assimilation of a street culture[c]	Various types of personal problems, including physical health, mental health, and substance abuse[c]	Childhood foster care placement; educational attainment; prior work history[c]; functional health status[c]; severe mental disabilities[c,d]; alcohol problem[c]; drug problem[c,d]
Resource utilization variables	Whether have earned income	Income	Not included in study	Recipiency of public assistance[c,d]; residence in subsidized housing[d]	Recipiency of welfare[c]	Formal support from service systems and social support[c]	Current wages or employment status[d]; cash benefits level or enrollment status[c,d]; residence in subsidized housing[d]; receipt of social services[d]

[a]Information on the effects of particular personal deficit and resource utilization variables is in prepublication status and thus not available.
[b]Significant predictors of length of shelter stay or type of housing placement.
[c]Significant predictors of exit from homelessness.
[d]Significant predictors of return to homelessness among exiters.

Basic demographics

Age. Four studies found age to be a significant predictor of exit from homelessness or homeless shelters. For both single homeless people and families in New York City, younger age is associated with a higher probability of discharge from homeless shelters (Culhane and Kuhn 1998; Wong, Culhane, and Kuhn 1997). Similar correlations were found among single homeless shelter users in Philadelphia. Moreover, among the three panel studies reviewed in this article, two—the Course of Homelessness Study and the Alameda County study—reported a significant correlation between age and exit from homelessness.[14] The direction of the age effect identified in these panel studies is consistent with that identified in shelter-based studies.

Apparently, as results of two studies indicated, younger people tended to leave homeless shelters or homelessness at a faster rate (Wong, Culhane, and Kuhn 1997; Wong and Piliavin 1997). However, among those in these studies who had exited, older people were less likely to seek readmission to public shelter and were more likely to stay in their domicile.

Race and ethnicity. Six studies reported race and ethnicity as significant predictors of residential outcomes. Irrespective of the specific outcome measure used, most studies found membership in a minority group to be associated with a less favorable residential outcome.[15]

Being white was associated with a higher probability of obtaining permanent housing placement (Rocha et al. 1996), a higher probability of leaving single homeless shelters (Culhane and Kuhn 1998), and a higher rate of making a transition from

---

provide some descriptive information on the seasonality and time trend of shelter use, their interpretability is questionable without adequate knowledge of the operation of shelter facilities and the larger policy context. None of the studies that examined these variables analyzed their data in reference to the policy and organizational contexts where the shelter facilities were located.

[14] According to personal communication with Paul Koegel, younger age was associated with a higher rate of independent 30-day exits and all 30-day exits in the Course of Homelessness Study. Pooled-sample analysis in the Alameda County study also found younger age to be a significant predictor of faster exits, even after controlling for the effect of gender, family status, and other personal deficit and resource utilization variables (Wong and Piliavin 1997).

[15] The only exception is the Course of Homelessness Study, in which the researchers found that being African American was associated with a higher rate of all 30-day exits.

homelessness to domicile (Piliavin et al. 1996). Further, Wong, Culhane, and Kuhn (1997) found that African-American families had shelter discharge and readmission patterns similar to those of Hispanic families. Compared with the "other" racial and ethnic group—which is predominantly white—these families had a lower rate of all four modes of discharge as well as a higher rate of readmission to homeless shelters. Consistent with the above findings, the Alameda County study observed that single African-American men had a lower rate of exit from homeless spells than men of other racial categories, and that single African-American women had a higher rate of return than their non-African-American counterparts (Wong and Piliavin 1997).

Household composition. Having more dependent children in a family was associated with less favorable residential outcomes. Rocha et al. (1996) found that families with more children were more likely to be placed in temporary housing than in permanent accommodations. Wong, Culhane, and Kuhn (1997), on the other hand, documented that larger families—those with more adults or more dependent children—had a lower rate of leaving homeless shelters as well as a higher rate of shelter readmission. The same study did not, however, identify female headship (relative to other family forms) as a significant predictor of either shelter discharge or readmission.

Other demographic variables. Contrasting gender effects were identified in two panel studies on primarily single homeless people. The Course of Homelessness Study found a higher rate of leaving homelessness for women than for men, and female sample members in the Minneapolis study were observed to experience a higher return rate than their male counterparts (Piliavin et al. 1996). In the only study that explored the effect of pregnancy status (Wong, Culhane, and Kuhn 1997), no consistent patterns were identified for the rate of various modes of discharge, although pregnancy status at the time of shelter stay was associated with an increased risk of shelter readmission.

Homelessness-related variables

Reason for homelessness. Kelly, Mitchell, and Smith (1990) found the sort of reason families gave for being homeless to be an important predictor of length of shelter stay.[16] Families

---

[16] Kelly, Mitchell, and Smith's study did not report the statistical significance of the variables included in their regression model. The researchers reported the two most important predictors of shelter stay length: (1) time of the year for shelter admission and (2) reason for homelessness.

reporting rental and tenant difficulties experienced shorter shelter stays than families attributing their homelessness to other reasons. Wong, Culhane, and Kuhn (1997) found that the reasons shelter users gave for being homeless were variably associated with different modes of shelter discharge. While families that reported domestic abuse and environment-related problems were more likely than families that reported economic problems to be discharged to their own housing, to subsidized housing, and to other exit destinations, they were less likely to be discharged to unknown arrangements. Moreover, the researchers found that families reporting environment-related problems were less likely than the "economically homeless" to seek shelter readmission.

Incidence and length of homeless episodes. Variables indicating the incidence of prior homeless episodes and length of current homelessness were included in six out of seven multivariate studies. Apparently, these variables are not robust predictors of residential outcomes. Only two significant findings were identified: Experience of a prior homeless episode was associated with (1) a lower rate of exiting homelessness in the Minneapolis study (Piliavin et al. 1996) and (2) a higher rate of returning to homelessness in the Alameda County study (Wong and Piliavin 1997).

Personal deficit variables

Measures of personal problems and disabilities were variably available in the studies reviewed in this article. Of the four shelter-based multivariate studies, only Culhane and Kuhn (1998) systematically examined the effects of personal deficit variables on exits from homeless shelters. All three panel studies used various types of personal problems and disabilities in modeling the process of exit from and return to homelessness.

Research results on the effects of personal deficit variables were mixed and inconclusive. The Minneapolis study (Piliavin et al. 1996) provided only partial support for the relevance of personal deficit variables in predicting homeless-domicile transitions. Of the 16 variables that represented four forms of deficit,[17] only 3— recent employment, vocational training, and identification with other homeless people—correlated with exiting homeless spells.

---

[17] The four forms of deficit used in the Minneapolis study were (1) institutional disaffiliation, (2) emotional and physical disabilities, (3) human capital deficiencies, and (4) acculturation to street life.

Only one deficit attribute—work history—was associated with returns to homelessness.

The lack of significant effects of personal deficit variables was documented by Wong and Piliavin (1997) in their endeavor to account for gender and family status differences in homeless-domicile transitions among members of the Alameda County study. However, in the same study, the researchers noted more positive results for personal deficit variables when analyses were conducted separately for single men, single women, and families. Interestingly, the Course of Homelessness Study offered some counterintuitive findings on the effects of personal deficit variables by noting that personal problems were associated with a higher rate of exit from homelessness.

Among the four multivariate studies that included personal deficit variables, Culhane and Kuhn's study provided the most consistent results in support of the relevance of personal deficits in predicting residential transitions. Specifically, the researchers found that physical health problems, mental health problems, and substance abuse were all associated with a lower probability of exiting from both the New York City and Philadelphia shelter systems. But Culhane and Kuhn's findings should be interpreted with caution because exits were restricted to discharges from public shelter only. Exit patterns, therefore, might be driven largely by shelter policy. Public shelters might be used as an asylum for people with physical and behavioral health problems—as a form of substitute care that would otherwise be provided by other institutionalized settings such as hospitals and other rehabilitative facilities.

Resource utilization variables

Although all but one study included some measures of institutional resources in their multivariate analyses, only the Alameda County study systematically tested the importance of material resources for facilitating exit from homelessness and attaining residential stability (Wong and Piliavin 1997). The Alameda County study was also unique in that it went beyond baseline predictor measures to incorporate resource utilization status during domicile in modeling the process of returning to homelessness.

As table 5 shows, almost all resource utilization variables were to some degree associated with residential status or homeless-domicile transitions. On the one hand, the direction of the effects was consistent with the assumption that access to resources increases a homeless person's chance of leaving homelessness and obtaining stable domicile. On the other hand, the effects of particular resource utilization variables seemed to vary according to the homeless subpopulations studied as well as whether the outcome variable used was exit or return.

Receipt of cash benefits was associated with an increased likelihood of exiting to subsidized housing among family shelter users in New York City, to independent exits among primarily single homeless people in Minneapolis, and to any exits among women in Alameda County.[18] Interestingly, although cash benefits had no effect on the exit rate among single men in Alameda County, they were associated with a lower rate of returning to homelessness. Moreover, among single men who exited their homeless spells in Alameda County, being gainfully employed was associated with a lower rate of returning to homelessness. For female family heads and single females in Alameda County, receipt of housing subsidy—rather than employment status—emerged as the most important predictor of residential stability. A similar effect was noted among family shelter users in New York City; the researchers documented that families discharged to subsidized housing units had a remarkably lower readmission rate than families discharged to other types of locations. Finally, among female family heads in the Alameda County study, receipt of social services was associated with a lower rate of returning to homelessness.

Summary and policy implications

This review of the longitudinal studies on the residential status and homeless-domicile transitions of the contemporary urban homeless suggests several findings that are relevant to social policy and service program design.

First, as other researchers have previously noted, homelessness is neither a short-term crisis nor a long-term situation for most homeless people. It is part of an experience of residential instability that involves a patchwork of various housing strategies stitched together by people in dire housing situations. Public shelter facilities represent one of the resources homeless people use in coping with their housing crisis. But most homeless people

---

[18] Researchers in the Course of Homelessness Study also found that individuals who had access to resources through jobs and benefits programs were more likely than those who did not to exit homelessness (personal communication).

use shelter facilities on a short-term, recurrent, or strategic basis, suggesting that other housing arrangements are an equally important part of homeless people's survival strategies. Indeed, all three panel studies reviewed in this article found the majority of the homeless population to be capable of making a transition from the streets by renting their own apartments, by doubling up with family and friends, or by procuring admission to rehabilitative and treatment facilities. These studies, however, show that the hold on conventional housing among those who exited their homeless spells was tenuous, since the majority would return to the streets within the limited duration of the studies. The challenge for social policy, therefore, is not only to develop programs that help people to leave homelessness, but also to prevent recurrence of homelessness among people with extremely limited resources to lay a claim on stable housing.

Second, demographic characteristics, including age, race and ethnicity, and household structure, are associated with the process of exit from and return to homelessness as well as with the type of domicile obtained after leaving homelessness. These easy-to-identify indicators can help policy makers and social service providers target programs to assist those among the homeless who experience more difficulty in locating and maintaining conventional housing. Among different demographic groups, homeless families with dependent children experience the most favorable residential outcome, as reflected by their higher rate of leaving homelessness, lower rate of returning to the streets, and higher incidence of placement in permanent housing. Understanding the process by which homeless families with children make their transition to permanent housing would illuminate the course of action that needs to be taken in order to enable members of other groups to achieve residential stability.

Third, access to material resources has a strong influence on facilitating exit from homelessness as well as on preventing the recurrence of homeless episodes. It also accounts for more favorable residential situations—higher incidence of permanent housing placement and lower rate of returning to homelessness—of homeless families relative to people who are not living with their dependent children.[19] Moreover, it is clear

---

[19] Wong and Piliavin (1997) found that institutional resource variables account for a higher rate of exiting homelessness and a lower rate of returning to homelessness among families, when compared with single individuals. Wong, Piliavin, and Wright (forthcoming) reported that families were more likely than single individuals to obtain permanent housing. This is attributable to families' access to more stable and generous benefits from the public income support system.

that resources procured from the social welfare system have stronger and more consistent effects on enabling people to leave homelessness than resources derived from participation in the labor market. Among the different cash and near-cash social programs, subsidized government housing emerges as the most effective program for facilitating the residential stability of previously homeless families and single females.

These findings are hardly surprising given that homelessness is at its roots a housing problem attributable to low income and shortage of affordable housing (Burt 1992). As numerous studies have shown, many homeless people have either few marketable skills or profound personal problems that make gainful employment difficult. Even among those who actively engage in paid employment but who experience low wages and erratic work, income supplements from the social welfare system represent an essential resource for maintaining their hold on housing.

In conclusion, the recent wave of longitudinal research on the residential patterns of the urban homeless provides empirical support for the concept of a prevention-oriented approach proposed by researchers, policy makers, and advocates for the homeless (Culhane et al. 1997; Jahiel 1992; Lindblom 1997; U.S. Department of Health and Human Services 1991). As the findings of this review imply, the design of a comprehensive homelessness prevention strategy should embody several characteristics. First, homelessness prevention services should be community based rather than shelter based. Second, prevention services should be differentially designed and targeted to different population groups according to their specific strengths, needs, and problems. Third, outreach effort should be planned to include not only currently homeless people, but also previously homeless people who are currently domiciled but have characteristics indicating a high risk of recurrent homelessness. Finally, intervention programs, in addition to focusing on the training and rehabilitative needs of homeless people, should emphasize the creative mobilization and interface of resources from both the formal and informal systems.

Author

Yin-Ling Irene Wong is Assistant Professor of Social Work at the University of Pennsylvania. The author wishes to acknowledge Paul Koegel of the Rand Corporation for his generosity in sharing information on the Course of Homelessness Study.

References

Arce, A. A., Marilyn Tadlock, Michael J. Vergare, and Stuart H. Shapiro. 1983. A Psychiatric Profile of Street People Admitted to an Emergency Shelter. *Hospital and Community Psychiatry* 34(9):812–15.

Bane, Mary J., and David T. Ellwood. 1986. Slipping Into and Out of Poverty: The Dynamics of Spells. *Journal of Human Resources* 21(1):1–23.

Burnam, M. A., and Paul Koegel. 1988. Methodology for Obtaining a Representative Sample of Homeless Persons: The Los Angeles Skid Row Study. *Evaluation Review* 12(2):117–52.

Burt, Martha R. 1992. *Over the Edge: The Growth of Homelessness in the 1980s.* New York and Washington, DC: Russell Sage Foundation and Urban Institute Press.

Burt, Martha R. 1994. Comment on Dennis P. Culhane et al.'s "Public Shelter Admission Rates in Philadelphia and New York City: The Implications of Turnover for Sheltered Population Counts." *Housing Policy Debate* 5(2): 141–52.

Burt, Martha R., and Barbara E. Cohen. 1989. Differences among Homeless Single Women, Women and Children, and Single Men. *Social Problems* 36(5):508–23.

Calsyn, Robert J., and Gary A. Morse. 1990. Homeless Men and Women: Commonalities and a Service Gender Gap. *American Journal of Community Psychology* 18(4):597–608.

Culhane, Dennis P., Edmund F. Dejowski, Julie Ibañez, Elizabeth Needham, and Irene Macchia. 1997. Public Shelter Admission Rates in Philadelphia and New York City: The Implications of Turnover for Sheltered Population Counts. In *Understanding Homelessness: New Policy and Research Perspectives*, ed. Dennis P. Culhane and Steven P. Hornburg, 101–34. First published in 1994 as *Housing Policy Debate* 5(2):107–40.

Culhane, Dennis P., and Randall Kuhn. 1998. Patterns and Determinants of Shelter Utilization among Single Adults in New York City and Philadelphia. *Journal of Policy Analysis and Management*, forthcoming.

Freeman, Richard B., and Brian Hall. 1987. Permanent Homelessness in America? *Population Research and Policy Review* 6:3–27.

Grigsby, Charles, Donald Baumann, Steven E. Gregorich, and Cynthia Roberts-Gray. 1990. Disaffiliation to Entrenchment: A Model for Understanding Homelessness. *Journal of Social Issues* 46(4):141–56.

Jahiel, René I. 1992. *Homelessness: A Prevention-Oriented Approach.* Baltimore: Johns Hopkins University Press.

Kelly, Elinor, J. C. Mitchell, and Susan J. Smith. 1990. Factors in the Length of Stay of Homeless Families in Temporary Accommodation. *Sociological Review* 38(4):621–33.

Koegel, Paul, M. A. Burnam, and Rodger K. Farr. 1988. The Prevalence of Specific Psychiatric Disorders among Homeless Individuals in the Inner City of Los Angeles. *Archives of General Psychiatry* 45:1085–92.

Koegel, Paul, M. A. Burnam, and Sally C. Morton. 1996. Enumerating Homeless People: Alternative Strategies and Their Consequences. *Evaluation Review* 20(4):378–403.

Koegel, Paul, Elan Melamid, and M. A. Burnam. 1995. Childhood Risk Factors for Homelessness among Homeless Adults. *American Journal of Public Health* 85(12):1642–49.

Kuhn, Randall, and Dennis P. Culhane. 1998. Applying Cluster Analysis to Test a Typology of Homelessness by Pattern of Shelter Utilization: Results from the Analysis of Administrative Data. *American Journal of Community Psychology*, forthcoming.

Lindblom, Eric N. 1997. Toward a Comprehensive Homelessness-Prevention Strategy. In *Understanding Homelessness: New Policy and Research Perspectives*, ed. Dennis P. Culhane and Steven P. Hornburg, 265–334. First published in 1991 as *Housing Policy Debate* 2(3):957–1025.

Link, Bruce, Jo Phelan, Michaeline Bresnahan, Ann Stueve, Robert Moore, and Ezra Susser. 1995. Lifetime and Five-Year Prevalence of Homelessness in the United States: New Evidence on an Old Debate. *American Journal of Orthopsychiatry* 65(3):347–54.

Marshall, Grant, M. A. Burnam, Paul Koegel, G. Sullivan, and Bernadette Benjamin. 1996. Objective Life Circumstances and Life Satisfaction: Results from the Course of Homelessness Study. *Journal of Health and Social Behavior* 37:44–58.

Piazza, Thomas, and Yu-Teh Cheng. 1993. Sample Design for the Study of the Alameda County Residents. Unpublished manuscript. University of California, Berkeley, Survey Research Center.

Piliavin, Irving, Bradley R. E. Wright, Robert D. Mare, and Alex H. Westerfelt. 1996. Exits from and Returns to Homelessness. *Social Service Review* 70(1):33–57.

Rocha, Cynthia, Alice K. Johnson, Kay Y. McChesney, and William H. Butterfield. 1996. Predictors of Permanent Housing for Sheltered Homeless Families. *Families in Society: The Journal of Contemporary Human Services* 77(1):50–57.

Rossi, Peter H. 1989. *Down and Out in America: The Origins of Homelessness.* Chicago: University of Chicago Press.

Rossi, Peter H. 1994. Troubling Families. *American Behavioral Scientist* 37(3):342–95.

Rossi, Peter H., Gene A. Fisher, and Georgianna Willis. 1986. *The Condition of the Homeless of Chicago.* Amherst, MA: Social and Demographic Research Institute and National Opinion Research Center.

Roth, Dee, Beverly G. Toomey, and Richard J. First. 1992. Gender, Racial, and Age Variations among Homeless Persons. In *Homelessness: A National Perspective*, ed. Marjorie J. Robertson and Milton Greenblatt, 199–212. New York: Plenum.

Shinn, Marybeth. 1992. Homelessness: What Is a Psychologist to Do? *American Journal of Community Psychology* 20(1):1–24.

Shlay, Anne B., and Peter H. Rossi. 1992. Social Science Research and Contemporary Studies of Homelessness. *Annual Review of Sociology* 18:129–60.

Snow, David A., Leon Andersen, and Paul Koegel. 1994. Distorting Tendencies in Research on the Homeless. *American Behavioral Scientist* 37(4):461–75.

Sosin, Michael, Irving Piliavin, and Herb Westerfelt. 1990. Toward a Longitudinal Analysis of Homelessness. *Journal of Social Issues* 46(4):157–74.

Stretch, John J., and Larry W. Kreuger. 1992. Five Year Cohort Study of Homeless Families: A Joint Policy Research Venture. *Journal of Sociology and Social Welfare* 19(4):73–88.

U.S. Department of Health and Human Services. 1991. *Homelessness Prevention Programs*. Washington, DC: Office of Policy Development and Research.

Wong, Yin-Ling I. 1995. Family Status, Use of Institutional Resources, and Residential Transitions among the Homeless. Unpublished doctoral dissertation. University of Wisconsin–Madison.

Wong, Yin-Ling I., Dennis P. Culhane, and Randall Kuhn. 1997. Predictors of Exit and Re-Entry among Family Shelter Users in New York City. *Social Service Review* 71(3):441–62.

Wong, Yin-Ling I., and Irving Piliavin. 1997. A Dynamic Analysis of Homeless-Domicile Transitions. *Social Problems* 44(3):408–23.

Wong, Yin-Ling I., Irving Piliavin, and Bradley R. E. Wright. Forthcoming. Residential Transitions among Homeless Families and Homeless Single Individuals: A Comparison Study. *Journal of Social Service Research*.

Wright, James D. 1989. *Address Unknown: The Homeless in America*. New York: A. de Gruyter.

Section 2:

The Causes and Prevention of Homelessness

Introduction
Martha R. Burt

Causes of the Growth of Homelessness During the 1980s
Martha R. Burt

Is Homelessness a Housing Problem?
James D. Wright and Beth A. Rubin

Where the Homeless Come From: A Study of the Prior Address Distribution of Families Admitted to Public Shelters in New York City and Philadelphia
Dennis P. Culhane, Chang-Moo Lee, and Susan M. Wachter

Toward a Comprehensive Homelessness-Prevention Strategy
Eric N. Lindblom

© Fannie Mae Foundation 1997. All Rights Reserved.

Section 2

The Causes and Prevention of Homelessness: Introduction

Martha R. Burt
The Urban Institute

In the early 1980s, as the population of homeless people on the streets of large American cities began to grow enough to become visible to the larger public, there was some hope that the phenomenon would be short-lived and was in some ways "new." A deep recession in 1981–82 had driven the poverty rates several points higher than they had been for a long time, unemployment was extreme, and traditional shelters and soup kitchens were reporting greatly increased demand, plus the presence of "the new homeless"—families with children who could not make ends meet. These circumstances initially suggested that the causes of this spurt of homelessness lay in the recession and related displacements. The passage of time and economic recovery were thought to be the best solutions, but in the meantime private charities and finally the federal government (through the Emergency Food and Shelter Program) responded with short-term measures to ameliorate the obvious distress.

As the decade wore on and, despite economic recovery, homelessness grew rather than disappeared, more questions arose about the possibility that major societal changes might justifiably be examined as possible underlying causes. Some advocates first went for the obvious, citing changes in housing costs and availability as the only cause of homelessness worth talking about, while others noted the high incidence of personal problems and disabilities among the homeless and chose to attribute homelessness to individual characteristics rather than to any of a number of structural causes, alone or in combination. Argument, rather than analysis, raged. And since efforts at prevention or reduction of homelessness hinge largely on theories of what causes it in the first place, various solutions were offered, depending on which causes one favored.

Two of the articles in this section represent efforts of the late 1980s and early 1990s to raise the level of argument to the level of analysis. Martha Burt creates a new database for large U.S. cities, with which she examines the influence of many structural factors on changing levels of homelessness from 1981 through 1989. James Wright and Beth Rubin analyze existing housing availability and cost data, compare them with the capacity of people to afford available housing in the early 1990s, and draw important conclusions about who is most likely to be left out of the housing market. Both articles seek to reconcile arguments that pit structural against personal reasons for homelessness by showing how the situation is not "either-or" but "both-and."

Burt proposes a model whose core is the concept of housing affordability, made up of balance or imbalance between house-hold incomes and housing costs. She identifies a number of factors affecting the income side, including household members' human and social capital, employment, and the availability of public benefits to augment household income. On the housing cost side, she identifies unit costs, unit availability, and public low-income housing policy as proximate factors, along with more remote factors affecting each of these, such as federal tax policy, housing investment policy, and interest rate policy, which affect housing cost and availability although they are not designed with the problem of homelessness in mind. Burt tests her model with data from the 147 U.S. cities that had populations of at least 100,000 in 1986 and were the largest in their counties. She identifies various processes that may produce homelessness in cities with different characteristics, such as a high cost of living and a squeeze on low-cost housing in cities experiencing general prosperity and high growth, or unemployment and generally depressed incomes in cities with stagnant or dwindling econo-mies and population loss.

Wright and Rubin directly address the question of whether homelessness is a housing problem, concluding that homeless-ness is *at least* a housing problem but that the people most likely to experience homelessness are those who are most vulnerable and therefore have the least capacity to weather even a minor crisis and remain housed. The authors therefore come down firmly in the "both-and" camp. They consider separately the circumstances of significant subgroups of homeless persons who have personal characteristics that some advocates have identi-fied as "the" cause of their homelessness, such as mental illness, chemical dependence, familial and social estrangement, and extreme poverty. They document the ways these subgroups have, often as a result of social policy changes, lost mechanisms of support (programmatic or financial) that sustained them in housing in the past. They also document changes in the housing market for the very low cost housing that members of these subgroups could afford. Wright and Rubin conclude that the combination of income loss, public program policy changes (particularly for the mentally ill), and reductions in the availability of low-cost housing units offers a sufficient reason for the increased levels of homelessness seen as the 1980s progressed.

Dennis Culhane, Chang-Moo Lee, and Susan Wachter use the capacities of the New York and Philadelphia shelter-tracking databases for families to address a critical question: Do homeless families come from all over, or even from all locations with many poor people, as might be expected if we believe that homelessness affects a wide spectrum of families? Or are there neighborhoods with particularly high likelihoods of producing homeless families, and if so, what are the characteristics of these neighborhoods? This information could be particularly important for the targeting of prevention efforts, revealing whether such efforts should be spread around a city or concentrated in a few high-risk neighborhoods. Culhane and his colleagues find that the addresses given by homeless families as their dwelling immediately before applying for shelter cluster strongly in certain neighborhoods characterized by extremely poor housing and very high proportions of families headed by young single mothers. Thus, these poorest of poor neighborhoods produce homeless families out of all proportion to the less distressed but still poor neighborhoods on their borders and in other parts of the city. These findings have important implications for service development.

The views and information presented in the first three articles in this section feed directly into the policy recommendations proposed by Eric Lindblom for preventing homelessness in the first place. One can approach the problem of prevention from a short-term or a long-term perspective. A short-term perspective means that one tries to identify people who are about to become homeless and intervenes as close to that moment as possible to forestall their having to go through that last drastic step. A long-term perspective means that one tries to change the social conditions that result in substantial numbers of people being so vulnerable to homelessness that the slightest reversal in their circumstances pushes them over the edge. Lindblom takes the short-term perspective. He carefully examines all the circumstances that might precede an episode of homelessness, considering different conditions that might affect the principal subgroups among the homeless. He suggests ways to identify the people who are vulnerable to imminent homelessness among all the people in those circumstances and describes interventions that could avert the impending crisis if offered in time.

From the perspective of the late 1990s, the policy recommendations presented in this set of articles are impressive in their hope that significant public investment might still be made in programs to prevent or reduce homelessness. Suggestions are made that, if followed, would take a good deal of new money, and such funding would have to be sustained over time unless the underlying conditions pushing people toward homelessness were to change dramatically. It is a measure of how far we have come down the path of lowered expectations for government action that, while many might still believe such massive interventions are necessary, fear of losing credibility and therefore influence would constrain most analysts and advocates from offering as sweeping a set of recommendations today.

Author

Martha R. Burt is the Director of the Social Services Research Program at the Urban Institute. She received her Ph.D. in sociology in 1972 from the University of Wisconsin–Madison. Since then she has been involved in research and evaluation pertaining to a wide variety of populations and issues. Her work on homelessness began in 1983, with an examination of the administrative structure of the first two waves of the Federal Emergency Management Agency's Emergency Food and Shelter Program. In 1987 she directed the first, and still the only, national survey of homeless individuals. That study focused on soup kitchen and shelter users in cities with populations over 100,000 and is reported in *America's Homeless: Numbers, Characteristics, and the Programs That Serve Them* (1989). In 1992 she published *Over the Edge: The Growth of Homelessness in the 1980s*, which analyzes why homelessness became a major social problem in that decade. Also in 1992 she compiled *Practical Methods for Counting Homeless People: A Manual for State and Local Jurisdictions*, which has been widely disseminated and used. She continues to be involved in research and policy work on homelessness and residential instability, analyzing the results from the 1996 National Survey of Homeless Assistance Providers and Clients, which is supported by the Interagency Council on the Homeless and 12 of its federal agencies, and data on residential instability from the National Survey of American Families, which is part of the Urban Institute's Assessing the New Federalism project.

© Fannie Mae Foundation 1991, 1997. All Rights Reserved.

Causes of the Growth of Homelessness During the 1980s*

Martha R. Burt
The Urban Institute

Abstract

This article presents an analysis of the factors that predicted 1989 homelessness rates in large U.S. cities. Data were collected to describe homelessness rates in the 182 cities with populations over 100,000. In addition, variables were assembled to represent many factors that have been hypothesized to cause homelessness, including each city's housing and income conditions, household resources, employment conditions, employment structure, available public benefits, and cost of living. The researcher used regression analysis to assess the impact of each hypothesized causal factor on between-city differences in 1989 homelessness rates for the 147 primary cities in the data set (excluding suburbs) and for subgroup breakouts based on level of manufacturing employment and population growth from 1980 to 1986. The article ends with a discussion of policy implications of the patterns discovered.

The growth of homelessness

For the first time since the Depression in the 1930s, homelessness resurfaced as a source of public concern during the recession of 1981–1982. Unemployment, as well as housing and other policies of the Reagan administration, were blamed at that time. However, such explanations increasingly seem simplistic, given the growth of homelessness during the remainder of the decade. This growth occurred despite the decrease in the official unemployment rate and the economic stability or growth that increasingly characterized the mid- and late 1980s. The pattern of increasing homelessness in the face of seeming national prosperity suggests that potential causes need to be explored at a more sophisticated level than has been done to date.

"Housing affordability" is one of the most frequently named culprits in the rise of homelessness. The assumption is that as housing has become less affordable, homelessness has resulted. This assumption is quite reasonable, but unfortunately for both policymakers and researchers, "housing affordability" is a slippery term. Housing can become more affordable because people

---

*Originally published in *Housing Policy Debate* Volume 2, Issue 3.

earn more but housing costs remain stable, or because people's earnings stay the same but housing costs decrease. It can become less affordable because people earn less although housing costs remain constant, or because people's incomes are constant but housing costs increase. People's incomes may change for many reasons, including unemployment; shifts in the pattern of employment between well- and poorer-paid jobs or between full- and part-time work; changes in eligibility for benefits or in the inflation-adjusted dollar value of benefits; and the availability for employment of more or fewer workers per household. Housing costs may change for equally diverse reasons: because a shortage of housing inflates the price; because building codes require more expensive construction; because national fiscal policy keeps interest rates high; or because localized economic downturns cause a glut of available housing. Each of these potential causes of a change in housing affordability implies a need for a different policy approach. This paper seeks the reasons behind shifts in housing affordability and their relationship to homelessness as a necessary first step in determining which policies to pursue.

However much homelessness may be affected by housing affordability, it will most likely be true that homelessness is *not only* a housing problem. Many of the people who fall off the bottom of the economic ladder may find themselves in this position because their disabilities and deficits (physical, mental, addictive, educational, social) make them more vulnerable and poorer than other people. They still need housing; however, their presence among the homeless represents a failure of social and mental health support programs and the absence of any coordinated efforts that include government housing resources.

With few exceptions, the homeless come from the ranks of the very poor.[1] One may hypothesize that as poverty increases, not only do single individuals find it harder to pay for housing on their own, but the relatives or friends with whom they might share housing are also stretched to the limit and less able to help. This line of reasoning suggests that increasing poverty and the decreasing effectiveness of safety-net programs strain all low-income households, reduce the personal and financial resources available to avert homelessness, and increase the probability of homelessness among the most vulnerable and poorest of the poor.

In discussions of homelessness, the factors consistently mentioned as contributing to the growth of homelessness include shifts in housing availability and affordability, increases in poverty, changes in the structure of the job market, public policy toward people with specific disabilities, and public program benefit levels.[2] In addition, researchers increasingly suspect certain demographic trends of contributing to homelessness, although popular treatments rarely acknowledge them. These trends include increasing age at marriage, decreasing tendency to marry at all, increasing numbers of female heads of families with children, increasing numbers of people living alone, and the confluence of the baby boom generation's coming of age with changing mental hospitalization policy and increasing recreational drug use.

Although policy discussions consistently mention these contributory factors, surprisingly little scientific analysis has been done to document changes in these factors during the 1980s while also making explicit the tie-in to changes in homelessness. The obvious next step for research on the factors contributing to homelessness is to assemble the data that would make possible analysis over time and across jurisdictions. The analysis should meet several criteria. First, it should consider a broad range of potential influences on homelessness. Second, it should be performed with a big enough sample of jurisdictions to reveal associations among important variables. Third, it should simultaneously consider differences in the hypothesized causal factors and differences in rates of homelessness.[3] Work meeting these three criteria is reported in this article.

The various factors hypothesized to cause homelessness were included in a conceptual model depicted graphically in figure 1. At the heart of figure 1 is a relationship between household income and the availability and cost of housing—housing affordability. This relationship is depicted by the (in)equality symbols in the center of figure 1.

The complexities of the model pictured in figure 1 enter when one takes into account the many factors that influence the level of household income, on one side of the equation, and the availability and cost of housing, on the other. The model proposes that household income is influenced by social policy as it pertains to public benefit programs and to the treatment of people with disabilities; by the structure of the job market in a local area, local wages, and local unemployment; and by household resources. The factor "household resources" is in turn multifaceted, and any of its elements may be affected by structural or policy factors. Figure 1 lists household resources that might be expected to influence a household's risk of homelessness, as follows:

Figure 1. **Factors Influencing Homelessness**

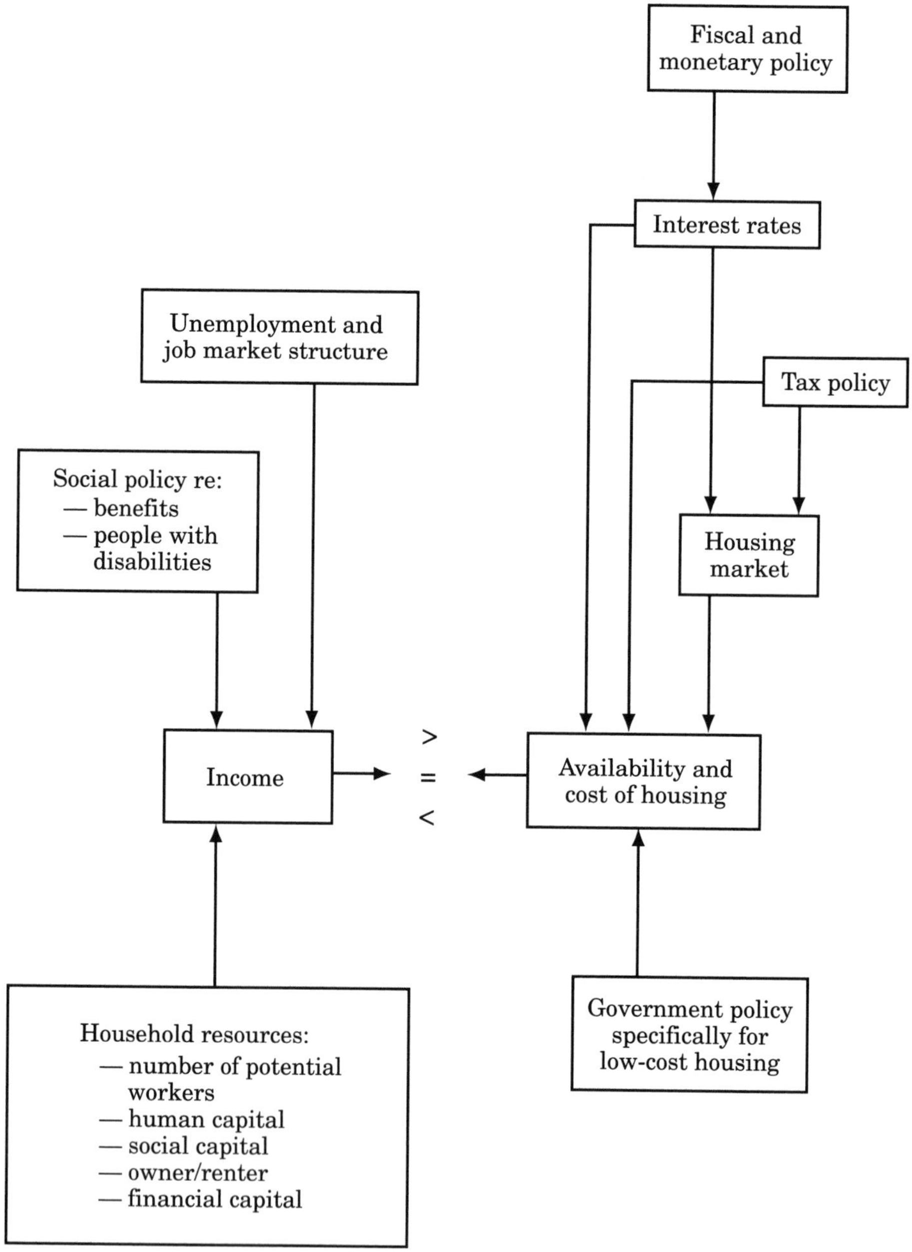

- The number of actual and potential workers in the household;

- The household's human capital (education, physical and mental health, work experience);

- The household's social capital (family resources, friendship resources, participation in supportive neighborhood networks);

- The household's ownership or rental of its dwelling (its physical capital);

- The household's financial capital (savings, pension rights, eligibility for and participation in public benefit programs).

The housing side of the equation is as complex as the income side. In the lower right of figure 1, government policy specifically focused on low-cost housing is shown as an influence on the availability and cost of housing. However, the factors in the upper right quadrant of figure 1 are hypothesized to have equal if not greater influence on housing cost and availability. The model shows fiscal and monetary policy affecting interest rates, interest rates and tax policy in turn influencing the housing market (construction, rehabilitation, maintenance, abandonment), and all three—interest rates, tax policy, and the housing market—affecting housing cost and availability. If these global factors do affect housing cost and availability as hypothesized, an exclusive policy focus on what has happened to targeted low-income housing subsidies may ignore the far more pervasive influences of fiscal, monetary, and tax policies on the housing market.

The model actually estimated (see figure 2) differs somewhat from the complete causal model shown in figure 1. Fiscal, monetary, and tax policies affecting the housing market are not represented because they were constant for the country as a whole and would add nothing to the analysis. In addition, variables had to be selected from the entire data set to represent each element in figure 1. Figure 2 shows the variables included in each block of the model actually estimated.

The income and housing variables shown in figure 2 as the immediate antecedents of homelessness rates parallel the income and housing blocks in figure 1 on either side of the affordability relationship. Both models propose, in effect, that the factors affecting housing affordability also affect homelessness. The blocks of variables to the right in figure 2 are assumed to be

Figure 2. **Causal Model to be Tested, Showing Hypothesized Relationships of Variables in the Data Set**

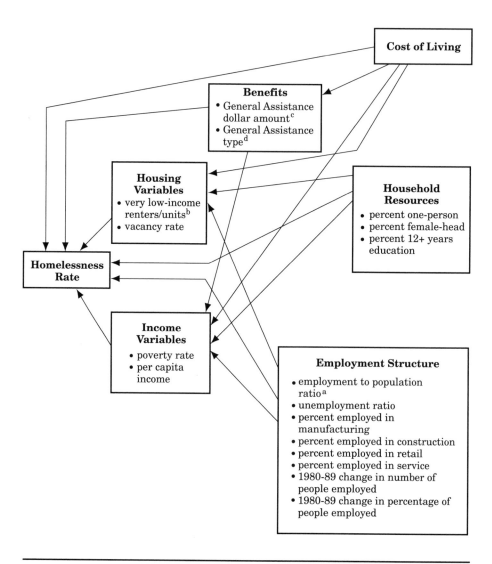

[a] Number of persons employed/total number of persons 16 years of age or older
[b] Ratio of very low-income renters to number of units they can afford, in the state
[c] Maximum dollar amount for single individual living independently
[d] Availability and type of General Assistance program in a particular county

antecedent to, and causal of, the variables to the left. The arrows in figure 2 represent hypothesized causal paths among blocks of variables. The figure 2 model depicts the exogenous variables (those on the right side) as affecting homelessness both directly and indirectly through the income and housing variables.

Methods

The task of assembling data to understand the growth of homelessness in the 1980s was governed by the model in figure 2. Measures were sought to represent each element in figure 2 that could vary among communities (because they were essentially uniform across the country, interest rates and tax policy were not included in the measures used to estimate the model). This effort was part of a larger study examining probable causes of homelessness in the 1980s.[4] The inquiry focused on the 182 U.S. cities that had populations of 100,000 or more in 1986, because the large majority of the nation's homeless are found in these cities.[5]

Because it was important to be able to examine changes in the 1980s that might have contributed to homelessness, data sources were sought that could supply parallel indicators for early and late in the decade. The result is a data set that includes, where available, parallel data elements for the early and late 1980s (usually 1980 and 1987–1989), and that contains variables pertinent to each factor hypothesized to affect homelessness. With the exception of General Assistance program availability and benefit levels and the dependent variable to be used (homelessness rates based on shelter bed counts), the data were all assembled from published sources, federal government statistical agencies, or other researchers' analyses of publicly available data (e.g., the 1980 census, the American Housing Survey). Where possible the data are at the city level. When city-specific data were not available, county-level data were sought. In some instances state-level data are used, either because there is no within-state variation (e.g., Aid to Families with Dependent Children benefit levels) or because no data exist for local jurisdictions.

The dependent variable

No easily available statistics exist on numbers of homeless people in cities, or city homelessness rates, to serve as this study's dependent variable. The only figures that would meet the criteria of availability for early and late in the decade, for the 182 cities over 100,000 in population, and for a consistent method of data collection across cities and years were counts of shelter beds within a clearly defined geographical area for which the population was known (so a rate could be calculated).[6]

To get accurate counts of shelter and voucher-subsidized beds, the research team called virtually every shelter provider in all

182 cities.[7] Initial contact was usually made with the person responsible for the local Comprehensive Homeless Assistance Plan (CHAP) submitted to the Department of Housing and Urban Development (HUD) prior to receipt of HUD's McKinney Act funding. Lists of shelters operating in 1989 were first obtained from the CHAPs, and were supplemented in most instances with lists from local coalitions or coordinators of services for the homeless. Contacts were also obtained for any public or private voucher or payment systems available to the homeless (e.g., for welfare hotels or motels). In most cities, each provider was contacted and asked three questions:

- What is your current bed capacity (or the number of people who get vouchers)?

- When did you open (or when did you first offer shelter services, if the facility had an earlier history of offering different services)?

- What was your bed capacity in 1981?

In several cities (e.g., Boston; Detroit; Washington, DC) the person supplying the list was able to provide answers to all three questions for many facilities. When this happened, the researchers directly contacted only those facilities for which they did not have all the information needed.

The researchers were able to get complete information on 1989 shelter bed capacities. The first official answering the phone at each shelter usually could supply the shelter bed capacity for the shelter's current operations. If not, researchers were referred to the program director, who supplied the data. For the 37 percent of all shelters that had been operating in 1981, the program director was asked to provide information on bed capacity in 1981. The capacity of most shelters is determined by the buildings they occupy. In answering the question, directors often referred to the fact that they were in the same building, and therefore their capacity was the same. They could date program expansion or reduction to a move from one building to another, to renovations on a building that expanded its capacity, or to new licensing or regulatory activity that changed the official capacity. In a number of instances, directors who did not know the shelter's history consulted official records or referred the researchers to past directors.

All shelters were able to report whether the shelter was operating in 1981 or had opened later in the 1980s. If a shelter had

opened after 1981, it was counted as having no beds in 1981.
However, for 12 percent of the shelters opening after 1981
(8 percent of all shelters counted), the researchers could not
learn the opening year. The distribution of shelter openings by
year for the 88 percent of post-1981 shelters with known opening
dates was used to interpolate shelter bed counts for 1983 and
1986 for the remaining 12 percent of post-1981 shelters. Otherwise, a shelter that first opened, for example, in 1984 was
counted as adding all of its 1989 shelter beds to the city's total
bed count in 1984 and was assumed to have maintained those
beds in subsequent years. The researchers also determined
whether or not a shelter was a battered women's shelter. Although many cities list battered women's shelters in their roster
of resources for the homeless, many cities do not, even if they
have these shelters. Because of this inconsistency, battered
women's shelters were excluded from the counts used in this
research.

The independent variables

The independent variables included in the analysis and their
sources are shown in table 1. All of the housing variables included in the data set index characteristics of the local housing
market.[8] The most direct reflection of the mismatch between
rental housing costs and the ability of poor people to pay those
costs is the statewide excess of very low-income renters to rental
units they could afford.[9] This variable is based on 1980 census
income and rent data for metropolitan statistical areas (MSAs).
For the purpose of this study it is a very rough measure, because
it is available only at the state level. It was derived by first
estimating the incomes of households that would qualify as very
low-income renters according to HUD standards, that is, those
with incomes of less than 50 percent of the median renter household income for the MSA. A series of constants was applied to
update these income and rent levels to 1985 equivalents. Rents
were then examined to determine how many units were available
for less than 30 percent of the average very low-income renter
household's income. Although this index was published as a 1985
figure, it is really more appropriate for this analysis to consider
it as reflecting 1980 conditions. The figures are given in terms
of *excess* percentage; "12 percent" means there are 112 very
low-income renter households for every 100 rental units they
can afford at 30 percent of their income.

Low rental vacancy rates are usually taken to mean a local
housing market in which rental housing is scarce and demand

Table 1. Variables in the Analysis

Variable	Year(s) Data Represents	Source
Housing variables		
Rental vacancy rate, 1980[a]	1980	HC, Tables 9 and 12
Rental vacancy rate, 1988	1988	Estimates of National Association of Home Builders, based on 1987 American Housing Survey
Excess of very low-income renters over units they can afford in the state	1980	LIHIS, 1985
Income Variables		
Percentage of persons in poverty	1980	CCDB, city item 40
Per capita income	1979, 1985	CCDB, city items 38;36
Benefits variables		
County General Assistance maximum for one person living independently	1981, 1989	Telephone survey done for this research
Type of General Assistance program in the county	1981, 1989	Telephone survey done for this research
Household resource variables		
Percentage of one-person households	1980	CCDB, city item 18
Percentage of female-headed households	1980	CCDB, city item 17
Percentage of adults 25+ with 12+ years of education	1980	CCDB, city item 34
Employment variables		
Unemployment rate	1980, 1989	PC, Table 120; DOL/BLS unpublished data
Number employed	1980, 1989	PC, Table 120; DOL/BLS unpublished data
Employment-to-population ratio		
no. employed	1980, 1989	PC, Table 120; DOL/BLS
no. 16 and older	1980, 1989	unpublished data

Table 1. **Variables in the Analysis** *(continued)*

Variable	Year(s) Data Represents	Source
Number employed for week of March 12, by sector, for county employment: total, mining, construction, manufacturing, transportation/ communications/utilities, wholesale trade, retail trade, financial/ insurance/real estate, services[b]	1980, 1987	CBP, Table 2
Cost of living	1985-1987	ACCRA

Sources: ACCRA = American Chamber of Commerce Researchers Association, quarterly *Cost of Living Index*; CCDB = *County and City Data Book: 1988*; HC = *Census of Housing, 1980*, HC80-2-58/380; LIHIS = *Low Income Housing Information Service, The Rental Housing Crisis Index*, Washington, DC: LIHIS,1985; PC = *Census of Population, 1980, PC80-1, General Social and Economic Characteristics*; CBP = *County Business Patterns, 1980* and *1987*, U.S. Bureau of the Census, 1982 and 1989; DOL/BLS = Department of Labor, Bureau of Labor Statistics.
Note: All variables are for the city, unless specifically noted.
[a]Vacant rentals divided by vacant plus occupied rentals.
[b]Used to construct the proportion of employment in each sector (e.g., manufacturing employment/total employment = percent manufacturing).

may force prices higher. The rental vacancy rate for 1980 was calculated, using data from the *1980 Census of Housing* for each of the 182 cities,[10] as the number of vacant-for-rent units divided by the sum of the number of vacant-for-rent units plus the number of renter-occupied units. No such calculation was possible for each city for 1988. However, the Census Bureau estimates vacancy rates for the 50 largest MSAs based on the American Housing Survey. These MSAs include a large proportion of all cities with populations over 100,000, and generalization was possible to the remaining cities on the basis of their proximity to MSAs with known rates.

Income variables included the percent of individuals in poverty for each city for 1980 (the only year available) and per capita income for each city for 1979 and 1985. Both variables were taken from the *County and City Data Book: 1988*.[11]

Benefit variables are represented by General Assistance (also called General Relief, Public Relief, Home Relief, Public Aid, and other variations). General Assistance (GA) is probably the public benefit program most relevant to the people at risk of homelessness. Of all the cash assistance benefit programs, it is the only one that may serve single, nondisabled people, and most homeless individuals fall into this category. GA, where it exists, is usually a county program, and individual counties set eligibility criteria as well as benefit levels; a few states operate programs that are consistent throughout the state. The General Assistance grant amount for a single individual living independently was obtained for 1981 and 1989 through a telephone survey of General Assistance offices in the counties serving all 182 cities in the sample (or the independent cities, when they functioned as counties for this purpose). The General Assistance program type was obtained through the same survey and is coded "0" for no program (or emergency one-time grants only), "1" if eligibility is limited to people who cannot work, and "2" if employables are eligible.

Household resources are represented by three variables: the percentage of one-person households in a city, the percentage of households with female heads, and the percentage of adults (25 and older) with 12 or more years of education.[12] These data are available only for 1980.

Employment structure is represented by eight variables. Each city's average unemployment rate for 1980 was taken from the *Census of Population: 1980* for each state.[13] The standard definition of unemployment rate was used for this variable—those people who are out of work but looking for work as a proportion of the labor force (those working plus those looking for work). Parallel data for 1989 were obtained from the Bureau of Labor Statistics, U.S. Department of Labor.

A common criticism of the standard unemployment rate is that it overlooks discouraged workers—those who are no longer looking or never began to look, although they are of working age. Therefore the employment-to-population ratio was also used. This employment-to-population ratio for 1980 for each city was calculated as the number employed divided by city population age 16 and older.[14] Parallel data on number employed in each city for 1989 were obtained from the Bureau of Labor Statistics, U.S. Department of Labor, and used to calculate the employment-to-population ratio for 1989. The "number employed" figures for 1980 and 1989 were also used to calculate the 1980–1989 change in number employed (1989 employment minus 1980 employment) and proportional change in employment (change in number employed/1980 employment).

Services sector employment, manufacturing sector employment, construction sector employment, and retail trade sector employment, each as a percent of total county employment, were obtained for each city's county (or the independent city, if the city and county are one) from each state's *County Business Patterns* for 1980 and 1987.[15] They represent employment for the week containing March 12 in 1980 and 1987 (the latest year available). These four variables represent the sectoral structure of the local labor market.

The final variable included is a very rough measure of cost of living. It was considered essential from a theoretical standpoint to have some measure of cost of living, but no highly reliable measure exists that would differentiate all of the cities in the sample for this study. The only data available are from the *Cost of Living Index,* published quarterly by the American Chamber of Commerce Researchers Association (ACCRA).[16]

Results

Homelessness rates

The information on shelter bed availability was gathered to form the numerator in a homelessness rate. When homeless counts have been turned into rates they usually appear as a rate per 10,000; this study follows that convention. Because all the beds are within the city limits and clearly serve city residents, the denominator is the city population (1980 population for 1981 and 1983 rates; 1986 population for 1986 and 1989 rates). Table 2 gives the city homelessness rates (shelter bed rates) for 1981, 1983, 1986, and 1989.

Taking all 182 cities as a group, homelessness rates tripled between 1981 and 1989, from 5.0 per 10,000 to 15.0 per 10,000. The primary cities had substantially higher rates than the suburbs.[17] In fact, the 1989 rate for the suburbs is still less than the 1981 rate for the primary cities, and the suburban cities did not undertake any major expansion of shelter capacity until 1986.

Table 2 also gives the breakouts of homelessness rates (shelter bed rates) by region and city size for the 147 primary cities in the data base. Cities in the Northeast and West clearly had higher rates from mid-decade onward, although the Northeast began the decade with the lowest rates of any region. City size is not quite as clear a determinant of homelessness rates. If there is any trend by city size, it appears to be that the cities of moderate size (250,000 up to one million) have led in the development

Table 2. **Homelessness Rates by Region and City Size for 1981, 1983, 1986, and 1989**

	Homelessness Rates per 10,000 Population*			
	1981	1983	1986	1989
147 primary cities only				
Region				
Northeast (22)	4.2	8.8	15.3	20.5
Midwest (35)	6.1	7.9	12.3	15.6
South (59)	5.9	7.5	10.2	15.3
West (31)	7.6	10.7	15.4	22.2
City size				
100-249 K (89)	5.7	7.7	11.3	16.2
250-499 K (35)	7.9	10.2	14.9	20.1
500-999 K (15)	4.6	8.9	14.0	20.3
1 million + (8)	4.4	7.5	13.3	18.0
Totals				
All 182 cities	5.0	7.0	10.6	15.0
147 primary cities	6.1	8.4	12.6	17.6
35 suburbs	0.7	1.0	2.2	4.5

Source: Burt, *Over the Edge*, Table 7-4.
Note: Number of cities is shown in parentheses.
* The homelessness rate is calculated by dividing the number of shelter beds in the city by the *city* population (in 10,000s).

of shelters for their citizens, and hence in increases in the homelessness rates according to the measure used here.

To make this concept more concrete, we can consider how many primary cities, and which cities, had extremely low or high rates at different times during the decade. Nineteen cities had rates of zero in 1981, while 31 additional cities had rates of 3 per 10,000 or less. Thus slightly more than one-third of the 147 primary cities had very low homelessness rates in 1981. The number of cities with rates of zero shrank to 13 in 1983, 6 in 1986, and none in 1989. The number of cities with rates of less than 3 per 10,000 (including those with rates of zero) decreased from 50 in 1981 to 31 in 1983, 11 in 1986, and 3 in 1989.

At the high end, only five cities (Atlanta; Grand Rapids, Michigan; Eugene, Oregon; Salt Lake City; and Seattle) had rates of homelessness exceeding 20 per 10,000 in 1981. By 1983 these five had been joined by another six (Birmingham, Alabama;

Boston; Minneapolis; St. Louis; Reno, Nevada; and Yonkers, New York), two of which had rates of over 30 per 10,000. The real growth in shelter capacity can be seen in the big difference between 1983 and 1986 rates. In 1986 there were 24 cities with rates of over 20 per 10,000, again more than doubling the number of cities with rates this high. Eleven of these 24 cities had rates higher than 30 per 10,000; 2 of the 11 exceeded rates of 40 per 10,000.

The final year of the inquiry, 1989, had the largest number of cities with very high rates, as one would expect. Forty-five cities had rates of over 20 per 10,000; of these, 19 cities' rates exceeded 30 per 10,000 and 7 cities (Washington, DC; Atlanta; Boston; Reno, Nevada; New York City; Eugene, Oregon; and Seattle) had rates of over 40 per 10,000. Thus, for the 147 largest cities in the country, the decade saw a shift from 34 percent with homelessness rates under 3 per 10,000 in 1981 to 31 percent with rates over 20 per 10,000 in 1989—a dramatic increase by any standard.

Predicting 1989 homelessness rates

Regression analysis was used to test the adequacy of the causal model presented in figure 2. Table 3 presents the results for the 147 primary cities. In table 3, independent variables are arranged as column headings in the same order as the order in which the groups of variables are displayed to the right of Homelessness Rate in figure 2 (housing and income variables, benefits variables, household resources and employment structure variables, and cost of living). The rows in table 3 also follow this order of presentation. Each row presents the *beta* coefficients of a predictive equation for every variable in figure 2 that has arrows pointing to it, symbolizing that other variables in the model are epxected to affect it. Rows 1 through 6 present these equations for the two benefits variables, two housing variables, and two income variables. Rows 7 through 11 present predictive equations for homelessness rates, each of which includes only one group of predictor variables: benefits variables, household resources variables, employment variables, or cost of living.

Row 12 presents all the potential predictors of homelessness in the full model. Row 13 shows the model eliminating variables that do little to predict homelessness. In deciding which variables to drop for this "best" model, two criteria were used. The first was whether deletion of the variable caused a substantial reduction in the explained variance (R^2); if the reduction was

Table 3. **Antecedents of 1989 Homelessness Rates in Primary Cities (*N* = 147)**

Row No.	Dependent Variable	Independent Variables										
		VLI R/U	Vac. Rate	% Pvty.	PCI	GA $	GA Type	% One	% FH	% 12 Yrs+	Emp/ Pop	% UE
1.	GA $	—	—	—	—	—	—	—	—	—	—	—
2.	GA type	—	—	—	—	—	—	—	—	—	—	—
3.	Vac. rate	—	—	—	—	—	—	-.186	-.372	-.220	.093	.329
4.	VLI R/U	—	—	—	—	—	—	.449	-.512	-.632	-.090	.007
5.	% Pvty.	—	—	—	—	-.018	-.107	.174	.533	-.292	-.255	.077
6.	PCI	—	—	—	—	-.132	-.025	.143	-.077	.455	.267	-.155
7.	HL rate	.089	-.231	.236	.296	—	—	—	—	—	—	—
8.	HL rate	—	—	—	—	.647	-.417	—	—	—	—	—
9.	HL rate	—	—	—	—	—	—	.451	-.085	.109	—	—
10.	HL rate	—	—	—	—	—	—	—	—	—	.148	.112
11.	HL rate	—	—	—	—	—	—	—	—	—	—	—
12.	HL rate	-.209	-.124	.052	-.102	.570	-.413	.235	-.178	.119	.138	.339
13.	HL rate	-.213	-.118	—	-.119	.569	-.417	.248	-.151	.112	.129	.340

Table 3. **Antecedents of 1989 Homelessness Rates in Primary Cities** (*N* = 147) *(continued)*

Row No.	Dependent Variable	% Mfg.	% Cns.	% Rtl.	% Srv.	Change (No.)	Change (%)	COL	R²	AR²
1.	GA $	—	—	—	—	—	—	**.512**	**.262**	.257
2.	GA type	—	—	—	—	—	—	**.400**	**.160**	.154
3.	Vac. rate	**-.224**	.138	-.089	.052	.115	-.038	**-.363**	**.433**	.382
4.	VLI R/U	**.347**	.202	**.511**	.128	**.321**	-.096	.152	**.366**	.261
5.	% Pvty.	**-.164**	**-.147**	.093	.087	-.012	**.301**	-.011	**.789**	.767
6.	PCI	.044	.078	-.052	.018	-.007	**-.192**	**.300**	**.690**	.657
7.	HL rate	—	—	—	—	—	—	—	.130	.106
8.	HL rate	—	—	—	—	—	—	—	.143	.131
9.	HL rate	—	—	—	—	—	—	—	.226	.210
10.	HL rate	**-.243**	-.226	**-.388**	.188	-.113	.072	—	**.294**	.253
11.	HL rate	—	—	—	—	—	—	**.304**	.093	.086
12.	HL rate	-.189	-.113	**-.360**	.115	.133	.147	.113	**.461**	.385
13.	HL rate	-.196	-.120	**-.357**	.111	-.133	.161	.119	**.461**	.390

Source: Burt, *Over the Edge,* Table 9-2.

Notes: A bold coefficient is significant at p = .05 or better; an underscored R^2 indicates an *F* significant at p = 0.5 or better.

HL rate = 1989 homelessness rate per 10,000 city population; VLI R/U = very low-income renters/units (degree of shortage of affordable housing); Vac. Rate = 1988 rental vacancy rate; % Pvty. = 1980 percent of individuals below poverty line; PCI = 1985 per capita income; GA $ = 1989 maximum benefit for single individual living independently; GA Type = none/disabled only/also employables; % One = percent of one-person households in 1980; % FH = percent of households that were female-headed in 1980; % 12 Yrs.+ = percent of population 25 or older who had 12 or more years of education in 1980; Emp/Pop = ratio of employed to population 16 and older, 1989; % UE = percent unemployed, 1989; % Mfg., % Cns., % Rtl., % Srv. = proportion of employment in county that was in the manufacturing, construction, retail, services sector, respectively; Change (No.), Change (%) = 1980-1989 change in people employed in the city, expressed as a number and as a percentage of 1980 employment; COL = cost of living. See text for full description of variables.

2 percent or more, the variable was retained. The second criterion was the significance level of the variable. In general, variables were retained if their significance was $p < .30$. This is obviously a much higher, or less significant, cutoff than the usual $p < .05$. However, a significance level of $p < .30$ still means that the odds are 7 to 3 that the variable is a significant predictor of homelessness. In this exploratory work, it seemed more important to retain possible predictors and understand their action than to reject them. In table 3, variables that meet the conventional significance level of $p < .05$ are indicated by underscoring of coefficients that meet or exceed that criterion.

The final two columns of table 3 present the predictive power of the equation both as R^2, the proportion of variance in the dependent variable explained by the model, and as AR^2 (R^2 adjusted for the degrees of freedom absorbed by the number of variables in the equation).

Effects of each block acting alone

There is much to note in table 3, beginning with the five equations predicting homelessness using each group of variables separately (rows 7–11). The housing and income variables together predict 10.6 percent of the variance in homelessness, but the equation contains some surprises. First, the effect of affordable housing shortages (very low-income renters/units, VLI R/U) is small and nonsignificant, contrary to expectation. Second, rental vacancy and poverty rates behave as expected, with tighter rental markets and higher poverty rates associated with more homelessness. However, per capita income is also positive and significant, meaning that higher per capita incomes and higher homelessness seem to go together. This is contrary to expectation; in fact, because poverty rates and per capita income are negatively related to each other, it is quite surprising to observe that they have the same sign in this equation.[18] Yet in this analysis and in those to follow, poverty rates and per capita income usually display the same sign, whether positive or negative.

General Assistance. General Assistance payment levels (GA $) and type of General Assistance (GA Type) also display anomalous behavior in this analysis of all cities (and will continue to do so). Both are significant, and together they explain 13.1 percent of the variance in homelessness. Higher payment levels predict higher homelessness. This effect appears to occur because the local cost of living drives GA payment levels.[19] Yet even the highest payment levels do not provide enough resources to meet living costs. The effects of the type of GA are negative once payment levels have been taken into account. Cities with no GA seem to have higher homelessness rates than those with some type of GA, and cities whose GA program includes employables as eligibles have lower homelessness rates than those that exclude employables but still serve disabled people and families.

Leaving payment level out of the equation usually reduces the coefficient for GA program type to nonsignificance, whereas leaving out program type merely reduces the size of the coefficient for payment level. The interaction effect suggested by these results is that payment levels supply the larger effect; the type of GA program contributes its importance only after payment levels have accounted for their share.

Household resources. Among household resources variables, which together account for 21.0 percent of the variance in homelessness, the proportion of one-person households in a city is highly significant. The more one-person households, the higher the homelessness. Not only may some one-person households be very vulnerable to homelessness (people living in single-room occupancy [SRO] dwellings are counted as one-person households), but given a fixed number of dwelling units, when more of them are occupied by one-person households, the housing market will be tighter and more people will have to fit into the remaining units. Thus, even if the one-person households are affluent and not at risk of homelessness, their presence may affect the vulnerability of others.

Employment structure. Of the employment structure variables, lower proportions of manufacturing, construction, and retail employment are all associated with higher homelessness. When this set of variables is taken by itself, as it is in row 10 of table 3, it accounts for 25.3 percent of the variance in homelessness. Furthermore, the unemployment rate and employment-to-population ratio are not significant when the employment variables are considered by themselves. Note, however, that the coefficients of both are positive. This is another case, similar to that of poverty rates and per capita income, of two variables with a negative relationship to each other operating in the same direction in a predictive equation. This anomaly, too, persists in subsequent analyses and will be discussed in more detail after all the results are presented. Finally, the higher a city's cost of living, the higher its homelessness; cost of living accounts for 8.6 percent of the variance in homelessness rates.

The full model

Once all sets of predictor variables are combined in an equation representing the full model, together they account for 38.5 percent of the variance in homelessness. The two GA benefits variables, percentage of one-person households, and the size of the retail employment sector retain their influence and significance in this full model. In addition, several interesting and important changes occur. The coefficients of the three significant housing and income variables shrink in size and significance, suggesting that variables earlier (to the right) in the model are responsible for the apparent effects of these housing and income variables on homelessness. Also, the effect of affordability shortages becomes significant and negative, quite contrary to expectation. Finally, the unemployment rate becomes significant, and the effects of several other factors are reduced in size and significance. The "best" model, presented in row 13 of table 3, drops only one variable from the full model—the poverty rate—and the effects of other variables remain essentially what they were in the full model.

Direct and indirect effects

The effects on homelessness of the significant factors in the final equation can be traced through the blocks of other variables in the model, represented in rows 1 through 6 of table 3. Public benefits, represented in the model by General Assistance grant levels and program type, are affected by the cost of living, have a direct effect on homelessness rates, and do not display any indirect effects through the income or housing blocks. Variables in the household resources block affect homelessness both directly and indirectly through income and housing variables. The proportion of one-person households has the most consistent effects, decreasing the rental vacancy rate, increasing the shortfall of affordable units, increasing both poverty and per capita income, and increasing homelessness even when the intervening variables are part of the predictive equation.

Labor force participation variables also appear throughout the model. A higher employment-to-population ratio is negatively associated with the poverty rate and positively associated with per capita income, but has little influence on the housing variables in the model. Higher unemployment and rental vacancy rates occur together, and higher unemployment rates are associated with lower per capita incomes and more homelessness. The sectoral structure of employment also figures prominently, with the proportion of employment in manufacturing contributing to lower vacancy rates and a greater shortfall of affordable units, but also to lower poverty rates and lower homelessness when employment-related variables are considered separately. When cost of living is considered as a sole predictor, it affects benefit levels, vacancy rates, per capita income, and homelessness.

Intervening variables or spurious associations?

Two patterns can be discerned in the set of equations shown in table 3. In one, effects of one antecedent variable that are significant when the variable appears on its own are reduced in the presence of a second, more proximate variable, suggesting that the first variable produces its effect on homelessness through the second variable. The effects of cost of living follow this pattern. Cost of living significantly affects the two benefits variables and homelessness when it appears alone in the equations for each dependent variable. But when the benefits variables and cost of living are all in the equation for homelessness, the benefits variables retain their significance and cost of living loses its direct impact.

In the second pattern, the more proximate variable is significant by itself, but loses its significance in the presence of a second, more antecedent variable. One example of this pattern is the effects of rental vacancy rates in the presence of the percentage of one-person households and the unemployment rate. Both the unemployment rate and the proportion of one-person households significantly predict rental vacancy rates, and rental vacancy rates initially predicted homelessness. However, when all are in the same equation, the effect of rental vacancy rate is reduced in size and significance, but the effects of unemployment are strengthened. This pattern suggests that the initial association of vacancies and homelessness was spurious in a causal sense, because both seem to be caused by their common antecedents of one-person households and unemployment.

Plotting the results

A visual representation of regression results always helps to translate the meaning of coefficients into readily graspable effects (see figure 3). The findings just reported can be used to calculate how much of a difference in homelessness rates would result from a difference in one or more predictor variables. These figures were calculated for all cities using 5, 10, 15, 20, and

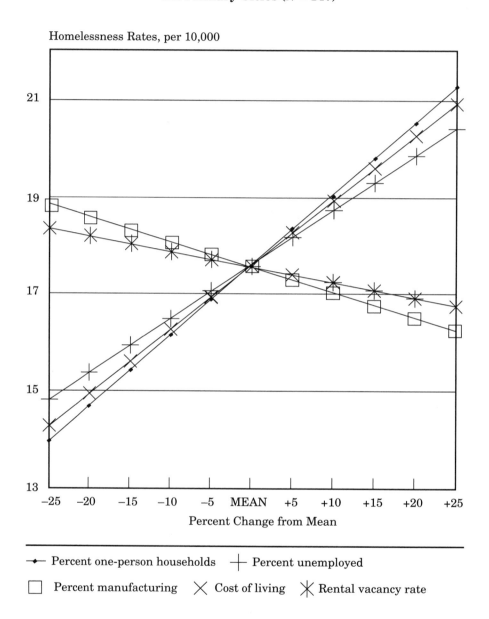

Figure 3. **Predictors of 1989 Homelessness Rates**
All Primary Cities (*N* = 147)

Homelessness Rates, per 10,000

Percent Change from Mean

-●- Percent one-person households   -+- Percent unemployed

☐ Percent manufacturing   ✕ Cost of living   ✳ Rental vacancy rate

25 percent increases and decreases in one-person households,
unemployment and vacancy rates, manufacturing employment,
and cost of living.[20]

The proportion of one-person households has the most dramatic
effect on homelessness, closely followed by the cost of living and

the unemployment rate. A 5 percent difference between cities in the proportion of one-person households (e.g., from the mean of 27.6 to 29.0) predicts a 4 percent shift in homelessness, the equivalent of 0.73 homeless persons per 10,000 city population. A 5 percent difference in the local cost of living has approximately the same effect (a shift of 3.8 percent). Likewise, a 5 percent difference in city unemployment rates (equivalent to adding or subtracting .293 to the mean unemployment rate of 5.86 for these cities) predicts a 3 percent difference in homelessness. The effects of other variables on homelessness are more modest but still apparent. A 5 percent difference in either the rental vacancy rate or the proportion employed in the manufacturing sector produces a 1 percent difference in the homelessness rate.

Subgroup analyses

As informative as the model in table 3 is, it reveals only one pattern of homelessness. Further analysis indicates that the causal antecedents of homelessness differ considerably depending on which subgroup of cities one examines. Several different subgroup breakouts were explored; the two breakouts ultimately selected were chosen because of the substantive importance of the grouping variable, and because the antecedents of homelessness in the two subgroups of cities in each breakout are quite different.

One breakout divides the original sample of 147 cities into two approximately equal groups based on their 1987 proportion of manufacturing employment (17 percent or more, $n = 71$; less than 17 percent, $n = 76$). In 1987, manufacturing employment ranged from 2.6 percent of employed persons to 42.3 percent. The second breakout divides the sample based on cities' population change from 1980 to 1986 (3 percent or more, $n = 68$; less than 3 percent, $n = 79$). During these years, these cities experienced population changes ranging from −11 percent to +47 percent. All but 12 of the 79 low-growth cities experienced population decline or stagnation.[21]

For all cities and for each subgroup breakout, the first panel of table 4 displays the effects on homelessness of the housing and income variables acting alone; the second panel displays the coefficients of the best equation for each breakout. Looking at the first panel, it appears that the effects of vacancy rates, poverty rates, and per capita income noted in the all-cities analysis are derived predominantly from the low-manufacturing and

Table 4. **Comparison of Antecedents of 1989 Homelessness Rates Across Subgroups of Cities**

Dependent Variable = HL Rate	Independent Variables										
	VLI R/U	Vac. Rate	% Pvty.	PCI	GA $	GA Type	% One	% FH	% 12 Yrs+	Emp/ Pop	% UE
Proximate Variables Only											
All cities	.089	-.231	.236	.296	—	—	—	—	—	—	—
High mfg.	.100	-.028	-.005	.093	—	—	—	—	—	—	—
Low mfg.	.121	-.349	.367	.345	—	—	—	—	—	—	—
High growth	.217	-.194	-.107	.075	—	—	—	—	—	—	—
Low growth	-.122	-.222	.465	.527	—	—	—	—	—	—	—
Best Models											
All cities	-.213	-.118	—	-.119	.569	-.417	.248	-.151	.112	.129	.340
High mfg.	.086	—	—	—	.554	-.505	.422	—	.264	—	.268
Low mfg.	-.228	.112	—	—	.422	-.195	.234	—	—	.214	.370
High growth	—	-.601	-.641	-.572	—	-.420	.349	—	—	.293	.693
Low growth	-.123	—	.105	—	.507	-.391	.270	—	.318	—	.195

Table 4. **Comparison of Antecedents of 1989 Homelessness Rates Across Subgroups of Cities** *(continued)*

Dependent Variable = HL Rate	Independent Variables								
	% Mfg.	% Cns.	% Rtl.	% Srv.	Change (No.)	Change (%)	COL	R²	AR²
Proximate Variables Only									
All cities	—	—	—	—	—	—	—	**.130**	.106
High mfg.	—	—	—	—	—	—	—	.021	.000
Low mfg.	—	—	—	—	—	—	—	**.259**	.217
High growth	—	—	—	—	—	—	—	**.160**	.107
Low growth	—	—	—	—	—	—	—	**.197**	.153
Best Models									
All cities	-.196	-.120	**-.357**	.111	.133	.161	.119	**.461**	.390
High mfg.	-.180	-.138	—	—	**-.237**	**.378**	—	**.405**	.306
Low mfg.	—	—	**-.368**	.150	-.109	—	.164	**.611**	.544
High growth	.175	—	—	**.386**	—	-.199	**.269**	**.531**	.438
Low growth	**-.274**	-.138	**-.309**	—	—	—	—	**.510**	.438

Source: Burt, *Over the Edge,* Table 9-7.

Notes: In the "All Cities" models a bold coefficient is significant at $p = .05$ or better; in the subgroup analyses, a bold coefficient is significant at $p = .10$ or better; an underscored R^2 indicates an F significant at $p = .05$ or better.

HL rate = 1989 homelessness rate per 10,000 city population; VLI R/U = very low-income renters/units (degree of shortage of affordable housing); Vac. Rate = 1988 rental vacancy rate; % Pvty. = 1980 percent of individuals below poverty line; PCI = 1985 per capita income; GA \$ = 1989 maximum benefit for single individual living independently; GA Type = none/disabled only/also employables; % One = percent of one-person households in 1980; % FH = percent of households that were female-headed in 1980; % 12 Yrs+ = percent of population 25 or older who had 12 or more years of education in 1980; Emp/Pop = ratio of employed to population 16 and older, 1989; % UE = percent unemployed, 1989; % Mfg., % Cns., % Rtl., % Srv. = proportion of employment in county that was in the manufacturing, construction, retail, services sector, respectively: Change (No.), Change (%) = 1980–1989 change in people employed in the city, expressed as a number and as a percentage of 1980 employment; COL = cost of living. See text for full description of variables.

low-growth subgroups. The subgroup effects of affordable housing shortages seem largely to cancel each other when subgroups are combined in the all-cities analysis.

The picture changes considerably, however, when the remaining variables are added to the model. The vacancy rate, poverty rate, and per capita income effects in low-manufacturing and low-growth cities largely disappear in the presence of the household resources and employment variables. One extreme shift comes in the high-growth cities, with the development of strong negative associations between poverty rates and per capita income and homelessness. The other clear shift is that from small positive associations of the shortage of affordable housing to significant negative associations in low-manufacturing cities and the disappearance of a once significant positive association of the same variable in high-growth cities. These two subgroup changes together produce a significant negative association between affordable housing shortages and homelessness in the all-cities analysis.

The interpretation of these changes in the proximate variables once the remaining variables are included in the equation is important, because there is some danger that these results will be read to mean that affordable housing shortages, poverty, and the other proximate variables are not "really" associated with homelessness. A more judicious reading of the results might be as follows.

There is some association of increased homelessness with lower vacancy rates, higher poverty rates, and higher per capita income in low-manufacturing and low-growth cities, and with more extreme shortages of affordable housing in high-growth cities. In all but high-manufacturing cities, where they have no effect, these proximate variables are able to explain between 11 percent and 22 percent of the variance in 1989 homelessness rates. However, once the more antecedent variables are included, it becomes apparent that some of them are responsible for much of the association between the proximate variables and homelessness. Thus, the proximate variables are important indicators of homelessness, but often are not causal in the context of the model examined in this article. Any policy approach should, therefore, address the conditions represented by the antecedent variables.

The subgroup analyses highlight the very different processes that may produce homelessness under different urban conditions. In low-growth cities (and to a lesser extent in high-manufacturing cities), homelessness seems to be the result of general economic depression. Unemployment, job loss, and poverty are serious contributors to homelessness. But variables that might indicate a squeeze on the poorer population by the more economically advantaged—cost of living and the rental vacancy rate—are not significant. The picture is quite different in high-growth cities. In these cities the evidence suggests that the well-being of the majority of people puts pressure on those who cannot or do not participate in the growth economy. Cost of living is a significant factor in increased homelessness, as is a tight rental housing market (low vacancy rates). Furthermore, a positive employment-to-population ratio coupled with a positive unemployment rate suggests that most adults are working, leaving those who are not to fall further behind the general standard of living. Finally, the association of smaller poverty populations with higher homelessness conveys the picture of small enclaves of poverty unable to obtain consideration of their needs in the midst of a generally prosperous population.

The consistent effects of the proportion of one-person households in the population and of the unemployment rate are shown clearly in the best models in the second panel of table 4. Whoever these one-person households are, even if they are elderly persons and young professionals, their effect on the housing market seems to be strongly related to affordable housing shortages and to homelessness. By occupying units that might house more people, they contribute to the tightening of the housing market. In addition, some of these individuals, such as those in SRO housing, may themselves be vulnerable to homelessness.

The unprecedented levels of unemployment and financial hardship experienced by many households during the recession of 1981–1982 occasioned the first public concern with homelessness as a social issue for the 1980s. Unemployment remains a significant factor contributing to homelessness in every subgroup examined. It is most important in high-growth cities, but its presence is felt everywhere.

Policy makers cannot do much to affect the proportion of one-person households in the population, but they can influence levels of unemployment. Also, more importantly for short-term crises that the unemployed may face, policymakers can create or enhance programs that ameliorate the effects of unemployment until new jobs can be secured. Unfortunately, public policies have moved in the opposite direction during the 1980s. One result of this retrenchment may be increasing homelessness among people with work histories who would have been protected in previous decades.

Discussion

The results of the final models suggest that short-term policy efforts to alleviate homelessness might best be directed toward protecting the poor and near-poor from the effects of both generally depressed economies and economic squeezes. Appropriate mechanisms include ameliorating the immediate impact of unemployment through improved benefits and coverage, providing General Assistance benefits to single employables, improving assistance levels to match local costs of living, and providing more complete coverage of poor households through housing assistance programs. If benefit levels were set high enough, the effects of the cost of living on homelessness might be offset. Similarly, if eligibility for benefits were extended to more poor people, they would have greater resources for coping with increased living costs. The most immediate effect would probably be felt if increased benefits were specifically targeted to subsidizing rental costs in those cities where the cost of housing absorbs unacceptably high proportions of the income of poor households, including one-person households.

Long-term policy attention should be directed toward improving the ability of the disadvantaged to earn enough to achieve a decent standard of living. The two tacks necessary to accomplish this involve improving the human capital of the disadvantaged (including displaced workers) and developing and making accessible the types of jobs that pay a living wage.

Changing a city's employment structure is considerably more difficult to do than taking direct action to change benefit levels. But a more favorable employment structure should reduce poverty and stimulate population growth in the long run. Many cities and states already have very active policies in place to try to increase the availability of well-paid jobs. But these local efforts may not yield as much as would be yielded by a consistent national strategy, if one could be devised, that includes developing human capital as well as increasing investment in plant, equipment, and research and development.

A variety of events and local conditions can precipitate an episode of homelessness for any given person or family. In a few cities, such as New York, Boston, or Los Angeles (where much of the early research on homelessness was done), there may be an actual shortage of units for low-income households. Viewed from these cities, the construction or rehabilitation of low-cost rental units may truly appear to be the cure for homelessness. However, many other cities in the nation have supplies of housing at reasonable cost, but unemployment or the average wage of available jobs reduces household incomes to levels that cannot afford even quite cheap housing. In these cities, the appropriate response would be not to build more housing, but to apply a range of remedies including housing subsidies, job development, retraining of unemployed workers, and supported housing for the disabled. Still other cities are faced with tremendous increases in the drug-addicted population—particularly those addicted to crack—whose members swell the ranks of the homeless. They may need a greatly expanded drug treatment capacity, but they also need the resources to develop programs that offer those most vulnerable to drugs viable alternatives to drug taking.

An examination of the hypothesized causes of the increase in homelessness during the 1980s leads to the conclusion that many societal changes converged during the decade to make it increasingly difficult for poor people to maintain themselves in housing. Few of the factors examined in this paper lend themselves to easy solutions. But most of the factors affect large numbers of Americans in addition to the literally homeless; the existence and extent of homelessness may index the changing fortunes of the United States as a whole.[22] Certainly the policy options that would address the two most intransigent of the factors identified in this paper—employment structure and the increasing mismatch between incomes and cost of living—are also the ones under discussion to recover and maintain a standard of living that many Americans have not seen since the early 1970s. The level of homelessness in the United States shows us how far we have to go.

Author

Martha R. Burt is Director of the Social Services Research Program at The Urban Institute, Washington, DC. This article is based on findings and conclusions from a book, *Over the Edge: The Growth of Homelessness in the 1980s,* by Martha R. Burt (New York and Washington, DC, Russell Sage Foundation and Urban Institute Press, 1991).

Endnotes

1.   Martha R. Burt and Barbara E. Cohen, *America's Homeless: Numbers, Characteristics, and the Programs that Serve Them* (Washington, DC: The Urban Institute Press, 1989); Peter H. Rossi, *Down and Out in*

America: The Origins of Homelessness (Chicago: University of Chicago Press, 1989); Michael R. Sosin, Paul Colson, and Susan Grossman, *Poverty and Pathology, Social Institutions and Social Change* (Chicago: Chicago Community Trust, 1988).

2.   Michael S. Carliner, "Homelessness: A Housing Problem?" in *The Homeless in Contemporary Society,* Richard D. Bingham, Roy E. Green, and Sammis B. White, eds. (Beverly Hills: Sage, 1987); Institute of Medicine, Committee on Health Care for Homeless People, *Homelessness, Health and Human Needs* (Washington, DC: National Academy Press, 1988); H. Richard Lamb, "Deinstitutionalization and the Homeless Mentally Ill," in *The Homeless Mentally Ill: A Task Force Report of the American Psychiatric Association,* H. Richard Lamb, ed. (Washington, DC: American Psychiatric Association, 1984); F. Stevens Redburn and Terry F. Buss, *Responding to America's Homeless: Public Policy Alternatives* (New York: Praeger, 1987); Rossi.

3.   The data collected by the Department of Housing and Urban Development (HUD) in 1984. (*A Report to the Secretary on the Homeless and Emergency Shelters,* Washington, DC: Department of Housing and Urban Development, Office of Policy Development and Research, 1984) were used as the basis for four intercity analyses of homelessness rates. These are William Tucker, "Where Do the Homeless Come From?" *National Review* (September 25, 1987): 32-43; Richard P. Appelbaum, Michael Dolny, Peter Dreier, and John Gilderbloom, "Scapegoating Rent Control: Masking the Causes of Homelessness" (Washington, DC: Economic Policy Institute, Briefing Paper, December 1989); John M. Quigley, "Does Rent Control Cause Homelessness? Taking the Claim Seriously," *Journal of Policy Analysis and Management* 9 (1990): 88-93; Marta Elliott and Lauren J. Krivo, "Structural Determinants of Homelessness in the United States," *Social Problems* 38 (1991): 113-131. HUD collected data on homelessness in 60 Rand-McNally statistical areas. Each of the four studies used only 40 to 50 of these areas for its analysis. The first three studies were concerned with the effects of rent control on homelessness; the last was concerned with general causes of homelessness. All used very simple models that included only a limited range of potential causal factors, and each used only one change factor (Tucker—rent control plus one additional variable; Quigley—rent control plus five other variables; Appelbaum—rent control plus seven other variables; Brown and Krivo— seven or eight variables in initial models, four or five variables in final models).

4.   Martha R. Burt, *Over the Edge: The Growth of Homelessness in the 1980s* (New York and Washington, DC: Russell Sage Foundation and The Urban Institute Press, 1991). This book provides a review of major housing, income, employment, public benefit, and mental health/chemical dependency policy changes during the 1980s, along with more extensive analysis of the causes of 1989 homelessness rates and the change in rates from 1981 to 1989.

5.   Cities were selected as the unit of analysis for two reasons: (1) There are more of them, so the sample size could be large enough for more complex analyses; and (2) cities were the most reasonable jurisdiction for which, with reasonable effort, I could get accurate counts of shelter beds for both 1981 and 1989 to provide the basis for the dependent variables—

homelessness rates per 10,000 population, and the change in rates between 1981 and 1989.

6. The flaws in this measure are numerous. They are described here so the reader will understand the biases inherent in this measure, as in any other measure of homelessness currently available.

The problems with the measure lie in its unknown relationship to the true number of homeless individuals in a given jurisdiction, and in its confounding of local responsiveness to the homeless problem (by building shelters) with the extent of the problem itself. There is also its potential for missing some shelters that existed earlier in the decade but which had gone out of business by 1989 and therefore were not on any lists.

The first problem is that, on any given night, many homeless people do not use shelters, so the shelter bed count will underestimate the true number of homeless people. A corollary problem is that different communities have undertaken the development of shelters at different rates, so there is every reason to believe that the ratio of shelter beds to the true number of homeless people will differ in each city by an unknown amount. If the issue were the development of a national estimate of the number of homeless, the number of shelter beds could be multiplied by some factor to account for the unsheltered. But the issue of interest in this study was the intercity associations of rates with other variables. In the absence of an accurate correction factor for each city, no multiplier was applied to the shelter bed counts obtained, because such a multiplier would only magnify each city's shelter bed count by a constant that would be the same across all cities.

Another problem with the measure is that the official bed count for a facility may be an inaccurate reflection of the number of homeless individuals served even for the facility itself. It may be too high (if the shelter operates at less than 100 percent capacity most of the time) or too low (if the shelter operates at overflow capacity most of the time). The overflow part of this problem was handled by recording separately the excess number of people sheltered at peak times, if a shelter accepted people beyond its official capacity. Rates were calculated with and without these overflow capacities, but the issue was dropped when no differences emerged in the results of regression analyses with the two different sets of rates. If a given facility was an "overflow shelter," operating only at peak demand, its entire capacity was included as a regular shelter. The same was true for shelters that operated only in the winter. No attempt was made to correct for underutilization of shelters (shelters operating below capacity), because any count of shelter beds would underrepresent the city's total homeless population, and reducing the estimate still further to correct for underutilization seemed unnecessary.

Quite a different issue is whether any measure based on shelter bed counts reflects the actual level of homelessness, or only a jurisdiction's willingness or ability to respond to the problem. There is plenty of evidence that some jurisdictions have been reluctant to open shelters. In some cities, lawsuits were required to make the city respond to the need for shelters. These realities probably mean that shelter counts from early in the decade are a more highly variable reflection of the true underlying rate of homelessness than are later shelter counts.

Even with all of the problems with using shelter bed counts as a measure of homelessness, for the purpose of the present study they will suffice, if one can have confidence that homelessness rates based on these counts provide a reasonably accurate reading of the relative degrees of homelessness in different cities. This confidence is bolstered by two correlations that can be calculated from data that provide independent readings of shelter beds and numbers of homeless people. The 1987 study by Burt and Cohen (*America's Homeless*) provides one of these correlations. That study obtained readings on the number of shelter beds from interviews with providers, and on the number of homeless individuals from interviews with homeless people. The correlation between the two was .934. The second correlation is based on 42 of the 60 cities that were in the sample used in HUD's 1984 study; these 42 cities are also in the universe for the present study of cities over 100,000. Calculations using the midpoint of HUD's "most reasonable range" of estimates of the homeless population for these 42 cities and the 1983 shelter bed counts obtained for the present study showed that their zero-order correlation was .827. These two very strong correlations lend credence to the use of homelessness rates based on shelter bed counts for the purposes of the present study.

The method used to obtain shelter bed counts relied on lists of shelters operating in 1989. It is likely that some shelters in existence prior to 1989 had closed their doors by early 1990, when the data were collected for this study. They would, therefore, not be included on the lists used to contact shelters, and our methods would have omitted them from the counts in the years during which they did operate. Although it is almost certain that this happened, it is also very likely that the number of shelter closings was small and that the consequent undercount of shelter beds in earlier years is very small when considered in light of the overall growth in shelter capacity. Virtually every city in the country was straining to supply shelter beds during the 1980s; the story is overwhelmingly one of growth, both in the number of new shelter facilities and in the capacity of existing facilities.

7.   The enormous number of telephone calls this involved was supported by grants from the Federal National Mortgage Association and from the Rockefeller Foundation. Christopher Vaz and Garth Green made the calls, with help from Laura Bonanomi and Jennifer Parker.

8.   The model in figure 1 also shows governmental housing policies as affecting the local housing market. The two measures of these policies contained in the data set—per capita public housing units (1981 and 1989) and per capita Section 8 units (1981 and 1989)—were excluded from the analysis because of their strong associations with a city's poverty rate, and the resulting problems of multicollinearity.

Rent control was considered but not selected for inclusion as a variable. From a pragmatic viewpoint, most of the cities in the data set would have had values of zero, because only a few have any type of rent control. From a theoretical viewpoint, the work of Appelbaum et al. ("Scapegoating Rent Control") and Quigley ("Does Rent Control Cause Homelessness?") has demonstrated the inadequacies of Tucker's analysis of rent control and homelessness ("Where Do the Homeless Come From?").

9.   Low Income Housing Information Service, *The Rental Housing Crisis Index* (Washington, DC: Low Income Housing Information Service, 1985).

10.   U.S. Bureau of the Census, *Census of Housing (HC80-2)* (Washington, DC: U.S. Government Printing Office, 1982). For each city, the number of vacant-for-rent units was obtained from table 12; the number of units currently occupied by renters was obtained from table 9.

11.   U.S. Bureau of the Census, *County and City Data Book: 1988* (Washington, DC: U.S. Government Printing Office, 1988).

12.   Census Bureau, *County and City Data Book: 1988.*

13.   U.S. Bureau of the Census, *Census of Population* (Washington, DC: U.S. Government Printing Office, 1982), for each state, table 57.

14.   Data come from *Census of Population: 1980* for each state, table 57.

15.   U.S. Bureau of the Census, *County Business Patterns: 1980; County Business Patterns: 1987* (Washington, DC: U.S. Government Printing Office, 1982; 1989), table 2.

16.   American Chamber of Commerce Researchers Association (ACCRA), *Cost of Living Index* (Alexandria, VA: ACCRA, 1985–1987). Every quarter, members of the Chambers of Commerce in more than 200 cities price a consistent "shopping bag" of goods and services (including housing). Cities of all sizes participate, including many that are not in the data base for this study. The ACCRA index reported is based on the number of cities participating for the quarter—a number that varies from quarter to quarter. The index is calculated by taking the average cost of the shopping bag for all cities participating for that quarter as 100, and showing the deviations from that average. It thus measures the relative cost levels for consumer goods and services in participating areas. A city with a very high cost of living compared with that of other cities participating in that quarter might have an index of 130; a city with a low cost of living might have an index of 94.

   The index figures are not strictly comparable across quarters, because the average depends on which cities are included for the quarter. It would thus be best to take all the data from a single quarter's reports. This was not possible because some of the cities in the sample for this study did not report to ACCRA in every quarter, or even in every year. The base period for the data used in this study was the fourth quarter of 1985; data were sought only for the 147 primary cities in the sample. The ACCRA report for the fourth quarter of 1985 contained information for about 75 percent of these 147 cities. It was therefore necessary to take some data from other quarterly reports, staying as close to the fourth quarter of 1985 as possible. This combining of ACCRA data from different quarters is not strictly legitimate, but without it there could be no cost-of-living indicator in the data base. It was hoped that the cities' standings relative to each other would not vary so much from quarter to quarter that combining the data from different quarters would constitute a great distortion. As will be seen, this cost-of-living indicator, however rough, does relate to other variables as one would expect.

17. When a county included more than one city with a population of 100,000 or more, the largest city in the county was designated the "primary city"; the remainder were designated "suburbs." Examples of primary cities and suburbs, respectively, include Miami and Hialeah; Dallas and Plano; Phoenix and Scottsdale; San Diego and Chula Vista; Los Angeles and Inglewood.

18. If individuals or households were the unit of analysis, this would not happen. But the unit of analysis here is cities; and it is quite possible for some people in cities to be poor while the higher incomes of others have the effect of raising the average per capita income.

19. Other than cost of living, region is the most important factor affecting GA payment levels (including levels of zero for counties that have no GA program). Payment levels are higher in the Northeast and West, and lower in the South. So is homelessness, as shown in table 2. Together, cost of living and region produce an adjusted R^2 of .628 for 1989 GA payment levels. These regional differences themselves are proxies for the political philosophies and histories of local governments.

20. These calculations were made to translate the results into readily comprehensible and comparable effects of each predictor variable on homelessness. Simply plotting standardized regression coefficients would be one way to do this, but standard deviation units are not readily comprehensible by a lay audience. As a more intuitive substitute, the percentage change in each of five important predictors was plotted. For variables with low mean values, such as the unemployment rate (5.86) and the rental vacancy rate (9.06), a 5 percent difference (.293 and .453, respectively) is quite small. For variables with higher mean values, such as the percentage of one-person households (mean of 27.6), a 5 percent difference (1.38) is larger. Yet the meaning of a 5 percent difference is the same in both cases, giving us the ability to compare the size of the effects of each variable in graphic form.

21. The relationship between the two variables used to create subgroups— proportion of manufacturing employment and a city's population growth or decline—is significant ($r = -.401, p < .001$). The chi-squared statistic for the two-by-two association of high or low manufacturing with high or low growth is 14.10 ($p = .0002$), with most high-manufacturing cities being low-growth and most low-manufacturing cities being high-growth. But 30 percent of high-manufacturing cities grew enough during the first half of the 1980s to be categorized in this analysis as high growth, and 31 percent of high-growth cities are categorized as high manufacturing. Among low-manufacturing cities, 37 percent are low growth by the definitions used here, and about 38 percent of low-growth cities are low-manufacturing. These differences are enough to make analyses of both subgroup breakouts interesting.

22. See, for example, Gary Burtless, ed., *A Future of Lousy Jobs? The Changing Structure of U.S. Wages* (Washington, DC: The Brookings Institution, 1990); Council on Competitiveness, *America's Competitive Crisis: Confronting the New Reality* (Washington, DC: Council on Competitiveness, 1987); Michael L. Dertouzos, Richard K. Lester, Robert M. Solow, and the MIT Commission on Industrial Productivity, *Made in America: Regaining the Productive Edge* (Cambridge: The MIT Press, 1989); Frank Levy and Richard C. Michel, *The Economic Future of American Families: Income*

and Wealth Trends (Washington, DC: The Urban Institute Press, 1991); Benjamin Friedman, *Day of Reckoning: The Consequences of American Economic Policy in the 1980s* (New York: Random House, 1988); William Greider, *Secrets of the Temple: How the Federal Reserve Runs the Country* (New York: Simon & Schuster, 1988).

© Fannie Mae Foundation 1991, 1997. All Rights Reserved.

Is Homelessness a Housing Problem?*

James D. Wright and Beth A. Rubin
Tulane University

Abstract

Homeless people have been found to exhibit high levels of personal disability (mental illness, substance abuse), extreme degrees of social estrangement, and deep poverty. Each of these conditions poses unique housing problems, which are discussed here. In the 1980s, the number of poor people has increased and the supply of low-income housing has dwindled; these trends provide the background against which the homelessness problem has unfolded. Homelessness is indeed a housing problem, first and foremost, but the characteristics of the homeless are such as to make their housing problems atypical.

Introduction

The question of whether homelessness is a housing problem is perhaps best approached by asking, If homelessness is not a housing problem, then what kind of problem might it be? Most agree that the number of homeless people in the cities increased significantly in the 1980s. Was there any corresponding decline in the availability of low-cost housing? What besides a dwindling low-income housing supply would account for the trend? Even if one concludes that homelessness is not *just* a housing problem, there seems to be little doubt that inadequate low-cost housing must have something to do with the problem, and it is useful to ask just what that "something" is.

Superficially, the answer to our question is both clearly yes and obviously no. Homeless people, by definition, lack acceptable, customary housing and must sleep in the streets, double up with friends and family, or avail themselves of temporary overnight shelter. The lack of acceptable housing, in short, is implied in the very definition of homelessness. On the other hand, it can be argued that housing is not the real problem, because there is plenty of housing to go around. The problem, instead, is that homeless people cannot afford the housing that is available to people of sufficient means.[1] In this sense, homelessness is not a housing problem but a money problem; the root causes are

---

*Originally published in *Housing Policy Debate* Volume 2, Issue 3.

poverty, unemployment and underemployment, inadequate wages, and the insufficient income provisions of the welfare state.[2] It is, of course, foolish to pose the question in these either/or terms. A more useful question concerns the intersection of housing and economics and can be phrased thus: To what extent is the problem of homelessness caused by an insufficient supply of housing of the sort that homeless people need and could afford to live in?

Homeless people themselves readily identify the lack of housing and money as the source of their troubles. Ball and Havassy asked a sample of homeless people in San Francisco to identify "the most important issues you face or problems you have trying to make it in San Francisco or generally in life."[3] The most common responses were "No place to live indoors" (mentioned by 94 percent), followed by "No money" (mentioned by 88 percent). No other response was chosen by as much as half the sample.

Housing and money are by no means the only problems homeless people face. Many are mentally ill, many more are chemically dependent, some are physically disabled, and most are profoundly estranged from family and friends.[4] And, of course, they are among the poorest of the poor, surviving on a mere fraction of the poverty level income in most cases. These characteristics are of critical importance in specifying exactly what kind of housing problem homelessness is, but they do not negate the principal conclusion, that the most fundamental need is for housing.

If not housing, what?

What kind of problem might homelessness be, if not a housing problem? One common although profoundly wrong theory can be dismissed at once—the opinion expressed by Ronald Reagan and others that the homeless are homeless by choice. The implication of this viewpoint is that homelessness results from an exercise of personal will, not from mental illness, substance abuse, or an inadequate supply of low-income housing. In this view, homelessness is simply not a problem and the homeless are perceived, perhaps, as romantic vagabonds who have traded the rat race of modern urban civilization for a life uncomplicated by mortgage or rent payments, ringing telephones, surly bosses, nagging spouses, and truculent children.

However widespread such a viewpoint may be, no credible scholar who has studied the problem of homelessness takes it seriously. One does read occasionally about a homeless person with a locker full of cash in the bus station, or about a former Wall Street stockbroker who cashed it all in for the romance of life on the road, but in the overwhelming majority of cases, homeless people live as they do because they lack the means to live in any other way, not because they have positively chosen a life of destitution and degradation over some attainable alternative means of living.

Consider what a homeless person would choose by choosing to be homeless. The rate of AIDS infection among the homeless exceeds that in the general population by a factor of 10; the rate of sexual assault on homeless women exceeds that of women in general by a factor of 20; the rate of tuberculosis among the homeless exceeds that in the population at large by a factor of about 100; and the average age of death for homeless men is somewhere around 53 years old.[5] One does not "choose" to sleep in the gutters or scavenge food from Dumpsters.

The 1980s witnessed an impressive outpouring of research on who the homeless are, how they got to be homeless, and what could or should be done to help them. This research has not answered every outstanding question, but a substantial number of issues have been put to rest. One surprising result from this decade of research is that the homeless are not a homogeneous population. The homeless prove to be men, women, and children; young, middle-aged, and old; black, white, Hispanic, and Asian. Some are veterans, others are not. Many are mentally disturbed, many are astonishingly lucid. Half abuse alcohol and drugs, the other half do not. Some receive welfare benefits, most do not. In searching for the causes of homelessness, one looks for common threads woven through the lives of most homeless people, and these, it seems, are three in number:

First, rates of personal disability among the homeless are extremely high. About a third are mentally disabled; about a tenth are physically disabled; about half are substance abusive. Probably two-thirds to three-quarters of the total suffer from one or more of these conditions.[6] Other than lack of housing, these alcohol, drug, and psychiatric problems are probably the most commonly cited causes of homelessness; thus, these issues are taken up in detail later, mostly because they have obvious implications for the kind of housing problem the disabled homeless face.

Second, homeless people routinely show high levels of family and social estrangement. Few have ever been married; most who have been married were subsequently separated or divorced. Contact with the family of origin is minimal to nonexistent in most cases; indeed, many become homeless when their families can no longer support them. Lacking the safety net of familial and other social ties, they have nothing to catch them when they stumble, so they fall into the shelters and streets.

Finally, the homeless are characterized by extreme poverty. Many have no regular or steady means of support and live day to day by availing themselves of free food at the soup kitchens, clothing at the missions, and beds in the shelters. Among those with any income, the average income is somewhere between 25 percent and 40 percent of the poverty level for a single individual.[7] The exceedingly low income levels characteristic of the homeless have obvious implications for their housing needs, because even most low-income housing is priced well beyond their means.

There is, of course, a fourth commonality to emphasize: because of their extreme poverty, personal disabilities, and social estrangement, all homeless people are unable to secure or retain adequate housing. Is this to suggest, then, that homelessness is not a housing problem, but rather a poverty problem, a disability problem, and an estrangement problem? Surely not: instead, these facts explain why homelessness is a housing problem at its very core, and they also help to explain just what kind of housing problem homelessness is.

Mental illness

It is often argued that homelessness is mainly a mental health problem, one caused in substantial measure by inadequate discharge planning during the process of deinstitutionalization and by other related changes in society's treatment of the mentally ill. Supporting this interpretation is the now commonplace finding that the rate of psychiatric disorder is sharply elevated among the homeless compared with the domiciled population, especially among homeless women.[8] At the same time, only about a third of the homeless have clinically significant psychiatric disorders, leaving two-thirds whose homelessness must result from other factors altogether. It would be misleading to suggest that homelessness is mainly a mental health problem when most of the homeless are not mentally ill.

It is wrong to infer from the high rate of psychiatric disturbance among the homeless that homelessness is a mental health problem and, therefore, not a housing problem. The better conclusion is that many mentally ill people have housing needs that are not being adequately addressed and they are, therefore, homeless. Obviously, the housing needs of mentally ill homeless people are quite different from the housing needs of other homeless persons or of the poor in general, as was recognized at the beginning of the deinstitutionalization movement. The initial plan was to provide a large network of halfway houses, supported housing options, and community-based mental health centers to address the unique needs of the deinstitutionalized population. Although deinstitutionalization itself proceeded apace, and even accelerated during the sixties and seventies, little of this intended network was ever put in place; as a consequence, many former mental patients were returned to families and communities only to find that their families were unwilling or unable to provide for their care and that their communities lacked adequate provisions for their unique housing and other needs.

The housing problem posed by the existence of large numbers of mentally ill homeless people is that the current supply of supported, transitional, and extended-care housing for the mentally disturbed is insufficient or, in many places, simply nonexistent; the absence of an adequate supply of such housing is exactly why so many mentally ill people are homeless in the first place.

The housing problems faced by the mentally ill homeless cannot be addressed by the simple expedient of more flophouses or public housing projects. Adequate housing for this group requires on-site supportive social and psychiatric services, and because few could afford to pay rent, the necessary subsidies would be deep. These points, of course, only specify the nature of the housing problem that mentally ill homeless people face; they do not imply that the housing problem is of lesser causal significance than mental illness.

Stated simply, people do not become homeless just because they are mentally ill. Mentally ill people become homeless because housing that meets their needs is in extremely short supply and because they do not have sufficient financial resources to translate their evident needs into a housing demand that would stimulate additions to the supply. In the absence of capable advocacy and case management, the homeless mentally ill fall easily through the cracks—and the housing crack is one that they have fallen through in distressingly large numbers. It is, of course, correct to say that the mentally ill homeless require more than just housing, but it is also correct to say that the absence of acceptable housing lies at the root of their problems.

Indeed, it is a reasonable assumption that until the housing situations of homeless mentally ill persons are stabilized, efforts to address their many other problems will be largely fruitless. By themselves, counseling, therapy, and psychotropic medication cannot compensate for the psychic anguish and mental disordering that result from life on the streets. The point is that in the absence of acceptable housing options along the lines sketched above, society cannot adequately address even the mental health problems of the homeless mentally ill, much less their housing, financial, and other problems.

Alcohol and drug abuse

Next to mental illness, alcohol and drug abuse are commonly cited causes of homelessness, but most of what has just been said about mental illness also applies to substance abuse. As with psychiatric disturbance, rates of alcoholism and drug dependence among the homeless are admittedly quite high, on the order of 50 or 60 percent.[9] But 40 or 50 percent are not substance abusers, and their homelessness must, therefore, result from other factors.[10]

Also in parallel with the case of mental illness, it is misleading to conclude from the high rate of substance abuse among the homeless that homelessness is mainly an alcohol and drug problem and, therefore, not a housing problem; the better conclusion is that alcohol- and drug-abusing poor people have great difficulties maintaining their hold on acceptable housing and, therefore, become homeless in disproportionate numbers.

Homeless alcoholic men and women have existed in all times and places throughout American history; this aspect of the larger homelessness problem is scarcely new. In times past, however, most urban areas contained an informal social system that provided for the housing and other needs of the alcohol-abusing poor, the system called skid row. Skid row areas, of course, continue to exist; indeed, these are the places where the homeless tend to concentrate in most cities. But if skid row areas continue to exist, the skid row social system has all but disappeared; this disappearance has posed a formidable housing problem for the homeless alcohol- and drug-abusive poor.[11]

Skid row was always inhabited by unattached, unaffiliated single men, many of them alcoholic. There were many significant elements to the old skid row, but two are of particular interest: the flophouses, rooming houses, missions, and similar places that provided extremely cheap housing to the skid row population, and the day-labor outlets that provided casual employment.

The employment provided through the day-labor outlets was largely unskilled work; loading and unloading trucks, trains, and boats was perhaps the most common form of employment. The income to be earned through such work was minimal. At the same time, the flops were extremely cheap, and cheap meals were also widely available. Often, rooms could be rented for as little as 50 or 60 cents a night; a dime would purchase a sandwich and a cup of coffee. In those times and in that particular social system, one could pick up a dollar or two a day working at casual labor; more to the point, one could get by on a dollar or two a day. It was unquestionably a poverty-level existence, but it provided some level of nutrition and housing, even for the alcohol-dependent.

The single-room occupancy (SRO) hotels and the flophouses, of course, have largely disappeared, victims of urban renewal, gentrification, and the "revitalization" of downtown areas. Hartman and Zigas estimate that these processes have resulted in the loss of over one million units of SRO housing in the past two decades.[12] Some of the city-by-city figures are of interest: In San Francisco, 17.7 percent of the existing SRO units were destroyed or converted in a four-year period in the late 1970s, with further losses since. Similarly, in New York City there was an overall 60 percent loss of SRO hotel rooms between 1975 and 1981. The number of New York hotels charging less than $50 per week declined from 298 to 131 in that period; of hotels dropping out of that price range, the majority are no longer even hotels and have been converted to other uses, mainly to condominiums. Denver lost 29 of its 45 SRO hotels between 1971 and 1981, Seattle lost 15,000 units of SRO housing from 1960 to 1981, and San Diego lost 1,247 units between 1976 and 1984. The loss of SRO housing was described as a nationwide trend even in the late 1970s, a trend that has doubtless accelerated since.[13]

Day-labor outlets have also been disappearing. Most of the work once done by day laborers has been mechanized; many hundreds of thousands of day-labor opportunities were wiped out by the invention and widespread adoption of the forklift truck, by containerized shipping, and, of course, by the unions. The unionization of the construction and stevedore industries in particular has made day labor in these sectors obsolete. The function formerly served by the day-labor outlets has been assumed by large "temporary-help" corporations such as Manpower. These are sanitized temporary-help outlets located far from the skid row areas; they are no longer part of the skid row social system, at least not in most North American cities.

Thus, the flops and the SRO hotels of skid row are largely gone, their housing function taken over by the large, temporary over-night shelters that now exist in nearly every city. Opportunities for casual day labor are also largely gone, and the income-generating function of casual labor has been replaced by scav-enging from trash cans and panhandling. The social system of skid row, in short, has been replaced by the disorganized exist-ence of homelessness, and nowhere has this change been more problematic than among the alcohol- and drug-abusing homeless. With the housing of last resort now decimated, the alcoholic and drug-addicted poor end up living, essentially, in the streets.

Thus, in the final analysis, the homelessness of the alcoholic and drug-dependent, like that of the mentally ill, is also a housing problem, although here too, the nature of the housing problem is unique. If homeless alcoholics or addicts are no longer going to live in skid row, out of the sight and mind of society at large, then they will have to live among us, and this in turn requires reintegration into the norms and behaviors of normal middle-class society. Thus, to understand the exact nature of the hous-ing problem of chemically dependent homeless people requires an understanding of the alcohol and drug treatment programs that are normally available to those of limited means.

In most cities homeless alcohol and drug abusers who seek treatment can normally be placed, after a waiting period of weeks to months, in three- to seven-day detoxification programs. These programs provide an opportunity to get clean or sober (or often, both), food and shelter for the duration of the program, some introduction to Alcoholics Anonymous or Narcotics Anony-mous, some medical care, and limited group and individual counseling. Access to detoxification programs is itself problem-atic; the need for treatment slots exceeds the capacity almost everywhere. Still, when interviewed, many homeless substance abusers are found to have been detoxified dozens of times. The problem lies less in the limited availability of detoxification treatment slots than in the nearly complete absence of appropri-ate aftercare facilities, where any positive steps taken during detoxification can be encouraged and reinforced.

Most specialists in the treatment of chemical dependency disor-ders now recognize that the key to success lies in providing a therapeutic environment in which sobriety and independence are valued. This, needless to add, is not the environment that homeless alcohol and drug abusers encounter on the streets. Yet the modal treatment package for homeless substance abusers nationwide, as we have already noted, is seven days of detoxification followed by release back to exactly the environment that precipitated or exacerbated the abuse in the first place.

The ultimate housing problem of the homeless alcoholic or drug addict is thus to be found in the near-total absence of residentially based, transitional, and extended aftercare facilities that promote sobriety, encourage economic independence, and provide a stable residence during an extended recovery period. One promising, although relatively costly, approach is the so-called alcohol-free SRO hotel that has been the subject of experimentation in California and other areas. These facilities provide permanent (or at least long-term) housing to recovering homeless substance abusers and have appropriate job training, job placement, counseling, and social services on-site; in these respects, they are similar to the supported-housing options often recommended for the homeless mentally ill. Quantitative evaluations of the effectiveness of such facilities are inconclusive, but experimentation continues.[14] Certainly, "total care" approaches such as these—with secure, stable housing as the centerpiece—stand a far greater chance of success than the treatment modalities that are now common.

As with the mentally ill, it is obvious that homeless alcoholics and drug addicts need more than just housing. Their need for housing is entangled with their need for treatment; their need for treatment, in turn, is itself not unitary. They need assistance in overcoming their substance dependencies; job training and placement services; supported work environments, at least for a period of transition; counseling in money management and social skills; and even retraining in acts of daily living such as bathing, personal hygiene, and dress. Again, although homeless alcoholics and drug addicts need more than just housing, they do have a housing problem and unique housing needs. Without a solution to this housing problem, efforts to address their many other needs will be largely fruitless. Living in the streets is a powerful incentive to get high or drunk and stay that way.

Mention must also be made of the "dually diagnosed" homeless, who have recently begun to receive a great deal of research attention. These, of course, are the unfortunate souls who are both chemically dependent and mentally ill. Their unique problems are that most alcohol and drug treatment programs refuse admission to persons with co-occurring psychiatric disorders (on the not unreasonable grounds that these programs are not properly equipped to deal with mental problems) and that most mental health programs refuse admission to those who are also drinking or using drugs (on the same grounds). The dually diagnosed need both the stabilizing residential care needed by the mentally ill and the alcohol- and drug-free living environment needed by the substance abusers. Several of the National Institute of Alcohol Abuse and Alcoholism Round Two demonstration programs (see note 14) are targeted entirely or in substantial part to this population.

Familial and social estrangement

Homeless people are usually profoundly estranged from family and friends. The housing implication of this fact is that they are rarely able to draw on networks of kin and friends to sustain them through periods of social, economic, or psychological crisis. Most people, if they found themselves about to be homeless or newly homeless, would have someone to whom they could turn as they weathered the storm and got back on their feet. In general, the homeless are those who do not have such a support system.

There are two different types of estrangement among the homeless, both of which are well illustrated by certain findings from Rossi's survey of the homeless in Chicago (see notes 2 and 7). Homeless persons in that survey were asked whether they would like to return to their families, and if so, whether they thought their families would take them in. In general, the men said they would like to return but knew they would not be welcome; the women had no wish to return in the first place. Thus, the estranged are either family rejects who have exhausted the patience or resources of their kin networks, or family leavers who have fled a domestic situation so troubling or so abusive that life on the streets is the preferred alternative.

Many of the family rejects, of course, have been expelled because of their alcohol and drug abuse or because of other personal problems (chronic unemployment, troubles with the law, etc.). If their rejection is not to lead to homelessness, then they need rooming or boarding houses (or SRO rooms) appropriate to single individuals of limited means. Without a sufficient supply of such units, they end up on the streets. The family leavers have different needs: sanctuaries, battered women's programs, halfway houses, and transitional programs, all coupled with social and psychological services to address their troubled histories.

The role that family and kin networks play in housing the poor is not usually appreciated. Data from Chicago provide an illustration. There are approximately 100,000 general assistance recipients in the city. Most are single, unaffiliated, nonwhite males—in short, extremely poor persons who do not qualify for Aid to Families with Dependent Children (AFDC), Supplemental Security Income, Social Security Disability Insurance, or other forms of welfare.[15] A study of general assistance recipients by Stagner and Richman found that half resided with family or friends; without this housing assistance, as many as 50,000 additional Chicagoans could well be homeless.[16] Given this finding, the surprise is not that there are so many homeless people, but that there are so few.

In general, the welfare state provides for the unfortunate only what families, friends, and communities do not; one's social "safety net" is the first line of defense against misfortune of all sorts, and the welfare state safety net is the second. In general, the homeless have fallen through both. In some cases, certainly, and perhaps in many cases, the "hole" in the social safety net is due to lack of resources; families simply run out of money and turn their adult children out onto the streets. It is therefore possible that subsidies to families with dependent adult members, a program referred to elsewhere as Aid to Families with Dependent Adults,[17] might be sufficient to prevent the homelessness of many.

Extreme poverty: Poverty and housing in the 1980s

Finally, of course, the homeless are extremely poor, so poor that the poverty line would represent a standard of affluence to many of them. This is true of essentially all homeless people, regardless of their other problems. Even if there were a way to stabilize the mentally ill homeless, or treat the alcoholic and drug-addicted homeless, or reintegrate the estranged homeless with their families and friends, almost all would still be poor. And as poor people, they would then face the same housing problem that all poor people face—an insufficient and dwindling supply of low-income housing. This is the ultimate sense in which homelessness is a housing problem, and it is appropriate to conclude with a discussion of the trends in poverty and low-income housing over the past decade.

The 1980s were neither kind nor gentle to the nation's poor and destitute. During the decade, poverty increased and the supply of low-income housing dwindled. The trends in these directions were obvious even in the early 1980s and have, if anything, become more pronounced in the years since.[18]

From 1978 to 1985, there was a 25 percent increase in the number of households below the poverty line, and also an increase in just how poor the poor were. For example, in 1985 the median income of poor families was $4,000 beneath the poverty line; in constant dollars, those families were $600 deeper into poverty than poor families in 1978.[19] That the poor are getting poorer has been the theme of countless recent newspaper and magazine articles.

Over the past thirty years, the number of Americans living below the official poverty line has varied from a high of nearly 40 million in 1960 to a low of about 23 million in 1973. The number of the poor declined steadily throughout the 1960s, from nearly 40 million at the beginning of the decade to about 25 million at the end. Throughout the 1970s, the number of people living in poverty fluctuated around the 25 million mark, with no obvious trend in either direction. Then, starting in 1978, the number of the poor began to increase, reaching the 35 million mark in 1983 and hovering close to that number since. The 1983 figure is of historical significance because it represents the largest number of persons in poverty recorded since the beginning of the War on Poverty in 1964. In the five years from 1978 to 1983, the gains of the previous two decades were totally erased.[20]

Not only has the number of the poor increased, but their poverty has deepened. The total share of national income going to the poorest tenth of the population has declined by more than 10 percent in recent years; the share going to the most affluent 20th has increased by 37 percent. Accordingly, the gap between the poverty line and the median U.S. family income has widened. In 1980, this "income deficit" for the poor (the difference between the three-person-household poverty level and the median income) was $14,458; the corresponding figure in 1988 was $22,755—a 57 percent increase.

As the number of the poor has increased and their poverty has worsened, the supply of housing for low-income people has declined. A comparison of the number of units renting for less than $250 a month (30 percent of a $10,000 annual income) and the number of households with annual incomes under $10,000 reveals that in 1985, there were four million fewer units than renter households needing units, with the discrepancy between the number of poor families and the number of very low-income rental units evident in every state.[21] In the nation as a whole, there are nearly twice as many very low-income renter households as there are low-cost units to accommodate them.

Despite this gap, Department of Housing and Urban Development (HUD) funding levels for subsidized housing assistance declined sharply, from $26.6 billion in 1980 to $7.4 billion in 1989. In contrast to frequent claims by "Reagan administration enthusiasts" that HUD has played a major role in solving the housing crisis through an infusion of funds into the system, HUD officials have indicated that they are "backing out of the business of housing."[22] Recent downward trends in the federal obligation to subsidize the construction of low-income housing reverse a historical commitment dating to 1937.[23]

What has happened to the low-income housing stock in urban areas? The essential developments have been abandonment, arson, gentrification, conversion, and displacement. Despite the growing poverty population and the increased need for low-income housing in the 1980s, the decade witnessed considerable loss of low-income housing through arson and abandonment, outright destruction through urban renewal and the revitalization of downtown areas, and much more conversion of low-income to upper income units through the process of gentrification.[24] In general, "demolition, rehabilitation, abandonment, and condominium conversion have lessened the number of low-rent housing units in most major cities."[25]

Thus, the revitalization of downtown areas has been a mixed blessing. The razing of rotted urban slums and their replacement by attractive boutiques, elegant restaurants, upscale condominiums, and the like are positive developments, as is the ensuing increase in the urban tax base. At the same time, these processes have displaced large sectors of the poverty population and have destroyed much low-income housing, particularly (as already noted) the SRO housing that once served as the housing of last resort for the most down-and-out among the urban poverty population. With little federal funding available to subsidize the replacement of lost low-income units, many of the displaced have come to be permanently displaced, which is to say, homeless.

Unfortunately, the destruction of SRO housing is only part of a larger process of displacement. Based on data from the Annual Housing Survey, Huttman estimates that somewhere between 1.7 and 2.4 million persons are being displaced annually through outright destruction of units.[26] Razed units are predominantly low-income units; replacement units frequently are not. For example, in 1987, 346,500 new apartments were built nation-wide. Of these, only 23,900 (7 percent) rented for less than $350 a month. The median rent for new units constructed in 1987 was nearly $550 per month, well beyond the reach of low-income families and hopelessly beyond the reach of the homeless poor.

It is, of course, true that the federal government continues to subsidize the housing costs of the poor, mainly through the Section 8 housing voucher program. Section 8 provides qualify-ing low-income households with housing vouchers that can be used in lieu of cash for rent. In order to qualify as a Section 8 unit, an apartment must rent for less than a designated "fair market value." To prevent obvious abuses, the unit must also meet certain housing quality standards. Landlords providing such units receive what amounts to a guaranteed clientele whose rents are being paid by the federal government. In theory, Sec-tion 8 enhances the housing purchasing power (housing demand) of the poor, and this demand should, in turn, cause landlords to increase the supply of eligible low-rent units, either through new construction or through renovation of existing units to bring them up to the mandated quality standards.

Perhaps the most serious problem with the Section 8 program is that the housing vouchers are not entitlements given to every qualifying family; a limited number of vouchers are available each year and they are given mainly to AFDC recipients. Thus, only about one-tenth of the poverty population is actually subsi-dized via Section 8. It is possible that more complete coverage of the poverty population would appreciably enhance the demand for low-income housing and thus elicit the necessary supply, but this clearly has not happened with the existing level of coverage. As matters stand, few apartments are good enough to satisfy the quality standard but cheap enough to satisfy the rent standard, and nearly half the households that receive a Section 8 voucher in any given year must return it unused because an acceptable unit cannot be found. With the supply of low-income housing continuing to shrink and the need continuing to grow, it is not surprising that the waiting lists for public housing have become prohibitively long. The U.S. Conference of Mayors recently sur-veyed public housing waiting lists in 27 large cities. The average waiting time from application to occupancy of a subsidized unit was 22 months. In Chicago, the average applicant will wait 10 years for subsidized housing; in Washington, DC, 8 years; in New York, 17 years; in Miami, 20 years.[27] The Conference of Mayors' survey also showed that waiting lists for assisted housing had been closed in 65 percent of the surveyed cities due to excess demand.

Tucker has argued in an influential article that rent control in many cities has depressed the supply of low-rent units, and therefore has contributed to the homelessness problem.[28] His evidence consists of a modest statistical correlation between the estimated number of homeless in a city and whether or not the city exercises rent control. It is rather difficult to take this analysis seriously. First, the number of homeless people is not known with sufficient precision in any city to allow a compelling test of the hypothesis. Available estimates of the number of homeless often vary greatly. Second, the analysis is strictly bivariate, with no possible confounding factors taken into account. It is plausible to suppose that artificially low rents depress the motivation to build new units and thus depress the low-income housing supply; it is also possible that rent control keeps housing within the means of persons and families who would otherwise be on the streets. Probably, both processes occur simultaneously, but the evidence necessary to test for such effects is simply not available.

Conclusion

The general trend of the 1980s was that more poor people were competing for less low-income housing, a trend noted and remarked upon by many observers. The result has been a serious low-income housing squeeze. According to Dolbeare, there were two low-income units for each low-income household in 1970, and two low-income households for each low-income unit in 1983 (see note 24). In 1975, about 4 million low-income renters paid more than 30 percent of their incomes for rent; in 1983, 16 million low-income renters paid more than 30 percent of their incomes for rent.[29]

Most rental housing in urban areas has come to be priced well beyond the means of the poor. But even poor people have to live somewhere, and increasingly, "somewhere" has meant on the streets. Homelessness, then, is unquestionably a housing problem in that the loss of low-income housing and the growth in the urban poverty population have created a situation in which some are destined to be without housing. This situation suggests that the homelessness problem would be formidable today even in the complete absence of mental illness, alcohol and drug abuse, and all the other disabling conditions to which the homeless are prone.

It is essential in this connection to distinguish between the rules of the game and the characteristics of those who happen to lose when they play the game. Asking if homelessness is a housing problem is rather like asking whether bad luck is why people lose their money in Las Vegas. It is obvious that bad luck or insufficient skill cause some people to lose; likewise, good luck and skill are why some win.

But the laws of probability and the rules of the game ensure that someone must lose and that the losers must outnumber the winners. That there must be more losers than winners has nothing to do with luck or skill; it is the rule by which the game itself is played.

So, too, with homelessness. Recent trends in the poverty rate, in the concentration of the poor in the central cities, and in the low-income housing supply have created an urban housing "game" that some are destined to lose. Who in fact loses is an entirely separate issue, and it should not be surprising that the losers in the housing game turn out to be the most disadvantaged and debilitated sectors of the poverty population: the mentally impaired, the physically disabled, the substance-abusive, the disaffiliated, and the estranged.

Is homelessness just a housing problem? Certainly not. There is a long list of contributing and complicating factors that have been discussed in order to specify the nature of the housing problem. Still, an inadequate supply of low-income housing provides the backdrop against which these other factors unfold. With a large and growing urban poverty population and an inadequate and shrinking supply of low-cost housing, the problem is destined to worsen, and only more housing will make a difference.

In the final analysis, it is fairly obvious that personal disabilities, social estrangement, and extreme poverty will make it difficult for people to secure and retain acceptable housing in the private market. As the number of "competitors" (poor people) grows and the number of "prizes" (housing units) declines, the difficulties become more troublesome still. A diminished federal commitment to low-cost housing, an increasingly punitive attitude toward those on welfare, and a troubled, recessional economy add further to the housing problems of the poor.

Of course, homelessness and housing interact in many other ways. Racial minorities are heavily overrepresented among the homeless and would no doubt face significant discriminatory housing practices even if they were not disabled, estranged, or impoverished. Also, considering that the incomes of the homeless are nearly zero, any housing that is to be provided to them will require deep, if not total, subsidies; in the absence of these subsidies, it is not reasonable to expect the private market to respond with an adequate housing supply. Some have argued from this point to the conclusion that the zero-rent overnight shelters are exactly what is needed, but the problems with the shelters are such that many homeless people intentionally avoid them. The halfway point between an overnight shelter and an SRO hotel is a cubicle hotel providing minimum floor space and other amenities and some degree of privacy. But local building, health, and safety codes often rule out such an option; these are still other "housing" issues that impinge upon the problem of homelessness. A final point to note is that most homeless people are single, unaffiliated men; most housing money in existing federal homelessness programs, in contrast, is devoted to helping homeless families or homeless women with dependent children.

It is not written in stone that mentally disturbed people must be homeless. Adequate supported transitional and extended-care housing would be sufficient to undo this troubling pattern. No social or economic laws dictate that alcohol- and drug-abusive people have to be homeless, either. Adequate residentially based treatment and extended-care programs would be sufficient to eliminate most of the homelessness within this group. Even the extremely poor do not have to be homeless; an ample supply of subsidized low-cost housing would obviously prevent this from being the case. There are, in short, many routes by which people become homeless, but every route out of homelessness must sooner or later pass through stable, secure, affordable housing.

Authors

The authors are in the Department of Sociology, Tulane University, New Orleans. James D. Wright is the Charles and Leo Favrot Professor of Human Relations and Beth A. Rubin is an associate professor. [1997]

Endnotes

1. See Charles L. Heatherly and Barten Pines, eds., *Mandate for Leadership III* (Washington, DC: Heritage Foundation, 1989).

2. The real purchasing power of Aid to Families with Dependent Children (AFDC) and other welfare provisions has been approximately halved in the past two decades; see Peter H. Rossi, *Without Shelter* (New York: Priority Press, 1989).

3. J. F. Ball and B. E. Havassy, "A Survey of the Problems and Needs of Homeless Consumers of Acute Psychiatric Services," *Hospital and Community Psychiatry* 35(1984):917–21.

4.   For evidence on each of these points, see James D. Wright, *Address Unknown: The Homeless in America* (New York: Aldine de Gruyter, 1989), and many other sources cited later.

5.   These data are from James D. Wright and Eleanor Weber, *Homelessness and Health* (Washington, DC: McGraw-Hill, 1987). See also Philip W. Brickner et al., *Under the Safety Net: The Health and Social Welfare of the Homeless in the United States* (New York: W. W. Norton, 1990); Institute of Medicine, *Homelessness, Health, and Human Needs* (Washington, DC: National Academy Press, 1988).

6.   Peter H. Rossi, *Without Shelter,* 1989.

7.   Peter H. Rossi, James D. Wright, Gene Fisher, and Georgia Willis, "The Urban Homeless: Estimating Composition and Size," *Science* 235, no. 4794(1987):1336–41.

8.   The literature on homelessness and mental illness is vast. Useful overviews include James D. Wright, "The Mentally Ill Homeless: What is Myth and What is Fact?" *Social Problems* 35(1988)182–91; Joseph P. Morrissey and Deborah L. Dennis, *Homelessness and Mental Illness: Toward the Next Generation of Research Studies* (Washington, DC: National Institute of Mental Health, 1990).

9.   The academic literature on alcohol and drug abuse among the homeless is also extensive. See James D. Wright and Eleanor Weber, *Homelessness and Health* (Chapter 5), for an overview.

10. Also, some homeless alcoholics (and drug addicts) are substance-abusive because they are homeless, not the reverse. In a study of homeless Los Angeles alcoholics, Paul Koegel and Audrey Burnham found that although three-quarters had had significant alcohol problems before they became homeless, the other quarter experienced their first bouts of problem drinking after the initial onset of homelessness. See Paul Koegel and Audrey Burnham, "Traditional and Non-Traditional Alcoholics," *Alcohol Health and Research World* 11(1987):28–33.

11. The best available treatment of the disappearance of skid row as an indigenous urban social system is Charles Hoch and Robert A. Slayton, *New Homelessness and Old: Community and the Skid Row Hotel* (Philadelphia: Temple University Press, 1989).

12. Chester Hartman and Barry Zigas, "What's Wrong with the Housing Market?" (Paper presented to the Institute for Policy Studies, Conference on Homeless Children and Youth: Coping with a National Tragedy, Washington, DC, 1989). See also Hoch and Slayton, *New Homelessness and Old;* Philip Kasinitz, "Gentrification and Homelessness: The Single Room Occupant and Inner City Revival," in Jon Erickson and Charles Wilhelm, eds., *Housing the Homeless* (New Brunswick, NJ: Center for Urban Policy Research, 1986); Elizabeth Huttman, "Homelessness as a Long-Term Housing Problem," in Jamshid A. Momeni, ed., *Homelessness in the United States,* Vol. 2, *Data and Issues* (New York: Greenwood Press, 1989).

13. See Special Committee on Aging, *Single Room Occupancy: A Need for National Concern,* an information paper prepared for the U.S. Senate Special Committee on Aging (Washington, DC: U.S. Government Printing Office, 1978).

14. In 1988, the National Institute of Alcohol Abuse and Alcoholism (NIAAA) funded nine community demonstration programs, each involving expanded residentially based alcohol and drug treatment services for the chemically dependent homeless. Results from these nine programs are summarized in a special issue of *Alcoholism Treatment Quarterly* 7(1990), Milton Argeriou and Dennis McCarty, eds. See also Sue Korenbaum and Gina Burney, "Program Planning for Alcohol-Free Living Centers," *Alcohol Health and Research World* 11(1987):68–73.

    In 1990, NIAAA announced funding for 14 new (Round Two) demonstration programs, all of them again involving long-term, residentially based treatment programs for the chemically dependent homeless. These are three-year programs and each has a randomized, experimental component to assist in judging program effectiveness, but even preliminary results will not be available for a few years.

15. Wright, *Address Unknown,* 21–22.

16. Michael Stagner and Harold Richman, *General Assistance Families* (Chicago: National Opinion Research Center, 1985).

17. Peter H. Rossi and James D. Wright, "The Determinants of Homelessness," *Health Affairs* 6(1987):19–32.

18. James D. Wright and Julie A. Lam, "Homelessness and the Low-Income Housing Supply," *Social Policy* 17(1987):48–53.

19. Hartman and Zigas, "What's Wrong with the Housing Market?" 3.

20. For comparative purposes, the poverty rate is more revealing than the raw numbers. The 30-year trend shows that the highest poverty rates— in excess of 20 percent of the population—preceded the War on Poverty. From the early 1960s through 1973 (that is, from the beginning of the War on Poverty to the first Arab oil embargo and the ensuing collapse of the world economy), the rate of poverty in America was halved (falling from 22.2 percent to 11.1 percent). From 1973 through the end of the decade, no further progress was made, and beginning about 1980, the rate began to increase, reaching a post-1965 peak of 15.2 percent in 1983 and remaining at mid-1960s levels since. Thus, the secular trends in the poverty rate are much the same as the trends in the total numbers; overall, the pattern is one of progress in the 1960s, stagnation in the 1970s, and deterioration in the 1980s.

21. Beth Rubin, James D. Wright, and Joel A. Devine, "Unhousing the Urban Poor: The Reagan Legacy," *Journal of Sociology and Social Welfare* (forthcoming, 1991).

22. Access, "Federal Monies Support Transitional and Permanent Housing," Washington, DC: *Access,* 1990.

23. See Barry Zigas and Chester Hartman, "What's Wrong With Our Housing Programs?" (Paper presented to the Institute for Policy Studies, Conference on Homeless Children and Youth: Coping with a National Tragedy, Washington, DC, 1989); Sar Levitan, *Programs in Aid of the Poor* (Baltimore: Johns Hopkins University Press, 1985).

24. On the effects of gentrification, see Michael Carliner, "Is Homelessness a Housing Problem?" in Bingham, Green, and White (eds.), *The Homeless in Contemporary Society* (Beverly Hills: Sage Publications, 1987). On the related processes of arson and abandonment and their effects on low-income housing, see James Brady, "Arson, Urban Economy, and Organized Crime: The Case of Boston," *Social Problems* 31(1983):1–27. Cogent analyses of the low-income housing supply and its effects on the problem of homelessness include Cushing Dolbeare, "The Low-Income Housing Crisis and its Impact on Homelessness" (Paper presented at Assisting the Homeless: State and Local Responses in an Era of Limited Resources, U.S. Advisory Commission on Intergovernmental Relations, Washington, DC, 1988); Marjorie Hope and James Young, "The Politics of Displacement: Sinking into Homelessness," in Jon Erickson and Charles Wilhelm, eds., *Housing the Homeless* (New Brunswick, NJ: Center for Urban Policy Research, 1986); Michael Lang, *Homelessness Amid Affluence: Structure and Paradox in the American Political Economy* (New York: Praeger, 1989).

25. Elizabeth Huttman, "Homelessness as a Long-Term Housing Problem," 84.

26. Ibid.

27. Gerald Daly, "Programs Dealing with Homelessness in the United States, Canada and Britain," in Jamshid A. Momeni, ed., *Homelessness in the United States*, Vol. 2, Data and Issues (New York: Greenwood Press, 1989).

28. William Tucker, "Where Do the Homeless Come From?" *National Review,* September 25, 1987:32–43.

29. Kathryn P. Nelson, "Assisting Low Income Families: Policy Implications of Priority Housing Needs" (Paper presented at the annual meeting of the American Sociological Association, Washington, DC, 1990).

© Fannie Mae Foundation 1996, 1997. All Rights Reserved.

Where the Homeless Come From: A Study of the Prior Address Distribution of Families Admitted to Public Shelters in New York City and Philadelphia*

Dennis P. Culhane, Chang-Moo Lee, and Susan M. Wachter
University of Pennsylvania

Abstract

This study investigates hypotheses regarding the association of census tract variables with the risk for homelessness. We used prior address information reported by families entering emergency shelters in two large U.S. cities to characterize the nature of that distribution.

Three dense clusters of homeless origins were found in Philadelphia and three in New York City, accounting for 67 percent and 61 percent of shelter admissions and revealing that homeless families' prior addresses are more highly concentrated than the poverty distribution in both cities. The rate of shelter admission is strongly and positively related to the concentration of poor, African-American, and female-headed households with young children in a neighborhood. It is also correlated with fewer youth, elderly, and immigrants. Such areas have higher rates of unemployment and labor force nonparticipation, more housing crowding, more abandonment, higher rates of vacancy, and higher rent-to-income ratios than other areas.

Keywords: Homeless; Housing; Neighborhood

Introduction

Researchers and policy makers have increasingly emphasized the structural and dynamic nature of the homelessness problem (Burt 1992; Interagency Council for the Homeless 1994; Piliavin et al. 1993). Research on the structural factors associated with homelessness has used primarily intercity homelessness rates (point prevalence) as the dependent measure, attempting to identify the associated housing, population, income, and policy factors (Appelbaum et al. 1991; Gilderbloom et al. 1992; Burt 1992; Elliot and Krivo 1991; Quigley 1991; Tucker 1987). This research has yielded significant though inconsistent results, particularly regarding many predicted housing and income variables. This article addresses the same issue, using intracity

---

*Originally published in *Housing Policy Debate* Volume 7, Issue 2.

data, aggregated by census tract, based on the prior addresses of homeless families in two large U.S. cities.

Literature review

Basic research on contemporary homelessness has employed primarily cross-sectional survey methods designed to enumerate the population and document its demographic characteristics. While providing a detailed profile of the population and many of its needs, this method has had limitations. It has produced a static representation of a dynamic problem; it has identified where and in what condition people end up as homeless, but not where they come from or go to; and while it has identified the characteristics of individuals that increase their vulnerability to the condition, the data have not been well suited to assessing the social processes that contribute to that vulnerability. To some extent, public policies and programs designed to address homelessness have shared these limitations. Most homelessness program development has focused on expanding the availability of residential and supportive services that target currently homeless persons and families. Program development has focused less on forestalling the housing emergencies of the many more individuals and families who, without intervening assistance, will move in and out of homelessness over time. Homelessness programs have also targeted individuals for intervention, and not the communities or institutions from which they come or the social and economic forces that have put these individuals at risk. However, evidence has emerged of a shift in both the research and policy sectors toward a greater understanding of the structural and dynamic nature of the homelessness problem.

In the research sector, several investigators have applied or argued for the use of geographic methods to study structural aspects of the homelessness problem (Kearns and Smith 1994; Wallace 1989, 1990; Wolch and Dear 1993). Most commonly, researchers have attempted to identify the socioeconomic factors that correspond to the spatial distribution of homelessness, using data on intercity homelessness rates as the dependent variable (Appelbaum et al. 1991; Gilderbloom et al. 1992; Burt 1992; Elliot and Krivo 1991; Quigley 1991; Ringheim 1990; Tucker 1987). Based on this research, homelessness appears to vary by socioeconomic conditions, although specific study findings have been inconsistent. Tucker (1987), in one of the first applications of this method, argued that cities with rent control had higher homelessness rates, based on data from an early

survey of city shelter capacity by the U.S. Department of
Housing and Urban Development (HUD 1984). Appelbaum and
colleagues (1991; Gilderbloom et al. 1992) identified major flaws in
Tucker's approach and provided counterevidence that low vacancy
rates, as a proxy for tight housing markets, were more closely
related to HUD's intercity homelessness rates. Elliot and Krivo
(1991), using the same data, found that the availability of low-
income housing and lower per capita expenditures on mental health
care were significantly related to homelessness rates but that
poverty and unemployment rates were not. In a test of several more
carefully specified models of intercity homelessness rates, Burt
(1992) found that per capita income, the poverty rate, and the
proportion of single-person households combined to explain more
than half the variation in homelessness rates in high-growth cities,
interpreted as evidence that more affluent households and a
greater number of households with single people put pressure on
the housing choices of poorer people.

A limitation of this research, and perhaps an explanation for
study differences, is the reliability and validity of the dependent
variable. While perhaps the most widely attainable proxy for the
size of the homelessness problem across locales, point prevalence
measures are difficult to obtain reliably from place to place. The
HUD estimates (1984) used by Tucker (1987), Appelbaum et al.
(1991), Elliot and Krivo (1991), and Quigley (1991) were based
on a key informant survey in 60 cities. HUD officials asked field
staff to report on the capacity of localities' emergency shelters
and the estimated number of street homeless in their areas;
thus, these estimates were not based on a systematic count. The
comparability of study findings based on the HUD estimates is
further complicated by the various authors' use of different
jurisdictional boundaries in calculating rates. The Urban Institute estimates used by Burt (1992) were derived from results of a
larger, more systematic survey of shelter providers and based on
a hypothetical ratio of street homeless to sheltered homeless; but
again, they were not derived from an actual count.

Even if estimates were reliably obtained across jurisdictions,
their validity as comparable measures of the extent of homelessness across locales would be confounded by the highly variant responses of those locales to the problem of homelessness. To
a significant degree, the daily size of the sheltered population,
typically the largest component of the homeless count, is supply-
and policy-driven (Burt 1994; Culhane 1992). The elasticity of
the supply of shelter beds defines access to the shelter system,
which in turn is a function of local policies governing admission

criteria, length-of-stay limits, and the flexibility of resources to meet demand. Other policies, such as copayment requirements, sobriety checks, and treatment mandates, as well as the overall quality of facilities, are also likely to influence some clients' perceptions of whether accepting accommodations in a shelter has relative appeal over other options, and for what duration. Likewise, opportunities for exiting homelessness will affect the duration of episodes; in general, more programs to facilitate exit from homelessness should decrease time to exit and correspondingly produce a lower daily census.[1] Each of these factors is likely to exercise a systematic influence on a city's average shelter stay and shelter capacity, which in turn will play a determining role in the point prevalence of homelessness.

Recent longitudinal research has suggested the potential relevance of a structural and dynamic model of homelessness and has raised questions about the adequacy of point prevalence data for measuring the homelessness problem. Analyses of administrative data (Burt 1994; Culhane et al. 1994), a national telephone survey (Link et al. 1994), and a housing survey in New York City (Stegman 1993) have all found that as much as 3 percent of the population experienced an episode of "literal" homelessness between 1988 and 1992, suggesting a high degree of turnover in the homeless population. Longitudinal research based on tracked samples of homeless persons (Fournier et al. 1994; Koegel and Burnam 1994; Piliavin et al. 1993; Robertson, Zlotnick, and Westerfelt 1994; Wright and Devine 1995) has also documented the often transitory, intermittent nature of homelessness. Most shelter users appear to mobilize resources and community ties to avoid the shelters most of the time. Hopper (1990, 1995) has characterized these informal networks as the "economies of makeshift." Unfortunately, the nature of these support systems, and the factors that strain or enhance their supportive capacity, are not well understood (see related discussions in Burt [1994], Piliavin et al. [1993], and Rossi [1994]).

In the policy sector, recent proposals have discussed the dynamic and structural aspects of the homelessness problem. Most recently, the Clinton administration's plan *Priority Home: The Federal Plan to Break the Cycle of Homelessness* (Interagency Council for the Homeless 1994) offers a social and economic analysis of the causes of homelessness, as well as a distinction

---

[1] Paradoxically, the opposite could also occur, as may occur in some programs that require a minimum stay to become eligible for exit programs, or as may occur as a result of increased demand for emergency shelter to obtain access to exit programs.

between chronic and episodic homelessness.[2] Based on this analysis, the plan argues for making homelessness prevention a priority for future federal policy. The Clinton plan describes broad legislative initiatives intended to approach that goal, such as the administration's health care and welfare-reform proposals, expansion of the earned-income tax credit, and increased homeownership and rental-assistance opportunities.[3] In addition, the plan's core policy objective—that localities establish an organized "continuum of care" for the homeless service system— acknowledges the need for preventive and long-term housing stabilization efforts, as well as traditional remedial strategies, to reduce the prevalence of homelessness.

The plan does not address how localities might plan for prevention programs and offers few specifics regarding implementation other than in the broad terms of the major legislative initiatives described above. Given that many of the proposals in the federal plan are placed in the context of the scientific literature, the gap in the plan could well be a reflection of a gap in prior research. Some conceptual elaboration of homelessness prevention programming has appeared in the literature (Jahiel 1992; Lindblom 1997), but the available empirical literature is limited (U.S. Department of Health and Human Services 1991). The literature on program targeting has been comparably sparse (Knickman and Weitzman 1989). Researchers have not provided a method for helping policy makers to determine where homelessness prevention resources should be targeted, nor have they clearly documented the factors they should focus on.

Our present study is an attempt to contribute to the continuing integration of a structural and dynamic model of homelessness in the research and policy sectors, both by beginning to answer the "where to target" question facing the planners of homelessness prevention programs and by adding to researchers' tools for investigating the structural correlates of homelessness (or the "what to target" question facing planners). This study uses the prior-address information reported by persons admitted to the Philadelphia and New York City shelter systems to construct an intracity index for the rate of homelessness by census tract and identifies census tract variables that correspond to that

---

[2] Kondratas (1994) observed that the Bush administration plan also emphasized homelessness prevention and the integration of homeless populations into mainstream social programs.

[3] Regardless of the particular merits or shortcomings of many of these proposals, their future is uncertain in light of recent changes in the composition of the U.S. Congress.

distribution. An intracity measure has the following methodological advantages over the intercity point prevalence measures
described above: (1) in general, it is concerned not with the
exactness of a count for a given day but with identifying a
representative sample of persons from whom prior-address
information can be obtained over a given period of time; and
(2) it is not confounded by local policies and regulations that
affect shelter supply and stay patterns because those factors
would presumably have a similar impact across a city's jurisdiction, particularly in centrally administered shelter systems such
as those studied here. While intercity analyses permit researchers to assess the policy and social factors that vary in relation to
homelessness rates among cities, an intracity approach allows
them to characterize spatial variations within a city. Thus, an
intracity approach may contribute to an understanding of the
"makeshift economies" that beget homelessness and of the processes that contribute to the success or failure of the makeshift
economies in mediating housing instability.

Social selection processes of homelessness

To develop a theory for generating hypotheses, our study builds
on previous theoretical work (Blau 1992; Burt 1992; Culhane
1990; Hopper and Hamberg 1986; Jahiel 1992; Rossi 1989;
among others). Briefly, the model argues that homelessness is a
consequence of a combination of housing, income, population,
and policy factors that have significantly increased the probability that poor persons will live in precarious housing arrangements. Among the precariously housed, a shelter admission is
most likely to occur following some household crisis (e.g., job
loss, marital separation, benefit termination, utility disconnection, hospitalization, incarceration, family conflict) and most
frequently occurs among persons who have the least amount of
familial, social, or public support. These people include unemployed single mothers who are caring for young children and do
not receive child support payments; adults with disabilities,
including people with mental disorders and people addicted to
drugs or alcohol; the undereducated and underemployed, particularly those ineligible for unemployment insurance or general
assistance welfare programs; and people with weak familial
supports, such as those fleeing abusive families and individuals
who were reared in foster care or otherwise unsupportive family
environments. The precariously housed are expected to be concentrated in certain areas, because of both selective migration
and restrictions on their housing choice.

A family crisis or household disruption does not necessarily lead to shelter use, but such a result is more likely in the context of shortages of affordable and suitable housing for people with very low incomes. The risk of homelessness would likely be greater if the disruption were preceded by residence in poor-quality housing or if it resulted in a subsequent move to such housing. Thus, one would expect to find that public-shelter admissions are most often generated in the lowest rent neighborhoods where poor people exhaust the opportunities most accessible to them. Such areas are more likely to have generally distressed housing conditions, as indicated by more vacancies and abandonment. Moreover, despite having the lowest-cost housing available, such areas may nevertheless be "unaffordable" to the people who live in them, leading some to live in crowded or doubled-up arrangements (in subfamilies).

The relevance of the other major component to the housing affordability problem—low income—is likely to be evident by the higher rates of poverty and joblessness in such neighborhoods. Problems with access to the labor market are indicated by higher rates of unemployment, less full-time employment, and less participation in the labor force. Public assistance presumably reduces the risk of homelessness in an area (compared with poor areas where people receive less public assistance), but it also may be associated with an increased risk of homelessness to the extent that receipt of public assistance indicates very low income and less participation in the labor market.

It is presumed that the housing and income problems described above have differentially affected African Americans because of historical patterns of migration, economic development, residential segregation, and discrimination. Other ethnic minorities, such as Hispanics and immigrant groups, may also face increased risk of homelessness due to poverty, restricted labor market access, and segregation in poorer-quality housing.

Hypotheses and research questions

First, our study explores the spatial distribution of the residential origins of homeless families through spatial statistics and thematic maps, permitting us to compare the degree of clustering and segregation in those distributions between cities and among boroughs within New York City. The descriptive analyses also identify the degree to which the homeless and poverty distributions differ in their concentration, unevenness, and clustering, to further qualify the nature of the prior-address distribution of homeless families.

To understand the marginal effect of various factors on the spatial distribution of homeless families' prior addresses, we used cross-sectional data from the 1990 decennial census (measuring demographic composition, economic status, and housing and neighborhood factors) in a regression analysis to test some of the assumptions of the theoretical model regarding an area's potential risk. We hypothesize that the variables defined in table 1 will be significantly associated with the rate of family shelter admission by census tract.

Table 1. **Variable Definitions and Hypotheses**

Variable	Definition	Expected Sign
Demographic		
RBLACK	Ratio of black persons	+
RSPAN	Ratio of Hispanic persons	+
RUNDER18	Ratio of persons under 18	+
ROVER64	Ratio of persons over 64	+
RNOHIGH	Ratio of persons without high school diploma	+
RFHHOLD	Ratio of female-headed households	+
RFYOUCHD	Ratio of female-headed households with children under six years old	+
ROLDFAM	Ratio of families with householder over 64 years old	+
RSUBFAM	Ratio of subfamilies	+
RGRPQUAT	Ratio of noninstitutionalized persons in group quarters	+
RFRBRN70	Ratio of the foreign-born who immigrated after 1970	+
Economic		
RUNEMP	Ratio of unemployment	+
MNHHPAI	Mean household public assistance income	+
MEDHHINC	Median household income	−
RNOPOV	Ratio of persons below poverty level	+
RNOWORK	Ratio of persons not in labor force	+
RTMPWORK	Ratio of persons working under 18 hours per week	+
Housing and neighborhood quality		
MEDVALUE	Median property value	−
MEDCOREN	Median contract rent	−
RRENT	Ratio of rental units	+
RENTHINC	Ratio of median contract rent to median household income	+
RCROWD	Ratio of housing units with more than two persons per room	+
RVAC	Ratio of vacant units	+
RBOARDUP	Ratio of boarded-up housing units	+

Note: Dependent variable is log(ratio of homelessness occurrence +1). All ratios are in percent.

We expected variations by city to affect our results, given known differences in several housing market factors such as population loss, a much higher proportion of single-family housing, and overall lower housing costs in Philadelphia. We also explored differences between low- and higher-income areas to test for factors that may differentially expose persons to homelessness in areas disaggregated by median income.

Procedures

Database development

Data sources. New York City and Philadelphia systematically register all users of public shelters through automated client management information systems (see Culhane et al. 1994). As part of the shelter admission process, families in New York City and all households in Philadelphia are asked to report their "last address." This question may be variously interpreted by families requesting shelter. For purposes of the present study, we assume the addresses, through their aggregation, to be a proxy for the areas in which families entering the shelter have had some recent residence. For consistency between sites, only data on families were included in the study. To create an admission record in Philadelphia, clients must present two forms of identification that together must include a social security number and a Philadelphia street address.[4] The Philadelphia database begins December 21, 1989, and is current to April 1, 1994. It includes records for 9,160 families. In New York City, shelter admission information for families may be verified against a family's information in the New York State Welfare Management System at the time of admission, if the family is registered in that system. The data from New York used for this study begin April 1, 1987, and are current to April 1, 1994. They include records for 71,035 households.

Geocoding procedures. To construct a database of addresses aggregated by census tract, we overlaid the addresses from the

---

[4] Some persons may be admitted to a shelter with a non-Philadelphia street address because they can otherwise prove that they have been in Philadelphia for a minimum of six weeks (thereby meeting the residency requirement), because they are sheltered as part of the mandatory shelter provision policy in effect on extremely cold or hot days, or because they have been admitted in violation of policy. Some persons do not report a prior address because they enter the shelter system after-hours (after 5 p.m.), thereby avoiding the complete intake interview. Families are permitted to avoid the intake interview if they stay for only one night; they are required to complete the intake interview if they stay for consecutive nights.

Philadelphia data set with the census tract coverage from the TIGER/Line file (U.S. Department of Commerce 1993). We processed the address data from New York City through Geosupport, a program for normalizing street addresses and for producing geocodes for census blocks and tracts maintained by the New York City Department of City Planning.

For both cities, we first matched client address data to the respective base map files (see table 2). For New York City, 70 percent of the cases had an address that matched the Department of City Planning's geographic files. Shelter addresses were removed to produce the study population. The unmatched cases constitute 30 percent of the total and include rejected in-city addresses, in-state non–New York City addresses, out-of-state addresses, and missing addresses. In Philadelphia, 59 percent of the cases had an address that matched the TIGER file. Again, shelter addresses were removed to produce the study population. The unmatched cases (41 percent) include rejected in-city addresses, in-state non–Philadelphia addresses, and out-of-state addresses, but are composed largely of missing addresses. We conducted further analyses to determine the representativeness of the study population, including comparing the race and ethnicity of matched versus unmatched cases, comparing the geographic distribution of in-city addresses (both those that did and those that did not match the respective base maps by zip code), and comparing the prior addresses of households with single and multiple admissions to shelter (see appendix for a more complete discussion).

Descriptive measures of area variations in homelessness rates

Concentration by census tract. To analyze the two-dimensional concentration of the prior addresses of homeless households with thematic maps by census tract, we used the location quotient (LQ). The LQ is frequently used to identify the proportionate distribution of a given object group among areas (Bendavid-Val 1983). The LQ refers to the ratio of the fractional share of the subject of interest at the local level to the same ratio at the regional level (see appendix). This article uses the census tract as the equivalent of the local unit and the city or borough as the equivalent of the regional unit.[5]

---

[5] Census tracts with populations under 100 were omitted from both the descriptive and the regression analyses to avoid the outlier effects produced by small denominators.

Table 2. **Qualification of Study Populations**

	New York	Philadelphia
Address-matched sample	49,604	5,375
Shelter addresses	481	319
Family	49,123	5,056
Nonmatched sample	21,431	3,785
In-city[a]	9,990	858
In-state (not in city)[b]	429	24
Out-of-state[c]	2,120	42
Missing[d]	8,892	2,861
Total households	71,035	9,160

[a] In-city rejected addresses represent 16.8 percent of the total in-city addresses reported in New York City. The rejected addresses correlate with the matched addresses by zip code at $r = 0.877$. For Philadelphia, the rejected addresses represent 13.8 percent of the in-city addresses and correlate at $r = 0.972$ with the matched addresses by zip code.
[b] In New York, the most frequent counties of origin outside New York City are Westchester (48 cases), Suffolk (46 cases), and Ulster (20 cases).
[c] Outside of New York, the most frequent states/territories of origin are Puerto Rico (422 cases), New Jersey (244 cases), Pennsylvania (137 cases), California (117 cases), South Carolina (93 cases), North Carolina (90 cases), Connecticut (83 cases), and Massachusetts (81 cases).
[d] 12.5 percent missing in New York City, and 31.2 percent missing in Philadelphia.

Although the LQ is used to examine the two-dimensional aspects of a spatial distribution, other indices are required to quantify the relational aspects of that spatial distribution within and among jurisdictions. For this study, we selected three additional indices to measure these relational aspects: unevenness, contiguity, and clustering.

Unevenness. Unevenness refers to how unequally an object or social group is distributed among defined areas in a given jurisdiction. For example, a minority group is said to be "segregated" if it is unevenly distributed over census tracts in segregation studies (Massey and Denton 1988; White 1983). The most widely used measure of unevenness is the index of dissimilarity. It measures departure from evenness by taking the absolute deviation of the population-weighted mean of every census tract's object-group proportion from the city's object-group proportion and expressing that quantity as a proportion of its theoretical maximum (James and Taeuber 1985) (see appendix).

Contiguity. A second distributional attribute is the degree of spatial contiguity. While unevenness deals with the distribution of an object group within a set of areal units overall, contiguity is concerned with the similarity in concentration between adjoining areal units. In this study, we used an index of spatial autocorrelation, Moran's I (Odland 1988), to measure the degree of contiguity (see appendix).

Clustering. The third dimension to the spatial distribution of an object group is clustering. The contiguity index captures some aspects of clustering because it identifies the extent to which adjoining areas have similar concentrations of a given phenomenon. However, when the object group forms highly segregated enclaves in space, the contiguity index would fail to distinguish that type of clustering. Unfortunately, a proper measure of clustering for lattice data is not available in the literature. Therefore, we developed a clustering index based on our own definition of clustering, referring to the close spatial association of areas with a high concentration of that object group (see appendix).

Regression analyses

As stated in the conceptual model, we assume the number of the prior addresses of the shelter users in each census tract to be a function of demographic composition, economic factors, and housing and neighborhood characteristics in the census tract. The mathematical form of the model can be denoted as follows:

$$\log(HR_i) = a + b(X_{1i}) + c(X_{2i}) + d(X_{3i}) + \epsilon_i, \tag{1}$$

where HR_i is the rate of shelter admission with the number of households in tract i; X_{1i} is the set of demographic variables in tract i; X_{2i} is the set of economic variables in tract i; X_{3i} is the set of housing and neighborhood variables in tract i; a is intercept; b, c, and d are sets of the coefficients corresponding to the sets of the explanatory variables, X_1, X_2, and X_3, respectively; and ϵ_i is the error disturbance in tract i. Sample statistics for the variables are shown in table 3.[6]

The ordinary least square (OLS) estimation is based on the assumption of constant error variance. However, data based on census tract contain sources of unequal error variance. Every

---

[6] In terms of explanatory variables, median property value (MEDVALUE) is missing in 99 census tracts in New York. The census tracts are mostly low-income neighborhoods that are our main areas of interest (the mean of MEDHHINC in the 99 tracts is $20,090, while the mean of all the tracts is $31,532). MEDVALUE is presumably missing in these tracts because it measures owner-occupied property values, and these areas may have too few owner-occupied properties. We dropped MEDVALUE in the final model specification, since MEDVALUE was not statistically significant in the exploratory model specifications and the loss of the observations is so large that it may produce a biased result.

Table 3. **Sample Statistics**

Variable	New York			Philadelphia		
	N	Mean	Corr.*	N	Mean	Corr.*
Demographic						
RBLACK	2,107	28.675	0.67	342	39.712	0.71
RSPAN	2,107	21.985	0.46	342	4.990	0.06
RUNDER18	2,107	21.823	0.64	342	22.027	0.46
ROVER64	2,107	13.427	−0.50	342	15.523	−0.24
RNOHIGH	2,107	21.433	0.46	342	22.225	0.36
RFHHOLD	2,107	19.325	0.82	342	31.992	0.79
RFYOUCHD	2,107	5.352	0.76	342	9.167	0.64
ROLDFAM	2,107	10.451	−0.44	342	18.676	−0.24
RSUBFAM	2,107	5.193	0.58	342	8.562	0.69
RGRPQUAT	2,107	1.000	0.09	342	2.507	−0.04
RFRBRN70	2,107	18.912	−0.05	342	3.810	−0.22
Economic						
RUNEMP	2,107	9.632	0.63	342	11.079	0.67
MNHHPAI	2,107	1,986	−0.52	342	3,897	−0.21
MEDHHINC	2,107	31,532	−0.58	342	25,783	−0.51
RNOPOV	2,107	19.268	0.75	342	20.028	0.68
RNOWORK	2,107	2.321	0.47	342	2.383	0.54
RTMPWORK	2,107	1.773	−0.11	342	2.101	−0.08
Housing and neighborhood quality						
MEDVALUE	2,008	203,004	−0.48	337	65,580	−0.45
MEDCOREN	2,107	489.000	−0.57	341	364.173	−0.56
RRENT	2,107	65.143	0.42	342	39.669	0.24
RENTHINC	2,107	1.720	0.54	341	1.542	0.15
RCROWD	2,107	1.657	0.34	342	0.383	0.31
RVAC	2,107	5.367	0.12	342	10.875	0.54
RBOARDUP	2,107	0.336	0.36	342	2.378	0.72
RNOHMLS	2,107	1.530	NA	342	1.239	NA
LRNOHMLS**	2,107	1.812	1.00	342	0.495	1.00

Note: NA = not applicable.
* Correlation coefficient with the dependent variable (LRNOHMLS).
** LRNOHMLS is calculated as log(RNOHMLS + 1) to avoid missing values.

census tract does not have the same physical size or equal population. Therefore, the shelter-admission rate in less-populated census tracts tends to fluctuate more than the rate in more-populated census tracts. This situation can worsen when sheltered households are concentrated in smaller census tracts.

To test the existence of heteroskedasticity, we assumed the error variance to be a decreasing function (negative exponential) of the number of households in each census tract. Technically, the log of squared residuals from the OLS estimation is regressed with the number of households. The White test for the pooled OLS estimations reveals the existence of heteroskedasticity (New York: $\chi^2 = 35.6$, p value = 0.00; Philadelphia: $\chi^2 = 2.66$,

p value = 0.10). To overcome heteroskedasticity, we used the square root of the estimated error variance for the weight for the final weighted least square (WLS) estimations.

Results

Descriptive measures

In both cities in the aggregate, the distribution of homeless origins is more highly concentrated than the poverty distribution. Both cities have a lower proportion of census tracts with an LQ greater than or equal to 1.01 for homelessness than for poverty, but a higher proportion of tracts with an LQ greater than 2.00 for homelessness than for poverty (see tables 4, 5, and 6 and figures 1, 2, 3, and 4). Thus, while the poverty distributions are characterized by areas that are more broadly distributed but have moderately high concentration (LQ $\geq$ 1.01), the homeless distributions are characterized by areas that are less broadly distributed but have higher concentration (LQ > 2.00). Accordingly, poverty is a modest proxy for homelessness. The correlation coefficient between the two distributions (by LQ by census tract) is 0.558 in New York City and 0.640 in Philadelphia, as the relative shares of poverty are more widely distributed than the relative shares of homeless origins.

Within each city, the concentrations of homeless origins yield visually evident clusters as well, as shown in figures 1 and 3. Nearly two-thirds (61 percent) of all homeless families from New York City from 1987 to 1994 were from the three major clusters: Harlem (15 percent of total), South Bronx (25 percent), and the Bedford-Stuyvesant–East New York neighborhoods (21 percent). Philadelphia also has three major clusters accounting for 67 percent of the homeless families' prior addresses: North Philadelphia (primarily west of Broad Street) (38 percent), West Philadelphia (20 percent), and South Philadelphia (primarily west of Broad Street) (9 percent).

The calculated indices of unevenness, contiguity, and clustering are given in table 7. For unevenness, Staten Island scores the highest, and the Bronx scores the lowest among the five boroughs in New York. The homeless families' addresses are highly segregated in Staten Island, whereas in the Bronx, where a broad set of areas is affected, homeless origins are not highly segregated. With the exception of the Bronx, each of the boroughs has much higher unevenness, or more segregation, in the distribution of the homeless than of the poor. In New York

Table 4. **Shares of the Homeless among Boroughs in New York (1987–1994) and Philadelphia (1990–1994)**

	New York						Philadelphia
	Manhattan	Bronx	Brooklyn	Queens	Staten Island	Total	
Number of families	305,368	291,978	563,283	495,625	99,464	1,755,718	381,339
Number of homeless families	11,207	15,475	16,875	4,927	639	49,123	5,056
Homeless/families (%)	3.67	5.30	2.99	0.99	0.64	2.80	1.33
Location quotient	1.31	1.89	1.07	0.36	0.23	NA	NA

Note: NA = not available.

Table 5. **Location Quotients of the Homeless (Number of Tracts and Percent of Total)**

	New York						Philadelphia
Location Quotient	Manhattan	Bronx	Brooklyn	Queens	Staten Island	Total	
Zero	40	50	162	192	30	474	229
	13.84%	14.84%	21.07%	29.31%	30.61%	22.07%	65.62%
≤ 1.00	151	154	381	257	39	1,048	8
	52.25%	45.70%	49.54%	39.24%	39.80%	48.79%	2.29%
≥ 1.01	98	133	226	206	29	626	112
	33.91%	39.47%	29.39%	31.45%	29.59%	29.14%	32.09%
Total	289	337	769	655	98	2,148	349
Missing*	7	18	19	18	3	65	18

* The number of census tracts with population under 100.

Table 6. **Location Quotients of the Poor (below Poverty Level) (Number of Tracts and Percent of Total)**

Location Quotient	New York						Philadelphia
	Manhattan	Bronx	Brooklyn	Queens	Staten Island	Total	
Zero	7	12	13	20	4	56	15
	2.36%	3.45%	1.66%	2.99%	4.00%	2.55%	4.18%
≤ 1.00	152	185	483	413	87	1,387	198
	51.18%	53.16%	61.84%	61.83%	87.00%	63.22%	55.15%
≥ 1.01	138	151	285	235	9	751	146
	46.46%	43.39%	36.49%	35.18%	9.00%	34.23%	40.67%
Total	297	348	781	668	100	2,194	359
Missing*	1	7	8	5	1	22	8

* The number of census tracts with population of zero.

Table 7. **Indices of Unevenness, Contiguity, and Clustering of the Homeless and the Poor**

	New York						Philadelphia
	Manhattan	Bronx	Brooklyn	Queens	Staten Island	Total	
Unevenness							
Homeless	0.56	0.40	0.49	0.56	0.63	0.54	0.58
Poor	0.39	0.40	0.33	0.29	0.36	0.40	0.37
Contiguity							
Homeless	0.59	0.61	0.21	0.63	0.59	0.62	0.52
Poor	0.50	0.64	0.59	0.31	0.37	0.65	0.54
Clustering							
Homeless	0.81	0.84	0.87	0.83	0.80	0.86	0.85
Poor	0.75	0.84	0.79	0.73	0.72	0.80	0.72

Figure 1. **Census Tract Map of the Distribution of the Prior Addresses of the Homeless in Philadelphia, 1990–1994**

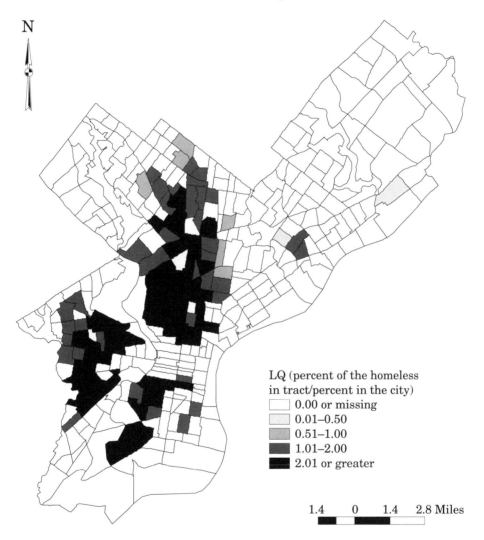

overall, the unevenness index is 35 percent higher for the homeless distribution than for the poverty distribution, and in Philadelphia, the index is 57 percent higher for the distribution of homelessness than for poverty.

According to the clustering index created for this study, in four of the boroughs (Manhattan, Brooklyn, Queens, and Staten Island) and in both cities overall, origins of the homeless are, again, more clustered than those of the poor. The Bronx is the only jurisdiction with an equal clustering score for poverty and homelessness, again consistent with the other evidence showing

Figure 2. **Census Tract Map of the Distribution of the Poor in Philadelphia, 1990**

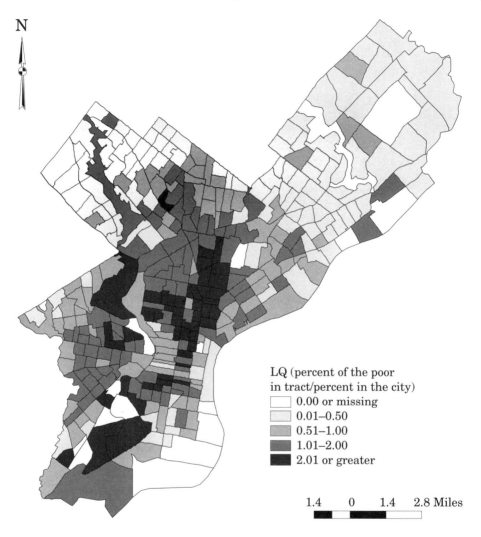

N

LQ (percent of the poor in tract/percent in the city)
- 0.00 or missing
- 0.01–0.50
- 0.51–1.00
- 1.01–2.00
- 2.01 or greater

1.4   0   1.4   2.8 Miles

a more widespread area of risk of homelessness that more closely parallels the poverty distribution.

Regression results

New York, pooled sample. Among the demographic variables, indeed among all variables in the model, the proportion of African-American persons in a tract is the most important predictor, in terms of the standardized coefficient (table 8). The ratio of female-headed households with children under age six is

Figure 3. **Census Tract Map of the Distribution of the Prior Addresses of the Homeless in New York City Boroughs, 1987–1994**

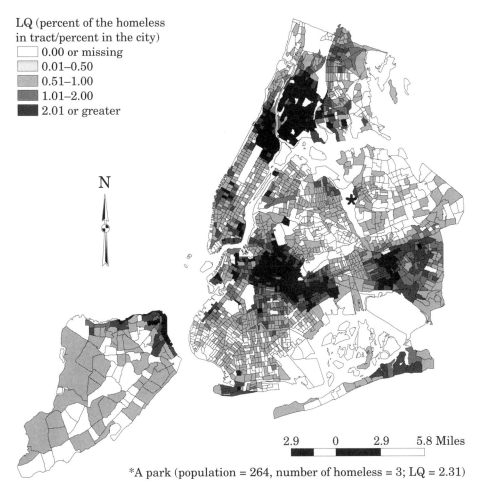

LQ (percent of the homeless
in tract/percent in the city)
☐ 0.00 or missing
☐ 0.01–0.50
☐ 0.51–1.00
☐ 1.01–2.00
■ 2.01 or greater

N

2.9   0   2.9   5.8 Miles

*A park (population = 264, number of homeless = 3; LQ = 2.31)

the second strongest predictor among demographic variables, even though a variable for the ratio of female-headed households is included and is nearly significant in the predicted direction ($\beta = 0.040$, $p = 0.110$). Contrary to our hypothesis, tracts with more immigrant households are less likely to have shelter admissions. When this variable is removed in New York Model II, the sign for crowding reverses to become negative, suggesting that there is a positive relationship between immigrant communities and crowding that reduces the likelihood of shelter admissions. Coefficients for other demographic variables—such as the ratio of persons without a high school diploma, the ratio of subfamilies (families with children who are part of a larger household), and the ratio of Hispanic households—are significant and in the

Figure 4. **Census Tract Map of the Distribution of the Poor in New York City Boroughs, 1990**

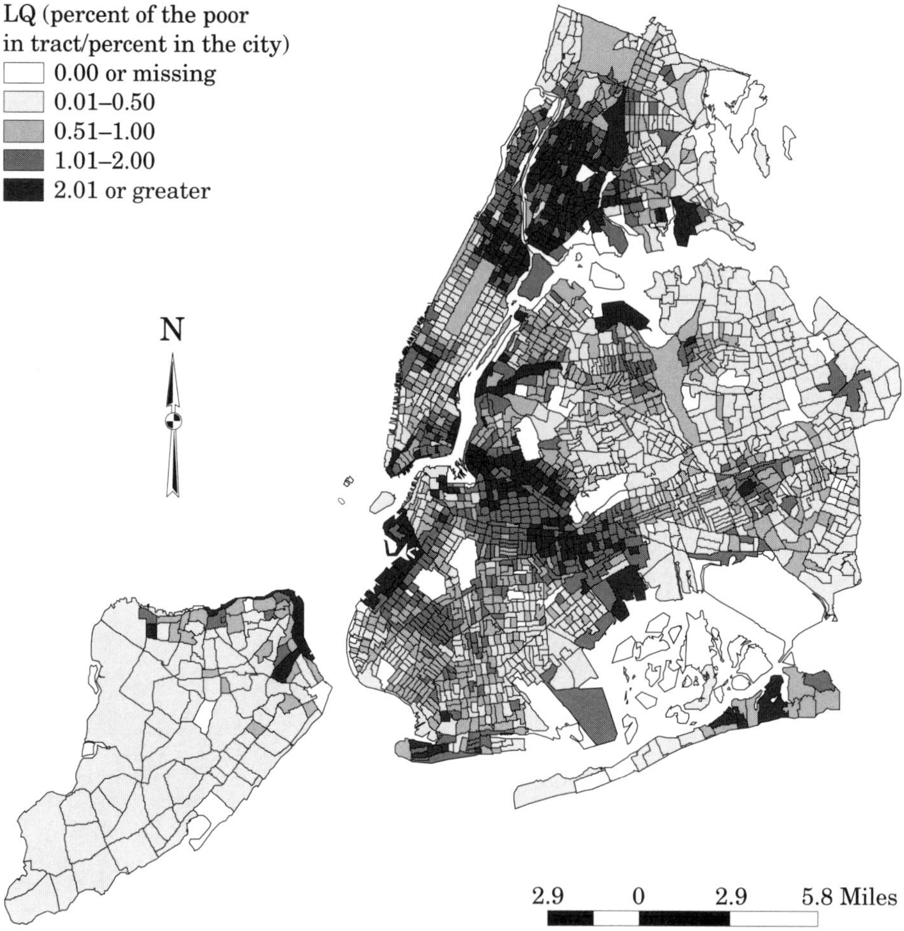

LQ (percent of the poor
in tract/percent in the city)
☐ 0.00 or missing
☐ 0.01–0.50
▨ 0.51–1.00
▨ 1.01–2.00
■ 2.01 or greater

N

2.9   0   2.9   5.8 Miles

predicted positive direction, though of relatively lower magnitude. The ratio of persons under 18 was negatively associated with shelter admissions (opposite the predicted direction), as was the ratio of persons over the age of 64. The coefficient for the variable for older families with children is in the predicted direction, and the coefficient for the variable for persons in group quarters is opposite the predicted direction, but neither is statistically significant.

Among economic variables, the ratio of poor households is the most important factor. The coefficient for the rate of labor force nonparticipation is also significant and in the predicted direction. The effect of the ratio of temporarily employed persons is

Table 8. **WLS Estimation Results for the Pooled Samples**

Variable	New York I Standard Coefficient	p	New York II Standard Coefficient	p	Philadelphia Standard Coefficient	p
Demographic						
RBLACK	0.363***	0.000	0.342***	0.000	0.219***	0.001
RSPAN	0.098***	0.000	0.081***	0.000	0.029	0.594
RUNDER18	-0.038**	0.033	-0.058***	0.001	-0.041	0.525
ROVER64	-0.121***	0.000	-0.124***	0.000	-0.025	0.771
RNOHIGH	0.080	0.000	0.057***	0.000	0.016	0.833
RFHHOLD	0.040	0.110	0.085***	0.001	0.201**	0.042
RFYOUCHD	0.186***	0.000	0.196***	0.000	0.007	0.928
ROLDFAM	0.014	0.448	0.008	0.659	0.050	0.449
RSUBFAM	0.091***	0.000	0.083***	0.000	0.089	0.121
RGRPQUAT	-0.003	0.791	-0.002	0.831	-0.047	0.234
RFRBNRN70	-0.148***	0.000			0.013	0.699
Economic						
RUNEMP	-0.001	0.980	0.018	0.472	0.201**	0.022
MNHHPAI	0.040*	0.072	0.064***	0.005	-0.024	0.702
MEDHHINC	0.062**	0.023	0.095***	0.001	-0.066	0.465
RNOPOV	0.204***	0.000	0.248***	0.000	0.264***	0.007
RNOWORK	0.042***	0.050	0.024	0.272	-0.181**	0.013
RTMPWORK	0.006	0.565	0.006	0.553	0.084*	0.051
Housing and neighborhood quality						
MEDCOREN	-0.080***	0.001	-0.128***	0.000	0.029	0.723
RRENT	0.008	0.666	-0.025	0.183	0.034	0.573
RENTHINC	0.072***	0.000	0.082***	0.000	-0.150**	0.027
RCROWD	0.049***	0.001	-0.034***	0.005	-0.135**	0.031

Table 8. **WLS Estimation Results for the Pooled Samples** *(continued)*

Variable	New York I		New York II		Philadelphia	
	Standard Coefficient	p	Standard Coefficient	p	Standard Coefficient	p
RVAC	0.080***	0.000	0.094***	0.000	0.014	0.809
RBOARDUP	0.058***	0.000	0.058***	0.000	0.252***	0.000
N	2,107		2,107		341	
R^2	0.828		0.819		0.704	

* $p < 0.10$. ** $p < 0.05$. *** $p < 0.01$.

not significant but is in the predicted direction. Effects of the ratio of unemployed persons and the mean household public assistance income variables are not significant, although the public assistance variable is nearly significant in the positive direction. The effect of median household income, which is opposite the predicted direction and statistically significant, may proxy for housing market tightness.

Among the housing and neighborhood quality factors, the rent-to-income ratio is significant and positively associated with the rate of shelter admission. The association of median contract rent is negative and significant, as expected. The effect of the ratio of rental units in an area is not significant. All of the other neighborhood quality variables are significant and positively associated with the rate of shelter admission, including the vacancy rate, the ratio of boarded-up buildings, and the ratio of housing crowding.

Philadelphia. In general, the Philadelphia regression results produced findings qualitatively similar to those of New York, though fewer variables achieved a level of statistical significance. Once again, the proportion of African-American persons produced the most significant positive coefficient among demographic variables and, in Philadelphia, is the second most important predictor as measured by the standardized coefficient. The effect of the ratio of female-headed households is also significant and positive. Coefficients for the other variables are in the same direction as in New York (with the exception of percent foreign born) but do not reach statistical significance.

Among the economic factors, again, the ratio of poor persons is an important predictor (and the largest standardized coefficient in the Philadelphia model). Median household income is negatively associated but not significant. The impacts of the unemployment rate and the proportion of temporary workers are also significant (nearly significant in the case of temporary workers, $p = 0.051$) and positively correspond to the rate of shelter admission, although neither was significant in New York. The coefficient for mean public assistance income is not significant. The coefficient for persons not in the labor force is negative, opposite that found in New York.

Among the housing and neighborhood variables (including median contract rent as a control variable), the most significant predictor (and among the most important variables in the Philadelphia model overall) is the proportion of boarded-up buildings. Coefficients for both the crowding and the rent-to-income ratio variables are significant, but with negative signs (opposite that found for New York), suggesting that homeless families in Philadelphia come from areas that are less crowded and more "affordable" than other parts of the city, perhaps because of the low neighborhood quality and the comparatively lower cost of housing in Philadelphia. Coefficients for the vacancy rate and proportion of rental units variables are not significant.

New York, comparison between low-income areas and higher-income areas. We used median household income to define low- and higher-income areas in New York, with the citywide median value of each tract's median household income as the break point. In New York, census tracts that have a median household income lower than $30,609 are categorized as low-income neighborhoods and the remainder as higher-income.[7]

Results for most demographic variables are similar to those of the pooled sample (table 9). Coefficients relating to the proportion of African-American persons, Hispanics, female-headed households with young children, subfamilies, immigrants, and persons lacking a high school education are all significant and have the same sign in both areas as in the pooled sample.

Among economic factors, effects of the poverty rate and the rate of labor force nonparticipation are also positive and significant in both areas. However, the mean household public assistance income is now significant and positive in predicting shelter admissions in high-income areas, but negative (though not significant) in low-income areas. Unemployment and temporary work remain not significant.

Among the housing and neighborhood variables, the impact of the proportion of rental units is now significant in both areas, though positively associated in high-income tracts and negatively associated in low-income tracts. The positive association of homelessness to an area's rent-to-income ratio holds only in low-income tracts. The neighborhood quality variables (crowding, vacancy, boarded-up buildings) are all positively associated and significant.

---

[7] We did not make a similar comparison for Philadelphia because there were too few observations. We used the Chow test to check for structural differences with the null hypothesis that the regressions of the low- and high-income groups are identical. The results show that there are structural differences at a statistically significant level ($F_{22, 2107} = 6.12$, $p = 0.00$).

Table 9. **WLS Estimation Results
for Low- and Higher-Income Areas in New York**

	Higher-Income Tracts		Low-Income Tracts	
Variable	Standard Coefficient	*p*	Standard Coefficient	*p*
Demographic				
RBLACK	0.567***	0.000	0.362***	0.000
RSPAN	0.150***	0.000	0.096***	0.000
RUNDER18	−0.015	0.553	−0.038	0.158
ROVER64	−0.173***	0.000	−0.104***	0.001
RNOHIGH	0.068***	0.007	0.075***	0.000
RFHHOLD	−0.015	0.663	0.037	0.325
RFYOUCHD	0.079***	0.001	0.187***	0.000
ROLDFAM	−0.019	0.570	0.031	0.213
RSUBFAM	0.226***	0.000	0.082***	0.000
RGRPQUAT	−0.050**	0.026	0.030*	0.053
RFRBRN70	−0.203***	0.000	−0.130***	0.000
Economic				
RUNEMP	−0.058	0.208	−0.050	0.151
MNHHPAI	0.168***	0.000	−0.041	0.231
MEDHHINC	−0.028	0.660	0.045	0.429
RNOPOV	0.120***	0.000	0.149***	0.000
RNOWORK	0.100**	0.025	0.077**	0.012
RTMPWORK	−0.002	0.916	0.002	0.901
Housing and neighborhood quality				
MEDCOREN	0.053	0.380	−0.161***	0.000
RRENT	0.076***	0.007	−0.064***	0.004
RENTHINC	−0.028	0.616	0.091**	0.011
RCROWD	0.069***	0.007	0.043**	0.029
RVAC	0.051**	0.020	0.093***	0.000
RBOARDUP	0.096***	0.000	0.041**	0.016
N	1,031		1,030	
R^2	0.704		0.809	

* $p < 0.10$. ** $p < 0.05$. *** $p < 0.01$.

Discussion

While homeless households appear to come from areas with high rates of poverty, areas with the greatest risk of homelessness are generally more densely clustered than poor areas. In both cities, the distribution of homeless families' prior addresses is more highly segregated than the poverty distributions. An exception to this pattern is the Bronx, where the rate of shelter admissions is more evenly distributed among the borough's poor neighborhoods, and where the level of risk appears generally high. But, in general, homeless families come primarily from a subset of poor neighborhoods where some additional set factors contribute to their increased risk of public shelter admission.

The regression results support several of the hypotheses concerning the neighborhood characteristics associated with the rate of public-shelter admissions among families. We will focus primarily on the New York regression results, which benefited from more observations (census tracts) and thus greater statistical power. We will discuss the Philadelphia results in light of differences between the two cities.

The rate of public-shelter admissions from an area increases with the proportion of African Americans and female-headed households (FHH), particularly those with young children, and to a lesser extent with Hispanic households. These results were predicted, based on previous research, which has shown that homeless families are disproportionately composed of minorities and FHH. Variables for race and FHH with young children continue to be strongly associated with the rate of shelter admission, even controlling for the rate of poverty, welfare receipt, educational attainment, and various housing and labor market variables, which indicates that such households face additional barriers to residential stability not specified in this model.

Areas with high concentrations of FHH may be at greater risk because of a higher level of risk among individuals in those areas, such as having more limited social network size, higher rates of substance abuse and mental-health problems, and other individual risk factors. However, research comparing housed and homeless Aid to Families with Dependent Children recipients in New York City has shown that there are few such differences in individual risk factors among public assistance recipients and that such individual risk factors affect a relatively small proportion of families entering shelters (Knickman and Weitzman 1989). In addition to these individual-level effects, it is likely that other social and economic barriers, such as restricted residential mobility, limited labor-market access, and various neighborhood effects, have a differential negative impact on FHH with young children and contribute to both their concentration in low-rent areas and their increased risk of public-shelter admission.

A similar set of dynamics may contribute to race and poverty concentrations in a neighborhood, which are among the most significant predictors of shelter admissions for both cities. Again, the increased risk of shelter admission may be partially attributable to a larger number of individual-level risk factors among such groups. However, research has found that race has an additional positive effect on public-shelter use that has not been explained by individual risk factors. For example, African-American single adults in Philadelphia have been found to have a significantly longer homelessness duration (controlling for history of mental-health and substance-abuse treatment), and African-American homeless families in New York City have been found to have a significantly higher probability of readmission to shelters (controlling for reason for homelessness and type of shelter discharge) (Culhane and Kuhn 1995; Wong, Culhane, and Kuhn forthcoming). Thus, apart from individual risk factors, other social and economic factors are likely to contribute to the differential exposure of predominantly African-American and poor neighborhoods to the risk of public-shelter admission. For example, the high degree of spatial clustering among homeless families' prior addresses found in the descriptive results and the significance of the effects of race and poverty concentration suggest that processes of racial and economic segregation contribute to the increased risk of shelter admission. Such an effect would be consistent with research on the impact of segregation on housing and neighborhood quality. Massey and Denton (1993) have found that increasing racial segregation has interacted with declining income to produce higher poverty concentrations among African Americans over the past two decades, which the authors argue has promoted disinvestment in these communities by concentrating tenants with a decreasing ability to pay market rents in financially distressed buildings. This concentration can produce a "hollowing out" effect, in which units and buildings are more likely to be left vacant or abandoned, a portrait consistent with the neighborhoods identified in this study as being at greatest risk of generating homelessness. Housing market forces and government policies may contribute to increases in spatial stratification by income and race (Schill and Wachter 1995).

The finding that homeless families come from areas with more subfamilies, together with the significance of the crowding variable, provides empirical support for the hypothesis that homelessness is one consequence of "doubling up" in an area. Families doubling up are presumably doing so because of a lack of income for independent household formation. Aside from being at greater risk of a housing emergency because of crowding, people in doubled-up arrangements may also expend sources of social support more quickly in the event of a crisis. For example, people in subfamilies are often already living with parents or other family members prior to public-shelter admission; thus, they have exhausted some of the housing alternatives to which others might have access in the event of a housing emergency.

The interesting exception to the heightened risk associated with crowding is found among recent immigrants. The reversal of the sign relating to the crowding variable in the New York Model II, when the ratio for foreign-born persons is excluded from the regression analysis, suggests that immigrant groups mitigate the risk of homelessness by increased crowding. Such groups may have developed adaptations to crowding that prevent or resolve housing emergencies. Alternatively, such persons may be less willing to seek the support of the public-shelter system, even though they may need its services. This area deserves further study, as immigrant communities' accommodations to crowding may help to inform the design of prevention efforts for other communities and families confronting crowding or, alternatively, may reveal a greater need for outreach to immigrant families in need of public shelter. Further research on accommodations to housing distress may also help to explain differences in shelter admissions by race and ethnicity.

The results provide support for hypotheses that family homelessness is related to housing and neighborhood conditions. Homeless families often come from deteriorated and low-rent neighborhoods, as measured by the ratio of boarded-up buildings (among the most important variables in the Philadelphia model) and the median contract rent. Homeless families are also more likely to come from neighborhoods with higher vacancy rates, suggesting that these areas are viewed as relatively undesirable and that the rental housing in these areas is at risk of under-maintenance and abandonment. Affordability matters as well, as indicated by the positive effect of the rent-to-income ratio, confirming the hypothesis that shelter admissions are more likely to occur in areas with a relatively greater rent burden.

The Philadelphia data generally support the findings from New York, though with less statistical significance. Some differences are worth noting, particularly because they might be a function of differences in housing and labor markets, as well as in public policies between the two cities. Among the demographic variables, the effect of the ratio of foreign-born persons immigrating since 1970 is not significant in Philadelphia, nor is the effect of the Hispanic variable. Hispanics constitute a relatively small proportion of the population in Philadelphia (5.6 percent versus 24.4 percent in New York) and are known to be underrepresented among shelter users there. Hispanics and recent immigrants in Philadelphia may be subject to dynamics similar to those of the recent immigrants in New York, whose relatively greater crowding may be an alternate accommodation to housing distress.

Among economic variables, unemployment is significantly related to shelter admission rates in Philadelphia but not in New York. This finding may indicate a relatively greater problem of unemployment in some of that city's neighborhoods. (However, the effect of the rate of labor force nonparticipation is significant and positively related to shelter admissions in New York.) The importance of labor market opportunities as a contributing factor in Philadelphia is amplified by the added positive significance of persons temporarily employed.

Finally, among the housing and neighborhood variables, the negative association between the rent-to-income ratio and the rate of shelter admission likely reflects the comparatively lower cost of housing in low-rent areas in Philadelphia (compared with New York), because population loss has resulted in higher vacancy rates. The relatively greater importance of abandonment as a predictor in Philadelphia compared with New York could also be related to Philadelphia's continuing population loss, as well as the higher rate of immigration in New York, where immigrants fill some of the low-cost housing that might otherwise have been left vacant. Differences between cities in the disposition of abandoned and tax-foreclosed properties may also help to explain the more limited effect of abandonment in New York, where local government has assumed more direct responsibility for the management and rehabilitation of tax-foreclosed properties.

Separating tracts by median income in New York also produced some interesting differences from the pooled sample. First, the model performed better for low-income than for higher-income tracts. However, among higher-income tracts, the ratio of African-American persons increases in importance in terms of the standardized coefficient, again raising concerns about the increased risk of homelessness among African-American communities, even those with relatively higher income. The effect of the proportion of rental units also appears more significant in these models, tending to be positive in the case of higher-income areas and significantly negative in low-income areas. This finding may suggest that in low-income areas, homeowner-related housing problems, such as the inability of aging parents or their adult children to maintain the costs of the home, may play a role in increasing the risk of homelessness. In higher-income areas, homelessness is more often related to problems with rental housing and its unaffordability.

From a policy perspective, this research offers two broad insights. First, because the risk of family homelessness is spatially and demographically concentrated, homelessness prevention and outreach efforts would likely benefit from a geographic- and population-targeted strategy. Policies designed to counteract residential segregation, concentrated poverty, and poor housing and neighborhood conditions, as well as more narrowly defined homelessness-prevention programs, could target the neighborhoods found to be at greatest risk for generating shelter admissions in this study and the population groups they overrepresent. Second, this study has identified some of the associated factors that could guide the substance of a prevention-oriented policy strategy. For example, improved household income, through expanded rental assistance, improved access to employment income, or increased public assistance benefits, would reduce the poverty and housing unaffordability that this study found to be associated with a higher rate of shelter admission. An income-support or housing-subsidy program could also reduce crowding, vacancies, and possibly abandonment, as well as the potential reinforcing effect of these problems on the risk of shelter admissions. Further research is needed to model and test the impact of such policy strategies.

Our study was limited in that the dependent variable represented an aggregation of homeless families' responses to a single query regarding their prior address. Although intake forms for both cities' systems provide some standardization for collecting information, there are no scripts for collecting information from people seeking shelter admission. Some unknown rate of false reporting could also occur because people are responding to questions that partly determine their access to or eligibility for services. Moreover, having found significant and theoretically consistent associations among neighborhood-level variables, the study's results do not diminish the importance of other levels of causal influence, such as intercity effects, emergency-assistance policies, household dynamics, behavioral adaptations, or other individual risk variables. Each of these may influence who among the persons in these areas is at greatest risk of shelter admission and how that risk is distributed geographically. A multilevel or hierarchical analysis would be necessary to examine the differential impact of these factors in a more systematic manner.

Finally, future research should further develop and refine this analytic approach for studying homelessness. This study was limited in treating shelter-admission data and predictive variables cross-sectionally, whereas a more time-sensitive treatment of these variables would be better able to capture the dynamics of change, including population composition, neighborhood quality, and housing conditions. This study was also limited by an aggregation of variables at the level of the census tract, whereas further analyses could examine the block-group-level predictors or even the characteristics of specific properties associated with the risk of shelter admission. The analysis could also be further refined by including various spatial measures in the specification of the regression model. Researchers should consider replicating this work in other localities. Such research could be undertaken in areas without computerized shelter-tracking systems by selecting a representative sample of shelter admissions over a given period of time and surveying people about their housing history. The prior-address data could be enhanced by including more detailed questions regarding the housing arrangements of clients. Such an approach would bring greater depth to the understanding of the interaction of neighborhood- and household-level dynamics of housing instability than we could discern with the data available for this study.

Conclusion

This study has provided empirical support for several hypotheses regarding the influence of housing and income problems in generating homelessness in New York City and Philadelphia, particularly as they disproportionately affect women with young children and African Americans. The rate of public-shelter admission was found to be associated with housing crowding, residence in subfamilies, poverty, restricted access to the labor market, rent burden, and poor neighborhood quality. Future public policies should consider the role of geographic and demographic variations in the risk of homelessness in designing interventions to reduce that risk.

Appendix

Qualifications of the study population. To assess the degree of bias in the selection of the matched versus unmatched cases, we conducted t tests comparing the groups in each respective city by race and gender of household head (see table A-1). In New York, the matched addresses were significantly more likely to be composed of African-American households ($t = 11.445, p < 0.0001$). The matched addresses were also significantly less likely to be composed of Hispanic households ($t = -7.851, p < 0.0001$). However, as shown in table A-1, none of the mean differences between groups was large enough to warrant great concern with

Table A-1. **Demographics of Matched and Nonmatched Samples in Philadelphia and New York**

		African American	Hispanic
Philadelphia			
Matched sample	Proportion	0.917	0.036
	N	5,332	5,098
Nonmatched sample	Proportion	0.875	0.058
	N	3,745	3,497
t test for H0	t	41.897	23.181
	p	0.000	0.000
	Result	Can reject H0	Can reject H0
New York			
Matched sample	Proportion	0.651	0.325
	N	36,296	36,296
Nonmatched sample	Proportion	0.593	0.364
	N	12,427	12,427
t test for H0	t	11.445	−7.851
	p	0.000	0.000
	Result	Can reject H0	Can reject H0

Notes: Total number of observations varies due to missing values. H0 = null hypothesis. The means between matched and nonmatched samples are the same.

the representativeness of the study population (+5.8 percentage-point difference for African American and −3.9 for Hispanic). Nevertheless, study findings will remain qualified by the fact that the study population for New York City is slightly more likely to represent African-American households and slightly less likely to represent Hispanics than the overall homeless family population.

In Philadelphia, the address-matched group (the study population) is more likely to include African-American households ($t = 41.897$, $p < 0.0001$) and to underrepresent Hispanic households ($t = 23.181$, $p < 0.0001$). Again, the mean differences are not large (+4.2 percentage points for African American and −2.2 for Hispanic).

We undertook an additional procedure to assess whether a geographically distributed bias operated in the matching and rejection of reported addresses *within* each city by the geocoding procedures. It is possible that inaccurate base maps or systematically unconventional address reporting resulted in a biased distribution of matched versus rejected in-city addresses. Matched and rejected addresses within each city were thus geocoded by zip code, and the correlation coefficient was computed between the distributions (see table A-2). The matched and rejected addresses are highly similar in distribution in New York City ($r = 0.877$) and nearly identical in Philadelphia

Table A-2. **Correlations between the Number of Homeless Families in Each Zip Code in New York and Philadelphia**

Pair of Comparison	New York	Philadelphia
Address-matched and nonmatched sample	0.877	0.972
Single and multiple admissions	0.992	0.999

($r = 0.972$), showing that the geographic distribution of the study population in both cities is highly representative of all households reporting in-city addresses, at the zip code level (see table A-2).

Finally, because these systems were designed for management and not research purposes, both systems are limited in that households with multiple admissions to shelters have their prior address information overwritten at the time of subsequent re-admissions. In other words, an address history is not retained for households with multiple shelter admissions. It is conceivable that households readmitted to shelters may have a significantly different locational distribution than households presenting to shelters for the first time. For example, households with multiple admissions may be disproportionately discharged by shelter programs to housing in more or less stable areas relative to the locational origins of households with a single admission. To assess the degree of bias introduced by this possibility, and to assess whether single- and multiple-admission households should be separated for the purposes of the distributional measurements for this study, the correlation between the distribution of prior addresses for households with single versus multiple admissions by zip code for all matched addresses was computed in both cities. Again, however, the distributions are highly similar in New York City ($r = 0.992$) and Philadelphia ($r = 0.999$), suggesting that such a locational difference does not occur at the zip code level and would not warrant further adjustment (see table A-2).

Measures of area variations in homelessness rates include the location quotient, unevenness, contiguity, and clustering.

The location quotient (LQ). The LQ cannot have a value less than zero. When the LQ in a locality is greater than 1.00, the locality has a higher concentration of the subject of interest relative to the other localities of the region combined. Thus, the LQ is used to identify census tracts that contain a higher percentage share of the prior addresses of the homeless, the poor (people below poverty level, as reported in 1990 census), and minority poor than that of Philadelphia or New York as a whole. Because of its unitlessness and absolutivity, the LQ also permits intercity and interborough comparisons of the spatial distribution of the subject of interest.

Unevenness. The dissimilarity index varies between 0 and 1, and conceptually it represents the proportion of an object group that would have to change its location to achieve an even distribution. The dissimilarity index is calculated as follows:

$$\text{Dissimilarity} = \sum_i \left[\frac{t_i |r_i - R|}{2TR(1 - R)} \right], \tag{A.1}$$

where t_i is population of areal unit i; r_i is homeless proportion of areal unit i; and T and R are the total population and the proportion of an object group in the whole, respectively.

Contiguity. The difference between contiguity and unevenness is well illustrated by comparing the case of the "checkerboard problem" (White 1983); highly concentrated areas are located in a scattered fashion like the dark squares on a checkerboard, with a pattern in which the dark and light areas are each clustered together to form two halves on the board (one light, one dark). Both patterns yield the same unevenness index value, although they clearly have different distributional patterns in terms of spatial association. A contiguity index is used to capture this difference in spatial association. In this study, we used an index of spatial autocorrelation to measure the degree of contiguity. If objects that are similar in location also tend to be similar in attributes, the pattern as a whole is said to show positive autocorrelation. Conversely, if objects that are close together in space tend to be more dissimilar in attributes than objects that are farther apart, then negative spatial autocorrelation is displayed (Shen 1994). Moran's I is used to calculate spatial autocorrelation, and its mathematical notation is as follows (Odland 1988):

$$I = \frac{n}{\sum_i \sum_j w_{ij}} \frac{\sum_i \sum_j w_{ij} \left(p_i - \bar{p} \right) \left(p_j - \bar{p} \right)}{\sum_i \left(p_i - \bar{p} \right)^2}, \tag{A.2}$$

where n is the number of census tracts; the double summation indicates summation over all pairs of tracts; p_i is the ratio of an object group of tract i to the population of tract i; $\bar{p}$ is the mean of p_i; and w_{ij} is a proximity weight for the pair of tract i and tract j, which is 0 when i equals j.

In the geographic literature, the quantity w_{ij} refers to an element in "contiguity matrix" that equals 1 when census tracts i and j are contiguous and 0 otherwise. In this article, adjacent tracts of every census tract were identified by using a geographic information system.

Clustering. As a first step in creating a clustering index, we divided census tracts into two groups, based on the LQ: highly concentrated census tracts and census tracts with low concentrations. When two highly concentrated tracts are adjacent to each other, the common boundary lines are deleted and the two polygons of the tracts are merged to form one polygon. If this merging process keeps going, a few polygons that represent highly concentrated areas are obtained. The more unevenly distributed an object group is, the smaller number of tracts categorized as the highly concentrated area will be. The more clustered the highly concentrated tracts are, the more common boundaries are erased, and the smaller the ratio of the sum of the perimeters of the merged polygons to the sum of the perimeters of the original areal units will be. In this concept, the clustering index (CI) can be denoted as follows:

$$CI = 1 - \frac{\sum_{i'} \sum_{j'} b_{i'j'}}{\sum_{i} \sum_{j} b_{ij}}, \tag{A.3}$$

where b_{ij} is the length of common boundary between census tracts i and j before polygon merging; i' and j' are a pair of census tracts that form the boundaries between the highly concentrated areas and the sparsely concentrated areas.

In the checkerboard example, the sum of the perimeters of highly concentrated polygons persists after the merging process, and CI will be 0. In the opposite extreme, when the object group is concentrated in a few census tracts adjacent to one another, a single highly concentrated polygon will remain after the polygon merging process, and CI will be close to 1 but will not exceed 1 (see Lee and Culhane [1995] for diagrammatic examples).

Recently, Wong (1993) formulated a new segregation index that uses the length of the common boundary of two areas as an indicator of the degree of social interaction between the residents of the two areas. In a similar context, the total length of common boundaries between the two areal groups (for racial segregation, minority area, and majority area) may be interpreted as the total possibility of social interaction between the two groups. The total length of the common boundaries between the areas belonging to the same areal group may be interpreted as the total possibility of social interaction within a group. Therefore, the clustering index measures how small total social interaction between the two groups is compared to the sum of total interaction between the two groups and total interaction within groups.

Authors

Dennis P. Culhane is Associate Professor in the School of Social Work and Research Associate Professor in the Center for Mental Health Policy and Services Research at the University of Pennsylvania. Chang-Moo Lee is Senior Fellow at The Wharton School Real Estate Center of the University of Pennsylvania. Susan M. Wachter is Professor of Real Estate and Finance at The Wharton School of the University of Pennsylvania.

This research was supported by a grant from the Edna McConnell Clark Foundation, Program for New York Neighborhoods. The authors gratefully acknowledge the assistance of Mon Louie of the City of New York Human Resources Administration, Heide Lange-Joe of the City of New York Department of Homeless Services, and Joseph Henry and June Averyt of the University of Pennsylvania for their assistance with this project.

References

Appelbaum, Richard, Michael Dolny, Peter Dreier, and John Gilderbloom. 1991. Scapegoating Rent Control: Masking the Causes of Homelessness. *Journal of the American Planning Association* 57(2):153–64.

Bendavid-Val, Avrom. 1983. *Regional and Local Economic Analysis for Practitioners*. New York: Praeger.

Blau, Joel. 1992. *The Visible Poor: Homelessness in the United States*. New York: Oxford University Press.

Burt, Martha. 1992. *Over the Edge: The Growth of Homelessness in the 1980s*. New York and Washington: Russell Sage Foundation and The Urban Institute Press.

Burt, Martha. 1994. Comment. *Housing Policy Debate* 5(2):141–52.

Culhane, Dennis P. 1990. The Social Selection Processes of Homelessness. In *On Becoming Homeless: The Structural and Experiential Dynamics of Residential Instability*, 135–47. Unpublished doctoral dissertation. Boston College.

Culhane, Dennis P. 1992. The Quandaries of Shelter Reform: An Appraisal of Efforts to "Manage" Homelessness. *Social Service Review* 66(3):428–40.

Culhane, Dennis P., Edmund F. Dejowski, Julie Ibanez, Elizabeth Needham, and Irene Macchia. 1994. Public Shelter Admission Rates in Philadelphia and New York City: The Implications of Turnover for Sheltered Population Counts. *Housing Policy Debate* 5(2):107–40.

Culhane, Dennis P., and Randall Kuhn. 1995. Patterns and Determinants of Shelter Utilization Among Single Adults in New York City and Philadelphia: A Longitudinal Analysis of Homelessness. Paper presented at the Annual Meeting of the Eastern Sociological Association, March 31, Philadelphia, PA.

Elliot, Marta, and Lauren J. Krivo. 1991. Structural Determinants of Homelessness in the U.S. *Social Problems* 38(1):113–31.

Fournier, Louise, Malijai Caulet, Gilles Cote, Jean Toupin, Maurice Ohayon, Micheline Ostoj, and Isabelle Laurin. 1994. Longitudinal Study of the New Homeless: Preliminary Results. Paper presented at the Annual Meeting of the American Public Health Association, November 1, Washington, DC.

Gilderbloom, John, Richard Appelbaum, Michael Dolny, and Peter Dreier. 1992. Debating the Causes of Homelessness: Sham Rent Control Research: A Further Reply. *Journal of the American Planning Association* 58(2):220–24.

Hopper, Kim. 1990. The New Urban Niche of Homelessness: New York City in the Late 1980s. *Bulletin of the New York Academy of Medicine* 66(5):435–50.

Hopper, Kim. 1995. Definitional Quandaries and Other Hazards in Counting the Homeless: An Invited Commentary. *American Journal of Orthopsychiatry* 65(3):340–46.

Hopper, Kim, and Jill Hamberg. 1986. The Making of America's Homeless: From Skid Row to New Poor, 1945–1986. In *Critical Perspectives on Housing*, eds. Rachel Bratt, Chester Hartman, and Ann Meyerson, 12–40. Philadelphia: Temple University Press.

Interagency Council for the Homeless. 1994. *Priority Home: The Federal Plan to Break the Cycle of Homelessness*. Washington: U.S. Department of Housing and Urban Development.

Jahiel, René. 1992. Toward the Prevention of Homelessness. In *Homelessness: A Prevention Oriented Approach*, ed. Rene Jahiel, 315–36. Baltimore: The Johns Hopkins University Press.

James, David R., and Karl E. Taeuber. 1985. Measures of Segregation. In *Sociological Methodology 1985*, ed. Nancy Tuman, 1–32. San Francisco: Jossey-Bass.

Kearns, Robin A., and Christopher J. Smith. 1994. Housing, Homelessness and Mental Health: Mapping an Agenda for Geographical Inquiry. *Professional Geographer* 46(4):418–24.

Knickman, James, and Beth Weitzman. 1989. *Forecasting Models to Target Families at High Risk of Homelessness*. New York: New York University Health Research Program.

Koegel, Paul, and M. Audrey Burnam. 1994. The Course of Homelessness Among Homeless Adults in Los Angeles. Paper presented at the Annual Meeting of the American Public Health Association, November 1, Washington, DC.

Kondratas, Anna. 1994. Comment. *Housing Policy Debate* 5(2):153–62.

Lee, Chang-Moo, and Dennis P. Culhane. 1995. The Spatial Distribution of Homelessness Occurrence and the Efficacy of Shelter Programs in Philadelphia. Wharton Real Estate Center Working Paper Series No. 213. University of Pennsylvania.

Lindblom, Eric N. 1997. Toward a Comprehensive Homelessness-Prevention Strategy. In *Understanding Homelessness: New Policy and Research Perspectives*, ed. Dennis P. Culhane and Steven P. Hornburg, 265–334. First published in 1991 as *Housing Policy Debate* 2(3):957–1025.

Link, Bruce G., Ezra Susser, Anne Stueve, Jo Phelan, Robert E. Moore, and Elmer Struening. 1994. Lifetime and Five-Year Prevalence of Homelessness in the United States. *American Journal of Public Health* 84:1907–12.

Massey, Douglas S., and Nancy A. Denton. 1988. The Dimensions of Residential Segregation. *Social Forces* 67(2):281–315.

Massey, Douglas S., and Nancy A. Denton. 1993. *American Apartheid: Segregation and the Making of the American Underclass*. Cambridge, MA: Harvard University Press.

Odland, John. 1988. *Spatial Autocorrelation*. New York: Sage Publications.

Piliavin, Irving, Michael Sosin, Alex H. Westerfelt, and Ross L. Matsueda. 1993. The Duration of Homeless Careers: An Exploratory Study. *Social Service Review* 67:576–98.

Quigley, J. 1991. Does Rent Control Cause Homelessness? Taking the Claim Seriously. *Journal of Policy Analysis and Management* 9:89–93.

Ringheim, Karen. 1990. *At Risk of Homelessness: The Roles of Income and Rent*. New York: Praeger.

Robertson, Marjorie J., Cheryl Zlotnick, and Alex Westerfelt. 1994. The Course of Homelessness Among Adults and Families in Alameda County. Paper presented at the Annual Meeting of the American Public Health Association, November 1, Washington, DC.

Rossi, Peter. 1989. *Down and Out in America*. Chicago: University of Chicago Press.

Rossi, Peter. 1994. Comment on Dennis P. Culhane et al.'s "Public Shelter Admission Rates in Philadelphia and New York City: The Implications of Turnover for Sheltered Population Counts." *Housing Policy Debate* 5(2): 163–76.

Schill, Michael H., and Susan M. Wachter. 1995. Housing Market Constraints and Spatial Stratification by Income and Race. *Housing Policy Debate* 6(1): 141–67.

Shen, Qing. 1994. An Application of GIS to the Measurement of Spatial Autocorrelation. *Computer, Environment, and Urban Systems* 18(3):167–91.

Stegman, Michael A. 1993. *Housing and Vacancy Report: New York City, 1991*. New York: Department of Housing Preservation and Development.

Tucker, W. 1987. Where Do the Homeless Come From? *National Review*, September, pp. 32–45.

U.S. Department of Commerce. 1993. *TIGER/Line 1992*. Washington, DC: Bureau of Data User Services Division.

U.S. Department of Health and Human Services. 1991. *Homelessness Prevention Programs*. Washington, DC: Office of the Inspector General.

U.S. Department of Housing and Urban Development. 1984. *A Report to the Secretary on the Homeless and Emergency Shelters*. Washington, DC: Office of Policy Development and Research.

Wallace, Roderick. 1989. "Homelessness," Contagious Destruction of Housing and Municipal Service Cuts in New York City: 1. Demographics of a Housing Deficit. *Environment and Planning A* 21:1585–1603.

Wallace, Roderick. 1990. "Homelessness," Contagious Destruction of Housing and Municipal Service Cuts in New York City: 2. Dynamics of a Housing Famine. *Environment and Planning A* 22:5–15.

White, Michael J. 1983. The Measurement of Spatial Segregation. *American Journal of Sociology* 88(5):1008–18.

Wolch, Jennifer, and Michael Dear. 1993. *Malign Neglect*. San Francisco: Jossey-Bass.

Wong, David W. S. 1993. Spatial Indices of Segregation. *Urban Studies* 30(3):559–72.

Wong, Irene, Dennis P. Culhane, and Randall Kuhn. Forthcoming. Predictors of Shelter Exit and Return among Homeless Families in New York City. Available from authors, University of Pennsylvania.

Wright, James D., and Joel A. Devine. 1995. Housing Dynamics of the Homeless: Implications for a Count. *American Journal of Orthopsychiatry* 65(3): 320–29.

Toward a Comprehensive Homelessness-Prevention Strategy*

Eric N. Lindblom
U.S. Department of Veterans Affairs

Abstract

Because of the misery and deprivation suffered by homeless persons, the initial response to homelessness in the United States focused first on quickly addressing the dire need for emergency food and shelter, and then on providing additional assistance to already homeless persons—ideally to help them move out of homelessness. New preventive measures to help people avoid becoming homeless were largely ignored or put off.[1] But now that efforts to provide emergency food and shelter are well under way throughout the country, many more experts, policymakers, and service organizations have begun focusing on homelessness prevention.[2] Nevertheless, actual prevention efforts are still tentative and somewhat haphazard. In support of a more rapid expansion of effective homelessness-prevention activities, this paper discusses the benefits of prevention, develops an initial framework for a comprehensive homelessness-prevention strategy, and, using this framework, evaluates existing prevention efforts and suggests new initiatives.

Why homelessness prevention?

As long as there are substantial new entries into homelessness, helping only the already homeless cannot significantly reduce the size of the problem. Bailing out the boat can keep the problem from getting worse (and, if done well, might even gain some ground), but bailing will never solve the problem until the leaks are fixed. Failing to fix these leaks (and reduce the size of the homeless population) through homelessness-prevention initiatives risks further declines in both public compassion for homeless persons and in the critical, still substantial popular support for government and private efforts to address the problem.[3] It also risks the permanent institutionalization of both homelessness and the already large network of related programs and bureaucracies. Indeed, there are some indications that benefits and services for homeless persons that are not available (or as readily available) to others may have prompted some marginal families and individuals to become homeless, and that people

*Originally published in *Housing Policy Debate* Volume 2, Issue 3.

and institutions are more likely to terminate their support for otherwise homeless persons when they expect that such persons will be picked up by homeless shelters and services.[4]

Besides counterbalancing any existing incentives to become or remain homeless, expanded prevention efforts also hold the promise of avoiding or reducing significant costs associated with homelessness. In other words, an ounce of prevention may actually be worth a pound of cure. It is often less expensive to help a person or family avoid homelessness than it is to let them become homeless and then provide them with emergency shelter, other homelessness services, and help getting out of homelessness. Moreover, while people living in near-homeless situations face a wide range of basic problems and challenges, preventing them from becoming homeless can keep the existing problems from escalating and can block a host of new ones (thereby avoiding a corresponding increase in the need and demand for costly public and private assistance).

On any given day, there are probably between 350,000 and 750,000 literally homeless persons.[5] By reducing the number of homeless persons, prevention efforts would not only reduce the expense of providing emergency food and shelter and other services to them, but also cut the direct social costs from such things as policing and cleaning up after them. Although no precise calculations exist, direct homelessness assistance from federal, state, and local governments already exceeds $2.5 billion each year. Considerably larger amounts come indirectly from nonhomeless-specific programs,[6] and policing and cleanup costs annually total in the tens (if not hundreds) of millions of dollars.[7]

Reducing the size of the homeless population enough to lower these costs significantly and produce the many associated benefits and savings will not occur without the federal, state, and local governments, together with the private and nonprofit sectors, implementing a range of new and expanded homelessness-prevention initiatives. To develop a framework for such prevention activities (at whatever level), these questions need to be answered as well as possible:

1. Who are the most at risk of becoming homeless, and how can they be identified? (To help target the prevention assistance most effectively, identify characteristics that make homelessness more likely, and develop strategies for reducing the size of the most-at-risk pool.)

2.   Where do homeless persons come from; where were they housed prior to becoming homeless? (To help identify possible sites for intervention assistance.)

3.   What events precipitate or cause individuals and families to become homeless? (To help develop prevention assistance that will either keep such events from occurring or enable the most-at-risk to weather them without falling into homelessness.)[8]

This approach focuses on identifying those types of people most at risk of becoming homeless and then developing proposals on how to help them avoid homelessness. An alternative prevention approach might first identify the major causes of homelessness (in a more macro sense) and then develop broad policies to address these causes.[9] However, the approach chosen here is more useful for developing the kind of targeted, practical (and cheaper) intervention strategies at the local level that can immediately begin helping those most at risk to avoid homelessness. Moreover, by identifying possible approaches to each of the major problems that the most-at-risk face, this approach addresses all the major "causes" of homelessness as well.

Who are the "most at risk of becoming homeless"?

The term *most at risk* refers to those who are either clearly at *immediate* risk of becoming homeless (for whatever reasons) or the most likely to become homeless at some point because of their inherent characteristics. This group differs from those who, despite their poverty or even their risk of losing their current housing, do not, as a definable group, face any special, significant risk of soon ending up in shelters or on the street. It is often said that "everyone is one or two paychecks away from homelessness"; but, thanks to family and friends, savings, and other resources, relatively few people actually are. At the margin, homeless persons become homeless because of a variety of disadvantages and counterproductive personal characteristics that most people either do not face or do not share to the same extent. This analysis focuses on those persons who are most at risk of becoming homeless because they do share these same disadvantages and characteristics.

Extreme poverty: the common denominator

Almost all individuals and families with nonpoverty incomes
have more or less stable housing, and the most fundamental
characteristic shared by the homeless and at-risk populations is
their extreme poverty.[10] However, the vast majority of extremely
poor persons in the United States are not homeless. For example,
census data show that approximately 12 million people in the
United States live below 50 percent of the poverty line,[11] but
even the most generous estimates of the homeless population
are only a small fraction of that number. Accordingly, extreme
poverty can be seen as a necessary but not sufficient cause of
homelessness. Similarly, poor education and weak work experience reflect major causes of extreme poverty that do not have
any special, further impact on whether extremely poor persons
also become homeless.[12]

Secondary characteristics: the predictors of homelessness

When compared to the nonhomeless extremely poor, homeless
persons have a much higher incidence of a range of secondary
characteristics. Insofar as these characteristics are not caused by
homelessness itself, they can be seen not only as predictors of
the likelihood of homelessness but as either actual causes of
homelessness or direct reflections of causes. Determining these
secondary characteristics identifies the problems that increase
the likelihood of becoming homeless, which is the first step
toward developing effective preventive interventions.[13] Moreover, identifying those nonhomeless, extremely poor persons who
also have these secondary characteristics can make it easier to
target cost-cutting preventive assistance to those most at risk of
becoming homeless. These secondary characteristics, however,
are associated not only with moving from extreme poverty into
homelessness but also with becoming extremely poor in the first
place: A person with one or more of these characteristics is more
likely than an otherwise similar person, first, to fall into (or stay
in) extreme poverty and, second, to fall even further into
homelessness.

Prior homelessness. While some portion of the homeless population is homeless only once and then leaves that state, never
to return, studies have found that between 35 percent and
67 percent of currently homeless persons have experienced at
least one (and often several) prior, separate episodes of homelessness.[14] Accordingly, while it tells little about what causes
homelessness, *one of the most accurate predictors of whether*

someone is likely to become homeless is whether he or she has been homeless before.

Solitary males. Solitary (single, unattached) adult males make up about 70 percent of the adult homeless population but fewer than 10 percent of all adults living below the poverty line.[15] Although simply being a solitary male might only slightly increase one's chances of moving from extreme poverty into homelessness, homelessness appears significantly more likely among extremely poor divorced or separated solitary males than among never-married single males.[16]

Solitary women with children. About 80 percent of all homeless families are headed by solitary women, as opposed to about half of all poor families. Intact two-parent families with children are rare among both the homeless and the extremely poor populations. Half of the homeless women with children have never been married, which parallels the marriage rate among the nonhomeless extremely poor, but the divorce rate among homeless women who have been married (over 72 percent) is much higher.[17]

Unattached youths. While most homeless or most-at-risk preteen children are in families, a significant number of unattached youths (usually teenagers) are in both categories.[18] Unfortunately, little is known about their other characteristics. Undoubtedly, many unattached youths are victims of child abuse, neglect, or abandonment who have separated from their parents or left their foster care situation and have few resources. This situation suggests a strong likelihood of their ending up homeless or at risk.

Mental illness. About one-third of the homeless adults have spent time in a mental institution, as opposed to less than 5 percent of the general public and probably less than 10 percent of the nonhomeless extremely poor. Accordingly, mental illness can be seen as a strong predictor of homelessness among the extremely poor (and comparisons of other mental health indicators substantiate this view).[19]

Alcohol and other drug problems. Approximately one-third or more of homeless adults suffer from chronic alcohol problems, and 10 percent to 20 percent have other drug-dependency problems (and these latter percentages may be rising).[20] Although the percentage of nonhomeless poor who suffer from these problems is not known with any precision, the incidence of these problems is considerably lower among all nonhomeless persons

than among homeless persons.[21] There is also some indication
that alcohol problems often precede homelessness.[22]

Health problems. More than one-fourth of the homeless population are too disabled to work, and about 40 percent report themselves in poor health, compared with only 20 percent of the U.S.
poor. Some studies have concluded that preexisting health
problems may be a significant cause or predictor of homelessness.[23] But, more than with any other trait, it is likely that much
of the poor health of homeless persons comes from the ravages
of homelessness itself, suggesting that it is less useful as a
homelessness predictor.

Institutional histories. Homeless and most-at-risk persons are
much more likely than the extremely poor who have never experienced homelessness to have a history of mental hospitalization,
inpatient treatment for alcohol and other drug problems, foster
care, or time spent in jail or (to a lesser extent) prison.[24]

Weak support networks. Compared with other extremely poor
persons, homeless and most-at-risk families and individuals
have far less extensive or helpful support networks of family and
friends who might provide them with housing or other assistance. For example, a 1989 survey of 56 homelessness studies
done by expert Peter H. Rossi calculated an average finding from
the studies that roughly a third of the homeless population have
no contact with any family members and another third have no
friends of any kind. (The survey did not report the amount of
overlap between these two groups.)[25] Moreover, Rossi's own 1986
study in Chicago determined that the contact that does exist
between homeless persons and their family or friends is often
rare or superficial.[26] In contrast, available data indicate that,
unlike the homeless, the nonhomeless poor often live with family
or friends and have much more frequent, direct, and
nonsuperficial contact with them.[27]

The quality of an extremely poor person's support network is
considered one of the key determinants of whether he or she is
likely to become homeless. Many of the other differences between
the homeless and the nonhomeless extremely poor can be seen as
factors directly affecting the size and quality of one's support
network. For example, family and friends are probably less likely
to share their housing or provide other sustained assistance to
people who abuse alcohol or other drugs, have criminal records,
or suffer from severe mental illness. Similarly, the Chicago
Community Trust study found that time spent in foster care,
mental hospitals, or the armed services were strong predictors of

ever becoming homeless, primarily because people with those experiences tended to be more solitary and less likely to live with others, and to have fewer friends or family to turn to in a crisis.

Using the most-at-risk profile

Although not all extremely poor persons with one or more of the most-at-risk characteristics become homeless, they are significantly more likely to become homeless than otherwise similar extremely poor persons who do not have them, and the likelihood increases along with the number of most-at-risk characteristics a person has.

Moreover, virtually all homeless persons have several of the most-at-risk characteristics,[28] which indicates that the most-at-risk profile (although somewhat overinclusive) will at least identify the lion's share of those extremely poor persons who will enter or reenter homelessness if they do not receive outside help. Accordingly, the preceding list of characteristics offers the most accurate means available of targeting preventive assistance to most-at-risk persons (i.e., by screening applicants for certain types of public or nonprofit services or assistance, or by identifying the most-at-risk persons among the populations at promising prevention-intervention points where such persons are known to be prior to becoming homeless).

Where do homeless persons come from?

Available studies have identified several institutional and home settings that homeless persons are likely to pass through immediately prior to becoming homeless, at some earlier point, or between episodes of homelessness.

Mental hospitals

Almost one-fourth of the homeless population have been in a mental institution prior to becoming homeless, and more than half of those with prior mental hospitalization have been hospitalized more than once.[29] The latest available nationwide survey of the homeless found that 20 percent of solitary men, 24 percent of solitary women, and 8 percent of single women with children had a prior history of mental hospitalization.[30] Not surprisingly, the equation works both ways: A significant portion of all extremely poor discharged mental patients experience homelessness either immediately or at some later point.[31] Taken together, the studies on homelessness and mental hospitalization suggest a "typical" path that homeless persons with a history of mental hospitalization take into homelessness: They experience their *first* stay in a mental hospital prior to ever having been homeless, follow that stay with some sort of housed living, and then eventually (possibly with one or more intervening stays in mental hospitals and various types of housed living) descend into homelessness with subsequent additional intervening stays in various types of housed living and mental institutions—with some unknown portion of such persons eventually leaving homelessness for good.[32] A significant portion of persons experience homelessness prior to their first hospitalization—and then follow the same basic pattern.[33] Either way, mental hospitals offer extremely useful sites for locating and assisting about one-fourth of the most-at-risk population.

Other health institutions

About 29 percent of homeless persons have been in some sort of detoxification program prior to their current episode of homelessness;[34] and the latest available national study of the homeless found that 37 percent of solitary adult males, 19 percent of solitary females, and 7 percent of all women with children had a history of prior inpatient chemical dependency (mostly detox).[35] Although no studies have tried to determine what portion of those discharged from inpatient detoxification programs or from alcohol- or chemical-dependency units becomes homeless, a Chicago study reported that roughly half the extremely poor persons found in alcohol-, drug-, or health-treatment programs for the indigent were found to be otherwise homeless.[36] No similar data exist regarding either the extent to which homeless persons have previously been inpatients at hospitals and other health facilities for *physical* ailments or the number of otherwise homeless persons in such inpatient situations. Nonetheless, temporary stays in health facilities are likely to precede or interrupt some persons' periods of homelessness.[37]

Prisons and jails

More than half of all homeless persons have previously been in local jails, and (with some overlap) about one-fifth have been in prison. For example, in the most recent national study of the homeless, 60 percent of solitary men, 22 percent of solitary women, and 15 percent of single women with children had been in jail for five days or more; and 29 percent of homeless solitary men and 2 percent each of homeless solitary women and solitary women with children had been in prison.[38] No studies have determined what portion of those released from prison or jail eventually enters or reenters homelessness or what portions of the jail or prison populations were formerly homeless, but the close relative sizes of the homeless population with jail or prison experiences and the current jail and prison populations indicate that a significant portion of those released from jail or prison eventually become homeless.[39]

Armed services

Recent studies suggest that between 29 percent and 47 percent of homeless adult males have served in the armed forces prior to becoming homeless, but there are virtually no homeless female veterans.[40] There are no studies on the paths that homeless veterans take from discharge into homelessness or on how long the process takes; but because members of the armed forces receive a steady income for some time before discharge, it is unlikely that many become homeless soon afterward. Moreover, approximately 250,000 people leave the armed services each year, and there are more than 25.6 million veterans, which indicates that only a minor percentage ever becomes homeless.[41]

Foster care

While only about 2 to 3 percent of the general adult population have experienced foster care, studies have found levels of prior foster care among the homeless population ranging from 14.5 percent to 39 percent.[42] Many of the approximately 360,000 children now in foster care will return to their original families (or will run away) rather than proceed through the system to "emancipation" (usually at age 18). However, in a study of youths in San Francisco and Sacramento who had been emancipated from the foster care system, 29 percent reported periods when they either had no home or were moving at least every week, and 39 percent reported sometimes, or often, having problems with housing.[43] Because this study could not locate about one-quarter of the sample, the actual homelessness percentages might be significantly higher. About 37 percent of those released from foster care in the San Francisco/Sacramento study reported difficulties finding their first place to live, but available studies provide little information on the paths taken after emancipation (or escape) from foster care into homelessness. However, because foster care experiences usually predate initial entries into homelessness, foster care offers an especially promising site from which to prevent homelessness before it ever occurs.

Interestingly, in one New York and two Chicago studies, none of the homeless persons surveyed was found to have been in foster care, jail, a state hospital, or any other kind of institution *immediately* before becoming homeless.[44] Although other studies indicate that at least some people move directly into homelessness upon release from institutional stays, the New York and Chicago studies suggest that, for those who ultimately become homeless, discharge from institutional living is typically only an early step toward homelessness, and that the actual entry usually does not occur until after some period of intermediate housing (e.g., temporary stays in the homes of friends or family, in single-room occupancy [SRO] hotels, or in other cheap rental housing).

Rental units and shared housing

A New York City study of families seeking shelter in homeless facilities for the first time found that, during the night prior to seeking shelter, about 20 percent of those not already homeless had come from their own apartments and 80 percent had been doubled up with family or friends (with more than half of this latter group never having had their own home).[45] The Chicago Community Trust study of homeless adults in families or alone (with roughly two-thirds solitary adults) found that, immediately prior to becoming homeless, 55 percent were living with their immediate families, relatives, or friends and 45 percent were solitary adults living alone.[46] Taken together, these studies indicate that solitary adults are more likely than families to live by themselves immediately prior to becoming homeless (mostly in day-to-day or week-to-week accommodations) and much less likely to be living in shared housing. In addition, most households become homeless because of informal or formal evictions (mostly for nonpayment of rent) or because of arguments or problems with spouses or housemates. Problems with their prior residence (such as condemnation, fire, or no heat) are also a significant factor. Family households were more likely to lose their prior housing because of problems with others in shared housing, whereas solitary adult households were more likely to be evicted.

The special role of SRO hotels

Cheap SRO hotels, which can be rented day-to-day or week-to-week, are usually the lowest-cost housing option available to very poor and near-homeless solitary adults, and even families. SRO hotels often provide temporary housing for otherwise homeless solitary adults (especially males), a significant portion of whom move back and forth between periods of literal homelessness and temporary stays at SRO hotels (and possibly with family and friends).[47] The destruction of many low-cost SRO units by urban renewal, gentrification, and other forces is often cited as one reason behind the emergence of today's homelessness.

Preventing homelessness at the sources

The information on "sources" of homelessness shows where prevention interventions could be located, and the most-at-risk profile provides guidance on how to target assistance to the most-at-risk persons leaving those sources. Without meaning to implicitly establish priorities, this analysis develops, suggests, and evaluates some prevention interventions (or guidelines) for each source, starting with interventions directed at those families and individuals found right on the brink of homelessness and then working back to more remote precursors.

Preventing evictions

The just-discussed studies of where homeless persons stayed immediately prior to becoming homeless indicate that as many as half of all homeless adults (well over half of solitary homeless adults and more than one-fifth of homeless families) make the final move from housed living into homelessness because of an eviction or some other landlord or rent problem. The New York study found that a significant portion of the families who enter homelessness from shared housing for reasons unrelated to evictions were previously forced into the shared-housing situation because of an earlier eviction or other landlord or rent problem (usually within the past month).[48] Other studies reached similar conclusions.[49] Accordingly, helping these families and individuals (or the people putting them up) to avoid eviction could reduce the direct flow of persons into homelessness by more than half.

Solving notice problems. Government agencies and organizations that want to prevent improper or unnecessary evictions of most-at-risk households must receive sufficient advance notice, but most evicted low-income individuals and families neither receive any such notice themselves nor contact any public or private social service agencies or government officials prior to losing their residence. For example, in the Chicago Community Trust study, only 24 percent of the sample threatened with imminent homelessness contacted a social service agency in an attempt to secure new housing. Formal eviction papers filed with the courts could provide some notice, but the Community Trust study found that fewer than 15 percent of the extremely poor who became homeless because of an eviction for nonpayment of rent were evicted through a formal court order.[50] Most left because the landlord "asked" them to leave. (The study does not indicate how polite these requests were.)

Prompting larger portions of most-at-risk tenants facing nonformal eviction to require that their landlords use formal eviction proceedings would improve the notice situation, as well as provide tenants with at least a chance of asserting and protecting their legal rights.

Simply informing tenants both of their rights and responsibilities under the formal eviction process and of where they can get help would most likely reduce the number willing to leave merely because their landlord asks or threatens them and increase the portion of eviction attempts that would go through the formal process. Making sure that at-risk tenants get this information and receive the assistance they need could be done in a number of ways, including:

1. Requiring landlords to provide all tenants periodically (or when the tenants are being requested to leave) with an information sheet that explains the tenant's and landlord's rights and responsibilities regarding eviction and lists organizations that will provide assistance.

2. Publicizing tenants' rights and responsibilities, and eviction-prevention programs and assistance (e.g., by establishing and publicizing a 24-hour hotline that low-income residents faced with eviction or rent payment problems can call for assistance).

3. Requiring landlords to notify an appropriate government agency or nonprofit organization prior to asking any low-income tenants to leave (either formally or informally) and whenever their low-income tenants fall behind in their rent (which means the tenant is at risk of eviction).

To be useful, eviction notices must be provided in a timely enough fashion to allow both the tenants and the support agencies to respond. Yet 22 percent of the homeless persons who lost their residence to eviction, as reported in the Chicago Community Trust study, had no prior notice, and another 28 percent had fewer than six days to find new housing before eviction. Even those tenants who receive formal court eviction papers from their landlord often do not realize that filing responsive papers with the court will give them more breathing room or do not know how to file such papers. By educating tenants about their rights and informing them how to obtain assistance, some of the suggested measures regarding notice would also help tenants know that they either have or can get more time to respond to the threatened eviction. In addition, the form and content of three-day notices and similar court papers should be made clearer. Formal eviction procedures could also provide tenants with a more reasonable amount of time after receiving the summons and complaint to find and get help and to file their answer.

Assuming that such measures improve the chances that the targeted at-risk population will link up with an eviction-prevention agency in time, effective assistance still must be provided to keep these people in their dwellings. Eviction-prevention programs now fall into two basic types: those that provide legal assistance related to the eviction process, and those that provide cash assistance to pay all or part of the rent owed (sometimes with complementary landlord-tenant mediation or casework-type assistance).

Tenant legal assistance programs. Only about 20 to 30 percent of all tenants in formal eviction proceedings (and much fewer among those most at risk) have legal representation, as opposed to more than 80 percent of landlords; and roughly one-third to one-half of all tenant defendants never file any responding papers and simply lose by default.[51] Addressing this lack of legal representation among tenants could be an extremely effective homelessness-prevention tool. A Berkeley study, for example, determined that tenants in eviction proceedings won less than 6 percent of the time when they did not have legal representation but won 58 percent of the time when they had it. Four legal assistance eviction-prevention projects in New York City kept their low-income clients in the clients' apartments in 84 percent of the first 675 cases they completed.[52] These and other examples show that providing legal representation to low-income tenants threatened with eviction does not just gum up the works and give tenants who cannot pay the rent some free time. Instead, in most cases such assistance can successfully enable tenants to assert their legitimate rights and defenses, gather available resources to pay any past-due rent, and either negotiate settlements agreeable to the landlords or win in court.[53]

Eviction-defense legal assistance can also be cost-effective. For example, using conservative estimates of how many of the projects' clients would have otherwise ended up homeless and of how much it would have cost to house them in New York's emergency housing and shelter system, the Bar Association of New York City estimated that, during their first 18 months of operation, the four New York legal assistance eviction-prevention projects mentioned earlier saved $3.3 million in direct federal, state, and local homelessness assistance expenditures at a cost to the city of less than $1.9 million for legal assistance. It calculated an even larger return of almost $8 for every dollar spent over the first two full years of the projects' operation.[54] Given the projects' guidelines, which explicitly target families on public assistance who are not only threatened with eviction but also separately considered at risk of entering the city's shelter system, these savings estimates are probably reasonable. Even if the projects were only half as successful as the Bar Association's estimates, they would still be cost-effective—especially after factoring in all the indirect costs to society from the increased homelessness that would otherwise have occurred. Among other indirect benefits, the projects preserve low-cost housing by keeping low-income families in apartments that might otherwise have been rented out at a higher rate, force landlords to repair substandard units and bring them up to code and even create new jobs.

The New York projects appear to be cost-effective despite (or because of) providing especially comprehensive, direct legal assistance from the beginning to the end of the eviction process, along with other services to their clients (e.g., help in getting public assistance benefits). Other legal assistance programs either do not have the resources to provide such intensive assistance or have chosen to provide less intensive assistance so they can reach a larger number of needy people. These other programs primarily provide guidance and advice so that tenants threatened with eviction can represent themselves and meet the court deadlines; they directly represent tenants only in rare situations (e.g., at trial).[55] Because they neither help tenants obtain available public assistance or other benefits that might enable them to pay the rents owed, nor negotiate payback arrangements with landlords that will keep the tenants in their homes, these programs usually just help buy a little time before the eviction actually occurs. At the same time, their low per-tenant costs and the potential savings from delaying a household's entry into the homeless emergency assistance network might make these low-intensity legal assistance programs cost-effective (although, in some cases, such delay only shifts the burden of providing shelter onto the landlords).[56] These programs' per-client costs are usually well under $100, and a survey by the U.S. Department of Health and Human Services (HHS) Office of the Inspector General of shelter costs in eight major cities found that keeping a solitary person out of city shelters for a month can save $225 to $375; and keeping a family of three or four persons out of the shelters can save at least $675 to $1,500.[57] In New York, providing emergency shelter or housing for a homeless family can range from $2,500 to $3,700 per month.[58]

Nevertheless, both the greater general success rates of tenants with full legal representation and the experience of the New York projects indicate that establishing more eviction-defense programs patterned after the New York models of intensive legal representation and other assistance would be more productive from a homelessness-prevention viewpoint than increasing the availability of the less intensive legal assistance. To most effectively prevent homelessness, however, these new programs would have to also assist solitary-person households instead of only families. Although the disproportionate number of families among the homeless and at-risk in New York support the existing programs' family focus, there are still a large number of solitary adults in the city's homeless and most-at-risk populations who also need assistance. More significantly, throughout the country solitary homeless adults are not only the largest segment of the homeless and at-risk populations but also the most likely to become homeless because of an eviction. Indeed, significant reductions in the growth or size of the homeless population will be impossible without aggressive efforts to prevent homelessness among solitary adults.

Unfortunately, providing intensive legal assistance to solitary-person households might be less successful and cost-effective than helping families. Most-at-risk solitary adults usually have more disadvantages and less access to resources than most-at-risk families (making it harder to keep them in their rental units), and it is much cheaper to house solitary persons in homeless shelters. Despite these problems, providing intensive legal assistance to prevent the eviction of solitary most-at-risk adults is still a useful tool, especially if combined with increases in other assistance to most-at-risk solitary adults that will enable them to afford the saved housing (e.g., increases in access to public assistance or in rental subsidies adequate to enable them to pay rent regularly).

The effectiveness of the New York model legal assistance programs could be increased (and the overall cost reduced) by using the most-at-risk profile to target the legal assistance more precisely to those most likely to become homeless without it. Changes in the law to require landlords to enter mediation with tenants prior to starting the formal eviction process could also enable the legal representation organizations to resolve problems much more quickly and cheaply than by providing tenants with full legal representation through the formal court proceedings.[59]

Cash assistance programs. As noted before, all efforts to help at-risk households faced with formal evictions will do nothing to help the larger group of at-risk households evicted outside of the formal procedures. Many at-risk tenants facing either informal or formal eviction (including some who receive legal help) will not be able to pay their current and past-due rent unless they receive funds from some other source. These two problems could be addressed by eviction-prevention programs that provide money to help tenants facing eviction catch up on their rent. Several such programs already exist, but how well they actually prevent homelessness is unclear. For example, New Jersey's Homeless Prevention Program, which has been used as a model by other states and private organizations, provides financial assistance to applicants who can prove they have lost income (e.g., from job loss or disability); are in an emergency situation; and need the money for rent, past rent, utility bills, or mortgage payments.[60] New Jersey state officials believe the program is cost-effective in preventing homelessness—estimating that it is three times cheaper than putting the families in a shelter and 30 times cheaper than putting them in a welfare hotel. However, the extent to which the program's clients would have actually become homeless without its assistance is not clear.

Most significantly, the New Jersey program targets the "working poor" and is not supposed to assist any household that will not be able to resume paying rent on its own once the assistance ends. But only a small portion of most-at-risk households could be considered among the working poor, and most are unlikely to be able to resume paying full rent on their own unless they are linked up with a new source of income or find a cheaper apartment. Most other eviction-prevention programs, whether public or nonprofit, have similar problems. For example, an evaluation of eight such programs (not including the New Jersey program) noted that each was restricted to serving families with a reasonable prospect of resuming a self-sufficient status. Most of the assisted families had incomes higher than $615 per month, almost half included someone who was employed, and all were normally "functional families capable of living in society autonomously" who had experienced some kind of severe economic disruption.[61] In contrast, the most-at-risk households are much poorer, usually dysfunctional, and seldom self-sufficient.

Nevertheless, it is probably still worthwhile, from a homelessness-prevention viewpoint, for the eviction-prevention programs to continue serving their comparatively better-off client populations. First, the aforementioned evaluation of eight such programs found that somewhere between 4 percent and 18 percent of the families receiving assistance from the programs still lost their homes within six months to a year after receiving help and either became homeless or found refuge with friends or relatives. These findings show that the program at least delayed these families' loss of their homes and suggest that some larger percentage might have ended up in a similar situation if no assistance had been provided.[62] Second, the assistance helped at least 80 percent of the families not only to avert eviction but also to escape the severe disruptions that inevitably accompany the loss of one's home (even when a replacement is quickly found). Even if most of the families would not have immediately become homeless, for some these problems might still have been their first step in a decline into homelessness, and all the families would have been weakened without help. Finally, by keeping virtually all the families in their own homes and in a stronger position to face the future, the eviction-prevention programs might have had the desirable side effect of making the families more able and willing to help their own needy friends and family. And, as discussed earlier, such private support network assistance is crucial in keeping people out of homelessness.

Although they typically serve only basically functional families (and usually only those with children), these eviction-prevention programs already face an enormous demand for assistance.[63] Nevertheless, they would be more effective at preventing homelessness if they also assisted solitary-person households. Expanding to serve most-at-risk households (however constituted) might also be productive. While there may be an intuitive resistance to providing emergency eviction-prevention payments to most-at-risk households that will likely be facing eviction again within a few months, any such households that received emergency help would have somehow paid for their housing before and might somehow be able to do so again when the emergency funds run out (even if exactly *how* is not apparent). At the same time, the majority of most-at-risk households are (by definition) in a continuing state of emergency and would probably be better served by some new, more adequate, and longer-term rental or housing subsidies designed specifically for them. Indeed, if such housing assistance were more readily available, more most-at-risk households could use it to resume paying their regular rent after receiving the emergency assistance and would thereby be eligible for the emergency assistance under existing rules. Until such new regular housing assistance is made available to most-at-risk households, however, providing them with one-time emergency help might be better than nothing.[64]

Put most simply, the homelessness-prevention cost-effectiveness of a cash assistance program can be calculated by comparing its cash assistance amounts with the alternative cost of placing those recipients *who would have become homeless without the cash assistance* in a homeless shelter for the average length of stay. Although data are scanty, the previously cited survey of eight eviction-prevention programs provides insight into the cost-effectiveness of cash assistance to various types of clients. The survey calculated that the programs provided an average total of $440 to their clientele of basically functional families, which amounts to less than 15 percent of the average cost of placing each of these families in a homeless shelter.[65]

Consequently, if at least 15 percent of the families would have become homeless without the cash assistance, the cost of providing the cash assistance was less than the avoided cost of providing shelter to those who would otherwise have needed it. Factoring in other indirect benefits and avoided costs from preventing homelessness (or just eviction) would increase the programs' calculated cost-effectiveness, as would reducing their costs by providing the cash assistance in the form of loans to those families capable of eventually paying them off.[66]

Because of their lower rents, the average cash assistance payments required by solitary-person households or poorer, most-at-risk households would be less than for basically functional families (e.g., less than the $440 family average in the eight-program survey). In addition, the savings multiplier for cash assistance programs serving solitary-person and, especially, most-at-risk households would be higher than that for those programs serving basically functional families because a larger portion of their clientele would become homeless without the assistance. At the same time, the avoided costs of sheltering solitary persons are lower than they are for families ($764 versus $2,978 in the eight-program survey); and most-at-risk households are less likely to be able to stay in their housing after the emergency assistance runs out. Nevertheless, delaying their descent into homelessness for only a month could still save one month's worth of shelter costs ($1,140 per family or $290 per solitary person in the survey).[67]

Half the programs in the survey also provided case management assistance (e.g., household budgeting training, family counseling, and help in obtaining public assistance benefits). Such assistance substantially increased the per-family cost of those programs and thereby significantly decreased their calculated cost-effectiveness. Because the survey found no difference in the success rates of those programs providing case management assistance and those that did not, it probably makes sense not to provide such services to the *currently eligible pool of recipients* except in special cases. To the extent that they are basically functional families, it appears they can do without it. In contrast, it is likely that most-at-risk households could benefit significantly from some case management assistance.[68] Given the serious disadvantages suffered by the most-at-risk families and individuals, their chances of actually becoming self-sufficient (or at least of avoiding another threatening emergency for a longer period of time after receiving emergency assistance rent) probably depend on case management or on some other additional assistance. Adding in the cost of case management, however, weakens the basic cost-effectiveness calculations and ultimately makes them dependent on whether the additional assistance can actually prevent, rather than just delay, the households from becoming homeless.[69] Indeed, simply providing the case management costs in the form of additional rent assistance to most-at-risk households might be more cost-effective in many cases.

As Connecticut's statewide eviction-prevention program shows, an inexpensive mediation component can help make these programs more cost-effective by significantly reducing the amount of money paid to landlords for past-due rent and sometimes even lowering the future rent levels, both of which make the recurrence of rent payment problems less likely.[70] Landlords are willing to make these concessions in mediation because the mediation process can save them the considerable time and expense of formal eviction proceedings and can enable them to receive at least some payment. (Formal or informal eviction proceedings usually only get the tenant out without necessarily getting the landlord any of the past-due rent.)

Another important component of these eviction-prevention programs is making referrals to other social service agencies and helping tenants obtain other available benefits (e.g., food stamps, general assistance, Aid to Families with Dependent Children [AFDC], housing subsidies). Receiving such benefits can enable the tenants to stay current with their rent more easily, and referrals to other public and nonprofit social service agencies can help the tenants address their problems and become more self-sufficient (e.g., through job training or placement assistance, family counseling, or alcohol or other drug treatment). Efforts to help tenants find cheaper housing, either directly or through referrals to other agencies, are especially constructive in avoiding future rent problems.

To minimize the risk of fraud and abuse, virtually all the programs make their payments directly to the landlords. The Connecticut program will not make any payments on behalf of tenants until the tenants have first paid their initial contribution to the mediated agreement, and other programs require matching tenant contributions toward the debt.[71] In addition, virtually all the programs limit the amount a tenant can receive and restrict tenants to receiving assistance only once a year or even less frequently. Centralized record keeping that tracks which tenants and landlords have received eviction-prevention payments from which sources (some areas might have multiple sources) helps prevent duplicate or repeated payments. It can also uncover patterns of use that suggest landlord fraud and other problems, as can case management, mediation, site visits, and follow-up.[72]

If the various benefits from cash assistance eviction-prevention programs do not spark sufficient expansion, the federal government could encourage their development by making some level of state participation in the federal Emergency Assistance (EA) program mandatory and by requiring states to use a portion of the EA funds for eviction prevention. The EA program provides states that *choose* to participate with a 50 percent financial match for any temporary financial assistance and services given to eligible families experiencing an emergency, but fewer than half the states use EA funds for homelessness prevention.[73]

Direct-payment programs. Though not designed to respond to eviction threats, programs that provide for portions of various types of public assistance payments to be paid directly to the recipients' landlords to cover rent can avoid nonpayment problems and related evictions.[74] Because landlords want the reliability of direct payments from the public assistance agencies, tenants often are able to negotiate greater forgiveness of past-due rent or even lower future rent levels in exchange for entering into the direct-payment system.[75] For one powerful example, the SRO program of San Francisco's Tenderloin Housing Clinic receives the monthly general assistance checks and Supplementary Security Income (SSI) checks of its clients (solitary adults living in SRO hotels), deducts its clients' monthly (negotiated lower) hotel fees from the checks, forwards payment to the hotels, and then pays the remainder to the clients. This system breaks the destructive cycle of general assistance recipients starting out each month with housing and cash, running out of money before the end of each month, not being able to pay for their hotel room, and becoming homeless until their next check comes along.[76] Similar direct-payment plan options could be developed and expanded for all major forms of public assistance (e.g., in public housing).[77] As a less administratively difficult alternative to direct-payment programs, public assistance programs could provide a portion of their benefits in the form of housing vouchers that landlords and SRO hotel owners could cash upon receipt.[78]

Keeping people in shared housing

More than one-fifth of homeless solitary adults and more than three-quarters of single-parent families are in some kind of shared housing immediately prior to becoming homeless. The eviction-prevention initiatives described above could help the portion of the at-risk households that lose their shared housing because their host tenants are evicted. However, more than two-thirds of the at-risk families and more than half of the solitary adults in shared housing immediately prior to entering homelessness left because of problems with the people with whom they were staying.[79] A significant portion of these problems concerned rent or the sharing individual's or family's contribution to the household; some stemmed from personality conflicts; and others entailed abuse or mistreatment.

Personality conflicts and abuse and mistreatment in shared-housing situations can sometimes be resolved through family counseling or third-party mediation of disputes.[80] The money and contribution issues could be addressed through such things as allowing public assistance recipients to live in shared housing (either as hosts or guests) without a corresponding reduction in their benefit levels. Under current laws, state general assistance and AFDC recipients often have their benefit levels reduced if someone else is living with them and helping with the rent, and public housing authorities and Section 8 subsidies have regulations that prohibit tenants from allowing others to live with them. Allowing low-income heads of household to list as dependents for income tax purposes at-risk adults and others who are currently ineligible could also reduce the economic burden on the hosts in some shared-housing situations (e.g., parents who house adult children). Some experts have even suggested a new program of aid to families with dependent adults to reduce the burden on low-income parents and others who provide housing for at-risk persons.[81]

Helping people who have been displaced from condemned or destroyed buildings

A significant portion of homeless persons (perhaps 10 percent or more) lose their previous place to stay because their building is condemned, destroyed by fire, or otherwise made uninhabitable. In these cases, unlike the situations with households facing eviction or expulsion from shared housing, working to keep the at-risk households in their current residences is impossible, and prevention efforts can only take the form of transition assistance (although more rigorous enforcement of existing building, safety, and fire codes and other efforts to preserve low-cost housing would reduce the likelihood of the condemnation, fire, or uninhabitability occurring in the first place). Fortunately, households placed at risk of homelessness because their housing has been destroyed (rather than because of their own inherent problems and disadvantages) are probably easier, as a whole, to help than other most-at-risk households.

In the case of condemnation, for example, some advance warning and assistance should be possible. The government agencies in charge of formally condemning buildings could be required not only to notify the tenants of the building (which is currently done to some extent) but also to notify other relevant public agencies and private organizations that could help the tenants find replacement housing and generally aid in the transition. As with the formal eviction notices, condemnation notices could be required to contain an emergency hotline phone number through which tenants could get more information and transition assistance. Of course, advance notice is more difficult when the building is lost through fire or some other sudden calamity; but ensuring that the fire and police departments provide displaced tenants with transition information, a hotline phone number, and the like (with special attention to those most-at-risk) would certainly help. Apparently, these things are not now being done or being done well—at least not in those areas where the at-risk and other extremely poor persons live.

General transition assistance to new housing

Once actually displaced from their own residence, whether
through eviction, the condemnation or destruction of their building, or any other means, most-at-risk households clearly need
help making the transition into affordable replacement housing.
So do those in shared-housing situations that are too crowded,
costly, or conflictual to maintain.

Security deposit guarantees. Because of inadequate funds, more
than 70 percent of those in the Chicago Community Trust study
who became homeless after being evicted either did not look for
alternative housing or were not able to find any. Several measures short of general increases in income or housing support
can address this problem. Many of the existing eviction-
prevention programs discussed earlier also provide funds both to
clear up past rent amounts (which is often necessary for persons
to qualify for new housing) and to cover security deposits or first
and last months' rent.[82] Other special security deposit programs
guarantee that they will pay landlords up to the amount of the
security deposit if the tenant defaults on the rent or damages the
apartment. (Typically, the tenant makes monthly payments into
the landlord's security deposit account until the full amount is
reached and the guarantee is removed.)[83] For most-at-risk tenants who are looking for new housing but have large debts from
past unpaid rents, some sort of expedited bankruptcy procedure
might clear the slate and make their transition easier.[84]

Information and referral services. Even with some money and
time, finding affordable housing can still be difficult. But information and referral operations that keep computerized records of
available low-cost housing and offer detailed rental information
on telephone hotlines can help match at-risk households that are
losing their housing with appropriate existing housing.[85] Other
programs that link evicted households with alternative housing
and support services have been established as part of formal
eviction processes.[86] To meet current needs, however, the supply
of such transition services needs to be expanded and better
publicized.[87]

The Homeless Prevention Directline and Network in Alameda
County, California, offers an effective, inexpensive model
for connecting more people with the available services and
assistance.[88] It provides information and referrals in nine separate areas (e.g., eviction prevention, rental assistance, legal
assistance, housing search, and independent living skills)
through a voice-mail system of prerecorded messages on a

24-hour computerized phone line. Similar systems could easily be established by other networks of homelessness-prevention services, or by government social service agencies that do not always have enough staff members to answer the phones (much less provide after-hours guidance).

A model program for transition assistance. The Los Angeles Early Intervention Demonstration Project for Recently Homeless and At-Risk Families (EIDP) works to coordinate government and community-based services in the Los Angeles area to (1) provide crisis intervention and short-term case management services to help stabilize at-risk or recently homeless families, (2) quickly stabilize these families in permanent housing, and (3) provide 12 months of intensive case management services leading to the families' economic and social self-sufficiency.[89] Unlike the previously described eviction-prevention programs, the EIDP targets families that need more than one-time emergency assistance. Rather than trying to keep its clients in current housing, the EIDP finds *new* affordable housing for families who are losing their current housing or living week-to-week in SRO hotels, with friends or family in overcrowded situations, or in apartments they can no longer afford.[90]

In its first year, 143 families (mostly solitary mothers with children) were referred to the program. Of those, 38 found alternative housing, moved out of state, or otherwise disappeared; the remaining 105 were placed in permanent housing (65 percent in subsidized housing). After 18 months, 10 of these 105 families had left permanent housing, 80 were still working with the program, and the remaining 15 had already successfully graduated. As noted earlier, the cost of putting a homeless family in emergency shelter or housing for a year in New York is more than $30,000, and the average annual cost of sheltering a family of four in the eight cities surveyed in the inspector general's report was more than $14,200. In sharp contrast, the EIDP costs less than $3,350 per family for more than a year of assistance.

The EIDP serves as a useful model for additional programs to help those facing homelessness obtain permanent housing and become self-sufficient—but with some qualifications. First, the EIDP serves only families and, even among families, screens out many of the most-at-risk. For example, the EIDP screened approximately 600 families to obtain the first batch of 150, rejecting many as simply too dysfunctional for the program to assist (although many other families simply were unwilling to participate). Second, the EIDP's success hinges on its ability to locate *already available* housing and supportive services from other sources, and it has received priority for its clients in a number of supportive programs and a significant amount of other special assistance (e.g., dedicated Section 8 vouchers). If the EIDP were expanded significantly, the already overburdened network of supportive services would be stretched even more, and special preferences for program clients would be less likely. This point simply emphasizes that the strategy of connecting at-risk individuals and families with existing services is limited and cannot work in any large-scale way to prevent homelessness unless the existing network of these services is fortified and expanded.

Expanding the EIDP to assist solitary adults would take only the decision to do it, but placing solitary adults in housing is much more expensive (per capita) and difficult than placing families. Most significantly, solitary adults are not eligible for AFDC or most Section 8 rental subsidies (major sources of housing funding for families in the EIDP and for at-risk families in general); and states' general assistance payments (basically the only public assistance available to nonelderly, nondisabled solitary adults) are almost always inadequate to pay for housing. EIDP-type programs could partially address these problems by placing solitary adults together in group homes when possible. However, fully serving solitary adults would require more supplementary income or housing assistance specifically for them or new, additional resources for the EIDP-type programs to supply housing directly. Similarly, the EIDP's costs and resource needs would increase if it screened out fewer dysfunctional or most-at-risk families and individuals, and its "success rate" might decline.[91]

A bare-bones version of the EIDP is California's Homeless Assistance Program (HAP), which provides shelter and move-in costs for newly homeless families but no casework and only the most basic referrals (if that). The HAP costs about $700 per family, and a recent study indicates that more than 60 percent of the homeless families were still in their new permanent housing six months after receiving the move-in assistance.[92] It is true that the HAP has a significantly lower success rate than the EIDP in placing and keeping families in permanent housing and that it does not produce the other longer-term benefits of the EIDP model. At the same time, modified HAP-type programs that specifically target most-at-risk families and individuals might offer a cheaper, quicker way to provide transition assistance to more of these largely ignored needy households—perhaps as the first stage in developing a larger scale EIDP-type system with more comprehensive assistance.

Developing prevention strategies regarding institutional releases

As the main identifiable and predictable places where the prehomeless come into direct contact with the system (and often come under its direct control), the previously discussed institutional settings offer remarkably stable, accessible environments for prevention interventions to assist the troubled, frequently hard-to-reach most-at-risk population. An effective strategy could (1) use the most-at-risk profile to identify the persons in the institutions who are most likely to become homeless after release; (2) provide appropriate assistance to these people while they are in the institution to improve their chances of avoiding homelessness; (3) provide them with transition assistance and referrals (e.g., to housing and other support services) during their release; and (4) when appropriate, offer the targeted most-at-risk persons the option of extending their stay until adequate housing outside the institution can be arranged.

The most-at-risk profile could identify the target population through personal interviews or questionnaires. For example, each member of the institution's population could be polled shortly before release (or earlier, when longer-term prevention support is available) to identify those who have any of these characteristics that correlate with an increased risk of homelessness:

1. Few assets or resources and poor income potential (i.e., poor education or weak work history), indicating the likelihood of continued extreme poverty;

2. History of prior homelessness;

3. Weak support network (i.e., few nonhomeless friends or close relatives outside);

4. Mental illness (e.g., history of mental hospitalization);

5. Alcohol or other drug problems;

6. Serious physical health problems;

7. Time served in prison and/or jail; and

8. History of foster care or out-of-home childhood.

Most simply, prevention assistance could then be provided to all those who exhibit both extreme poverty and at least one of the other characteristics (although other triage formulas could be developed). Statistically this group would be the most at risk of becoming homeless without prevention assistance. Although some of the people missed by this targeting might become homeless after discharge, since they would not (by definition) have any disadvantage-reflecting characteristics they would probably be among the most functional of the homeless, the easiest to help, and the most likely to leave homelessness quickly on their own. More important, providing prevention assistance only to those with the most-at-risk characteristics would most accurately target scarce resources to those disadvantaged persons both most at risk and most in need.

If the most-at-risk persons are identified well before their release date, steps could be taken to eliminate some of their most fundamental problems (e.g., through education, job training, treatment of alcohol or other drug problems, mental or physical health care, and contacting their relatives and old friends in an attempt to strengthen their support networks). Although these longer-term prevention efforts are impractical for those institutions with quite short average stays, some are already supposed to be part of the standard rehabilitative or developmental efforts in the institutions with longer-term stays (e.g., prisons, mental institutions, foster care, and the armed services).

Even when such longer-term prevention efforts are impractical, shorter-term assistance just prior to release could significantly reduce the targeted persons' risk of becoming homeless. Most simply, institution staff or volunteers could aggressively work to connect the at-risk persons with all available public assistance entitlements and other benefits, as well as with outside social services, physical and mental health treatment opportunities, education and job-training programs, and other assistance for which they are eligible—with special attention on securing appropriate, affordable housing prior to release. When housing cannot be secured, institutions could offer most-at-risk persons the opportunity (where appropriate and possible) to stay until housing is assured, even when their sentence or treatment has ended. In addition, persons identified as possibly being unable to fend for themselves because of mental illness or other incapacity could be thoroughly evaluated prior to release and, when necessary, referred to or committed into the care of a new institution that could assist them.[93]

Discharges from mental institutions. Homeless and at-risk persons with a history of mental hospitalization basically require the same kinds of assistance as other homeless or at-risk persons to get out or stay out of homelessness. However, their clinical needs usually require continued treatment after discharge from the mental hospital, and their mental illness can make it more difficult for them to obtain other required assistance.[94] Accordingly, it is especially important that mental institutions ensure that discharged most-at-risk patients have a stable, housed situation to go to, with access to community-based treatment that is clearly preferable to the institutional treatment. Unfortunately, mental institutions are not always this careful, and there is a critical shortage of community-based treatment linked with affordable housing for the indigent mentally ill. Developing more subsidized, supported housing and special transitional programs for these discharged mental patients would, of course, help. In the meantime, federal laws governing the states' use of federal funds for mental health care could be amended to prohibit the states from releasing any patients from state mental institutions unless the patients' housing and appropriate community-based treatment have both been ensured.[95]

Emancipation from foster care. Foster care can be a valuable refuge (and sometimes a tremendously positive experience) for neglected, abandoned, or abused children and youth; but foster care systems throughout the country are in a shambles.[96] More than half of all foster youths never graduate from high school, many do not develop even the most basic life skills, and emotional and physical health problems abound. Although much could be done to improve the entire foster care experience for many children, the focus here is on what could be done to help at-risk foster youths successfully make the transition out of foster care into self-sufficient, housed living and to reduce the disproportionate number of foster youths who end up homeless.

Foster care is supposed to be formally terminated at a court hearing when the youth reaches the age of emancipation (usually 18), but sometimes no notice comes until the foster parents stop getting the checks and begin making inquiries.[97] Suddenly, foster youths who have been given little previous responsibility or preparation are completely responsible for their own care and feeding, with hardly anyone to turn to. Much could be done along the lines of the basic transition assistance outlined for those leaving institutions (with similar targeting of the most-at-risk). Possible supplementary measures include:

1. Better training of foster parents to help prepare youths to be
    on their own; and more family counseling and mediation to
    maintain good relations between foster parents and foster
    youths, which could prevent early departures that place
    foster youths out on the streets in an even less prepared
    state.

2. Contacting members of the foster youths' natural families,
    where appropriate, and providing counseling and mediation
    toward rebuilding relationships and creating a support
    structure for the youths.

3. Raising the age of emancipation to 21, as some states have,
    and allowing youths to stay in foster care as long as they are
    in school or pursuing higher education (some states already
    allow foster youths to stay in the system until age 19 if they
    are still in high school or vocational training).

4. Providing at least two years of comprehensive, independent
    life-skills training (e.g., money management, job search
    skills, cooking, health care). Some current life-skills pro-
    grams are only two weeks long.

5. Raising the ceilings on how much money in savings foster
    youths are allowed to have at emancipation so they can
    better afford move-in costs.

6. Providing Section 8 rental subsidies to all emancipating
    poor foster youths (there are usually no special funds to help
    them afford housing).

7. Developing transitional housing that will offer continuing
    life-skills training and casework assistance for emancipated
    foster youths and will provide a support structure for
    them.[98]

The federal government could prompt many of these changes
through regulations associated with its Social Security Act Title
IV-E foster care maintenance payments and, more directly,
through its Independent Living Program (ILP). The ILP provides
more than $50 million each year to support local programs that
help foster youths make the transition to independent adult
living and avoid homelessness.

One especially promising homelessness-prevention model is
the Foster Youth Connection (FYC) of Los Angeles County, a
nonprofit organization created in 1989 by current and former

foster youths to assist foster youths in making the transition from foster care into adulthood.[99] Among other things, the FYC has already (1) established an emergency 800 phone number tended by foster youths that provides information and referrals, (2) created support groups and transition teams for foster youths approaching or going through emancipation, (3) increased public awareness of the problem and prompted governmental responses, (4) initiated a program to encourage senior citizens to provide housing to emancipated foster youths in exchange for support services, and (5) begun developing new transitional housing for foster youths.

Another strategy is to avoid putting (or keeping) children in foster care in the first place. This "family preservation" strategy—whereby social workers use intensive family counseling to try to remove the risk presented to the child in the family rather than remove the child from the family—has recently been gathering supporters in the child protective agencies throughout the country.[100] Michigan's statewide family preservation system cites costs of only about $4,500 per family (average total cost of the intervention), compared with roughly $10,000 per year for foster care. This same family preservation model could also be used to reunite runaway youths with their families, rather than turning them over to foster care or letting them fall into homelessness.[101]

Attacking the fundamental causes of homelessness

The many prevention interventions that directly assist specific at-risk families and individuals could, by themselves, significantly reduce the number of people who become homeless. They would be much more powerful, however, if supplemented by a variety of more general, macrolevel policies, and by changes in laws and regulations. As shown, many prevention programs and strategies rely on connecting their clients to other resources (such as public assistance benefits, housing subsidies, alcohol and other drug rehabilitation programs, and education and job-training programs) to keep or place them in stable housing and begin helping them become more self-sufficient. Such resources are scarce, and expanded prevention interventions will increase the demand for them. Increasing the availability of these resources and undertaking other, more macrolevel strategies will not only provide a more supportive environment for targeted prevention interventions but will also ultimately reduce the need for these interventions by simultaneously attacking the root causes of homelessness.

Most critical, perhaps, in this macrolevel effort to prevent homelessness is generally increasing the incomes of those extremely poor persons from which virtually all of our nation's homeless and most-at-risk come. In many cases, fairly moderate income increases can enable extremely poor people to afford more regular housing and, with luck, stabilize their lives and move toward self-sufficiency. The scarcity of affordable, very low cost housing in some areas, as well as the lack of appropriate supported housing for some especially disadvantaged groups among the most-at-risk, indicates that the supply side of the home procurement equation could also be improved. Confronting other underlying phenomena related to the perpetuation of homelessness—such as the mistreatment of children, the too-common breakup of (formal or informal) marriages, the related rise in single-mother families, and the general deterioration of the mutually supportive family—also makes sense.

Increasing the incomes of the extremely poor

The association between extreme poverty and homelessness is direct; and unemployment, reduced average wages, more restrictive eligibility standards for public assistance, and reduced benefit levels have helped produce much higher levels of poverty since the late 1970s.[102] Reversing these trends could be quite expensive. For example, bringing all the poor in the United States all the way up to the poverty line through direct public assistance payments might cost about $40 billion per year.[103] This large sum suggests more precise targeting of more moderate income assistance and the implementation of cheaper measures to increase incomes among the very poor. Indeed, studies indicate that, even when they do not bring a person out of poverty, relatively small increases in income can sometimes make the difference between homelessness and living at risk on the edge.[104] Nevertheless, substantial progress in preventing homelessness probably cannot occur without some substantial new investment of public and private resources.[105]

Public assistance: amounts. While the value of federal food stamps has more or less stayed the same since the early to mid-1980s, the value of federal-state AFDC and state general assistance benefits (the other two most important benefit programs for at-risk and homeless persons) has declined significantly.[106] Moreover, only about 34 states have statewide general assistance programs (11 others have some local programs).[107] In addition, AFDC and, especially, general assistance payments are often insufficient to cover even the lowest-cost, nonsubsidized housing options; and many states are cutting back on AFDC, general assistance, or various other benefits for the poor.[108] Unlike Social Security payment levels, public assistance benefits are not usually indexed for inflation and will become more inadequate over time, even if no actual cuts are made. (And some of the few jurisdictions that do index these benefits are eliminating the practice.)[109]

This situation could be improved by avoiding reductions in public assistance programs, indexing benefit levels to protect against inflation, establishing general assistance programs where they are absent, and increasing monthly AFDC and general assistance levels so that they at least equal the average fair-market rents where the recipients live. The federal government, for example, could set adequate minimum benefit levels in the basic federal-state AFDC program and establish a standardized package of other benefits that states must provide through AFDC. Other possibilities for maintaining and improving the real incomes of the most-at-risk and their support network of other poor families and individuals include:

1. Do not reduce benefits for at-risk families or individuals who receive other benefits or work income unless the sum exceeds 150 percent of the fair-market rent for the area they live in. Coordinate the various benefit programs to provide complementary assistance (with shared burdens), with total assistance increasing with the disabilities and disadvantages of the subject households and *gradually* phasing out as work and other nonbenefit incomes increase. Reducing disincentives-to-work income would not only help most-at-risk public assistance recipients to build their total income to a reasonable level, but could also reduce the overall cost of public assistance because more recipients might eventually work their way out.

2. Do not reduce benefits for otherwise eligible recipients (or at least for most-at-risk recipients) because they are living with others. Pooling resources might be the only way these people can afford housing, and reducing the ability of most-at-risk persons to contribute to their hosts in shared housing increases their chances of wearing out their welcome and being expelled.

3. Provide benefits from the federal Special Supplemental Food Program for Women, Infants, and Children (WIC) to all eligible persons. WIC provides supplemental foods and other assistance to low-income pregnant or breast-feeding women,

infants, and children up to age five, but reaches only about 60 percent of all eligible recipients. WIC enables at-risk women with children to use more of their other income on housing and other necessities, and by reducing medical problems among most-at-risk families, each dollar spent on WIC may save $3 in avoided costs for medical care.[110]

4. Ensure that food stamp allotments cover all the food needs of recipient households (leaving more of the recipients' other income available to pay for housing and other necessities).

Although implementing some of these options would require substantial additional funds, it could produce considerable prevention savings. For example, providing an additional $50 a month to some most-at-risk households could make the difference between their being able to obtain or stay in housing rather than go to a shelter (at a likely cost of at least $675 to $3,750 per month for families and $225 to $375 per month for solitary adults). Small increases in monthly assistance are also more efficient and possibly cheaper than periodic grants of larger emergency assistance amounts. In addition, up-front costs could be reduced by targeting increases in benefit levels specifically to the most-at-risk (at the cost of losing the prevention gains from providing additional benefits to the at-risk support network); and improved coordination between the various public assistance programs could ensure that no recipients would receive excessive amounts by qualifying for and receiving overlapping benefits. Problems and costs associated with fraud and abuse could be minimized by transferring more benefits in the form of rent vouchers, food stamps, and direct payments (e.g., to landlords), which could also reduce the problem of needy recipients having their money stolen after cashing their benefit checks.

Public assistance: eligibility. More than half of the poor receive food stamps; but fewer than half receive AFDC (with participation levels among the extremely poor and most-at-risk even lower), and participation in state general assistance programs is similarly low.[111] Moreover, the participation of homeless and most-at-risk persons in other assistance programs such as SSI, Social Security Disability Income (SSDI), Medicare, Medicaid, and veterans benefits are all well below eligibility levels.[112] Apparently, many eligible persons either do not know about these programs or do not consider themselves eligible, have their applications denied despite their eligibility, or are unwilling to go through the administrative hassles.[113]

Outreach efforts to connect more of the extremely poor and most-at-risk with available benefits are productive; and simpler application forms, better staffing of public assistance intake offices, and other administrative improvements could help, as could an increased availability of caseworkers, peer advocates, and benefits ombudsmen to assist at-risk families and individuals to obtain and to maintain benefits.[114] But significant increases in the number of deserving most-at-risk persons receiving the various benefits will not occur without legislative and regulatory changes.[115] Some possibilities include:

1. Coordinate eligibility tests for the major public assistance benefits (e.g., by creating separate "packages" of benefits based on income, family status, and disabilities), with eligibility for one benefit creating presumptive, or conclusive, eligibility for some or all of the others; and reduce overly rigorous standards of proof in eligibility determinations, especially those requiring extensive documentation.

2. Make quick initial determinations (i.e., within 24 hours) of whether applicants are likely to be eligible, and immediately begin delivery to all most-at-risk families and individuals in the "likely" category; or require more rapid processing of applications (with benefits accruing from the date the completed application is submitted, even if their actual delivery is substantially delayed by regular processing).

3. Restore or increase income-eligibility limits to include more of the very poor. For example, in 1980, a single parent with two children and with work income equal to 75 percent of the poverty line was eligible for some AFDC benefits in 42 states, but in 1990, that parent was eligible in only 9 states.[116]

4. More readily include mental illness and chronic severe alcoholism as "disabilities" that qualify most-at-risk persons for such benefits as Social Security, SSI, SSDI, Medicare, and Medicaid.[117]

5. Expand the range of workers covered by unemployment compensation to include more of those working in the marginal or secondary sectors of the economy where health insurance, fringe benefits, and unemployment compensation are rare; and increase the length of time that unemployment compensation is available.[118]

6. Modify work requirements associated with the receipt of benefits to make sure they are not creating an unreasonable barrier (e.g., by waiving the requirements for the unemployable, making it easier for persons with little or no prior

work experience or work habits to comply, and providing transportation to work sites).[119]

7. Provide more protection against improper decertifications of eligibility. The high success rate in getting benefits restored by those who appeal decertification suggests that cutoffs too often occur without adequate cause. The Chicago Community Trust study found that about three-fourths of all assistance cutoffs occur because of administrative issues not clearly related to financial eligibility, with a strong correlation between assistance cutoffs and becoming homeless.

The significant cost of these public assistance initiatives could be reduced by helping more public assistance recipients find income-producing work and by providing easier access to employment as an alternative to public assistance in the first place.

Employment. More unemployed poor persons could be connected to existing job openings by expanding and improving existing job-placement programs, assigning special caseworkers or job-placement officers to the most-at-risk population, and expanding job-training programs to prepare more poor and most-at-risk persons for jobs they are not yet qualified to do. Because the problems of at-risk persons resemble those of already-homeless persons, existing job-training and job-placement programs specifically for homeless persons could be expanded to help most-at-risk persons. However, significant success in placing more poor and most-at-risk persons in jobs probably will not occur until the supply of available jobs for such persons is increased.[120]

The federal government's macroeconomic policies are an indirect but powerful way to increase the supply of jobs. Without addressing the complexities of macroeconomic policy here, the government could, at least, pay more attention to reducing unemployment (and less to reducing inflation).[121] Other governmental decisions at all levels could also do more to promote job creation by favoring policy options that would create the most jobs. For example, a federal energy policy based on conservation and renewable resources would create many more jobs (especially for the less skilled) than one based on increased oil exploration and recovery or on nuclear power. Generally reducing the costs to businesses of hiring people or of choosing human capital over machinery (e.g., through tax credits or other incentives to businesses that hire new employees from the most-at-risk population, or through a reduction of the employer's contribution to Social Security) could also promote more job creation and full employment.[122]

New or expanded public employment programs could more directly increase the supply of jobs that match the unskilled pool of unemployed poor and most-at-risk persons. One option is to offer work for unskilled labor on a day-to-day basis to whoever wants it. A flat payment of, say, $5 per hour of actual work would be paid each day; no deductions would be taken out, no other benefits would be given, and no questions would be asked. (All who could do the work would be eligible, regardless of whether they received public assistance benefits.)[123] Administrative costs would be minimized, and the day-to-day nature of the job would enable poor, most-at-risk, and homeless persons unable to find or hold regular jobs (e.g., those with alcohol or other drug problems, or mental illness) to avoid going on welfare or to supplement their public assistance by doing some work for pay.[124] More comprehensive public employment initiatives could follow the model of the Civilian Conservation Corps and other jobs programs of the Great Depression. For example, a low-cost housing preservation corps could create teams of workers from the unemployed poor and most-at-risk population to rehabilitate and preserve low-cost apartment units, thereby addressing the homeless problem from two directions at once. The horrible condition of much low-cost housing shows the serious need for such an initiative, and the success of Habitat for Humanity and other organizations in cheaply fixing up such apartments primarily with unskilled workers suggests its viability.

Regardless of their particulars, any new public employment projects (and all existing job programs) should be sure to target the youngest among the most-at-risk population, such as those leaving school or foster care, to help them develop productive work habits and lifelong skills.[125] Indeed, the consistently high levels of unemployment among inner-city minority youths may have had a lot to do with the emergence of today's homelessness—not only by directly reducing the incomes and income potential of these youths, but also by indirectly contributing to other problems that contribute to homelessness, such as alcohol and other drug dependency and abuse, the breakup of formal and informal marriages (leading to single-mother families), and estrangement from families and friends.[126]

Various measures could also make working in public employment projects or other jobs more attractive to poor and most-at-risk persons, and easier for them to manage. For example, providing poor, single mothers with free day care while they are working (or looking for work) would make it easier for them to enter the work force; and working could be made more attractive if public assistance were structured so that work income did not drastically reduce public assistance benefit levels. (There might be, for example, a coordinated sliding scale whereby total public assistance would only gradually decline as work income increased.)[127] Tax reform to maximize the amount of earnings that very poor workers actually take home would also make working more attractive. By increasing the earnings of the already working poor, it would also reduce their risk of homelessness and improve their ability to support other most-at-risk persons.

Wages. The average hourly wage for private, nonsupervisory workers is now lower, after adjusting for inflation, than it has been since 1969. Whereas a mother working full time at the federal minimum wage could have raised her family of three out of poverty throughout most of the 1960s and 1970s, she would now fall short by more than $2,300 each year.[128] These statistics have prompted many to call for further increases in the minimum wage. However, because fewer than 20 percent of those working at the minimum wage are members of households with incomes below the federal poverty line, raising the minimum wage would be an expensive, poorly targeted way to try to prevent homelessness by increasing the wages of the working poor.[129]

A better, more precisely targeted alternative might be to raise the Earned Income Tax Credit (EITC), which provides a wage supplement for every hour a poor person works. More than 2.9 million of the families with children that live beneath the poverty line are headed by someone who works. Raising the EITC could bring all these families' incomes up to the poverty line (if food stamp benefits are counted as income) at an additional cost of about $3.8 billion, plus another $3.5 to $4.0 billion to provide food stamps to those families not already receiving them.[130] Although that may sound like a lot of money, the minimum wage would have to be raised to $6 per hour to have the same effect, would provide benefits to about 20 million of the nonpoor, and would increase labor costs by as much as $32 billion. Moreover, less dramatic but equally well-targeted improvements could be obtained by smaller increases in the EITC. As it stands, the EITC is not frequently used by those already eligible, and efforts to increase current participation would be constructive. Unfortunately, the modifications of the EITC enacted by Congress in 1990 have significantly complicated the process for applying for and receiving the EITC.[131]

Other targeted tax reductions could also increase the real or net wages of the working poor. For example, whereas raising the personal exemption would primarily provide larger tax reductions to nonpoor households, converting the personal exemption into a refundable tax credit would directly help more poor working families. Congress is considering reductions in the Social Security payroll tax that would also increase the take-home pay of the working poor (and, reportedly, create 299,000 or more jobs by reducing personnel costs).[132] However, those reductions could be better targeted to the most needy. For example, raising or eliminating the cap on payroll subject to the Social Security tax could be coupled (with or without a rate reduction) with raising the floor, so that there would be no Social Security tax at all on the first several thousands of dollars earned. Such a shift would target relief directly at the working poor and at those who hire them while still providing some help to middle-income wage earners.

Preparation for future job markets. Over the next decade and beyond, it appears that there will be a helpful, growing demand for workers, but most of the growth will be in jobs requiring advanced education and training.[133] Accordingly, to supply an adequately educated work force for tomorrow's job market and to keep the growth in new jobs from passing over the poor and most-at-risk populations, more must be done to ensure that the poor and most-at-risk receive an adequate education during their youth. Indeed, providing poor children with at least a solid high school education (which is not the same thing as a high school degree) significantly reduces their chances of becoming most-at-risk adults and is a necessary part of any longer term homelessness-prevention strategy. Suggesting how to correct the substantial deficiencies in our nation's educational system in regard to educating the poor is beyond the scope of this analysis, but expanding the successful Head Start program to reach all poor children could be a powerful first step.[134]

Creating more affordable housing

Some recent housing trends have been positive: The number and percentage of structurally inadequate and overcrowded low-cost units have been declining; vacancy rates for low-cost rental units indicate that there is no physical shortage of available housing in many areas; and, although the overall supply of low-cost rental housing has declined since the mid-1970s, federal housing subsidies have continued to increase.[135] At the same time, vacancy rates are still quite low in some areas, the supply of the most-needed, lowest-cost rental units (e.g., SRO hotels) has dropped significantly, and rent increases and income declines have forced low-income households to pay increasingly larger portions of their total income to cover their rent. (More than four million low-income families and individuals now pay more than 70 percent of their total household income for housing.)[136] There is also a continuing shortage of appropriate supported housing to serve poor persons with mental illness, alcohol or other drug dependency problems, or other disadvantages that make independent living impossible. Consequently, raising the incomes of poor and most-at-risk households might not be enough to meet their housing needs in all areas. Possible supplementary measures include direct housing subsidies; preserving, renovating, and encouraging more efficient use of the existing housing stock; and new construction.

Increasing the affordability of existing housing. Although generally increasing the household incomes of most-at-risk and other poor families helps, the most direct way to ensure that poor households can afford housing might be to increase the benefit levels and expand the coverage of existing programs (mostly federal) that provide direct housing subsidies. Indeed, low-income households living in subsidized housing pay significantly less of their total household income for rent than do otherwise identical households in nonsubsidized housing; but fewer than half (and possibly as little as a third) of eligible households receive housing subsidies, and many low-income households (e.g., most solitary persons) are not eligible.[137]

The federal Section 8 housing voucher and certificate programs (which provide rental subsidies) probably offer the cheapest, fastest way to provide housing subsidies to all low-income households not already receiving any.[138] Reaching these households would require additional funding, increased outreach, and expanded eligibility. For example, the Section 8 programs do not, for the most part, serve low-income households consisting of a solitary person or a group of unrelated persons, and some households are denied benefits because they live in substandard or overcrowded conditions.[139] Recent estimates indicate that the cost of expanding the Section 8 programs to reach all households with incomes below the poverty line or less than half of their area's average incomes would only total about $8 billion to $12 billion per year, and that cost could be drastically reduced by adopting one or more of the following options:[140]

1. Require households receiving Section 8 subsidies to contribute a larger portion of their total income toward the full rent. (They are now required to pay 30 percent.) Spreading the subsidy a little thinner to reach more needy households

could reduce the severe inequities that exist between those who receive federal subsidies and those (equally eligible) who do not, without damaging the integrity or basic usefulness of the assistance.

2. Target the full rental housing subsidy to *extremely* low income households only (e.g., those living below 50 percent of the poverty line). Providing full benefits to those at 50 percent of the poverty line and gradually reducing benefits as household incomes increase would produce a smaller but still substantial savings while also providing some assistance to the all-important support network of other low-income households.

3. Coordinate the rental housing subsidy with other federal, state, and local benefits to ensure an equitable sharing of total assistance costs. (To the extent that other programs provide households with income, those programs will increase the households' ability to contribute larger amounts toward rent, thereby reducing the size of the housing subsidy.)

Through a mixture of these cost-saving options, the federal Section 8 rental subsidy could be made into an entitlement for all low-income households at an additional cost to the federal government of possibly less than $5 billion each year. Such an entitlement would produce enormous benefits in increased access to housing, reduced rent burdens, and greater market incentives to maintaining or creating new low-cost rental housing.[141]

At the same time, just providing rental subsidies is not enough. Approximately 40 percent of Section 8 certificate and voucher recipients are still unable to secure housing promptly, either because they cannot find a unit that is affordable and satisfies program requirements regarding size and condition or because landlords refuse to rent to them.[142] Aggressive enforcement of ordinances prohibiting discrimination against Section 8 recipients could take care of part of this problem, as could changes in Section 8 requirements regarding unit suitability and size.[143] In some areas, however, additional steps must also be taken to preserve and expand the availability of low-cost units to meet the demand.

Preserving existing low-cost housing. Preserving existing low-cost housing is cheaper than constructing new low-cost units and can reduce the displacement of low-income and most-at-risk households. Most important, preservation efforts could block the destruction of the SRO hotels that provide a critical lowest-cost housing option for the most-at-risk. Possible preservation measures include:

1. Placing a moratorium (such as New York City's) on the demolition, conversion, or alteration of SRO units; and passing new local "housing preservation ordinances" (such as those in Hartford, Connecticut, and in San Francisco) that require developers either to replace low-cost housing destroyed by their projects or to contribute to a special fund used for creating new low-cost units.[144]

2. Increasing legal assistance to low-income tenants who are being harassed, improperly evicted, or otherwise forced out of their apartments by landlords who wish to convert the apartments into higher-income rental units.

3. Enforcing local building codes and habitability requirements more aggressively to ensure that low-cost rental buildings do not fall into such disrepair that it makes more sense to destroy them than repair them.

4. Providing owners with loans or other assistance (e.g., tax incentives) to rehabilitate and maintain low-cost rental units in exchange for contracted promises to keep the units as low-cost rentals.

5. Increasing funding, where necessary, for the maintenance and rehabilitation of existing public housing, and otherwise preserving existing government-supported subsidized housing.[145]

6. Providing incentives and support for nonprofit organizations to purchase and administer existing SRO hotels and other low-cost housing units in exchange for agreeing to keep them as permanent low-cost units.

7. Providing incentives for low-income tenants to acquire their own rental units and become homeowners (e.g., by allowing eligible households to use their Section 8 benefits to make monthly mortgage payments).[146]

Improving the use of existing housing stock. Special housing information and referral services, as well as more rigorous enforcement of antirental discrimination laws and other efforts to link poor or most-at-risk families and individuals with existing available housing, could promote the more efficient use of the current low-cost housing stock. Moreover, there are more than 4.7 million households in the United States with only one person living in a two- to four-bedroom home.[147] Encouraging such households with extra room to take in another person or family would, in effect, create new housing units from the existing housing stock without any construction costs. Some possible measures to encourage shared housing and otherwise create additional housing units within the existing housing stock include:

1.   Stop significantly reducing housing subsidies or other public assistance benefits for otherwise eligible persons who find housing with others, provided such persons contribute their housing subsidy or a significant portion of other benefits toward the household's rent and other costs.[148]

2.   Change those zoning laws that forbid shared housing by unrelated persons. More particularly, zoning laws should not prohibit homeowners from creating accessory apartments or independent living units within their single-family homes for renting out to others.[149] Tax incentives or special low-interest loans could further encourage the creation of these units or other shared-housing situations.

3.   Create or expand services that match persons with others offering shared housing arrangements (e.g., room in exchange for services).[150]

By expanding the overall supply of housing, which should also help to reduce rents, these (and other housing) measures can help prevent homelessness even when they primarily create additional housing opportunities for non-low-income households.

Creating new low-cost housing. Even with the previously discussed housing initiatives, some public funding for new construction is probably necessary to meet the need for low-cost housing in those areas with low vacancy rates, shortages of the least expensive SRO-type housing, or an inadequate supply of supported housing for special most-at-risk populations. But new construction of low-cost housing can also be encouraged without new public expenditures.

Many areas have counterproductive zoning regulations, building codes, and tax laws that forbid or inhibit the creation of new low-cost housing. For example, some zoning regulations simply prohibit SRO hotels or block the conversion of unused public buildings (e.g., former schools) into housing units.[151] Some counties tax newly constructed or existing low-cost housing developments more severely than they tax other housing projects (i.e., by taxing them on a per-unit basis, whereby low-cost units pay the same taxes as much more expensive luxury units, rather than on a rent-charged basis). Local licensing fees and building code requirements can also increase the cost of developing new low-cost housing. Although effective health and safety codes should not be eliminated, other building codes could be reviewed, along with zoning regulations and tax laws, to make sure that they do not place any unjustified obstacles in the way of private low-cost housing development.

Some policy analysts assert that rent control laws pose another regulatory obstacle to the creation of low-cost housing by reducing the incentives (i.e., the potential rents) to developers, and several analysts have even named rent control as a major cause of homelessness. However, other experts have pointed out serious flaws in these arguments (and in the underlying data collection).[152]

A real obstacle to developing low-cost housing, especially for disadvantaged populations, is the not-in-my-backyard (NIMBY) phenomenon, whereby residents block any "contamination" of their neighborhood by proposed low-cost housing. Several cities and states have passed "anti-NIMBY" or "anti-snob" legislation. This generally provides for such things as expedited processing of building permits, state overrides of local objections to otherwise acceptable low-cost developments, and requirements that localities meet the low-cost housing needs in their area. Of course, mediation, appropriate designs of the low-cost housing developments, and public education of NIMBY neighbors could also help avoid or diffuse many NIMBY situations.[153]

Although removing these obstacles could indirectly spark the creation of significant amounts of new low-cost housing, other, more affirmative steps are probably necessary in some areas. For example, the federal and state tax advantages for developers and owners of low-cost housing that are still available could be enlarged or introduced in those states that do not offer them.[154] Congress could fully fund the 1990 National Affordable Housing Act that, among other things, creates a new Community Housing Partnership Program to provide project-specific technical assistance and loans to help community-housing development organizations develop low-cost housing. The federal SROs for the Homeless Section 8 Moderate Rehabilitation Program, which already provides more than $100 million per year to rehabilitate and create new SRO housing with some support services for already homeless and at-risk solitary persons, could be expanded. More jurisdictions could replicate the various state and local initiatives to promote new SRO construction.[155] And more cities could follow the example of those that require developers of large commercial buildings to either build new low-cost housing or help finance such housing in exchange for building permits.[156]

Several federal programs provide funding and assistance for housing that serves various disadvantaged populations of the homeless and the at-risk (e.g., those with mental illness, physical handicaps, or alcohol or other drug dependency problems), and some states, localities, and private organizations have similar initiatives.[157] But a significant shortage persists. Expanding and replicating the successful existing programs could help, as could expanding the eligibility for the homeless-specific supported housing programs to include the most-at-risk. Another interesting idea is to create special public housing communities for disadvantaged most-at-risk populations following the model of existing senior citizen communities that (with considerable federal assistance) provide supported, yet independent, living situations.[158] However it is structured, an adequate supply of supported housing where the most disadvantaged of the most-at-risk population can receive the treatment and assistance they require is critical to both prevent homelessness among this group and deal with them humanely.[159]

Strengthening families

A large, disproportionate number of homeless adults have backgrounds of "out-of-family" experiences as children (such as living in foster care, being runaways, suffering from child abuse, or coming from single-parent families). In addition, many have similar out-of-family experiences as adults (such as undergoing divorces and separations from formal or informal marriages; suffering from spousal abuse; or finally wearing out their welcome with supportive family members because of lengthy periods of unemployment, alcohol or other drug abuse, or other troublesome behavior). These experiences often translate into serious emotional problems and weak or nonexistent family ties, which make homelessness more likely. Accordingly, preventing these family dysfunctions from occurring, or treating them before they precipitate a family breakup or the departure of an at-risk member, could significantly reduce the number of people who become most at risk of homelessness or, ultimately, homeless.

Possible earliest-stage interventions to prevent the formation of weak marriages (whether formal or not) or weak families include measures to prevent teen pregnancies or to somehow create a stronger culture of commitment and responsibility associated with parenting and, especially, fathering.[160] Once families come into being, efforts to ensure that the family will have stable housing, income security, and protection from financial emergencies (ideally through productive employment) could strengthen the foundation for family success and remove some of the stresses that can tear families apart emotionally or physically. Providing education, job training, and placement assistance to family members could also fight the disease of apathy and discouragement and help create more hope and optimism, a critical component for emotional health.[161] Other productive interventions could provide income support and training to enable families to care for dysfunctional family members (e.g., mentally ill adult children) or could immediately address dysfunctions that arise in poor families by providing counseling, medical treatment, and general casework and support services. Helpful models can be found in the family-preservation initiatives described earlier that make it possible for children to stay in their own families instead of being placed in foster care.

More general profamily government policies could also strengthen individual families and might help to create a stronger societal sense of the importance of families and the responsibilities of parents, especially fathers. This issue has received much attention lately (although more in relation to poverty or the plight of poor children than to homelessness), resulting in calls to make federal spending and tax policies more "family friendly."[162] Raising the personal and dependent exemption is one frequent proposal, but targeting such an increase to poor families with young children and making it a refundable tax credit would reduce costs, avoid subsidizing the wealthy, and reach more needy families.[163] Other suggestions include reducing the Social Security payroll tax or raising the EITC, removing the "marriage penalty" levied on persons receiving welfare who marry someone who is not receiving welfare, taxing single-parent families at the same rates that other families are taxed, instituting a parental leave policy that would allow new parents (or at least new mothers) to spend more time with their infants without risk of losing their jobs, providing more day care and Head Start programs, ensuring better health care for poor children, expanding the eligibility of welfare benefits to include two-parent families, and even offering special "dowries" for single mothers on welfare who marry.[164]

Another set of initiatives and proposals focuses on preventing divorce or separation and on ensuring proper child support when such disruptions occur. While providing family counseling and other assistance to poor couples facing separation or divorce would help, some analysts also suggest changing the law to make it more difficult for parents to divorce (e.g., by requiring waiting periods during which counseling would be provided).[165] Unfortunately, when divorces and separations do occur, so do problems with obtaining child support payments from the absent spouse. The federal government has expanded its Child Support Enforcement Program, which helps states track absent parents who fail to pay child support, and collection rates are increasing, yet many absent parents are still getting off the hook.[166] Better staffing and computerization would help collection efforts, as would more aggressive efforts to formally identify the fathers of newborn children at the time of birth; provision of financial incentives for single parents receiving public assistance to help track and obtain child support from absent spouses; penalties (e.g., required participation in job corps) for absent parents who cannot or do not make their child support payments; federalization of child support collection and enforcement; and more active garnishment of absent spouses' wages or other income.[167] However, because many absent poor parents simply do not have any income to share with their former spouse or children, the ultimate success of these measures is limited. Consequently, it has been proposed that the government step in to provide child support payments when no child support can be obtained from the absent parent despite the custodial parent's cooperative efforts.

Strengthening families could help to prevent future homelessness and most-at-risk situations, not only by strengthening family-support networks, but also by reducing poverty and preventing other problems (e.g., alcohol and other drug abuse, crime, mental illness, poor education) that predict homelessness and are linked with poor childhood experiences.[168] However, many homeless and most-at-risk persons with absent support structures (and many of these other problems) are already struggling with these problems. Although such persons are usually beyond the reach of these family-support measures, efforts to help them build new support networks or new "families" could help, such as measures to encourage and organize shared housing and group living. One promising nonprofit initiative creates a new support network for homeless families by matching them with teams of volunteers who provide one year of nonfinancial assistance and support in obtaining stable, permanent housing.[169] Similar initiatives could be designed to help most-at-risk families and individuals avoid homelessness.[170]

Resources directed at homelessness prevention

Although no comprehensive homelessness-prevention strategy
has been developed (much less implemented) at the federal or
state level, some significant prevention funding exists in both
the public and the nonprofit sectors.

Federal prevention funding

The 1988 McKinney Act Amendments added homelessness prevention as an eligible activity for three major McKinney programs, and several other federal homelessness programs provide
specific prevention assistance.[171] For example, in fiscal year (FY)
1990, more than 35 percent of the Federal Emergency Management Agency's $130 million Emergency Food and Shelter Pro-
gram was dedicated to prevention (mostly for rent, mortgage, or
utilities assistance); the Emergency Community Services Homeless Grant Program of HHS allows up to 25 percent of its grants
($21 million in FY 1990) to be used for homelessness prevention;
and HHS has also made grants totaling more than $1.2 million
from its Social Services Research Program's discretionary funds
to five homelessness-prevention demonstration projects for
at-risk families (including the Los Angeles EIDP profiled earlier). The 1990 McKinney Act Amendments raised the 20 percent
prevention spending limit of the U.S. Department of Housing
and Urban Development's (HUD's) Emergency Shelter Grant
program to 30 percent, permitting more of that program's funds
to support such eligible prevention efforts as emergency rent
assistance and mediation procedures for landlord-tenant disputes. (However, HUD estimates that only about 1 percent of the
program's funds went to homelessness prevention in FY 1990.)[172]
Overall, in FY 1989 and FY 1990, a little less than $50 million,
or about 6 percent of total FY 1990 federal *homeless-specific*
funding, went toward prevention, with some growth between the
two years.

Federal programs not specifically targeted at homelessness also
provide substantial direct and indirect support to prevention
efforts. Although improvements could be made, the federal-state
AFDC program is considered a major reason that more single-
parent families are not homeless, and many most-at-risk households receive assistance from a variety of mainstream federal
programs (e.g., food stamps). In addition, a number of states use
some of the funds they receive from the AFDC-related EA program to prevent evictions and otherwise help families stay in
their housing or quickly find new housing. HUD's various

housing subsidies (e.g., Section 8 vouchers) play a critical role in homelessness prevention, as do several federal block grants that fund efforts to increase affordable housing opportunities for low-income, at-risk populations or otherwise promote their self-sufficiency. And, on a smaller scale, the U.S. Department of Agriculture's Cooperative Extension Service family budgeting programs for low-income households help such households reduce their costs and improve their ability to manage their limited resources. Taken together, federal mainstream programs direct billions of dollars to a wide range of antipoverty and low-income housing initiatives throughout the country that promote self-sufficiency and unavoidably help to prevent homelessness.

Moreover, the *Goals and Objectives of the Federal Plan to Help End the Tragedy of Homelessness*, adopted by the U.S. Interagency Council on the Homeless in late 1990, identifies preventing nonhomeless families and individuals from becoming homeless as one of its two goals, and suggests a shift in attention to provide more early interventions to assist those persons who are at imminent risk of homelessness.[173] And in February 1991, a Homelessness Prevention Task Force of the Interagency Council issued nine recommendations to the full council for promoting homelessness prevention at federal, state, and local levels. The member agencies of the Interagency Council are now developing action items to implement the prevention objective and to follow through on both the task force's recommendations and the *Goals and Objectives of the Federal Plan*, including its prevention language.

State prevention funding

According to an ongoing study, state funding for targeted homeless assistance will total slightly more than $1.1 billion in FY 1991, with approximately $85 million (slightly less than 8 percent) of the total going for broadly defined homelessness prevention—primarily rent and utilities assistance.[174] Only 13 states reported any prevention spending; and, in a 1990 survey of the states and territories by HHS, only two states reported increases in homelessness-prevention funding during the past five years.[175] As noted earlier, several states plan to make significant cuts in public assistance programs, which are crucial in the effort to prevent homelessness, and homelessness spending is likely to be reduced because of the states' current fiscal difficulties.

Local government prevention funding

No national surveys of local government spending on homelessness prevention exist. The U.S. Conference of Mayors' annual survey of 30 cities' homelessness efforts, for example, does not mention prevention spending but focuses on efforts to help already homeless persons.[176] The survey does show, however, that cities largely depend on the federal government and the states for much of their homelessness-related spending. It indicates that the current economic slowdown has significantly increased demands on local homelessness services and could interfere with the cities' ability to meet those demands. Other, anecdotal evidence suggests that cities are, indeed, cutting back on their efforts to combat homelessness.[177]

Private, nonprofit prevention funding

Again, no national surveys are available that show the amount of private resources directed at homelessness prevention; but the many nongovernment programs mentioned earlier indicate considerable activity (although most nonprofits rely at least partly on public funding). One particularly powerful example of exclusively private or charitable funding for prevention efforts is the *San Francisco Chronicle*'s "Season of Sharing" initiative, in which the newspaper sponsors an annual fund-raising drive during the holidays to raise money for homelessness prevention (mostly rent and utilities assistance). The effort assists more than 1,500 households each year, and in 1990-91, the Season of Sharing fund topped $1.6 million.[178] Such a program could easily be replicated in other cities.

A new paradigm for combating homelessness

As all these public and private homelessness funding and program patterns suggest, the working model for combating homelessness has focused primarily on addressing the emergency food and shelter needs of already homeless persons and then looked at ways to address these people's problems and help them move out of homelessness. Prevention efforts, although growing, are still only an add-on component to this basic strategy. Determining the most optimal mix of emergency assistance, other help for already homeless persons, and prevention assistance for those most at risk of becoming homeless may be impossible, but the following model for comprehensive coverage provides a useful ideal:

1. Improve the quality and, where necessary, the availability of emergency homeless shelters; eliminate obstacles to their use; and increase other efforts to get more homeless persons into the shelters in order to connect them with the homelessness-assistance network.

2. Provide food and other emergency assistance (e.g., to address critical health problems) at the shelters, and use the shelters as the site for screening, referrals (e.g., to alcohol-treatment centers), and short-term assistance and stabilization (e.g., by connecting people with available public assistance benefits).

3. Help homeless persons into permanent housing (or into special transitional or supportive housing if they are too disadvantaged to live independently) as soon as possible, and then provide rehabilitative and developmental assistance (e.g., education and job training; longer-term mental health, alcohol, or other drug treatment; family counseling) either directly or through referrals.

4. Use the most-at-risk profile to identify and stabilize those persons most at risk of homelessness at their current homes or institutional residences (or, when necessary, in new permanent housing), and then provide similar rehabilitative and developmental assistance as needed.[179]

To avoid human suffering, providing adequate food and shelter to those who will otherwise go without must remain the top priority. But this model suggests, contrary to current practice, that other assistance should be more equally divided between the already homeless and the most-at-risk. Although helping already homeless persons clearly offers the most direct way to get people out of the homeless population, only prevention assistance to the most-at-risk can directly reduce new entries into the homeless population. Although it is impossible to precisely identify those special persons who will actually become homeless unless they receive help, prevention assistance to the at-risk still offers the potential of significant savings (per person actually prevented from becoming homeless) in both human and economic costs. Even if current funding were simply redirected from helping the already homeless to prevention assistance, the number of homeless persons receiving assistance could actually increase (assuming we define homeless to include those who would have become homeless without the prevention assistance). It is simply cheaper to help people before they become homeless than afterward, which means that more people can be helped with the same amount of funds. Moreover, prevention assistance can directly reach the large group of episodically homeless persons before they fall back into homelessness. At the same time, direct assistance to already homeless persons is the most effective way to reach the long-term or permanently homeless (although prevention efforts can help keep people from entering this category).

However allocated, assistance to already homeless and most-at-risk persons depends on other available resources; and there is little chance of reducing the need for both kinds of assistance unless steps are taken to attack the underlying causes (e.g., extreme poverty, shortages of affordable or appropriate housing, and the breakup of families) that provide the foundation for becoming homeless or most-at-risk. Accordingly, the model for comprehensively addressing homelessness should include two more elements:

1.   Strengthening the network of mainstream public assistance and social service programs to provide adequate assistance directly to homeless and most-at-risk persons and to attack the causes underlying homelessness.

2.   Creating more supportive policies and a less restrictive legal and regulatory environment for providing assistance directly to homeless and most-at-risk persons and for attacking the underlying causes.

Implementing and funding the new model

This paper has presented numerous effective no-cost and low-cost measures (e.g., changes in existing regulations or laws) that could be implemented immediately at federal, state, and local levels to create a more promising environment for homelessness prevention and begin to attack the causes underlying today's homelessness. It is simply a matter of taking the time and deciding to do it. However, eliminating the worst aspects of homelessness will also require substantial new investments to fund some mix of the other prevention measures that unavoidably come with significant price tags (despite the various measures outlined to minimize costs).

Ideally, new funding for prevention efforts would be added to current homelessness spending rather than diverted from it. For example, although it would be productive (from a prevention viewpoint) if public and private programs that currently provide other than emergency assistance to homeless persons expanded their scope to include most-at-risk families and individuals, increasing their funding to meet the additional demand would be more constructive than simply requiring them to serve a larger mix of clients with the same level of funds. Admittedly, obtaining new funding is extremely difficult; but spending on homelessness prevention is an investment that can pay off in actual dollar savings as well as in public benefits, and it may be the only way to eliminate homelessness as a significant social problem.

Because the various levels of government are still not only the primary source of substantial funding for homeless activities but also the best means for quickly effecting significant nationwide progress toward preventing homelessness, progress in preventing and eliminating homelessness in the United States depends on the funding choices made by government. However, because many state and city governments face serious, ongoing fiscal constraints, already rely largely on federal funding to support their homelessness efforts, and have shown little inclination to initiate prevention activities, they are unlikely to generate significant amounts of new prevention activity unless the federal government provides encouragement, coercion, or support. Accordingly, although preventing homelessness largely depends on locally based programs, new federal action is probably the best (if not the only) way to initiate and ensure the development of wide-ranging homelessness-prevention efforts throughout the nation.

As usual, it boils down to a matter of political will and budget priorities. If the focus is on how to most cost-effectively and productively end homelessness, prevention funding will increase and corresponding progress will be made. But if the focus is on short-term "fiscal restraint" and established patterns of government spending, only marginal improvements are possible. A much broader view than either of these, only hinted at in this paper, might see that aggressively pursuing a range of prevention-based initiatives to eliminate homelessness could have far-reaching effects that would dramatically strengthen the foundation and fiber of our society—which might be well worth the money.[180]

Author

Eric N. Lindblom is a policy analyst focusing on homelessness issues with the U.S. Department of Veterans Affairs and, in that capacity, is the primary author of the *1990 Annual Report of the Interagency Council on the Homeless.* The opinions expressed in this article are his own and not necessarily those of the VA or the Interagency Council. This article is a shortened version of a much more detailed paper on homelessness prevention that the author expects to complete soon.

Endnotes

1. Although preventing a currently homeless person from being homeless tomorrow could be considered homelessness prevention, this paper focuses exclusively on efforts to keep people not currently in the literally homeless population from joining (or rejoining) it.

2. From 1984 to 1988, public and private spending on homeless shelters increased from $300 million to $1.5 billion and the number of shelter beds increased from 100,000 to 275,000, and the average shelter occupancy rate was only 66 percent in 1988. Although improvements are still needed to meet excess demand in some areas, to improve shelter quality, and to remove obstacles to their use, the emergency response network is basically in place. U.S. Department of Housing and Urban Development, *The 1988 National Survey of Shelters for the Homeless* (Washington, DC: U.S. Department of Housing and Urban Development, 1989).

3. See Eric N. Lindblom, *1990 Annual Report of the Interagency Council on the Homeless* (Washington, DC: U.S. Interagency Council on the Homeless, 1991), for a discussion of softening public support for the homeless.

4. Randall K. Filer, "What Really Causes Homelessness?" *NY The City Journal*, no. 99(Autumn 1990):31–41; Robert C. Ellickson, "The Homelessness Muddle," *The Public Interest* (Spring 1990):45–60.

5. This paper uses the federal definition of homelessness that includes only the literally homeless (i.e., those living either in shelters or other homeless facilities or on the streets), but some of the cited studies may use broader definitions. For insight into the number of literally homeless persons on any given day, see Martha R. Burt and Barbara E. Cohen, *America's Homeless: Numbers, Characteristics, and Programs That Serve Them*, Report 89-3 (Washington, DC: Urban Institute Press, 1989); Martha R. Burt, "Developing the Estimate of 500,000–600,000 Homeless People in the United States in 1987" (Paper presented at the conference on "Enumerating Homeless Persons: Methods and Data Needs," sponsored by the U.S. Bureau of the Census, Department of Housing and Urban Development, and the Interagency Council on the Homeless in Washington, DC, November 1990); Peter H. Rossi, *Down and Out in America: The Origins of Homelessness* (Chicago: University of Chicago Press, 1989); the attempt to physically count homeless persons in the 1990 census, described in Barbara Vobejeda, "Census Spotted Nearly 230,000 Homeless People," *Washington Post*, April 13, 1991. These estimates and analyses of the number of homeless persons are all based on surveys or counts that precede the current economic recession, which has undoubtedly increased the size of the homeless population.

6. Lindblom, *1990 Annual Report;* Intergovernmental Health Policy Project, *Results from a Survey of State Initiatives on Behalf of Persons Who Are Homeless* (Washington, DC: George Washington University, 1988) and subsequent data collection and reports; U.S. Conference of Mayors, *A Status Report on Hunger and Homelessness in America's Cities: 1990* (Washington, DC: U.S. Conference of Mayors, 1990).

7. For example, as many as half of the homeless population have served five days or more in jail, at a cost of approximately $50 to $70 per day in big-city jails; and the costs of increased security, maintenance, and

cleanup made necessary by homeless persons' use of New York City
transportation facilities for temporary shelter total more than $20 mil-
lion each year; Burt and Cohen, *America's Homeless*. Cost information
from the American Jail Association, Hagerstown, Maryland; Nathan
McCall, "DC Inmates Glad to be 'Home,' " *Washington Post,* March 27,
1991; Daniel Machalaba, "Mobile Homes:Transit Systems Face Burden of
Providing Last-Resort Shelter," *Wall Street Journal,* July 18, 1990.

8.   Unfortunately, there has been little research in these areas. Still, much
can be done by piecing together data already available from existing
studies, which together provide a considerable amount of useful (but not
complete or always up-to-date) information.

9.   For one example of this approach, see J. R. Wolch, M. Dear, and A. Akita,
"Explaining Homelessness," *Journal of the American Planning Association* (Autumn 1988):443–53.

10. This and all other not otherwise footnoted information in the text
regarding the characteristics of the homeless population come from
Lindblom, *1990 Annual Report,* and the authorities cited therein.

11. The 1990 federal poverty line for a single-person household is $6,652, for
a two-person household, $8,512; for a three-person household, $10,419;
and for a four-person household, $13,360 (U.S. Bureau of the Census).

12. Poor education and weak work experience are shared equally by homeless persons and the nonhomeless extremely poor: see Burt and Cohen,
America's Homeless; Michael R. Sosin, Paul Colson, and Susan
Grossman, *Homeless in Chicago: Poverty and Pathology, Social Institutions and Social Change* (Chicago: Chicago Community Trust, 1988)
(hereafter cited as Chicago Community Trust study). Other characteristics associated with extreme poverty that apparently do not have any
additional, special relationship with homelessness include having had
low family income during childhood (which reflects socioeconomic background), being black or Hispanic, and not being elderly (see Chicago
Community Trust study).

13. Unfortunately, few studies have tried to compare the characteristics of
the extremely poor with those of persons who actually become homeless.
One of the most useful local studies that did is the Chicago Community
Trust study, which compares homeless persons who use soup kitchens
and other free meal services in Chicago with previously-but-not-
currently-homeless and never-homeless persons who use these same
services. However, although its information is extremely interesting and
helpful, the study is just one local effort.

14. Irving Piliavin, Michael Sosin, and Herb Westerfelt, "Tracking the
Homeless," *Focus* 10, no. 4(1987):20–25, report 58 percent; Roger K. Farr,
Paul Koegel, and Audrey Burnam, *A Study of Homelessness and Mental
Illness in the Skid Row Area of Los Angeles* (Los Angeles: Los Angeles
County Department of Mental Health, 1986), report 67 percent; and
Phoenix Consortium for the Homeless, *The Homeless of Phoenix: Who Are
They and What Should Be Done* (Phoenix, AZ: Phoenix South Community
Mental Health Center, 1983), reports 35 percent; all three studies are
cited in Barbara E. Cohen and Martha R. Burt, "The Homeless: Chemical
Dependency and Mental Health Problems," *Social Work Research and
Abstracts* 26, no. 1(1990), pp. 8–17. The Chicago Community Trust study

reports 52 percent; similarly, the Chicago Community Trust study of extremely poor persons using free meal programs found that about half of those not currently homeless had been homeless at least once before.

15. New York, which may have more homeless persons than any other city, has a significantly lower percentage of solitary males (and a higher percentage of homeless families) than is reflected in the national averages (Burt and Cohen, *America's Homeless*).

16. While there are no statistics directly on point, it appears that the pattern for not-formally-married couples with children parallels the pattern for those couples who do get formally married (Chicago Community Trust study; Burt and Cohen, *America's Homeless*).

17. Ibid.; see also Martha R. Burt and Barbara E. Cohen, "Differences among Homeless Single Women, Women, with Children, and Single Men," *Social Problems* 36(December 1989):508–24.

18. *Children and Youths: About 68,000 Homeless and 186,000 in Shared Housing at Any Given Time* (Washington, DC: U.S. General Accounting Office, 1989) estimates the one-day total of homeless unaccompanied youth to be 52,000 to 170,000; see also *Homeless and Runaway Youth Receiving Services at Federally Funded Shelters* (Washington, DC: U.S. General Accounting Office, 1989).

19. Rossi, *Down and Out in America;* Chicago Community Trust study. As discussed below, the onset of mental illness usually precedes homelessness.

20. Annual studies of homeless veterans by the Department of Veterans Affairs show a significant increase over the past three years in the incidence of past hospitalization for drug-dependency problems among homeless veterans and, by implication, among all homeless males. See Department of Veterans Affairs, Northeast Program Evaluation Center, *Reaching Out across America: The Third Progress Report on the Homeless Chronically Mentally Ill Veterans Program* (December 1989); *Healing Communities: The Second Progress Report on Domiciliary Care for Homeless Veterans Programs* (December 1989); and subsequent data collection.

21. See also the Chicago Community Trust study, which found that homeless persons are more prone to binge drinking and alcoholism than the never-homeless extremely poor but that nonalcohol illegal drug use among both groups is not statistically different.

22. Robert E. Drake et al., "Housing Instability and Homelessness among Rural Schizophrenic Patients" (Paper presented at the 143rd annual meeting of the American Psychiatric Association at the New Hampshire-Dartmouth Psychiatric Research Center, Hanover, NH, May 1990).

23. James Wright and Eleanor Weber, *Homelessness and Health* (Washington, DC: McGraw-Hill, 1987).

24. Chicago Community Trust study; Burt and Cohen, *America's Homeless;* Rossi, *Down and Out in America.* See also the discussion below regarding where homeless persons come from.

25. Peter H. Rossi, *Homelessness in America: Selected Topics,* study done for the U.S. Interagency Council on the Homeless (Amherst, MA: University of Massachusetts, Social and Demographic Research Institute, September 1989).

26. Rossi, *Down and Out in America,* which also found considerable alienation between homeless persons and existing family and relatives.

27. Ibid.; Chicago Community Trust study.

28. Burt and Cohen, *America's Homeless;* Rossi, *Down and Out in America;* Rossi, *Homelessness in America.*

29. Rossi, *Homelessness in America;* Rossi, *Down and Out in America.* There are also many formerly homeless persons among the patients in state mental hospitals. See Carol T. Mowbray, V. Sue Johnson, and Andrea Solarz, "Homelessness in a State Hospital Population," *Hospital and Community Psychiatry* 38(August 1987):880–82; Beverley G. Toomey et al., "Evaluating Community Care for Homeless Mentally Ill People," *Social Work Research and Abstracts,* no. 48(December 1989):21–26.

30. Burt and Cohen, *America's Homeless.*

31. Toomey et al., "Evaluating Community Care"; Robert E. Drake, Michael A. Wallach, and J. Schuyler Hoffman, "Housing Instability and Homelessness among Aftercare Patients of an Urban State Hospital," *Hospital and Community Psychiatry* 40(January 1989):46–51.

32. Ellickson, "The Homelessness Muddle" (citing a California study by Piliavin and Sosin); Chicago Community Trust study; Drake et al., "Housing Instability and Homelessness"; Irving Piliavin et al., *The Duration of Homeless Careers: An Exploratory Study* (Madison: University of Wisconsin, 1990).

    Many homeless persons resist institutionalization relating to mental or physical health, and a significant number of formerly homeless patients leave hospitals (often returning to homelessness) before their treatment is completed; see Luis R. Marcos et al., "Psychiatry Takes to the Streets: The New York City Initiative for the Homeless Mentally Ill," *American Journal of Psychiatry* 147(November 1990):1557–61.

33. A study of Minneapolis homeless persons found that those placed in mental institutions *after* their initial spell of homelessness have longer homeless career lengths than those hospitalized *before* their first homeless spell (although why is not clear). See Piliavin et al., *The Duration of Homeless Careers.*

34. Rossi, *Homelessness in America.*

35. Burt and Cohen, *America's Homeless.* Neither this study nor that of Burt and Cohen notes the extent to which these treatment episodes occurred before or after initial entries into homelessness.

36. Chicago Community Trust study.

37. Another category of health facility that might serve as a significant temporary residence for the prehomeless is battered women's shelters, but there is little available information.

38. Burt and Cohen, *America's Homeless;* Rossi, *Homelessness in America.*

39. Currently, there are about 400,000 persons in jail and 720,000 persons in prison at any one time. Further, there are annually about 9.6 million releases from jail (most involving repeat offenders and a time served of fewer than 72 hours) and over 540,000 releases from state and federal prisons (which also experience significant recidivism). Information comes from the American Jail Association in Hagerstown, Maryland, and the American Correctional Association in Laurel, Maryland.

40. Department of Veterans Affairs, Northeast Program Evaluation Center reports and data collection; see also Wright, *Address Unknown: The Homeless in America* (New York: Walter D. Gruyter, Inc., 1989).

41. Information from the Department of Veterans Affairs, Demographics Division of the Management Sciences Service of the Office of Finance and Planning, Washington, DC.

42. Piliavin et al., *The Duration of Homeless Careers* (38.6 percent); Chicago Community Trust study (14.5 percent); James R. Knickman and Beth C. Weitzman, *A Study of Homeless Families in New York City: Risk Assessment Models and Strategies for Prevention (Final Report: Volume 1),* prepared for the Human Resources Administration by the Health Research Program of New York University (September 1989) (20 percent among heads of families seeking shelter); David Wood et al., "Homeless and Housed Families in Los Angeles: A Study Comparing Demographic, Economic, and Family Function Characteristics," *American Journal of Public Health* 80(September 1990):1049–52 (35 percent among homeless mothers); Richard P. Barth, "On Their Own: The Experiences of Youth after Foster Care," *Childhood and Adolescent Social Work Journal* 7 (October 1990):419–40 (citing other studies finding 30 percent to 40 percent); and Ezra Susser, Elmer Struening, and Sarah Conover, "Childhood Experiences of Homeless Men," *American Journal of Psychiatry* 144(December 1987):1599–1601 (23 percent and 17 percent). See also J. C. Barden, "When Foster Care Ends, Home Is Often the Street," *New York Times,* January 6, 1991.

43. Barth, "On Their Own."

44. Knickman and Weitzman, *A Study of Homeless Families;* Chicago Community Trust study; Rossi, *Down and Out in America* (describing Rossi's own 1986 study of homeless persons in Chicago).

45. Knickman and Weitzman, *A Study of Homeless Families;* see also Beth C. Weitzman, James R. Knickman, and Marybeth Shinn, "Pathways to Homelessness among New York Families," *Journal of Social Issues* 46, no. 4(1990):125–40.

46. Rossi's 1986 Chicago study of homeless adults similarly found that, immediately prior to becoming homeless, 48 percent were living alone, 26 percent were living with their immediate family, 6 percent were living with other relatives, and 20 percent were living with friends. Rossi, *Down and Out in America.*

47. Ibid., which presents and analyzes the results of Charles Hoch and Diane Spicer, *SROs, An Endangered Species: Single-Room Occupancy Hotels in Chicago* (Chicago:Community Shelter Organization and Jewish Council

on Urban Affairs, 1985); Charles Hoch and Robert A. Slayton, *New Homeless and Old: Community and the Skid Row Hotel* (Philadelphia: Temple University Press, 1989); Nashville Coalition for the Homeless, *Nashville's SRO Hotels* (Nashville: Author, November 1988); Barrett A. Lee, "Stability and Change in an Urban Homeless Population," *Demography* 26(May 1989):323–24; T. J. Main, "What Do We Know about the Homeless," *Commentary* (May 1988):26–31.

48. Weitzman, Knickman, and Shinn, "Pathways to Homelessness."

49. Irene Bueno et al., *When the Rent Comes Due: Breaking the Link between Homelessness and Eviction: An Eviction Prevention Action Plan* (San Francisco: HomeBase Regional Support Center for Homelessness Policy and Programs, 1989) (hereafter cited as HomeBase report); Association of the Bar of the City of New York (NYCBA), Committee on Legal Assistance, *Report on the Prevention of Homelessness by Providing Legal Representation to Tenants Faced with Eviction Proceedings* (November 1988).

50. See also HomeBase report.

51. HomeBase report; NYCBA, Committee on Legal Assistance; Rebecca Hall, *Eviction Prevention as Homelessness Prevention: The Need for Access to Legal Representation for Low Income Tenants* (Berkeley, CA: Berkeley Community Law Center, May 1, 1991).

52. Hall; NYCBA, Committee on Legal Assistance.

53. For some powerful case histories that illustrate how legal assistance can protect low-income tenants from being unfairly steamrollered by unfamiliar procedures or by landlord attorneys' deceit and improper conduct, see NYCBA, Committee on Legal Assistance.

54. Ibid. See also New York State Department of Social Services, Office of Program Planning, Analysis, and Development, and Office of Shelter and Supported Housing Programs, *The Homeless Prevention Program Outcomes and Effectiveness* (Albany: New York State Department of Social Services, 1990).

55. Conversation with Roderick T. Field, attorney, Legal Aid Foundation of Los Angeles, February 21, 1991; conversation with Cathy Mosbrucker, staff attorney, Tenderloin Housing Clinic, Eviction Defense Office, San Francisco, February 13, 1991.

56. The Tenderloin Housing Clinic, for example, annually serves about 2,400 clients who are involved in over 1,900 unlawful detainer (eviction) actions and has an annual budget of about $100,000 to $110,000 (or less than $46 per client).

57. Office of the Inspector General, *Homeless Prevention Programs* (Washington, DC: U.S. Department of Health and Human Services [HHS], 1991) (hereafter cited as Inspector General's report).

58. NYCBA, Committee on Legal Assistance.

59. HomeBase report; conversation with Nancy Howard, associate director, Community Mediation, Inc., New Haven, CT, January 28, 1991;

Connecticut Department of Human Services, Bureau of Evaluation and Review, "Evaluation Report:Community Mediation, Inc. Eviction Prevention Program" (December 1990).

60. *Homelessness: Too Early to Tell What Kinds of Prevention Assistance Work Best* (Washington, DC: U.S. General Accounting Office, 1990) (hereafter cited as GAO prevention report); HomeBase report; Gen Ifill, "New Jersey Is Blunting the 'Knife Edge of Homelessness,' " *Washington Post National Weekly Edition,* March 19–25, 1990.

61. Inspector General's report; State of Connecticut, "An Act Concerning Programs to Prevent Homelessness," Public Act No. 90-257(July 1990); see also State of Connecticut, Department of Human Resources, "Eviction Prevention Program Guidelines" (January 1991).

62. The wide range of percentages results from the inability of the evaluation to locate all the families in its sample who received assistance, and there is no way of telling what portion of the not-found families became homeless and how many simply moved to other permanent housing.

63. GAO prevention report; Inspector General's report.

64. To facilitate the expansion of emergency rental assistance programs' eligibility requirements, the federal programs that support only those efforts directed at families could expand their coverage to efforts directed at solitary adults as well (or at least at those solitary adults who fit the most-at-risk profile). In addition, the 1990 federal McKinney Homeless Assistance Amendments Act and the other laws and regulations governing federal programs that currently provide some funding to eviction-prevention efforts could eliminate or modify their current requirements that assisted households must have a reasonable prospect of being able to resume rent payments on their own or otherwise escape their emergency situation within a reasonable time. U.S. House of Representatives, "Stewart B. McKinney Homeless Assistance Amendments Act of 1990," Conference Report, Report No. 101–951 (October 1990), Sec. 411(b); and GAO prevention report (regarding the nonhomeless-specific Emergency Assistance [EA] program).

65. Inspector General's report.

66. The New Jersey program uses loans for some recipients. Wright, *Address Unknown,* proposes a "rent emergency insurance program" that follows the model of national flood insurance to help finance these programs.

67. These figures are based on the average shelter costs per person and average size of family data reported in the Inspector General's report. As noted earlier, the cost of shelter in New York is much higher than the averages calculated here.

68. The eviction-prevention program run by the American Red Cross in San Francisco is a good example of a program that provides one-time rent assistance with short-term case management. Conversation with Martin Torow, director of social services, American Red Cross, San Francisco, February 14, 1991; American Red Cross of San Francisco, "Homeless Prevention Program Fact Sheet" (December 1990); correspondence from American Red Cross to California Department of Social Services regarding "Evaluation of DSS/ARC grant disbursement involving months April

through October 1990," November 15, 1990. For an example of a program that provides long-term intensive casework to at-risk families, see the description of the Los Angeles Early Intervention Demonstration Project (EIDP), below.

69. If the assistance levels stayed the same ($440) and the average case management costs ($2,223) were added in, the total cost of helping a most-at-risk family ($2,663) would total less than the average cost of putting that family up in a shelter for the average length of stay ($2,978). However, using these same figures, the cost of helping a solitary person ($2,663) would be significantly more than putting that person in a shelter ($764), but cash assistance levels and case management costs might be significantly lower for a solitary adult than for a family (Inspector General's report).

70. Connecticut Department of Human Resources, Bureau of Evaluation and Review. The Connecticut program, for example, simply provides about 18 to 20 hours of training for quasi-volunteer mediators (often former clients and law students) and pays them only $10 per mediation session. Other programs with mediation or less formal negotiation components also report savings on past-due amounts. Conversation with Sandy Weiner and Dawn Hasselbach of the Income Rights Project, San Francisco, February 13, 1991; conversation with Martin Torow; conversation with Georgia Berland, homelessness coordinator, Human Services Commission, County of Sonoma, Santa Rosa, California, February 15, 1991 (regarding Sonoma Rental Information and Mediation Services).

71. Inspector General's report.

72. For example, the Sonoma County People for Economic Opportunity organization in Santa Rosa, California, has just started developing a countywide, modem-connected computer network. Conversation with Robert Judd and Rivian Berlin regarding the rental guarantee program run by Sonoma County People for Economic Opportunity.

73. GAO prevention report; Lindblom, *1990 Annual Report*. The EA program could also be modified to permit the use of its funds to assist not only families with children but also other families and solitary adults.

74. For examples of direct-payment programs, see HomeBase report; Connecticut Department of Human Resources, Bureau of Evaluation and Review.

75. Conversation with Nancy Howard of Community Mediation; conversation with Sandy Weiner and Dawn Hasselbach.

76. Conversation with Randall M. Shaw, executive director, Tenderloin Housing Clinic, San Francisco, February 14, 1991.

77. HomeBase report. To avoid so-called welfare evictions, landlords could be required to notify the public assistance agency prior to initiating any eviction against tenants on a direct-payment plan (to make sure that the payment failure is not due simply to some administrative error).

78. For example, the Sonoma County Social Service Department in California distributes a portion of recipients' monthly general assistance benefits as a housing voucher. Conversation with Jerry R. Elder, chief of

general social services, Social Service Department, County of Sonoma, February 15, 1991.

79. Knickman and Weitzman, *A Study of Homeless Families;* Chicago Community Trust study.

80. For example, Connecticut's eviction-prevention program helps young single mothers who have left their families or been thrown out by providing special mediation services to try to strengthen family relationships and get these women and children back into the family home (Connecticut Department of Human Services, Bureau of Evaluation and Review).

81. Rossi, *Down and Out in America;* Peter H. Rossi, *Without Shelter: Homelessness in the 1980s* (New York: Priority Press Publications, 1989); Wright, *Address Unknown.*

82. Examples of such state programs include the New Jersey Homeless Prevention Program, as well as its separate EA program (GAO prevention report). An example of a nonprofit program is the Season of Sharing network in the seven counties of San Francisco's Bay Area. Telephone conversation February 12, 1991, with Diane Levy, Season of Sharing coordinator; see also "The Chronicle Season of Sharing Fund" (San Francisco: *San Francisco Chronicle,* September 1989).

83. Correspondence and program materials from Lisa Korwin, executive director, Eden Council for Hope and Opportunity, Hayward, California, February 12, 1991; conversation with Robert Judd and Rivian Berlin regarding the Rental Guarantee Program run by Sonoma County People for Economic Opportunity.

84. Chicago Community Trust study.

85. Conversation with Barbara Bernstein, executive director, and Catherine Behan, program coordinator, Eden I&R, Inc., Hayward, California, February 14, 1991; telephone conversation with Evie Ashcroft of Eden I&R, April 8, 1991.

86. The San Francisco Sheriff's Eviction Assistance Program, for example, gets high marks from the nonprofit tenants' rights community HomeBase report.

87. The Chicago Community Trust study, for example, indicates that fewer than a quarter of the at-risk population who are evicted contact a social service agency to try to obtain alternative housing or other transition assistance; even so, those agencies that provide assistance report an inability to meet the existing demand.

88. Conversation with Patricia Dominiquez-Greene, coordinator, Homeless Prevention Directline and Network, Oakland Citizens Committee for Urban Renewal (OCCUR), Oakland, California, February 14, 1991; Patricia Dominiquez-Greene, "Summary Report: DirectLine Community Service 1989–1990," report to Telecommunications Education Trust from Directline-OCCUR Community Information Service (July 1990).

89. The information relating to the Los Angeles EIDP comes from a conversation with Tanya Tull, president and chief executive officer of Beyond Shelter, Los Angeles, February 20, 1991, and from various program

material provided at that time, including the program's "Application for Federal Assistance," dated May 1, 1990.

90. A basic principle or belief of the program is that at-risk families must be stabilized in permanent housing with more-or-less confident access to life's necessities before any further progress can be made toward curing the family's problems and making the family self-sufficient. Otherwise, the family will simply be too distracted to provide the necessary commitment and energy into the developmental efforts. Moreover, establishing a family in a residential neighborhood and enrolling the children in the nearest school enables the family to begin creating its all-important support structure of friends and neighbors.

91. At some point, families and individuals are so dysfunctional that an EIDP-type program is not appropriate; such families should be referred to other, more appropriate programs (e.g., supported housing for the mentally ill or transitional housing for persons with alcohol or other drug problems).

92. How many will still be there at the end of a year or more was not determined, and there is no way to tell how many of the families would have left homelessness without the program assistance. California Department of Social Services, Statistical Services Bureau, "AFDC Survey of Homeless Assistance Applications Approved in California during May 1989: Social and Economic Characteristics of Families Approved to Receive Homeless Assistance Benefits" (December 1990).

93. This strategy might require a change in the standard for involuntary commitment from "dangerousness" to oneself or others to "helplessness." E. Fuller Torrey, "Thirty Years of Change: The Scandalous Neglect of the Mentally Ill Homeless," *Policy Review,* no. 48(Spring 1989):10–15; Marcos et al., "Psychiatry Takes to the Streets."

94. National Institute of Mental Health, *Deinstitutionalization Policy and Homelessness: A Report to Congress* (Rockville, MD: National Institute of Mental Health, 1990).

95. S. Anna Kondratas, "A Strategy for Helping America's Homeless," *Heritage Foundation Backgrounder No. 431*(Washington, DC: Heritage Foundation, 1985); Rossi, *Without Shelter.*

96. Barden, "When Foster Care Ends"; Barth, "On Their Own"; Paul Taylor, Programs Turn to Home as Children's Best Hope," *Washington Post,* March 31, 1991; Tracy Thompson, "Judge Calls D.C. Foster System 'A Travesty,'" *Washington Post,* April 19, 1991.

97. Conversation with Michael Olenick, Los Angeles regional coordinator of the Community College Foundation and president of the Board of the Foster Youth Connection of Los Angeles County, and his assistant, Eisha Mason, Van Nuys, California, February 21, 1991.

98. Some of these proposals and many others are contained in Barth, "On Their Own."

99. Conversation with Michael Olenick and Eisha Mason; Michael Olenick, "Foster Youth Connection of Los Angeles County," *Independent Living Resources-Daily Living* IV:3(Summer 1990).

100. Taylor, "Programs Turn to Home"; William Raspberry, "Saving Families, Saving Public Money," *Washington Post,* December 20, 1990.

101. The federal Runaway and Homeless Youth program provides about $30 million annually to support over 330 transition shelters in all 50 states. These shelters work to prevent runaway youths from becoming homeless by either reuniting them with their families or placing them in alternative living situations (such as foster care). HHS agency report; Lindblom, *1990 Annual Report.*

102. Although the numbers of the poor and extremely poor have declined slightly since peaking in 1983, the current recession will most likely produce a new surge in the poverty figures that exceeds the 1983 numbers.

103. Wright, *Address Unknown,* 136.

104. One of the clearest examples of how a small increase in income can help is the fact that many solitary adults living in SRO hotels become homeless for some short time at the end of each month when their monthly public assistance benefits run out, and then return to the hotels when they receive their next assistance check. See also Chicago Community Trust study, which found that a major difference between homeless and nonhomeless extremely poor persons is a slight difference in income levels, often caused by increased public assistance benefits received by the nonhomeless.

105. Overall economic health and growth in the nation's economy would, of course, help. But the failure of the prolonged expansion of the economy since the 1981–82 recession to have any significant impact on the numbers of extremely poor in society suggests that more direct assistance is necessary, even if the country enjoys an overall return to vibrant economic health. See Robert Greenstein, "Testimony of Robert Greenstein, Director of the Center on Budget and Policy Priorities," presented before the House of Representatives Committee on Ways and Means, March 13, 1991.

106. U.S. House of Representatives, Committee on Ways and Means, *Overview of Entitlement Programs: 1990 Green Book* (Washington, DC: U.S. Government Printing Office, 1990) (hereafter cited as *Green Book*); data from HHS; Lewin/ICF of Health and Sciences International and Jeff Bell Associates, "State and Local General Assistance Programs:Issues and Changes," a report prepared for HHS (November 1990); Spencer Rich, "Inflation's Bite on Benefits," *Washington Post,* May 14, 1991 (regarding 1991 *Green Book* data). Within federal guidelines, each state sets the benefit levels for AFDC and defines the benefits package within its boundaries, with the federal government providing matching funds for state AFDC expenditures; general assistance programs are funded exclusively by the states.

107. Lewin/ICF and Jeff Bell Associates, "State and Local General Assistance Programs."

108. Casey McKeever, "AFDC Grant Cut Hurts Children," Western Center on Law and Poverty Fact Sheet (February 1991); "Cutting Welfare: Close to Home," editorial, *Washington Post,* March 13, 1991; Paul Taylor and David S. Broder, "New Drive to Aid Children Often Cuts Adult

Programs," *Washington Post,* March 27, 1991; Jay Matthews, "Proposed Cuts in California Called Sharp Blow to the Poor," *Washington Post,* May 16, 1991.

109. Ibid.

110. Lindblom, *1990 Annual Report;* U.S. Department of Agriculture, Food and Nutrition Service, Office of Analysis and Evaluation, "The Savings in Medicaid Costs for Newborns and Their Mothers from Pre-natal Participation in the WIC Program" (October 1990). But see George C. Graham, "WIC: A Food Program That Fails," *The Public Interest* (Spring 1991):66–75.

111. *Green Book;* Burt and Cohen, *America's Homeless;* Chicago Community Trust study. See also Pat Doyle, *Food Stamp Program Participation Rates: August 1985* (Washington, DC: U.S. Department of Agriculture, Food and Nutrition Service, April 1990).

112. Rossi, *Down and Out in America;* Rossi, *Homelessness in America;* Burt and Cohen, *America's Homeless; Green Book,* Chicago Community Trust study.

113. *Food Stamps: Reasons for Nonparticipation* (Washington, DC: U.S. General Accounting Office, 1988).

114. Since 1984, the New York State Disability Advocacy Program has provided $10 million in legal representation to people whose federal Social Security disability benefits have been lost or denied, and it has obtained or recovered at least $30 million in benefits for more than 10,500 people (NYCBA, Committee on Legal Assistance). The Income Rights Project in San Francisco offers a good example of a peer-advocates system to help at-risk families obtain benefits and contest decertifications. Conversation with Sandy Weiner and Dawn Hasselbach.

115. Wright, *Address Unknown,* 127; Chicago Community Trust study, 361; *Food Stamp Program:Administrative Hindrances to Participation* (Washington, DC: U.S. General Accounting Office, 1988).

116. Robert Greenstein testimony.

117. Eligibility of the mentally ill for either SSI or SSDI was an underlying (unrealized) assumption of the deinstitutionalization movement of the 1960s and 1970s (Rossi, *Without Shelter,* 55).

118. Spencer Rich, "Fewer Got Jobless Aid in 1990," *Washington Post,* April 5, 1991; Robert Greenstein testimony; Wright, *Address Unknown,* 143–44; David S. Broder, "Their Last Unemployment Checks," *Washington Post,* March 17, 1991, stating that 262,512 people had their unemployment benefits "exhaust" in January 1991; Hobart Rowan, "Unemployment Benefits: Out of Sync," *Washington Post,* May 16, 1991.

119. The percentage of homeless and most-at-risk who are definitely or probably not employable is as high as 45 percent (Wright, *Address Unknown,* 153).

120. See Rossi, *Without Shelter,* 51–53, for a useful discussion of the problem with job-training programs as a solution to unemployment and the need for expanded public employment programs.

121. This issue is constructively analyzed in Alan S. Blinder, *Hard Heads Soft Hearts: Tough-Minded Economics for a Just Society* (Reading, MA: Addison-Wesley, 1987).

122. Approaching full employment is especially important because it forces employers to begin hiring more of the least trained and most disadvantaged workers (i.e., the unemployed most-at-risk).

123. Some federal and state labor and Social Security laws would have to be changed to make such a program legal.

124. Indeed, one perceived reason for both lower incomes and greater homelessness among today's most disadvantaged adults as compared with yesterday's Skid Row populations is that the spot market for unskilled labor in urban areas has dried up (Rossi, *Down and Out in America,* 186).

125. Rossi, *Without Shelter,* 51.

126. Ibid. In 1990, 34.4 percent of 16- to 19-year-old black males and 20.9 percent of those aged 20 to 24 were unemployed; and another half million young blacks wanted to work but gave up looking. U.S. Department of Labor, Bureau of Labor Statistics, *Employment and Earnings,* 1990 annual average tables (Washington, DC: U.S. Department of Labor, January 1991).

127. Head Start has just begun a $5 million demonstration program in which its programs in public housing will offer extended day-care services until the parents and guardians return from work (HHS, Administration for Children, Youth, and Families, Head Start Bureau). For a general discussion of day-care issues and descriptions of federal support for day-care activities, see Anne C. Stewart, *Child Day Care, Congressional Research Service Issue Brief* (Washington, DC: Congressional Research Service, 1990); Susan Schillmoeller and Sharon Stephan, *Child Day Care: Funding under Selected Programs, CRS Report for Congress* (Washington, DC: Congressional Research Service, 1988).

128. Robert Greenstein testimony.

129. Robert J. Shapiro, "An American Working Wage: Ending Poverty in Working Families," Progressive Policy Institute Policy Report No. 3 (February 1990); Robert J. Shapiro, "Work and Poverty: A Progressive View of the Minimum Wage and the Earned Income Tax Credit," Progressive Policy Institute Policy Report No. 1(June 1989).

130. Shapiro, "An American Working Wage."

131. Robert Greenstein testimony.

132. Spencer Rich, "Plan to Cut Payroll Tax Gains Support," *Washington Post,* March 15, 1991; Robert M. Ball and Robert J. Myers, "The Wrong Fix for Social Security," *Washington Post,* March 13, 1991; Robert J. Shapiro, "Cutting Social Security Taxes without Touching the Trust Fund or Increasing the Deficit," Progressive Policy Institute Economic Outlook No. 7(February 1991). But see also Tom Kenworthy, "Study Warns Against Payroll Tax Cut," *Washington Post,* April 12, 1991, which cites a Congressional Budget Office study that says that such a cut would slow economic growth if it increases the deficit.

133. U.S. Department of Labor, Bureau of Labor Statistics, *Outlook 2000*, Bulletin 2352 (April 1990); U.S. Department of Labor, Bureau of Labor Statistics, "Outlook 2000," *Occupational Outlook Quarterly* 33 (Fall 1989); William B. Johnston and Arnold H. Packer, *Workforce 2000:Work and Workers for the 21st Century* (Indianapolis: Hudson Institute, 1987).

134. DHHS, Administration for Children, Youth, and Families, Head Start Bureau, *Executive Summary: The Impact of Head Start on Children, Families and Communities: Head Start Synthesis Project* (Washington, DC: U.S. Government Printing Office, 1985); Monica Sorensen, ed., *Head Start Sucess Stories* (CSR, Inc., January 1990) (available from the Head Start Bureau at DHHS).

135. Lindblom, *1990 Annual Report;* data from HUD Office of Policy Development and Research. See also Irving Welfeld, "Our Nonexistent Housing Crisis," *The Public Interest* 101(Fall 1990):55–61.

136. Ibid.

137. HUD, Office of Research, Policy, and Development data; U.S. Congress, Congressional Budget Office, "Current Housing Problems and Possible Federal Responses" (December 1988). The United States provides housing assistance to a smaller percentage of its poor population than does any other industrialized nation. See Richard P. Appelbaum et al., "Scapegoating Rent Control: Masking the Causes of Homelessness," *Economic Policy Institute Briefing Paper* (October 1989).

138. Such an entitlement would also help to balance the inequitable treatment of renters as opposed to homeowners, who receive enormous federal subsidies through the mortgage interest deduction. See Paul A. Leonard, Cushing N. Dolbeare, and Edward B. Lazere, *A Place to Call Home* (Washington, DC: Center on Budget and Policy Priorities and the Low Income Housing Information Service, 1989).

139. In these cases, the subsidy could be provided first and the problems with substandard conditions or overcrowding could be addressed afterward— for example, by leaning on the landlord or by relocating to more appropriate housing (if available). Denying monetary assistance to households already suffering under substandard conditions or overcrowding (especially when no other options exist) hardly seems fair.

140. U.S. Congress, Congressional Budget Office, *Current Housing Problems;* Welfeld, "Our Nonexistent Housing Crisis."

141. U.S. Congress, Congressional Budget Office, *Current Housing Problems,* provides a number of useful calculations of the costs associated with different mixes of eligibility and recipient rent-contribution levels.

142. Ibid.

143. Some states (e.g., Massachusetts) have anti-Section 8 discrimination ordinances, and some localities in states without such ordinances offer landlords special economic incentives or other support (e.g., tenant screening or problem intervention) to encourage them to accept otherwise undesirable Section 8 tenants. David McKay Wilson, "Landlords Rewarded for Housing Homeless," *Standard Star,* June 25, 1990, regarding New York's Landlord Housing Incentive Program in Westchester County.

See footnote 138 regarding federal habitability and overcrowding restrictions.

144. Mary K. Nenno and George Colyer, *New Money and New Methods: A Catalog of State and Local Initiatives in Housing and Community Development* (Washington, DC: National Association of Housing and Redevelopment Officials, 1988); Mary K. Nenno, ed., *Assistance for Homeless Persons: A NAHRO Resource Book for Housing and Community Development Agencies* (Washington, DC: National Association of Housing and Redevelopment Officials, 1988); HUD, Office of Policy Development and Research, *Report to Congress on SROs for the Homeless Section 8 Moderate Rehabilitation Program* (Washington, DC: HUD, March 1990).

145. Rehabilitating vacant, uninhabitable public housing units costs, on average, less than 40 percent as much as constructing a new unit. U.S. Congress, Congressional Budget Office, cites HHS, *HUD Perspective on Public Housing Modernization* (March 1988). The 1990 National Affordable Housing Act provides new incentives to owners of low-cost rental housing projects with HUD-insured mortgages not to exercise their option to prepay the mortgages and thus become free to raise their rents (and get rid of their low-income tenants). The act also includes other measures to protect this low-cost housing and its tenants. Lindblom, *1990 Annual Report.*

146. For example, the National Affordable Housing Act's Housing Opportunities for People Everywhere (HOPE) provisions mean to encourage and assist tenants to purchase public housing.

147. Susan Vanhorenbeck, "Housing Low-Income Persons through Existing Use of Housing Stock," Congressional Research Service Report to Congress (August 1988).

148. The federal Section 8 rental-subsidy program currently provides assistance only to elderly or handicapped low-income individuals who wish to live in shared-housing situations.

149. Vanhorenbeck, "Housing Low-Income Persons." Perhaps as many as 1.75 million such units could be created if currently restrictive zoning laws were changed (citing Edith M. Netters, "Accommodating Accessory Apartments," *Urban Land* [April 1984]).

150. Project Match in San Jose, California, which placed over 7,000 persons over its first eight years, is one example of such a service; see also HomeBase report regarding ECHO Housing/Project Share.

151. For a discussion of the potential for public building conversion and "granny flats" to create substantial amounts of new low-cost housing, see Vanhorenbeck, *Housing Low-Income Persons.*

152. William Tucker, *The Excluded Americans:Homelessness and Housing Policies* (Washington, DC: Regnery Gateway, 1990); Appelbaum et al., "Scapegoating Rent Control: Masking the Causes of Homelessness," *Economic Policy Institute Briefing Paper* (October 1989); John M. Quigley, "Does Rent Control Cause Homelessness? Taking the Claim Seriously," *Journal of Policy Analysis and Management* 9, no. 1 (1990):89–93; Patrick J. Carty, "Preventing Homelessness: Rent Control or Rent Assistance," *Notre Dame Journal of Law, Ethics and Public Policy* 4(1989):365–83.

153. Lynn Nesselbush, *Neighbors, after All: Community Acceptance Strategies for Siting Housing and Services for Homeless People* (San Francisco: HomeBase, 1989), discusses the NIMBY problem and suggests a wide range of responses—with examples—beyond anti-NIMBY legislation.

154. U.S. Congress, Congressional Budget Office, *Current Housing Problems; Making Room at the Inn: Congregational Investment in Affordable Housing* (Washington, DC: Churches' Conference on Shelter and Housing, 1991) is a resource book for congregations and other community organizations that wish to develop low-cost housing; it also describes current nonprofit, low-cost housing efforts.

155. HUD, Office of Policy Development and Research, *Report to Congress on SROs;* Lindblom, *1990 Annual Report.*

156. Nenno, ed., *Assistance for Homeless Persons.*

157. Examples include the HHS–HUD–Robert Wood Johnson Foundation Joint Initiative; HUD's Permanent Housing for the Handicapped Homeless program (which primarily serves mentally ill persons), Transitional Housing program for mentally ill homeless persons, and Section 202 Direct Loans for Housing for the Elderly or Handicapped Program; and the Department of Veterans Affairs Comprehensive Work Therapy/Independent Living Housing program for homeless and at-risk disabled veterans. All these programs are described more fully in Lindblom, *1990 Annual Report.* For examples of state housing programs for the mentally ill, see E. Fuller Torrey et al., *Care of the Seriously Mentally Ill: A Rating of State Programs* (Washington, DC: Public Citizen Health Research Group and the National Alliance for the Mentally Ill, 1990).

158. This idea came from the Reverend Eugene L. Boutilier, Administrator, Los Angeles Emergency Food and Shelter Program Local Board, in a conversation on February 21, 1991.

159. In the absence of such community-based supported housing, those disadvantaged most-at-risk persons who simply do not have the ability to obtain or live in unsupported housing for more than short periods of time (e.g., the severely mentally ill) could be committed to existing institutional settings, such as state mental hospitals or nursing homes, so that they do not descend into homelessness (Torrey, "Thirty Years of Change"; Marcos et al., "Psychiatry Takes to the Streets").

160. Developing a stronger culture of commitment and responsibility among parents cannot be legislated, but laws that stress the importance of parenting and its attendant responsibilities could help; see Elaine Ciulla Kamarack and William A. Galston, *Putting Children First: A Progressive Family Policy for the 1990s* (Washington, DC: Progressive Policy Institute, 1990).

161. Toward this end, Congress enacted the Family Support Act in 1988 to help needy families with children obtain the education, training, and employment necessary to avoid long-term welfare dependence (HHS agency report; Lindblom, *1990 Annual Report).*

162. Paul Taylor articles in the *Washington Post:* "Conferees Urge Spending, Tax Policies to Reinforce U.S. Families," April 13, 1991; "Tax Code Increasingly Unfriendly to Families, Hill Committee Told," April 16,

1991; "Making Tax Policy 'Family Friendly,' " April 10, 1991; and "Family Seen as Key to Aiding Children," March 11, 1991. See also Kamarack and Galston; and "The Working Family Tax Relief Act of 1991: A Brief Summary," provided by the office of U.S. Representative Thomas J. Downey, one of the bill's main sponsors (May 1991).

163. Ibid.

164. Ibid.; Wood et al., "Homeless and Housed Families in Los Angeles."

165. Kamarack and Galston, *Putting Children First.* If filing for divorce becomes the triggering event for providing counseling and other assistance, more might be done to encourage couples to marry formally, thereby getting them into the family assistance system.

166. Paul Taylor, "Child Support System Called 'Abysmal,' " *Washington Post,* April 6, 1991; Spencer Rich, "Area Given 'D' in Child Support Enforcement," *Washington Post,* January 12, 1991.

167. Paul Taylor, "Catching Up with Absent Parents," *Washington Post,* April 5, 1991.

168. Studies indicate that two-parent households have higher incomes than single-parent households and that children from two-parent families have lower incidences of alcohol and other drug abuse, crime problems, teen pregnancies, suicides, and mental illness, and do better in school; see Kamarack and Galston, *Putting Children First,* and the authorities cited therein.

169. Letter to Maria L. Meaney from Michael E. DeVore, executive director, Service Outreach Ministry Education of Santa Rosa, California, with attached Initial Summary Letter Request that describes the Family Connection initiative (February 9, 1991); Clark Mason, "Teaming Up to Help Homeless," *The Press Democrat,* February 19, 1991.

170. For a private sector effort to prevent homelessness through strengthening entire neighborhoods or communities rather than individual families, see the Community Partnership for the Prevention of Homelessness of Washington, DC. (Correspondence and materials came from Sue Marshall, executive director, Community Partnership, April 10, 1991.)

171. Except where otherwise noted, all information on federal homelessness efforts comes from Lindblom, *1990 Annual Report.*

172. HUD officials are working with homelessness provider-organization representatives to promote greater use of these funds for prevention and to reduce regulatory obstacles to such use.

173. Lindblom, *1990 Annual Report.*

174. Intergovernmental Health Policy Project, *Surveys of State Initiatives.*

175. HHS, Office of the Inspector General, "State and Local Perspectives on the McKinney Act" (Washington, DC: December 1990).

176. U.S. Conference of Mayors, "Status Report on Hunger and Homelessness."

177. Nathan McCall and Kent Jenckins, Jr., "D.C. Votes to Limit Aid to Homeless," *Washington Post,* June 13, 1990; Thomas Morgan, "New York City Plans to Reduce Beds for Homeless," *New York Times,* 1991.

178. Telephone conversation with Diane Levy; "The Chronicle Season of Sharing Fund."

179. Because at-risk families and individuals would receive the same kind of benefits and assistance as homeless persons under this model, it has the additional benefit of not creating (as the current model sometimes does) any extra incentive for at-risk families or individuals to become homeless in order to qualify more quickly for more generous benefits.

180. For other discussions of addressing homelessness through more prevention activity, and for additional ideas on how that might be done, see Madeleine R. Stoner, *Inventing a Non-Homeless Future: A Public Policy Agenda for Preventing Homelessness,* American University Studies, series 11, vol. 29 (New York: Lang, 1989); and John R. Belcher and Frederick A. DiBlasio, *Helping the Homeless: Where Do We Go from Here?* (Lexington, MA: Lexington Books, 1990). In addition, the American Affordable Housing Institute of New Brunswick, New Jersey, will soon publish an in-depth study of homelessness-prevention programs in seven states, with brief descriptions of other state and local homelessness-prevention programs throughout the country.

Section 3:

Next Steps in Homelessness Research and Public Policy

Introduction
Nan P. Roman

Where to from Here? A Policy Research Agenda
Based on the Analysis of Administrative Data
Dennis P. Culhane and Stephen Metraux

Future Directions for Programs Serving the Homeless
Martha R. Burt

© Fannie Mae Foundation 1997. All Rights Reserved.

Section 3

Next Steps in Homelessness Research and Public Policy: Introduction

Nan P. Roman
National Alliance to End Homelessness

As a practical matter—and as it has evolved at the local, state, and federal levels—the development of public policy regarding homelessness has two dimensions: how to help people once they are homeless and, more broadly, how to place the phenomenon of homelessness within a framework of programs and policies that assist people who are very poor (the "mainstream" poverty programs). To date, homelessness policy in both these areas has been developed and implemented largely, although not entirely, in the absence of organized research. Furthermore, policy deliberations have not always been appropriately influenced by the research that *has* been conducted. As a result, the system that has emerged to assist homeless people is not as effective as it should be.

To develop more effective national policy on homelessness, research is needed to answer certain pressing and practical questions that confront policy makers. As they relate to homeless-specific programs, these policy questions include the following:

1. Does transitional housing, in which millions of dollars have been invested, work?
2. Do homeless people need some special package of social services in order to escape homelessness, and if so, which services work best for which populations?
3. How do we distribute targeted resources nationally to the places that have the most homeless people?
4. Which people are the mainstream poverty programs (such as the Job Training Partnership Act, Mental Health Block Grant, and Section 811 housing programs) systematically unable to serve, making them reasonable candidates for assistance from the homeless system?

As they relate to the mainstream system's impact on homeless people, policy questions include the following:

1. How do we identify those who are most at risk of imminent homelessness?
2. What will be the impact of welfare reform on homelessness, and how will people who are homeless and on welfare make out under the new systems?
3. What is the connection between homelessness and previous institutionalization (such as incarceration, foster care, hospitalization, or a combination of these)?

Not only must these questions be addressed, but ways must be found to ensure that policy properly incorporates the answers that research provides.

The two articles in this section discuss the important connection between homelessness research and homelessness policy. The authors describe some of the questions about homelessness that research *has* answered; discuss what they believe to be the policy implications of these findings, both to homeless-specific programs and to mainstream programs; and discuss a new way to develop homelessness data that may inform the policy debate.

Dennis Culhane and Stephen Metraux set the stage for using "administrative data" to answer many of the outstanding public policy questions. Around the country, more and more providers are collecting data on clients to meet the administrative needs of their own agencies. These data, the authors believe, could be compiled in ways that could address policy questions.

Culhane and Metraux begin by describing the shortfalls of many of the cross-sectional studies of the homeless population. Such studies provide a static picture of the problem and therefore have limited use in the development of public policy. The authors argue that the information provided by automated management information systems, which some service providers use, could be used to develop longitudinal data on homelessness. Longitudinal data better describe the dynamics of homelessness and can be more useful in the development of policy.

Culhane and Metraux raise the intriguing possibility that these administrative data could be integrated with data from other systems to investigate policy issues. Matching welfare caseload data with homeless shelter admission data, for example, would yield information about the impact of welfare reform on homelessness. Similarly, cross-referencing homeless shelter data with health services data (such as emergency room admissions) could show the costs to health systems of serving people who are homeless versus those who are housed.

Despite this promise, Culhane and Metraux point out that there are limitations to administrative data. Not every homeless person participates in services, nor does every service provider have the same skill level or opportunity to correctly collect client information. This can lead to some inconsistency in the data. There are also serious confidentiality issues, particularly when data are cross-referenced among systems. Finally, cross-referencing among systems may point out associations but, because it cannot express the dynamics of the homeless experience, may miss causalities.

Martha Burt's article reviews the 15-year history of federal homeless assistance programs; summarizes the research on the effectiveness of these programs; and proposes, partly on the basis of this research, some new directions for public policy. She begins with a history of federal homeless assistance efforts, starting with the first attempts to respond to what was seen, in the early 1980s, as a recession-related crisis. She explains that the McKinney Act of 1987 was originally designed as a fairly comprehensive, multiagency response to the problem. Over time, however, many of the programs of the McKinney Act were terminated, and homeless assistance eventually came to be concentrated in one agency, the U.S. Department of Housing and Urban Development (HUD). As a result, most public policy discussion about homelessness centers on HUD's Homeless Assistance Grant Program, which funds emergency, transitional, and permanent housing and services for homeless people. This situation persists despite the fact that homelessness is far too pervasive and pernicious to be "solved" by this relatively small ($823 million in fiscal year 1997) and limited program.

Burt describes existing research on the impact services have on various subpopulations of homeless people. She finds that while there is valuable research available on the service needs of long-term homeless people with chronic disabilities, there is significantly less information available on the service needs of homeless families and single people without disabilities. She rightly points out the irony of this, since most federal resources go to assist homeless families. She also notes that despite solid knowledge about what would work for long-term homeless people with disabilities, there has been steadfast resistance to bringing research-driven recommendations to scale.

Burt makes several recommendations about how to reorganize assistance targeted specifically to homeless people. In particular, she recommends reducing funding to geographic areas where research indicates no concentration of homeless people (specifically, suburban areas). She also recommends reducing the level of services offered by shelters (since their effectiveness has not been tested by research), thereby allowing more people to be sheltered. She identifies areas for additional research, such as the impact of services delivered to homeless families; the effectiveness of transitional housing; and the needs of single, nondisabled homeless people.

Burt concludes with a series of recommendations centering on the prevention of homelessness. She promotes experimentation with prevention programs for those who face imminent homelessness, recommending the HUD Homeless Assistance Grant Program as a funding source. For homeless people with severe and chronic disabilities, who tend to cycle in and out of the homeless system and absorb a disproportionately large share of its resources, Burt recommends the provision of permanent supportive housing. She interprets the research as indicating that this approach would successfully end homelessness for this group. Finally, Burt suggests that there is little public will to strengthen mainstream programs enough to protect all very poor individuals and families from becoming homeless. She believes that support could be developed, however, to target long-term comprehensive assistance to certain homeless families with children. This would prevent these children from becoming the next generation of homeless adults.

As both articles correctly point out, there have been many advances in research on homelessness since the early days of the crisis, when advocates and public agencies argued over whether there were 3 million homeless people or only 250,000. Sophisticated methods now allow more accurate enumeration of homeless people, more in-depth examination of the dynamics of their individual and cross-cutting experiences, and a more authoritative description of the population.

Despite great strides in describing a complex and diverse problem, however, many questions remain to be answered. The answers to these questions are needed if we are to design policy for both homeless-specific and mainstream programs that will *end* homelessness for as many people as possible. Only if researchers such as Culhane, Metraux, Burt, and their colleagues work together with policy makers to ask and answer the appropriate questions is there a hope of developing responsible and responsive public policy that will move us in this direction.

Author

Nan P. Roman is the Vice President for Programs and Policy of the National Alliance to End Homelessness (NAEH) in Washington, DC. NAEH is a national advocacy and capacity-building organization with more than 2,000 nonprofit and public sector members around the country. Ms. Roman has been with NAEH since 1987 and oversees all of its program and policy activities, including advocacy in Congress and federal agencies, training, technical assistance, publications, research, and other projects. She has worked on poverty and community organizing issues at both the local and national levels for 20 years.

© Fannie Mae Foundation 1997. All Rights Reserved.

Where to from Here? A Policy Research Agenda Based on the Analysis of Administrative Data

Dennis P. Culhane and Stephen Metraux
University of Pennsylvania

Abstract

This article outlines a policy research agenda based on the analysis of administrative data. Computerized records of client characteristics and their related shelter utilization patterns offer researchers a rich source of longitudinal data that makes possible a wide range of investigations and can be analyzed by using an array of multivariate statistical tools. Specifically, this article discusses the contributions administrative data can make to (1) enumerating and determining the characteristics of the homeless population, (2) understanding the effect of homelessness on related public systems, (3) gauging the effect of policy interventions on the use of homeless services, (4) evaluating the effectiveness of system-level delivery of homeless services, and (5) measuring the performance of individual homeless service providers.

The article concludes by commenting on several issues that policy makers might consider regarding the implementation of automated information systems among homeless service providers.

Keywords: Homelessness; Policy; Methods

Introduction

As data collection on users of homeless services in many U.S. localities becomes automated, the kind of research being conducted on homeless populations will likely change. Both individual homeless service providers and local homeless service systems have increasingly been turning to management information systems (MIS), also referred to as client tracking programs, to standardize their administrative records just as many public agencies have done. Using information systems to manage homeless programs is nothing new; some individual provider organizations have been using off-the-shelf applications or have had customized programs for these purposes for over a decade. There have even been several longstanding municipal and statewide systems (e.g., Columbus, OH; New York City; Philadelphia; Phoenix; St. Louis; and Rhode Island) that have collected uniform data on homeless service use. What is changing is that such systems are becoming both more prevalent and more standardized, thus making a broader range of research efforts possible on both local and multilocal levels. This research will greatly inform the planning and evaluation of legislation and programs affecting this population.

This article outlines a research agenda to accompany this expanded data capacity. Much of this agenda draws on research conducted at the University of Pennsylvania, where access to several years of administrative data from New York City and Philadelphia has created an opportunity for researchers to try a variety of analytical approaches. The agenda proposes ways to expand our understanding not only of how homeless persons and shelter systems interact, but also of how homelessness affects other related systems such as human services, health care, and criminal justice whose clientele frequently overlap. Specifically, the areas of research considered are (1) population enumeration and composition, (2) integrated database research, (3) time series analysis, (4) program evaluation, and (5) system management and administration. How the analysis of administrative data compares with or can supplement other information-gathering approaches is also discussed. The article concludes by considering measures both to facilitate the establishment of data infrastructures and to realize the potential for policy research that they can provide.

Population enumeration and composition

Perhaps no other research issues have consumed more resources or engendered greater debate than those that address the most basic policy and planning questions in this field: How many people experience homelessness, and what are their characteristics? Over the past decade, cross-sectional methods, also known as point-in-time methods, have become the predominant means of collecting data to describe and enumerate the homeless population. More recently, administrative data have been used to calculate period prevalence rates and to ascertain the characteristics of shelter users over time (see Culhane et al. 1997a).

Cross-sectional surveys of the homeless population elicit information over a very short period, usually between one day and one week. Their results offer point-prevalent "snapshots" and include a variety of specific methods, ranging from straightforward counts and basic sampling (Lee 1989; Metraux 1994; Robertson 1987) to more sophisticated sampling procedures (Burnam and Koegel 1988; Dennis 1993; Rossi et al. 1987). These methods have proved replicable across many localities, as demonstrated by the Urban Institute (Burt and Cohen 1989) and the Census Bureau (Burt and Taeuber 1991) in estimating or enumerating the population across the nation. Not only can these case-identification methods be applied over a broad variety of jurisdictions for purposes of enumeration, but they can also be used to gather in-depth data on individuals, for example, through the use of standardized diagnostic instruments. Specifically, administering such instruments to large, population-based samples has dramatically improved the accuracy of estimates of the prevalence of mental disorders and substance abuse in the homeless population (Fischer and Breakey 1991; Koegel, Burnam, and Farr 1988).

Cross-sectional studies have been the preferred approach to population enumeration and compositional analyses because they minimize a number of difficulties involved in surveying the homeless population, particularly the risk of double counting and of overrepresenting those who are easiest to find. The approach has been invaluable in producing defensible counts, acceptable to public officials and planning agencies. From the perspective of the information demands of public policy, however, the approach produces very basic data. Unless studies are conducted periodically, the primary use of these data is to inform the immediate planning of program or shelter capacity. Only indirectly can the number of persons homeless over longer periods be estimated on the basis of such data. Moreover, given the study frame (a single day), such data are unsuitable for tracking the service use patterns of subpopulations, for monitoring trends in shelter utilization over time, or for measuring the effect of various programs.

Automated MIS technology provides a promising alternative source of data on population size and characteristics. Homeless service providers are increasingly using MIS for two operational functions: program administration (managing the daily demand for shelter beds, complying with reporting or billing requirements, etc.) and service planning (providing information on individual homeless persons or families for case managers). If reliably maintained, such a system can record the dates and duration of service utilization, as well as a range of additional data on personal characteristics. These systems can thus be structured to produce a client-specific, provider-specific, and/or period-specific longitudinal data archive.

Such longitudinal data are well suited for answering a number of research questions on population enumeration and composition and for using an array of statistical procedures. From an epidemiological perspective, basic demographic data can be used to calculate prevalence rates by age, race, and sex, and the corresponding relative risk for shelter admission, for any selected time frame in a given jurisdiction (see Culhane et al. 1997a; Culhane and Metraux 1996). Multivariate regression approaches, including ordinary least squares regression, logistic regression, and event history analysis, can be used to estimate predictors of length of stay, repeat shelter use, or housing outcomes (Culhane and Kuhn 1998; Metraux and Culhane 1997; Wong, Culhane, and Kuhn 1997). One can also apply cluster analysis to define distinct patterns of shelter use and to measure their association with demographic characteristics (Kuhn and Culhane 1998). The effectiveness of past or proposed homeless policies on shelter utilization rates (prevalence) or on the service use patterns of subpopulations can also be estimated by analyzing census trends (see the section on time series analysis and Culhane, Metraux, and Wachter 1998).

In describing the advantages of administrative data, it is also necessary to point out certain limitations. Perhaps the most conspicuous disadvantage from an enumeration perspective is that administrative data can provide information only for persons who use the services being tracked. Undercounting can also result from service providers' declining to participate in the data collection system for various reasons (see Culhane et al. 1997a; Rossi 1994). Gaps in coverage and undercounting caused by those who do not use services can be mitigated through the expanded collection of data from tracking street outreach contacts or using survey methods to estimate the number or the proportional size of the non-service-using homeless population.

Another potential disadvantage, particularly for research on population characteristics, is the quality of administrative data. In many cases, data collection is part of an intake procedure in which many individuals and households must be processed quickly and in which interviewers are unlikely to have formal training in interviewing procedures. Given those circumstances, in-depth clinical interviews and lengthy survey instruments prove impractical, so self-reports are usually the only way to collect data on such areas as health status, substance abuse history, or mental health. But self-report questions can be misinterpreted or not answered truthfully when personally identifying data are collected along with data on these potentially sensitive issues. When combined with data from other service systems, however, administrative records can still be used to obtain such data, as discussed in the next section.

Integrated database research

The integration of administrative data for homeless services with data from other service systems offers a means of checking the reliability of self-reported individual characteristics and can also be used to investigate a range of policy-relevant issues. More specifically, integrated database research can examine how the policies and behaviors of other public systems influence the risk of shelter admission and the duration of episodes of homelessness, how homelessness affects individuals' interaction with other public systems, and what the costs that homeless persons incur for other systems are. Thus, data integration can expand tremendously the number and type of research questions that can be pursued and the research that may be directly relevant to the policies of the homeless service system, as well as to those of other public agencies.

A vast potential source of data exists for conducting such research. Because administrative data systems are usually organized by unique identifiers—Social Security number or some combination of name, date of birth, race, and sex—homeless services data can often be merged with a variety of other administrative record systems. A few of the more significant data sources and the research issues they could address are considered here.

Welfare

Perhaps no other policy area has aroused as much concern for its potential impact on homelessness than the recent passage of the Clinton administration's welfare reform legislation. Senator Daniel Moynihan's comment that "we will have children sleeping on grates" indicates the belief that recent changes in the welfare system will lead to an increase in homelessness, so the relationship between welfare and homelessness will undoubtedly figure prominently in future research evaluating the impact of policy changes on welfare recipients.

By matching the identifiers of people terminated from specific welfare programs against shelter registries, a change in the rate of public shelter use among those affected can be directly measured. For example, the shelter admission rate before and after termination of benefits for a particular cohort could be compared, or a group whose benefits were terminated could be compared with a control group of persons who remain on the rolls during a specified period. Culhane et al. (1997c) used both methods to

evaluate the impact on homelessness of two laws recently enacted by the Pennsylvania Legislature that severely restricted
access to General Assistance (GA) welfare benefits. Two data
sets were merged: one of persons from Philadelphia whose GA
benefits were terminated as a result of the two laws and the
other of persons using Philadelphia homeless shelters. Using
survival curves (Allison 1995), the study found that within a
year of termination, the rate of shelter admission among the
terminated cases had increased markedly, compared with the
persons themselves a year earlier and with a control group from
a year earlier.

If demographic or other characteristic variables had been made
available for all terminated cases, a multivariate model could
have been developed to identify the risk factors associated with
an increased probability of shelter admission among terminated
cases. Such information would be very useful for targeting assistance to those terminated cases at greatest risk of shelter admission. Future research could similarly compare the impact of
caseload terminations in Temporary Assistance for Needy Families, cuts in food stamps, eligibility restrictions in Supplemental
Security Income, and other changes on specific cohorts of
recipients.

For this type of research to be conducted, public assistance
agencies must either do the research themselves or be willing to
contribute the identifiers of affected cases to external research
organizations. Such data-sharing arrangements will require an
officially approved protocol for transferring data and protecting
confidentiality. If agencies are unwilling to contribute identifiers, the state or county welfare authority may be willing to
conduct the match, mask the identifiers, and then permit the
researchers to conduct the analysis on de-identified data. However it is done, research of this nature will be invaluable to
policy analysts attempting to measure the impact of these new
laws and regulations on homelessness and should be seriously
considered in any jurisdiction where automated shelter data are
available.

Public health

Public health is another major area of research that can benefit
from the integration of administrative data sources. Many public
health departments already conduct regular studies of specific
population groups by matching their identifiers to vital statistics

or other surveillance databases, and homeless persons are an important population to include in such research. For example, merging homeless data with vital statistics records would enable researchers to study the birth outcomes of pregnant women admitted to public shelters. Such studies could include analyzing how pregnancy outcomes vary as a function of the sequencing of the homelessness episode and the pregnancy, or how pregnant homeless women fare relative to nonhomeless women with similar characteristics (Culhane and Webb 1995). Mortality studies of infants as well as adults could be undertaken to examine any associations between admission to a shelter, duration of stay, or street outreach contact and mortality risk. Merges with other surveillance databases could examine other special populations, including children (vaccination and lead poisoning registries, poison or accidental injury databases), people with HIV/AIDS (Culhane et al. 1997b), or people with tuberculosis.

Research of this nature could affect how public health programs are funded, targeted, and evaluated. Results would be most directly useful for needs assessments and program design, as high-risk groups, including the homeless, are targeted for interventions. Specific cohorts of program participants could be tracked to determine whether existing or new interventions have a mediating effect on the health of homeless persons or on the rate of shelter admission for at-risk populations. A registry of public shelter users at local health departments could be used to identify residentially unstable persons who are consequently eligible for special programs. A prior history of homelessness could also be used as a risk indicator for vulnerable or at-risk populations in a variety of public health planning and research projects.

A prerequisite for conducting such research would be the establishment of protocols for maintaining the confidentiality of the service users, comparable to those used for databases on specific diseases that health departments already maintain. Confidentiality and informed consent are familiar to health officials who deal with this sensitive or legally protected health information. Again, external research organizations would likely require special approval to conduct such research, or else they may have to develop protocols whereby empowered health officials conduct the matching routines and then encrypt, strip, or mask the identifiers before investigators are permitted to perform their analyses.

Health services

Similarly, research can be conducted on the relationship between use of health services and shelter admission. Merges can be conducted with records from such sources as Medicaid claims, Medicare records, specific hospital or HMO files, Health Care for the Homeless databases, and public health center data to examine significant relationships between use of health services and homelessness. Data on diagnoses can be used to estimate the treatment rates for specific disorders in the homeless population and related trends over time. For example, two studies (Culhane, Averyt, and Hadley 1997, 1998) merged three years of Philadelphia shelter registry records with nine years of data on users of mental health services to assess the diagnostic distribution for mental disorders and substance abuse. These studies also used the merged data to examine the interrelationship and sequencing of hospitalizations, emergency room use, and episodes of homelessness.

In another study, Salit et al. (1996) examined records of homeless persons who used Health and Hospital Corporation facilities in New York City to compare the diagnoses of homeless and nonhomeless patients, the differential use of hospital days by diagnosis, and the estimated differences in costs of care. Such a method could also be used to ascertain the proportion of these costs, for both homeless and nonhomeless patients, that are paid by federal, state, or local sources or that are not compensated at all.

Research of this nature is valuable for health departments, state Medicaid offices, managed care organizations, hospital administrators, and other entities that study or plan health services for poor persons. The appropriateness of hospital discharge policies, the adequacy of access to primary health care in shelters, and the need for alternative residential programs are issues that can be studied or informed by this type of research. Patterns of health service use by homeless persons can also inform risk-adjustment procedures for this population, particularly since Medicaid recipients are increasingly required to enroll in privately managed health plans that face cost pressures to restrict hospital stays.

The health services data can also take the place of self-reports or diagnostic survey instruments in identifying subgroups of homeless persons with specific morbidities for more refined analyses. Through the creation of health status risk factors, then, it would be possible to gain a better understanding of how health issues

affect the service system involvement of different types of homeless persons. For example, the shelter stay history of persons
with severe mental illness could be tracked to determine the
pattern, frequency, and length of stay and the extent to which
shelters have become an ancillary feature of, or a surrogate for,
other types of treatment.

Again, given the sensitivity of health data and the laws protecting such information, research of this nature must be conducted
under carefully designed conditions, with the appropriate authorization from or participation of public agencies.

Housing

Housing is another major public policy area that can benefit
from this type of research. In this case, merging by individual
identifiers may not be as useful as merging by unique *geographic*
identifiers. Homeless services data systems will often collect
prior address information or a residential history as part of the
eligibility determination or assessment process. This information
can be used to identify the characteristics of a client's previous
housing or neighborhood. For example, most cities have automated records on property taxes and delinquencies, tax foreclo-
sures, and ownership; others may have automated data on
building type, age, history of code violations, and so on. Databases of public safety records, such as crime and fire data, social
service and welfare program utilization data, public health data,
court-ordered eviction data, and public or private utility termination data, are all likely organized by address or include an
address field, as well as the dates of various actions.

By using the digital geography of a particular area (by block or
parcel) and an address-matching routine (usually built into a
geographic information system program, such as ArcView),
researchers can match these addresses and create geography-
specific attribute tables that can then be used for further analysis by property or other geographic units, including blocks, block
groups, census tracts, or administrative districts and boundaries
(health districts, police precincts, city council districts, etc.). For
example, Culhane, Lee, and Wachter (1997) used multivariate
analyses to examine whether neighborhood variables could
account for the distribution of homeless families' prior addresses
by census tract in Philadelphia and New York City.

Such research would be valuable for designing, targeting, and
siting homelessness prevention programs. Multivariate studies

of neighborhood-level effects could inform the allocation of housing development resources or suggest the potential benefits of other policy strategies, such as those targeting crime prevention, mobility, antiabandonment, or fair housing enforcement, as a means of reducing residential instability and homelessness. Analyzing household migration patterns prior to shelter admission can help shape public policy interventions toward the residential instability process, of which homelessness is but one facet (Lee and Culhane 1996). Dynamic models of neighborhood change, including abandonment trends, gentrification, and neighborhood deterioration, could also be studied for their impact on shelter admissions (Culhane, Lee, and Song 1997).

One of the benefits of using a spatial database is that new area variables (e.g., code violations, tax delinquencies, crime) can take on geographic configurations different from those that have traditionally been available through census data. Customized areas of analysis can replace such standard and somewhat arbitrary units as census tracts, can be created to conform to underlying parcel-level data, and can also provide time intervals that are far more frequent (even continuous) than decennial census intervals. This capacity enables researchers to develop potentially rich, textured, and dynamic models of how housing and neighborhood conditions influence the frequency of housing emergencies and shelter admissions over time.

Criminal justice

People being discharged from jails and prisons are at high risk of shelter admission. Conversely, homelessness, particularly street homelessness, is likely a significant risk factor for arrest and incarceration. Some shelter operators have also reported an increased incidence of persons' being discharged from prisons directly to shelter facilities (Walker 1997). The nature of these pathways and the frequency with which they are traversed are potentially discernible through the integration of homeless services databases with arrest, conviction, and incarceration records.

Much like research on health services, this research could examine how people move between these systems, the costs of their movement, and the characteristics of persons at risk of homelessness or incarceration. The use of shelters as halfway houses by people coming from jails and prisons is of significant concern to agencies that view their mission as serving primarily the indigent poor and do not want to assume the responsibilities of serving ex-convicts. Municipal jails have also increasingly been forced to provide medication and mental health services to prisoners, possibly reflecting a heightened visibility of homeless mentally ill persons on the streets. Combining administrative data from homeless, health care, and criminal justice services could document the financial and human costs of such shifts in service delivery and provide a basis for designing more efficient alternatives.

Additionally, administrative data could help in assessing the relationships between homelessness, law enforcement, and crime. On one hand, homelessness is commonly associated with increases in both nuisance crimes committed by homeless persons attempting to fashion a private life in public spaces and more serious crimes committed against people or property. On the other hand, there is concern that homeless persons receive unfairly harsh treatment from police and the courts. Little empirical evidence currently exists to substantiate either position, but a better understanding of such links between homelessness, crime, and the criminal justice system would clarify both public safety issues and the need for providing better, more appropriate services in this area.

Among all the areas discussed here, integrating databases in criminal justice has perhaps the most potential pitfalls. There is undoubtedly a risk that an established association between crime and homelessness could further stigmatize the population and perhaps even lead to punitive measures. Establishing protocols that protect the confidentiality of the records used also takes on an added urgency, as merging shelter and police records could reveal information that might lead to the arrest of particular persons who use shelters. These risks have to be weighed against the potential benefits and considered in light of the legal and political context in which this work is conducted.

Limitations on integrated database research

As shown above, integrating databases offers a promising way to inform both research and policy in areas that are undoubtedly affected by homelessness. Gaining access to data from other agencies is often fraught with difficulties, however, and in many cases will be impossible. Legal restrictions present one obstacle that may prevent access to a particular data set. Another source of difficulty, of a more political nature, is obtaining the cooperation of agency heads, who will often decide whether to participate in data sharing on the basis of perceived self-interest for the agency or the current political administration. Technically, sharing databases often requires compatibility between different computer systems as well as the availability of information system personnel with the requisite time and technical skills. Finally, integrating data systems frequently necessitates the concurrence of shelter system administrators, directors of homeless programs, and services consumers that this research benefits them. Failure to meet any one of these conditions can stymie a request or introduce complex delays.

Time series analysis

Integrated database research, while perhaps the most powerful policy analysis tool associated with administrative data on homeless services, cannot address all the critical policy questions in this field. Many of the people affected by public policies, particularly those that restrict eligibility for welfare or health services, will not be registered in the corresponding administrative data systems. Their eligibility may have been denied, or they may never have applied for social benefits because they perceived that they would be denied them or punished for receiving them. Over time, this population of persons would likely grow larger than the population of terminated cases for which identifiers exist. Many social policies also have indirect or secondary effects that would not be measured or discernible by studying the direct effects on individuals in administrative record systems. For these reasons, other policy analysis tools that assess the aggregate impact of policy changes will need to be used. Again, administrative data are ideal for this purpose.

Time series analysis is one tool that can enable researchers to model the trend in a particular phenomenon, such as shelter admission rates, and to test the impact of a policy change or other events occurring along a time continuum, such as welfare caseload terminations, on those rates. Time series analysis takes into account both seasonality (common with shelter admissions) and preintervention trends in the data (e.g., increases in shelter admission rates may precede any effect from welfare cuts) and can specify the lag before the impact of a policy might be felt. Dependent variables of interest in such research might be the monthly rate of shelter admission, the readmission rate, the average length of stay and daily census, and the proportion of shelter users with certain characteristics.

Time series methods would enable a researcher to measure not only the aggregate impact of other system changes, such as welfare policy, but also the impact of *shelter system* policy changes. For example, if eligibility rules for shelter admission are tightened, this would likely lead to a decrease in admissions, but it could also reduce pressure on providers to discharge or place clients in housing and thereby increase the average length of stay. It could also change the case mix of persons admitted to shelters, increasing the population at greater risk for a long shelter stay and increasing the systemwide average length of stay. Administrative data, as opposed to data collected through traditional survey research methods, provide multiple measurements of variables over time and thus allow for the possibility of using time series analysis techniques to test such hypotheses.

New York City provides one example of how municipal homeless policy has been affected by a variety of noteworthy events, including a series of court cases, the availability of different types of subsidized housing programs and shelter accommodations, and three different mayoral administrations (Culhane, Metraux, and Wachter 1998). These dynamics continue, with recent changes including a diversion policy under which a family is denied shelter accommodations if on intake it is determined to have alternative housing options (Dehavenon 1996). Time series analysis would make it possible to estimate the significance of any association between these events and various indicators of shelter utilization.

Program evaluation

Program evaluations in the area of homeless services, as in most social service areas, are few and far between. Resources for services are usually slim and demand is great, so funding for program evaluations is typically scarce. Ideally, the evaluations involve experimental study designs to determine the outcome differences between two groups of randomly selected and assigned persons, where the only difference between the groups is the effect of the program in question. Unfortunately, experimental study designs are not always feasible, particularly if the intervention, such as a subsidized or supported housing placement, is costly to provide or has too little turnover to enroll enough subjects, or if random assignment is viewed as unethical or impractical. The controlled implementation of a particular intervention is also not always feasible in an applied setting, where funding constraints may require delayed, partial, or staged implementation or where sudden shifts in policy may mandate a shift in program capacity or activities. These factors typically mean that a relatively small number of persons are enrolled and followed in homelessness program evaluation research, if and when it is conducted.

Alternatively, even if an experimental design is not in place, the ongoing activities of a *system* of service providers, including the creation of special programs, can be evaluated if administrative data on services used and persons served are routinely collected. Administrative data systems can reduce the collection burden by using the operational infrastructure to record service activity and track client progress. Merges with other administrative data systems can examine the collateral impact on medical costs, incarceration rates, public assistance receipt, and so on. The lack of random assignment can be compensated for through quasi-experiments using the demographic characteristics of large numbers of subjects enrolled systemwide to control statistically for any preexisting differences in subject selection. Moreover, the large number of subjects potentially enrolled can afford more statistical power for determining the characteristics associated with a particular outcome by program type. Selected interviews or small-sample surveys can be used for supplementary information or validation studies. While such a method is not ideal for evaluating a program, the trade-off with statistical power, practicality, cost, and reduced data-gathering burden may make it the only feasible approach in many circumstances.

Such a research approach can be used to evaluate a broad set of program activities, including the effectiveness of "aftercare" case management programs in reducing shelter recidivism, the cost and benefit of supported housing programs relative to continued homelessness, the relative effects of transitional housing versus subsidized housing placements, and the effectiveness of various efforts to prevent homelessness. Hence, the availability of an administrative data system can help make such program evaluations a routine part of policy evaluation and program planning.

System management and administration

Managers of municipal shelter systems or networks of providers may wish to understand not only systemwide patterns of utilization and the effect of various policies and programs, but also the performance of providers in meeting program objectives. Administrative data can be used to compare various provider organizations and administrative units within them on performance objectives. For example, a system manager may wish to examine how well a set of shelter providers is moving families through its programs and into independent housing. Data on average length of stay can be used as a proxy for resource inputs and rates of housing placement as a proxy for program outputs. Other outcome measures (e.g., client satisfaction, residential stability, and income) could be used as well. Both average length of stay and readmission rate could also be used as dependent variables in a "best practice frontier" analysis to compare providers on these performance measures while controlling for differences in case mix and service provision.

Other management research techniques could be applied to study staffing patterns across the service system, to assess how funding changes affect staff qualifications or turnover. Data gathered about provider revenues and expenditures could also be matched to service utilization data to observe how differences or changes in funding patterns affect service delivery. For example, if federal funding drops, does this correspondingly increase dependence on other funding sources, thereby reducing the provision of certain types of services and affecting client outcomes?

Finally, these administrative data systems could be used to plan, implement, and monitor changes in reimbursement mechanisms or to create performance-based contracting systems. For example, some service systems may want to create incentives for providers to focus on timely discharge and resettlement assistance, as opposed to receiving reimbursement based solely on a client's continued stay. Administrative data can be used both to model the appropriate reimbursement rate and to devise case-mix adjustments. Once developed, administrative data can be used to monitor how providers and clients fare under such a system and to support modifications.

The chief benefit of these management research and planning approaches is that service system managers can increase the accountability of provider organizations and truly move the system toward agreed-on program objectives. Continuous shelter stays for which a provider can be continuously reimbursed could lead to the creation of dependence that is contrary to clients' best interests. Also, inappropriately long shelter stays deprive other clients of system resources, and failing to provide oversight and accountability and to measure outcomes could compromise the political viability of funding. If shelters are perceived as wasteful warehouses that accomplish little or nothing at great expense, they will lose their political appeal and could suffer funding cutbacks. Alternatively, well-managed programs that efficiently help people obtain permanent housing may be able to use those demonstrated outcomes to request increased funding and expanded programs.

Conclusions

The use of administrative data has great potential for shaping new research opportunities and public policy analysis in the area of homeless services. The research approaches described here, which take advantage of advances in MIS technology that enable quick compilation and efficient manipulation of large data sets on service use, have already shown that they can provide detailed, timely, policy-relevant information unavailable through traditional research methods. As homeless service agencies increasingly use MIS for record keeping, the data are, in many cases, already available, so performing the analyses described here would entail little additional cost.

Implementing an administrative information system for homeless services can be more difficult, however. One of the perceived barriers is the hardware, software, and system administration costs. While these systems can be expensive, their cost can be kept at reasonable levels, as many agencies have shown by their use of innovative, inexpensive tracking systems. In some cases, these systems are as simple as maintaining paper intake and census records at the provider level and sending them once a month to a central data entry site running standard database software on a single PC. With some modification, this is much like the system that has operated for more than six years in Philadelphia and has permitted a broad set of research and policy analysis projects. Of course, more complicated network configurations are also possible.[1]

Another frequently encountered problem is that homeless service providers, system managers, and clients are skeptical that benefits would outweigh the costs and additional work demands of implementing and maintaining an automated data collection system. This article has outlined the benefits of such a system mainly for researchers, policy analysts, system planners, and administrators. But a well-designed system can also make the day-to-day tasks of client and program management easier as it

---

[1] Dennis Culhane has been funded by the U.S. Department of Housing and Urban Development, the U.S. Department of Health and Human Services, the Fannie Mae Foundation, the University of Pennsylvania, and PRWT Services, Inc., to lead the development of a standardized homeless services software application known as the ANCHoR System (Culhane and Smith 1997).

helps with previously gathered information and produces useful output and reports. Clients benefit from fewer redundant services and forms to complete, a better-organized service system, better classification of their own personal information for case planning, and better accountability on the part of those intended to serve them.

From a research perspective, while the implementation of an information system will yield larger amounts of richer data, it will supplement, not supplant, other methods for gathering primary data. Primary data collection will continue to be the most effective method of carefully exploring client opinions, beliefs, characteristics, and so on. Administrative records also fail to capture what happens to people when they are not in contact with the service system, thus leaving major gaps in our understanding of informal support systems and resettlement patterns. Ideally, more in-depth interviews and follow-up studies on cases randomly selected by an administrative data system should be conducted. In this way, both basic research and more in-depth issues could be explored systematically, and results could be imputed for the larger population from which the sample is drawn.

In conclusion, administrative data systems have potential to inform public policy and research in the area of homeless services at a level of detail, cost-effectiveness, and timeliness not available with other methods. Federal, state, and local governments, which stand to gain an effective tool for evaluating both policy and program performance, should encourage the creation and implementation of such systems among local homeless service providers. As systems proliferate, government agencies will also have to consider the need for standards so that data from different sites are comparable and can be meaningfully aggregated across sites or jurisdictions. Also, setting up such systems will require establishing and adhering to protocols for maintaining the confidentiality and proper use of client records across agencies and research entities. Conducting research based on administrative data also invites collaboration between universities and public agencies to create dialogue on the policy implications such research would hold. Given the rapid change in the social welfare policy environment of the past two years, the creation of an information and analysis infrastructure would greatly enhance our understanding of the nature and causes of homelessness and possible solutions for the future.

Authors

Dennis P. Culhane is an Associate Professor of Social Work and Stephen Metraux is a Doctoral Candidate in Sociology at the University of Pennsylvania.

References

Allison, Paul D. 1995. *Survival Analysis Using the SAS System: A Practical Guide.* Cary, NC: SAS Institute.

Burnam, M. Audrey, and Paul M. Koegel. 1988. Methodology for Obtaining a Representative Sample of Homeless Persons: The Los Angeles Skid Row Study. *Evaluation Review* 12(2):117–52.

Burt, Martha, and Barbara Cohen. 1989. *America's Homeless: Numbers, Characteristics, and Programs That Serve Them.* Washington, DC: Urban Institute Press.

Burt, Martha, and Cynthia M. Taeuber. 1991. Overview of Seven Studies That Counted or Estimated Homeless Populations. In *Conference Proceedings for Enumerating Homeless Persons: Methods and Data Needs,* ed. Cynthia M. Taeuber, 31–75. Washington, DC: U.S. Department of Commerce, U.S. Bureau of the Census.

Culhane, Dennis P., June M. Averyt, and Trevor R. Hadley. 1997. The Rate of Public Shelter Admission among Medicaid-Reimbursed Users of Behavioral Health Services. *Psychiatric Services* 48(3):390–92.

Culhane, Dennis P., June M. Averyt, and Trevor R. Hadley. 1998. The Treated Prevalence of Behavioral Health Disorders among Adults Admitted to the Philadelphia Shelter System: Results from the Integration of Longitudinal Data. *American Journal of Orthopsychiatry,* forthcoming.

Culhane, Dennis P., Edmund F. Dejowski, Julie Ibañez, Elizabeth Needham, and Irene Macchia. 1997a. Public Shelter Admission Rates in Philadelphia and New York City: The Implications of Turnover for Sheltered Population Counts. In *Understanding Homelessness: New Policy and Research Perspectives,* ed. Dennis P. Culhane and Steven P. Hornburg, 101–34. First published in 1994 as *Housing Policy Debate* 5(2):107–40.

Culhane, Dennis P., Erica Gollub, Mark Shpaner, and Randall S. Kuhn. 1997b. The Co-Occurrence of AIDS and Homelessness in Philadelphia: Results from the Integration of Administrative Data. Unpublished paper. University of Pennsylvania.

Culhane, Dennis P., Meg Koppel, Stephen Metraux, and Irene Wong. 1997c. *Mitigating the Impact of State Welfare Cuts for Single Adults: The Implementation and Utilization of the Homelessness Prevention Pilot Project in the City of Philadelphia.* Philadelphia: University of Pennsylvania, School of Social Work.

Culhane, Dennis P., and Randall S. Kuhn. 1998. Patterns and Determinants of Shelter Utilization among Single Adults in New York City and Philadelphia. *Journal of Policy Analysis and Management,* forthcoming.

Culhane, Dennis P., Chang-Moo Lee, and Dayoung Song. 1997. Spatio-Temporal Analysis of Neighborhood Dynamics and Homelessness Incidence: The Effect of Neighborhood Deterioration, Gentrification, and Minority Segregation. Unpublished paper. University of Pennsylvania.

Culhane, Dennis P., Chang-Moo Lee, and Susan M. Wachter. 1997. Where the Homeless Come From: A Study of the Prior Address Distribution of Families Admitted to Public Shelters in New York City and Philadelphia. In *Understanding Homelessness: New Policy and Research Perspectives,* ed. Dennis P. Culhane and Steven P. Hornburg 225–63. First published in 1996 as *Housing Policy Debate* 7(2):327–65.

Culhane, Dennis P., and Stephen Metraux. 1996. Assessing Relative Risk for Homeless Shelter Usage in New York City and Philadelphia. Paper presented at Housing Is Not Enough: Helping Families Achieve Self-Sufficiency, Family Impact Seminar, Washington, DC, September 13.

Culhane, Dennis P., Stephen Metraux, and Susan Wachter. 1998. Homelessness and Public Shelter Provision in New York City. In *Housing and Community Policy in New York City: Facing the Future,* ed. Michael Schill. Albany, NY: SUNY Press, forthcoming.

Culhane, Dennis P., and Kirby Smith. 1997. *The ANCHoR System for Homeless Services: An Information System for the Continuum of Care (Resource Guide).* Philadelphia: University of Pennsylvania and PRWT Services, Inc.

Culhane, Dennis P., and David Webb. 1995. Homelessness and Birth Outcomes in Philadelphia. Paper presented at the Annual Meeting of the American Public Health Association, October 25, San Diego, CA.

Dehavenon, Anna Lou. 1996. *From Bad to Worse at the Emergency Assistance Unit: How New York City Tried to Stop Sheltering Homeless Families in 1996.* New York: Action Research Project on Hunger, Homelessness, and Family Health.

Dennis, Michael L. 1993. Coverage of a Service-Based Methodology: Findings from the DC*MADS Homelessness Study. Paper presented at Towards Census 2000: Research Issues for Improving Coverage of the Homeless Population, September 28–29, Arlington, VA.

Fischer, Pamela J., and William Breakey. 1991. The Epidemiology of Alcohol, Drug, and Mental Disorders among Homeless Persons. *American Psychologist* 46(11):1115–28.

Koegel, Paul, M. Audrey Burnam, and Rodger K. Farr. 1988. The Prevalence of Specific Psychiatric Disorders among Homeless Individuals in the Inner City of Los Angeles. *Archives of General Psychiatry* 45(12):1085–93.

Kuhn, Randall, and Dennis P. Culhane. 1998. Applying Cluster Analysis to Test a Typology of Homelessness by Pattern of Shelter Utilization: Results from the Analysis of Administrative Data. *American Journal of Community Psychology,* forthcoming.

Lee, Barrett. 1989. Stability and Change in an Urban Homeless Population. *Demography* 26(2):323–34.

Lee, Chang-Moo, and Dennis P. Culhane. 1996. Locating the Homeless: A Philadelphia Case Study. *GeoInfo Systems* 5(7):31–34.

Metraux, Stephen. 1994. *Enumerating the Homeless in Tarrant County, Texas: Practical Methods and Reliable Results.* Unpublished master's thesis. University of Texas at Arlington.

Metraux, Stephen, and Dennis P. Culhane. 1997. Family Issues and Recurring Homelessness among Women in New York City Homeless Shelters. Paper presented at the Eastern Sociological Association Annual Meeting, April 9–13, Baltimore, MD.

Robertson, Michael O. 1987. *Homelessness in Albuquerque.* Albuquerque, NM: City of Albuquerque, Department of Human Services.

Rossi, Peter H. 1994. Comment on Dennis P. Culhane et al.'s "Public Shelter Admission Rates in Philadelphia and New York City: The Implications of Turnover for Sheltered Population Counts." *Housing Policy Debate* 5(2): 163–76.

Rossi, Peter H., James D. Wright, Gene A. Fisher, and Georgianna Willis. 1987. The Urban Homeless: Estimating Composition and Size. *Science* 235:1336–41.

Salit, Sharon A., Evelyn M. Kuhn, Arthur J. Hartz, Jade M. Vu, and Andrew L. Mosso. 1996. The Healthcare Costs of Homelessness: Hospitalization Rates and Length of Stay among Homeless Persons in New York City. Paper presented at the annual meeting of the American Public Health Association, November 17–21, New York.

Walker, Adrian. 1997. Summer Fails to Thin Shelter Crowds: Youths, Freed Prisoners Said to Increase Shelter Populace. *Boston Globe,* June 18, p. B1.

Wong, Yin-Ling I., Dennis P. Culhane, and Randall S. Kuhn. 1997. Predictors of Exit and Reentry among Family Shelter Users in New York City. *Social Service Review* 71(3):441–62.

© Fannie Mae Foundation 1997. All Rights Reserved.

Future Directions for Programs Serving the Homeless

Martha R. Burt
The Urban Institute

Abstract

This article reviews federal involvement in funding homeless services during the 1980s: the impetus for federal action, the forms it has taken, and the retrenchment in recent years. It then summarizes what we know about the effectiveness of services for the homeless, examining in turn services for the long-term homeless with chronic disabilities, the short-term or episodically homeless single population, and homeless families, and discusses who appears to be willing, and who appears to be unwilling, to pay for these services.

It also examines possible directions for federal and other homeless policy, including targeting by homeless subpopulation and geography, taking a more extensive look at what works for homeless families, and paying serious attention to prevention. Finally, it discusses the ways in which the social safety net has frayed and is fraying ever faster and the likely consequences for people who face the possibility of homelessness.

Keywords: Homeless; Policy; Programs

Introduction

Many cities have had missions, flophouses, and soup kitchens serving the homeless and near homeless for more than a century. Virtually all of these programs have operated without funding from government agencies. The recession of 1981 to 1982 produced a dramatic and visible increase in the numbers of people using these resources and also altered the makeup of the homeless population. For the first time, public attention was focused on the presence of women and of families with small children among the homeless. The assumption at the time was that the recession had greatly increased the number of people in poverty and was largely responsible for the increase in these "new homeless." However, early programmatic responses quickly showed that this assumption did not reflect the new reality of people's vulnerability to homelessness.

This article summarizes the federal role in developing services for the homeless, what we know about the effectiveness of these

services, and how services are or are not funded. It ends with
implications for the direction of future policy.

Federal programs for the homeless

The federal government's first response to public pressure to "do
something" about homelessness was the creation of the Emergency Food and Shelter Program (EFSP), included as part of the
Emergency Jobs Act of 1983. This program, known colloquially
as FEMA (after the Federal Emergency Management Administration, where it is located), officially expired with its first wave
of funding because Congress assumed that the problem it addressed would disappear as the recession faded. After several
subsequent waves of funding, appropriated on the same emergency basis, the EFSP was folded into the Stewart B. McKinney
Homeless Assistance Act of 1987 and made into a permanent
program still run by FEMA. The McKinney Act, passed toward
the end of the Reagan administration, became the vehicle for
almost all federal programmatic efforts directed toward the
problem of homelessness.

The McKinney Act initially encompassed many programs:

1. A variety of emergency shelter and supportive housing
    programs at the Department of Housing and Urban Develop-
    ment (HUD)
2. The EFSP at FEMA
3. Projects for Assistance in Transition from Homelessness
    (PATH), a mental health services block grant for the home-
    less mentally ill, as well as a set-aside for homeless services
    in the Community Services Block Grant (CSBG) and demon-
    stration funds for mental health and substance abuse serv-
    ices for the homeless, all at the Department of Health and
    Human Services (HHS)
4. Programs for homeless veterans at the Department of Veter-
    ans Affairs
5. Adult education and assistance to homeless children to
    maintain school participation at the Department of
    Education
6. Job training programs at the Department of Labor
7. The establishment of an Interagency Council on the Home-
    less with many federal agencies as members

New programs such as Shelter Plus Care and Health Care for
the Homeless were authorized and included under the McKinney

Act's rubric as the need for them became apparent. However, even though many programs find a home under McKinney, the act specifically bars use of McKinney funds for prevention of homelessness, possibly because Congress was afraid that including the much larger "almost homeless" population would stretch available funding too thin to be effective. As a consequence, the only federal funds explicitly targeted toward prevention of homelessness are those earmarked for rent, mortgage, and utility assistance under the EFSP.

For the first few years (1988 to 1990), the programs under McKinney were funded at around $600 million per year, which constituted about 60 to 65 percent of the budget authorization. The most significant new programs incorporated into McKinney during the Bush administration were Health Care for the Homeless at HHS, which initially added about $50 million a year, and Shelter Plus Care at HUD, which initially added another $110 million to the McKinney total.

The first budget under the control of the Clinton administration made significant increases under McKinney for emergency shelter grants, supportive housing programs, rural homeless assistance, safe havens, and single-room-occupancy (SRO) housing. These changes added about $300 million in federal funds for fiscal year 1994 and an additional $350 million for 1995. However, those and subsequent years also saw the termination of funding for many of the McKinney Act's demonstration programs (for job training, alcohol and drug abuse services, and mental health services, including Access to Community Care and Effective Services and Support [ACCESS]). The rationale for these terminations was that the federal government's role, defined for these funding streams as demonstrating which types of programs worked, had been completed successfully. It was now up to other parties (state and local governments or the private sector) to supply ongoing funding for services. Some remaining federal programs serving the homeless (e.g., EFSP, PATH, and CSBG) have sustained budget cuts, but at least one has seen substantial increases (Housing Opportunities for People with AIDS went from $50 million in its first year, fiscal year 1992, to almost four times that in 1997).

Services, services research, and policy implications

In the process of spending billions of federal dollars over the course of a decade, we have learned some things about what works and what does not.[1] In contrast to the large number of studies whose purpose is to describe the homeless population, a much smaller body of research has addressed the complex issue of what might work to end homelessness for people who are already in that condition, and even fewer efforts have focused on documenting effective interventions to prevent homelessness. Even within the body of research on remedies, the focus has been skewed to particular subgroups within the larger homeless population. Over a year's time, homeless families comprise one of the largest subgroups among the homeless, largely because families are homeless for relatively short periods and many different families experience these short episodes during any given year (Burt 1994). Short-term homeless single people are the next-largest group, followed by episodically homeless singles and long-term homeless singles. A very large proportion of long-term homeless singles have serious chronic disabilities, such as mental illness or substance abuse problems, as well as many physical disabilities. The lion's share of research into services has focused on this last group, although it probably comprises only about 10 percent of single homeless people over a year's time and an even smaller percentage of the total homeless population if homeless families are also considered. Only a few studies have addressed service issues in reducing or preventing family homelessness, and no research known to the author has concentrated on assessing the effectiveness of actions that might prevent homelessness among short-term or episodically homeless single people.

Services for long-term homeless people with chronic disabilities

HHS agencies responsible for services to persons with certain disabilities (notably mental illness, drug abuse, and alcoholism) sponsored research demonstration projects to identify models of care and supported housing that could succeed in bringing some of the most difficult-to-help long-term homeless into stable housing situations. As a result, we know a good deal about creating programs that work to keep homeless people with chronic disabling conditions in stable housing, meet their needs, and

---

[1] State and local governments and private actors have spent much more on homeless services than the federal government has, but information about the extent and uses of this funding is not available for the 1990s. Further, despite the amounts they spend, state and local governments rarely have invested in documenting the impact, so no broad-based evaluation data are available from homeless service activities they support.

create satisfying living environments, thanks to program evaluation research funded by the National Institute of Mental Health (NIMH) and the National Institute on Alcohol Abuse and Alcoholism (NIAAA) (Fosburg et al. 1996; Morrissey et al. 1997; National Resource Center on Homelessness and Mental Illness 1992; Randolph et al. 1997; Shern et al. 1997; Sosin et al. 1994; Tessler and Dennis 1989).

The most remarkable thing we know is that the programs *do* work. Many have been able to retain around 80 percent of the previously homeless people they serve in decent, stable housing arrangements.

We also know that without services attached, the programs *do not* work. The critical services are negotiating with landlords and neighbors, handling situations of decompensation or "slipping off the wagon," ensuring that the rent is paid and the housing kept clean, and supplying tangible goods when necessary, such as furniture, transportation, and food.

Further, we know that without services, previously homeless people with serious disabilities not only lose their own current housing, but lose it in such a way—by antagonizing landlords and neighbors—that the housing unit itself is likely to remain unavailable for other homeless persons. Thus the program wastes the energy and resources already invested in finding and arranging the housing and has to start over with a bad track record. This setback is wasteful for all concerned and does little to build community goodwill toward homeless people with severe disabilities.

Most important, we know that local funders do not readily support the needed services. These critical services mostly are not available from other agencies in the community, nor are they the responsibility of any other agency. Federal programs, such as Shelter Plus Care, that have assumed the availability of locally funded services and the willingness of locals to provide them have had a difficult time obtaining necessary services for their clients.

Who has acted, and who should act? So, given that we know *what* to do for the homeless with severe disabilities, *where* should we do it, and *who* has the responsibility to see that it gets done? To answer these questions, we need to acknowledge a few things about the long-term homeless.

First, most long-term homeless single people with serious
chronic disabilities are concentrated geographically. They are
found overwhelmingly in large cities, to which they drift after
they wear out their welcome elsewhere and where their problems
are compounded by anonymity, disconnection, and isolation.
Concentrations of seriously disabled long-term homeless people
in other locations are found disproportionately in towns, often
rural, that have state mental hospitals or prisons. As a rule, we
do not find many of these people in the suburbs. Because the
location of long-term homeless people with serious disabilities is
identifiable, programs designed to serve them can be strongly
targeted to the geographic areas where they are found.

Second, we need to acknowledge that at present, nobody takes
effective responsibility for people with chronic and severe disabilities who may become homeless—even though we may be
able to identify federal, state, and local agencies with official
jurisdiction. The failure of government agencies to take effective
responsibility, especially for housing needs, is one reason many
people with such disabilities end up homeless.

The federal government has never had primary responsibility for
the direct care of persons with severe and persistent mental
illness or substance abuse problems. HHS does research on
mental health and substance abuse service issues through
NIMH, NIAAA, and the National Institute on Drug Abuse, which
is why we know as much as we do about what works for this
population. HHS also funded some services through Community
Mental Health Center and alcoholism and drug abuse formula
grants from the 1960s through the early 1980s, when the funds
were delivered to states through the Alcohol, Drug Abuse, and
Mental Health Block Grant. Even at its height, federal funding
for services was dwarfed by state funding in these areas.

Federal funding *has* played a significant supportive role for
homeless people with severe disabilities, such as chronic substance abuse and mental illness, through the Supplemental
Security Income program (SSI), which carries with it categorical
eligibility for Medicaid and food stamps. SSI has been the life-
blood of many severely disabled people in the community,
whether they are homeless or not. For homeless people with
qualifying disabilities, SSI provides the resources to leave
homelessness through direct cash grants, access to needed medical care through Medicaid, and usually (depending on the state)
state supplemental payments to augment resources for housing.
Most of the new and successful residential programs for the

severely disabled homeless (the mentally ill and substance abusers) have relied on SSI to supply the cash to pay for residential services. These arrangements are threatened by provisions enacted by Congress in 1996, which bar persons with a primary diagnosis of substance abuse from receiving SSI payments. Persons who could not be recertified with a different primary diagnosis have already lost benefits, and nothing exists to take their place.

State government agencies (i.e., health, mental health, substance abuse, and corrections) have some level of responsibility but generally have interpreted that responsibility as applicable only to people in their direct care in state mental hospitals or prisons. In recent decades, lip service has been paid to the idea of developing community alternatives to these large state systems and providing continuing supervision and support for people once they leave institutions. Some community-based programs have been developed, and some states and communities allocate almost half of their budgets to services in the community. However, it is still generally the case that this commitment covers outpatient services only and does not extend to housing and residential services. This is true even though state hospital capacity has been cut drastically and state mental health systems no longer provide the long-term residential environments they once did. It took decades (from 1965, when state hospitals began to empty in earnest, until the early 1980s) for this process of cutbacks to produce significant levels of homelessness in disabled populations. But eventually the effects became evident to most urban dwellers. State corrections agencies have taken even less responsibility for helping inmates once they leave prison. This lack of assistance occurs despite the fact that many have histories of homelessness, often suffer from mental illness or substance abuse or both, and have no stable residential options available to them when they are released.

The failure to assume responsibility and ensure the long-term well-being of their chronically disabled clients has gone so far that in some instances, state and local mental health, substance abuse, and corrections agencies actually discharge people directly to homeless shelters. These agencies may either give clients a shelter's address or contract with a particular shelter to take them. Agencies do not arrange for more stable, appropriate housing, because they have no resources available to provide that housing. Even when they are officially responsible for arranging for suitable accommodation and aftercare, agencies lack the supervisory capacity clients need.

A third point to be made is this: We need to recognize that recent reductions in income support programs may soon make matters much worse for the long-term single homeless population with disabilities. In addition to the failures already mentioned, both federal and state governments have taken actions in recent years to reduce important sources of income for the severely mentally ill and substance abusers. Most recently, congressional action changed SSI eligibility requirements to bar those with a primary diagnosis of substance abuse. SSI was the funding source enabling many such persons with a history of homelessness to stay in SRO housing. Without SSI, these people cannot pay for their housing. The programs offering it will not be able to cover the shortfall, because their budgets counted on contributions from clients receiving SSI. Further, loss of SSI means loss of Medicaid, so needed medical and mental health services will no longer be readily available to this population, despite its great need for such care. Federal legislation also recently imposed time limits on receipt of food stamps for unemployed singles, thereby cutting off another important source of income for many homeless people and people trying to forestall a return to homelessness.

In addition, a number of states have changed eligibility for their General Assistance programs in ways that bar any single non-elderly person who is considered "able-bodied" from receiving aid (Uccello and Gallagher 1997). Many people with undiagnosed disabilities maintained themselves in minimal housing through their General Assistance grants (and sometimes also through supplementary housing vouchers linked to General Assistance). Now they no longer receive these funds and have lost housing as a result (Bound, Kossoudji, and Ricart-Moes 1996).

What do these circumstances mean for how service funds should be used? The long-term homeless with serious, disabling mental illness or substance abuse problems have very little likelihood of leaving homelessness on their own. One top priority for federal, state, and local homeless funds should be to meet the housing and support needs of these individuals, now and in the future. A good deal of evidence suggests that this small percentage of the homeless population consumes emergency shelter services far in excess of its numbers—up to half of available days in some systems (Kuhn and Culhane 1998). However, their condition is clearly not an "emergency." The considerable funding used to sustain this population in emergency shelters could be redirected toward stable, permanent arrangements whose effectiveness has been demonstrated.

In addition, by targeting services to specific geographic areas, agencies can further direct needed services. In other words, they can put the most money where the most people are in need. To this end, Congress should revise its determination of which jurisdictions are directly eligible for HUD's homeless dollars. Of the approximately 320 Community Development Block Grant (CDBG) entitlement jurisdictions currently receiving Emergency Shelter Grants and Supported Housing funds from HUD, about 125 are what HUD calls "urban counties." These jurisdictions are what remains of a large county after its major city or cities are removed and given their own homeless grants (e.g., Harris County without Houston and Wayne County without Detroit). These "urban county" CDBG jurisdictions are mostly suburbs. They have relatively few homeless people on a per capita basis and even fewer of the long-term homeless with severe disabilities. Generally, they qualify as CDBG entitlement jurisdictions because they contain so many people, not because the people who live there have great needs. After funding for major cities is secure, the federal homeless funds that currently go to "urban counties" should be combined with the federal homeless funds that go directly to states. States can then use these funds to serve populations in greatest need, wherever they reside. This idea is in keeping with current trends toward devolution and local decision making and will most likely result in most funds going to the big cities and certain rural areas.

Services for short-term and episodically homeless single persons

This section is very short, because no one has invested either specialized service or research dollars in this part of the homeless population. Therefore, little can be said with certainty. Yet shelter tracking databases indicate that as many as 80 percent of single homeless persons could fall into the short-term category, with another 10 percent showing an episodic pattern of shelter use (Kuhn and Culhane 1998). Those in the latter category appear to be younger versions of the long-term homeless, that is, displaying significant levels of serious disability but unwilling to abide by the rules for using shelters or other services most of the time. They probably comprise most of the "street" homeless. The great need here is obviously for more concentrated attention to the characteristics and needs of homeless people in these subgroups. It is possible that the current emergency shelter system serves the short-term homeless quite well: They use it for brief periods and do not appear to need it again. However, the episodically homeless are probably not well served by any of the systems with which they interact. Shelters are often just one of the institutions through which these individuals pass during the course of a month or a year—others being jails, hospitals, detoxification units, and other treatment centers. Each entity in this nexus of services passes these episodically homeless people on to the next, usually with no thought given to what it would take to help clients achieve a more stable existence. Investment in transitional services to promote stability might make a big difference both to their individual lives and to the demands on a variety of service systems. Even if supported housing is expensive, significant cost savings might result when the outlays of all systems are considered. In addition, some private organizations, such as Delancey Street in San Francisco, appear to have had considerable success, not just in stabilizing drug-abusing street homeless, but in helping them become independent, employed, and contributing members of society.

Services for homeless and imminently homeless families

As previously noted, most of the research money has been invested in learning about what works for the long-term homeless with serious disabilities. We know considerably less about what works for families, because no federal funds have been earmarked for services research, despite the fact that the greatest proportion of federal homeless money has been spent on emergency and especially transitional housing for homeless families. Outcome research conducted for the Robert Wood Johnson Foundation and HUD's Homeless Families Program (Rog and Gutman 1997), the experiences of local diversion programs, and analyses of shelter tracking databases offer some insights into what services might be necessary.

Most families seeking shelter services experience relatively brief periods of homelessness. They usually do not return to the shelter system or, if they do, it is for another brief period within a few months of their first episode; they then leave for good (Burt 1994; Culhane et al. 1997). Even so, many encounter considerably more difficulties than housed families without a homeless episode (Bassuk et al. 1996; Salomon, Bassuk, and Brooks 1996; Weitzman, Knickman, and Shinn 1992).

The Homeless Families Program (Rog and Gutman 1997) demonstrated that with housing vouchers and certificates even the most troubled of these families can be maintained in stable housing, *outside of shelters*. However, additional supportive services arranged through case management have not been adequate to help these families achieve self-sufficiency or even significant labor force participation.

Less troubled families may be helped toward housing stability through payment of rent and other short-term interventions (e.g., first or last month's rent, rent arrearages, and security deposits), negotiations with landlords, budgeting assistance, or moving to less expensive quarters. This appears to be the experience of a number of diversion programs for families in New York City and New Hampshire (New Hampshire Department of Health and Human Services 1992), as well as those supported by the rent/mortgage/utility component of the Emergency Food and Shelter Program (Burt and Aron 1993). It is interesting to note that we have no evaluation research at all for the impact of transitional shelter stays on families' future residential stability, even though transitional family shelters absorb a significant proportion of federal shelter funding.

The paucity of research evidence for "what works" for homeless families leaves us on shakier ground in making policy recommendations than was the case for long-term homeless singles. The obvious recommendation is for some high-quality evaluation of transitional family shelter. The service packages to evaluate, and to compare with each other for effectiveness, are as follows:

1. Diversion with the provision of mental health, substance abuse, child care, education, parenting, and other needed services currently obtainable more easily through shelter than through generic service agencies, but without offering any housing-related assistance
2. Diversion with one-time housing-related assistance
3. Diversion with a long-term voucher or certificate and no additional supportive services
4. Diversion with a long-term voucher or certificate and with additional supportive services
5. Transitional shelter stays with facilitative and remedial services, but without a long-term voucher or certificate upon leaving
6. Transitional shelter stays with a long-term voucher or certificate upon leaving

Until we know through research the separate effects of residence in a transitional shelter facility, support services, and housing vouchers, we could be wasting a good deal of money on residence that might be better spent on vouchers or supportive services.

Of course, there is really no time to wait for this research before making policy decisions. But the array of service alternatives and research questions listed above carry with them the implication that perhaps we should give ourselves a chance to see whether *less* will work as well as *more*, since we have no evidence that *more* achieves better outcomes than *less*. Also, as is the case with homeless singles, the greatest resources appear to be invested in the households with the most problems. Again, questions arise. Should we reexamine the distribution of resources? Could we help many more homeless or near-homeless families if we assigned more resources to community-based rather than shelter-based interventions? This step, of course, would require a change in federal homeless policy that would allow federal funds to be used to prevent homelessness. A good argument can be made for reversing the trend toward *enriched* shelter environments and reverting back to making shelters fairly "bare bones," while at the same time ensuring that the services (other than a roof) many families seek by entering shelters are indeed available in the community. This consideration is especially worthy of thought as funding for homeless services stagnates or possibly even shrinks.

Discussion: Where do we go from here?

Virtually all federal programs concerned with homelessness focus on serving people who are already homeless. Under Republican and Democratic administrations, and with both Democratic and Republican control of Congress, federal funding has been restricted in this way. Republicans have offered somewhat less money, preferring to focus on personal problems as the cause of homelessness, whereas Democrats have offered somewhat more money and sometimes allow for the possibility of systemic causes. But neither party has been willing to invest in prevention, which deserves more serious consideration. Considering the costs of housing versus shelter, local governments are far ahead on this front, especially for families.

In addition, both political parties have operated under the assumption that federal leadership would stimulate localities to provide necessary ancillary services (see the rules for the Shelter Plus Care program) and fund new programs once their effectiveness had been demonstrated. Often this intended devolution has not occurred. For example, three-fourths of the job training for the homeless demonstration programs funded under McKinney are no longer operating, because local funding did not replace terminated federal resources. Further, a convenient myth persists that localities already have adequate levels of needed services. Legislation admonishes, forbids duplication, and requires coordination and interagency referrals: It repeatedly ignores the obvious fact that, even if a local system is perfectly coordinated, there are not enough services to go around. Further, many state and local governments are rushing even faster than federal entities to reduce programs for the poor or drop them entirely. The idea that devolution will put programs in the hands of state and local players who want to solve problems and take up the cause is probably wishful thinking in many cases.

Recommendations for increased funding and expanded programs that could be offered seriously a decade ago fall on deaf ears today. A different type of thinking may be necessary. One sensible recommendation that fits the current policy environment is that we carefully examine how we can do *the least that is effective*. Both parts of that phrase are important. The most important part is "that is effective." There is no point in wasting resources on services that do not help homeless people reach the goal of reduced homelessness. However, because at best we will have stagnant resources, and at worst shrinking resources, it is important for us to look at ways to do as much or more with less.

Perhaps a full continuum of care is not necessary for every community. Smaller communities and rural areas will probably not need or be able to afford separate facilities for single men, single women, and families. Transitional shelters may be inappropriate in locations where housing resources can be arranged and needed services offered through traditional community agencies. Regulations are needed to allow agencies to soften the definition of "literal homelessness," so they can offer more appropriate services or have more housing resources to offer the precariously housed without making them become literally homeless before help is available (Burt 1996; First et al. 1994; Kentucky Housing Corporation 1993). Certainly a three-week period of shelter residence for the purpose of conducting a full needs assessment is excessive at any time for most homeless people. In this policy climate it is essential that we consider alternatives that are nonresidential (not shelter based), faster, and more focused on immediate needs.

Also, we should take prevention seriously. We can think about prevention from three perspectives, two of which might attract policy attention. First, we can devise ways to avert homelessness among those for whom it is imminent ("proximate" prevention). Second, we can structure and invest in services to prevent homelessness among populations known to be at very high risk.

Both these approaches can probably be shown to be cost-effective if one considers costs to *all* public systems of care and support (including health, mental health, chemical dependency, and corrections, as well as housing). Third, we could commit societal resources to eliminating the conditions under which people grow up that increase their vulnerability to homelessness as adults. Many of these conditions are quite clear from the research evidence. The remainder of this discussion will consider these three approaches to prevention in turn.

Proximate prevention refers to efforts that occur as close as possible to the moment when someone is about to become homeless. The attraction of proximate prevention is that it involves the fewest people in a prevention effort—short of waiting for people to actually become homeless—and thus promises conservation of resources. The disadvantages are that (1) by the time intervention occurs, many people are in serious trouble, and (2) it is still not always easy to identify who is about to become homeless.

Lindblom (1997) details many options for proximate prevention, which will not be reiterated here. It is important, however, to point to screening activities at the state and local levels that divert as many as two-thirds of families applying for shelter to other forms of assistance that are less expensive and often more successful (e.g., negotiations with landlords, moving money, and security deposits). If HUD homeless funds are block granted without crippling restrictions, states and localities could use the money to experiment with more of these arrangements. If they do, analyses such as those conducted by Culhane and his colleagues (Culhane, Lee, and Wachter 1997; Wong, Culhane, and Kuhn 1997) can help identify where these services should be located and whom they should serve to do the most good. This flexibility is probably a good thing. A HUD homeless block grant should *not* restrict use of funds to bricks and mortar (of which we probably have enough) in ways that inhibit reasonable efforts at experimentation with more efficient approaches to assistance. It would be good, however, for HUD itself to retain sufficient funds to support a thorough evaluation of how well the various state and local efforts work at averting imminent homelessness and keeping people housed and out of shelters.

Preventing homelessness among high-risk populations could also have considerable payoffs. Episodically and long-term homeless people with severe and chronic disabilities use extensive amounts of homeless service resources, but usually still remain homeless. They also repeatedly pass through and use extensive, expensive resources in other systems, including health, mental health, substance abuse, and corrections agencies (Bray, Dennis, and Lambert 1993; Robertson, Zlotnick, and Westerfelt 1997). We could, quite literally, end homelessness for this group by investing in the types of proven supported housing arrangements described earlier in this article. To do this, each agency that routinely deals with this population would have to commit resources and create service structures to ensure that no one leaves a residential treatment or corrections institution without a place to live *and* the support necessary to keep him or her there. In addition, services located close to dwellings, such as SRO housing and boarding and lodging houses that house disproportionate numbers of this population (Bray, Dennis, and Lambert, 1993), could reach those who are not currently institutionalized.

Another high-risk population that could benefit from serious prevention efforts is the youth aging out of foster care. Many of them have no personal support system and little capacity to maintain themselves economically. Placement in foster care is a major predictor of future homelessness. Transitional living arrangements of adequate duration, with ancillary supports and education- or work-oriented activities, could help these youth avoid homelessness in the future.

Above all, we do not have to think that every severely disabled homeless person is a lifelong burden on the public purse. Some people will need long-term support, but they are people with conditions such as chronic and severe mental illness that should prompt us to offer that support. The systems officially responsible for people with these conditions should be required to fulfill those responsibilities. For many others, including long-term substance abusers, some program experiences have shown that with appropriate encouragement and support people can and do return to productive lives.

"Deep" prevention, in its most global interpretation, would involve eliminating the extreme childhood poverty and deprivation that are the forerunners of homelessness and a variety of other ills. Although resources to pursue this ultimate objective are not likely to be available, a more focused approach to "deep" prevention is, possibly, within our reach.

The characteristics found in today's homeless families are the very ones that show up repeatedly in research on childhood antecedents of adult homelessness. In particular, histories of foster care and other out-of-home placement, physical and sexual abuse (which often precede out-of-home placement), parental substance abuse, and residential instability and homelessness in the family are much more prevalent among people who have experienced adult homelessness than among people who have not (Bassuk et al. 1997; Caton et al. 1994; Herman et al. 1997; Koegel, Melamid, and Burnam 1995; Mangine, Royse, and Wiehe 1990; Susser, Lin, and Conover 1991; Susser, Struening, and Conover 1987; Weitzman, Knickman, and Shinn 1992; Wood et al. 1990). Therefore, one of the most direct ways to prevent future homelessness among the children of today's homeless families is to help them achieve housing stability and, better yet, some real capacity to function independently in the world. Over the course of even so short a period as a year, these children may comprise about 15 percent of the poor minority children in our nation's largest cities. We could conclude that stabilizing these families could make an appreciable dent in future homelessness, as well as in other problems associated with troubled youth. To enable future generations to escape homelessness, it seems worthwhile to support the idea of maintaining some of the most damaged families in housing, allowing them to receive cash benefits and participate in mental health and substance abuse recovery programs until their children are grown. Even if there is no expectation that the parent(s) will ever be self-sufficient, their children might be saved. The possible benefits of successfully helping homeless families might stimulate those who fund research to initiate comprehensive demonstration and evaluation agendas. These agendas would help us learn as much about how to help homeless families as we have learned about how to help people whose chronic disabilities lead to their long-term homelessness.

Finally, as already noted, income support programs such as SSI, food stamps, and General Assistance that have in the past helped some people avoid homelessness or return to stable housing have been or are being cut. To date, most of these cuts affect single people. But the very families most likely to experience homelessness while still receiving Aid to Families with Dependent Children are the same ones least likely to succeed under the coming strictures of welfare reform. They are the families most likely to hit time limits without having achieved self-sufficiency. They are the ones who will be left with no cash assistance when they could not make it even with such assistance.

Recommendations for more housing vouchers and certificates, however sensible, are certain to fall on deaf ears at the national level, where the number of available housing vouchers was frozen this year and debate raged for weeks about the advisability of renewing those that are left. In this policy environment, it is unlikely that any recommendations for helping homeless families will be forthcoming. For homeless singles, especially those with significant disabilities, we seem to be moving in a direction opposite to the one that will work. We are cutting supports out from under people, rather than providing additional, and more stable, ones. The thoughts presented in this article are offered in the hope that they may cause some people to question whether current policies may not make things worse, instead of better, for many high-risk people.

Author

Martha R. Burt is the Director of the Social Services Research Program at The Urban Institute.

References

Bassuk, Ellen L., John C. Buckner, Linda F. Weinreb, Angela Browne, Shari S. Bassuk, R. Dawson, and J. N. Perloff. 1997. Homelessness in Female-Headed Families: Childhood and Adult Risk and Protective Factors. *American Journal of Public Health* 87(2):241–48.

Bassuk, Ellen L., Linda F. Weinreb, John C. Buckner, Angela Browne, Amy Salomon, and Shari S. Bassuk. 1996. The Characteristics and Needs of Sheltered Homeless and Low-Income Housed Mothers. *Journal of the American Medical Association* 276(8):640–46.

Bound, John, Sherri Kossoudji, and Gema Ricart-Moes. 1996. The Ending of General Assistance and SSI Disability Growth in Michigan: A Case Study. In *The Social Security Administration's Disability Programs: Explanations of Recent Growth and Implications for Disability Policy*, ed. David C. Stapleton. McLean, VA: Lewin VHI.

Bray, Robert M., Michael L. Dennis, and Elizabeth Y. Lambert. 1993. *Prevalence of Drug Use in the Washington, DC, Metropolitan Area Homeless and Transient Population: 1991*. Rockville, MD: National Institute on Drug Abuse, Division of Epidemiology and Prevention Research.

Burt, Martha R. 1994. Comment on Dennis P. Culhane et al.'s "Public Shelter Admission Rates in Philadelphia and New York City: The Implications of Turnover for Sheltered Population Counts." *Housing Policy Debate* 5(2): 141–52.

Burt, Martha R. 1996. Rural Homelessness: A Report on the Findings and Implications of RECD's Rural Homelessness Conferences. In Rural Economic and Community Development/USDA, *Rural Homelessness: Focusing on the Needs of the Rural Homeless*. Washington, DC.

Burt, Martha R., and Laudan Y. Aron. 1993. *Assessment of the Rent / Mortgage / Utility Component of the Emergency Food and Shelter Program (EFSP): Findings from the Local Recipient Organization (LRO) Mail Survey and Site Visits.* Washington, DC: Urban Institute.

Caton, Carol L. M., Patrick E. Shrout, Paula F. Eagle, Lewis A. Opler, Alan Felix, and Boanerges Dominguez. 1994. Risk Factors for Homelessness among Schizophrenic Men: A Case-Control Study. *American Journal of Public Health* 84:265–70.

Culhane, Dennis P., Edmund F. Dejowski, Julie Ibañez, Elizabeth Needham, and Irene Macchia. 1997. Public Shelter Admission Rates in Philadelphia and New York City: The Implications of Turnover for Sheltered Population Counts. In *Understanding Homelessness: New Policy and Research Perspectives*, ed. Dennis P. Culhane and Steven P. Hornburg, 101–34. First published in 1994 as *Housing Policy Debate* 5(2):107–40.

Culhane, Dennis P., Chang-Moo Lee, and Susan M. Wachter. 1997. Where the Homeless Come From: A Study of the Prior Address Distribution of Families Admitted to Public Shelters in New York City and Philadelphia. In *Understanding Homelessness: New Policy and Research Perspectives*, ed. Dennis P. Culhane and Steven P. Hornburg, 225–63. First published in 1996 as *Housing Policy Debate* 7(2):327–65.

First, Richard J., Beverly G. Toomey, John C. Rife, and Elizabeth A. Stasny. 1994. *Outside the City: A Statewide Study of Homelessness in Nonurban / Rural Areas.* Final report. Columbus, OH: Ohio State University, College of Social Work.

Fosburg, Linda, Gretchen Locke, Laura Peck, and Meryl Finkel. 1996. *National Evaluation of the Shelter Plus Care Program.* Cambridge, MA: Abt Associates.

Herman, Daniel B., Ezra S. Susser, Elmer L. Struening, and Bruce L. Link. 1997. Adverse Childhood Experiences: Are They Risk Factors for Adult Homelessness? *American Journal of Public Health* 87(2):249–55.

Kentucky Housing Corporation. 1993. *Kentucky Homeless Survey Preliminary Findings.* Lexington, KY.

Koegel, Paul, Elan Melamid, and M. Audrey Burnam. 1995. Childhood Risk Factors for Homelessness among Homeless Adults. *American Journal of Public Health* 85(12):1642–49.

Kuhn, Randall, and Dennis P. Culhane. 1998. Applying Cluster Analysis to Test a Typology of Homelessness by Pattern of Shelter Utilization: Results from the Analysis of Administrative Data. *American Journal of Community Psychology*, forthcoming.

Lindblom, Eric N. 1997. Toward a Comprehensive Homelessness-Prevention Strategy. In *Understanding Homelessness: New Policy and Research Perspectives*, ed. Dennis P. Culhane and Steven P. Hornburg, 265–334. First published in 1991 as *Housing Policy Debate* 2(3):957–1025.

Mangine, Steven J., David Royse, and Vernon R. Wiehe. 1990. Homelessness among Adults Raised as Foster Children: A Survey of Drop-in Center Users. *Psychological Reports* 67:739–45.

Morrissey, Joseph, Michael Calloway, Matthew Johnsen, and Michael Ullman. 1997. Service System Performance and Integration: A Baseline Profile of the ACCESS Demonstration Sites. *Psychiatric Services* 48(3):374–80.

National Resource Center on Homelessness and Mental Illness. 1992. *Annotated Bibliography: Developing Housing for Homeless Persons with Severe Mental Illnesses*. Delmar, NY: Policy Research Associates.

New Hampshire Department of Health and Human Services. 1992. *Emergency Shelter Commission Annual Report, 1992*. Concord, NH: Division of Mental Health and Developmental Services.

Randolph, Frances, Margaret Blasinsky, Walter Leginski, Laurie B. Parker, and Howard H. Goldman. 1997. Creating Integrated Service Systems for Homeless Persons with Mental Illness: The ACCESS Program. *Psychiatric Services* 48(3):369–73.

Robertson, Marjorie J., Cheryl Zlotnick, and Alex Westerfelt. 1997. Drug Use Disorders and Treatment Contact among Homeless Adults in Alameda County, California. *American Journal of Public Health* 87(2):217–20.

Rog, Debra J., and Marjorie Gutman. 1997. The Homeless Families Program: A Summary of Key Findings. In *To Improve Health and Health Care, 1997: The Robert Wood Johnson Anthology*, ed. Stephen L. Isaacs and James R. Knickman, 209–31. San Francisco: Jossey-Bass.

Salomon, Amy, Shari S. Bassuk, and Margaret G. Brooks. 1996. Patterns of Welfare Use among Poor and Homeless Women. *American Journal of Orthopsychiatry* 66(4):510–25.

Shern, David L., Chip J. Felton, Richard L. Hough, Anthony F. Lehman, Stephen Goldfinger, Elie Valencia, Deborah Dennis, Roger Straw, and Patricia A. Wood. 1997. Housing Outcomes for Homeless Adults with Mental Illness: Results from the Second-Round McKinney Program. *Psychiatric Services* 48(2):239–41.

Sosin, Michael R., Jane Yamaguchi, Maria Bruni, Susan Grossman, Bernard Leonelli, Mairead Reidy, and Joan Schwingen. 1994. *Homelessness and Substance Abuse in Community Context: A Case Management and Supported Housing Demonstration*. Chicago: University of Chicago, School of Social Services Administration.

Susser, Ezra S., Shang P. Lin, and Sarah A. Conover. 1991. Childhood Antecedents of Homelessness in Psychiatric Patients. *American Journal of Psychiatry* 148:1026–30.

Susser, Ezra S., Elmer L. Struening, and Sarah A. Conover. 1987. Childhood Experiences of Homeless Men. *American Journal of Psychiatry* 144:1599–1601.

Tessler, Richard C., and Deborah L. Dennis. 1989. *A Synthesis of NIMH-Funded Research Concerning Persons Who Are Homeless and Mentally Ill*. Rockville, MD: National Institute of Mental Health, Division of Education and Service Systems Liaison, Program for the Homeless Mentally Ill.

Uccello, Cori E., and L. Jerome Gallagher. 1997. *General Assistance Programs: The State-Based Part of the Safety Net*. New Federalism Issues and Options for States, Series A, No. A-4. Washington, DC: Urban Institute.

Weitzman, Beth C., James R. Knickman, and MaryBeth Shinn. 1992. Predictors of Shelter Use among Low-Income Families: Psychiatric History, Substance Abuse, and Victimization. *American Journal of Public Health* 82:1547–50.

Wong, Yin-Ling I., Dennis P. Culhane, and Randall Kuhn. 1997. Predictors of Exit and Reentry among Family Shelter Users in New York City. *Social Service Review* 71(3):441–62.

Wood, David, R. Burciaga Valdez, Toshi Hayashi, and Albert Shen. 1990. Homeless and Housed Families in Los Angeles: A Study Comparing Demographic, Economic, and Family Function Characteristics. *American Journal of Public Health* 80:1049–52.